# Fix Schools First

## Blueprint for Achieving Learning Standards

**Jack E. Bowsher**
Former Director of Education
IBM
San Diego, California

AN ASPEN PUBLICATION®
Aspen Publishers, Inc.
Gaithersburg, Maryland
2001

Library of Congress Cataloging-in-Publication Data

Bowsher, Jack E.
Fix schools first : blueprint for achieving learning standards/Jack E. Bowsher.
p. cm.
Includes index.
ISBN 0-8342-1904-2
1. School improvement programs—United States.
2. Education—Standards—United States. I. Title.

LB2822.82.B69 2001
379.1'58'0973—dc21
00-067380

Orders: (800) 638-8437
Customer Service: (800) 234-1660

**About Aspen Publishers** • For more than 40 years, Aspen has been a leading professional publisher in a variety of disciplines. Aspen's vast information resources are available in both print and electronic formats. We are committed to providing the highest quality information available in the most appropriate format for our customers. Visit Aspen's Internet site for more information resources, directories, articles, and a searchable version of Aspen's full catalog, including the most recent publications: **www.aspenpublishers.com**
**Aspen Publishers, Inc.** • The hallmark of quality in publishing
Member of the worldwide Wolters Kluwer group.

Editorial Services: Ruth Bloom
Library of Congress Catalog Card Number: 00-067380
ISBN: 0-8342-1904-2

*Printed in the United States of America*

1 2 3 4 5

This book is dedicated to the memory of my father-in-law,
*Alfred Moore Clem*,
whose genuine love and dedication to teaching
for more than 45 years
inspired many students and teachers.
As a teacher, he honored the profession
with both respect and dignity.

I also dedicate this book
to his daughter and my wife, *Charmian*,
a former public school teacher,
who has worked with me over the past 14 years
to develop this document.

# TABLE OF CONTENTS

# FOREWORD

For two decades, many American citizens have been asked to invest their time and talents in the process of trying to improve our public schools. For me, the request came in 1981 when the Secretary of Education asked me to serve as the vice-chair for the National Commission on Excellence in Education. The Commission's purpose was to present a report on the quality of education in the United States to Terrel H. Bell, the Secretary of Education, and to the American people by April 1983.[1]

Our commission consisted of 18 members, all of whom were educators from K–12 schools and institutions of higher learning except for the retired chairman of the Bell Telephone Research Center, the former governor of Minnesota, and a member who represented parents. At the time, I was president of the San Diego School Board. Our group was led by David P. Gardner, who was president of the University of Utah and later became president of the University of California.[2]

We labored for nearly two years reading papers commissioned from experts on a variety of education issues; listening to administrators, teachers, students, representatives of professional groups, business leaders, public officials, and scholars; and reviewing notable programs and promising education approaches. In addition, we reviewed the existing analysis of problems in education and letters from concerned citizens, teachers, and administrators who volunteered extensive comments on problems and possibilities in American education.[3]

All of this input formed the foundation for the now landmark *A Nation At Risk: The Imperative for Education Reform* document that was published as an open letter to the American people on April 26, 1983. Dr. Bell, the Secretary of Education, and our commission met with President Reagan at the White House to review our recommendations. The document electrified the nation and brought the topic of public education to the forefront of every town, city, and state, as well as to Washington, D.C. The findings of the commission were the catalyst for extensive investigation from Maine to California by governors, superintendents, school board members, parents, teachers, students, taxpayers, and the media. Few government documents have had such an impact on our citizens and our country. Almost every professional educational group came forward to agree or disagree with the commission's conclusions. A few detractors defended the status quo, but the overwhelming opinion was that our nation's schools were indeed in need of a revolution, a renaissance, or systemic change.

Although we did not have formal discussions about how the fundamental changes that had to be implemented would be phased in, I am certain that most of us believed that substantial improvements would be made during the 1980s. When almost no progress occurred during that period, we were pleased to receive bipartisan support from political, business, and educational leaders for the eight national educational goals in the 1990s. During this period, I served from March 1992 until March 2000 as a member of the California State Board of Education, with three years as president of the board. Therefore, I feel qualified to state that our public schools, with few exceptions, are still "A Nation At Risk."

Progress has been made at the state level for learning standards and various methods of accountability, but few school districts have an integrated curriculum in place to achieve the learning standards. Many teachers continue to use their existing lesson plans and teaching methods that enable only about 50 percent of our students to be labeled successful learners. Textbooks are out of date in areas where funds have not been properly allocated, and although many computers are available in schools, few are being used as interactive tutors. Many schools have selected a few recommendations from our report that were relatively simple to implement, but they have ignored the fundamental changes that are necessary to achieve breakthroughs in student learning. Assessment systems are also inadequate. Therefore, the education revolution and progress that we need to achieve to move our nation forward is yet to be designed, developed, or implemented. This situation must change in the current decade.

Having said all that, I must tell you that the contents of this book are the most thoughtful and innovative material that I have read over the years on how our nation can reach the eight national educational goals and how most American students can be successful learners.

Almost everyone realizes by now that fine-tuning the existing teaching methods and management of schools will not fix the basic problems of student learning. Mr. Bowsher brings a new perspective to the challenge because he is not only an educator with 30 years of experience, but he is also an expert on how to solve major performance problems within large and complex organizations. He has a financial control background and was the director of a successful management development program in one of our nation's leading corporations. In addition, he has been involved in the evolution of technology systems for more than 40 years. Most important, he has a proven record on restructuring large education programs to achieve breakthroughs in student learning. He understands the process of learning as well as instructional systems design methods.

Some years ago, the former Assistant Secretary of Education, Chester E. Finn, Jr., criticized business executives involved in the education reform movement. He said:

> The most conspicuous feature of business involvement with the schools has been soft-headedness. Indeed, one sometimes gets the impression that when normally hard-nosed capitalists turn to education reform, they check all their business instincts at the door. They suspend the analytic habits that made for corporate success and instead embrace the assumptions and value system of the education profession. They go native. This doubtless endears them to the educationists. Failure to attend to the bottom line, however, yields bankruptcy in education as surely as in commerce.[4]

Chester Finn and other educators won't find that this executive, the author of *Fix Schools First*, suffers from soft-headedness. This book presents a bold statement on what the causes of poor performance really are in the American public school system. Bowsher tells us that the problems are in the schools and classrooms, not in society or parental involvement. He does not blame teachers or teacher unions; he makes it clear, instead, that administrators and boards of education have the primary responsibility to fix our schools. Their focus must shift toward achieving breakthroughs in student learning so that more than 90 percent of all students can meet the learning standards established by the state departments of education and local school districts.

Some educators will say that Jack Bowsher doesn't really understand all the barriers for changing the current teaching methods and managing schools. Not true. He has in-depth knowledge about how schools are managed today and knows that student performance cannot be improved unless fundamental changes are made. Some educators might be surprised that the process of learning must be managed in every classroom, every school, every district, and each state with a working partnership between the state, district, and school organizations. Futurist Joel Barker has stated that important shifts in paradigms will most often come from people who have not been entrenched in the existing paradigm. So it seems for the public school system.

Jack Bowsher is one of the few educators who insists that the job of teaching is not complete until all students have learned the lessons and have shown that they can apply them. He accepts no excuses for students not learning, and he believes that our schools are like any other successful organization: the senior management team must take responsibility for the performance of its workforce. Vice-presidents of sales cannot use the excuse that their sales personnel are incapable of making quota. They must take action to retrain their sales force and provide better support systems to the "front-line" employees who are having problems. Administrators must employ the same approach in every school where students are behind in grade-level expectations.

In addition to a new integrated curriculum, teachers need effective learning systems, tutoring systems, assessment systems, and administrative systems. Administrators need a new management system. Bowsher offers a new paradigm for these components so they can all contribute to major increases in learning. Just as he did in the field of employee training, Bowsher has emerged as a visionary leader who accepts no excuses for poor performance.

If public schools want millions and billions of dollars of additional funds in future years, they need to pay attention to the lessons in this book. It's time to stop throwing money at problems in our public schools. To warrant future investments of taxpayer funds, state school officers and district superintendents need to present a vision and plan of action for achieving genuine breakthroughs in student learning. Political leaders and business executives involved in school reform issues need to read the messages contained in *Fix Schools First*. Schools can be fixed, but the process requires a new paradigm and bold leadership. For years, people have been saying that educators must stop tinkering around the edges; however, no one has given them a "blueprint" to reach the goal of all children becoming successful learners. This book shows educators how to reach this realistic objective.

This book is timely. Jack Bowsher is one of the first educators to document a proven method for teachers and students in all schools to reach the learning standards that are being established in recent years by state departments of education and local school districts. The messages in this book must be given serious consideration if the proponents of high standards are going to survive the growing backlash by many educators who want to return to the world of only good intentions. If the standards can be achieved through other approaches, it is hoped that these approaches will be compared to the structured methods outlined in this document.

This book should receive an in-depth review by all colleges of education, state departments of education, and every school district in our country. These institutions must develop a vision and strategies for our schools to achieve the learning standards that are being established by the state departments of education and local school districts. Action programs to achieve the standards and the eight national educational goals must be implemented during this decade. The time for debate and task forces is over. School boards and administrators must provide great leadership for great change.

*Yvonne W. Larsen*
*Vice-Chair*
*National Commission on Excellence in Education*

## NOTES

1. National Commission on Excellence in Education (Washington, DC: U. S. Department of Education, April 26, 1983), letter page.
2. National Commission, 4 and 5 of Introduction.
3. National Commission, 1 and 2.
4. C. Finn, "Education As Funny Business," *National Review,* 24 February, 1989, 3.

# PREFACE

After 18 years of effort invested in the education reform movement and an unbelievable amount of money, student performance within the American public school system is still not acceptable. The political leaders and the President have established this crisis as a top priority. Student learning must be fixed, not just improved. Great progress has been made in establishing standards and accountability for learning in most states. The overall reason for this book's existence is to present a blueprint that enables public school students to achieve the learning standards that have been established by the state departments of education and the local school districts.

*Listed below are eight additional reasons for reading this book:*

1. ***Schools Damage Children.*** Schools continue to damage millions of children each year who are viewed as slow learners. Students should enjoy their school years, and most children should be successful learners. The lessons in this book eliminate this problem.
2. ***The Current Excuses for Inadequate Student Learning Must Be Eliminated.*** This book also shows how the excuses used by the education community for inadequate student performance, such as poverty, minorities, and low parental involvement, can be eliminated because they are valid only as a result of the current teaching methods and school management. Americans need to know that the inadequate performance in our schools is not the fault of teachers, unions, parents, or students.
3. ***The Education System Must Provide Equal Opportunity for All Students.*** The current school system has not provided equal opportunity for all races after 40 years of effort, so it is time to make fundamental changes. The vision in this book enables students of all races, genders, and socioeconomic backgrounds to be successful learners.

4. ***Teachers and Administrators Need an Embraceable Responsibility.*** Working conditions must be improved by defining appropriate responsibilities for each key position. The current attrition rates for education professionals are not acceptable.

5. ***Students Must Learn Their Lessons the First Time.*** This book presents a solution for eliminating the billions of dollars invested each year in thousands of remedial classes taught at our public schools, institutions of higher learning, and workplace training centers.

6. ***New People in Education Reform Need a Roadmap.*** Many educators, political leaders, and business executives who have been active in the school reform movement over the past 18 years have retired, passed away, or given up after developing several successful programs. This book discusses how the next generation of education reformers needs to use the lessons their predecessors learned as a foundation for fixing schools. It would be a terrible waste of time and resources to duplicate programs that have been tried and that failed.

7. ***Leaders of Public Schools Need a Blueprint.*** State school officers, school board members, district superintendents, and principals must be provided with a blueprint on how to fix the American public school system. This book provides such a blueprint based on education research studies as well as proven teaching and management methods. It is not an impossible task to achieve dramatic breakthroughs in student learning. This document clarifies who is responsible for fixing the public school system, with a detailed plan of action on how to succeed during this decade.

8. ***Failure Is Un-American—Taxpayers Will Not Indefinitely Support Ineffective Schools.*** For decades, taxpayers have been asked to support incremental funding for expensive programs that have been tried with the hope—and it's only a hope—that additional money will create more successful learners. With rare exception, this has not happened. As a result, a major taxpayer revolt against poor-performing schools could ensue during the next recession when state sales and income tax revenues decline.

This book describes a new vision, as well as the need for an integrated curriculum, new learning systems concepts, new tutoring systems, new assessment systems, and a new management system to achieve breakthroughs in learning. Our country did not achieve its national education goals by the year 2000. Jack Bowsher was motivated to write this book because the pace for fundamental change has been so slow over the past 18 years and the level of student learning so low that he believes that another wake-up call like *A Nation At Risk* is needed. This book contains a plan of action to fix the school system for the sake of future generations. One more effort must be made to lift the performance of the American public school system to a world-class status. The eight national goals must be reached by the year 2010, and this book provides a blueprint to do just that. During the past 18 years, almost 50 million children have struggled through an education system that was described by the educators in 1983 as mediocre. There must be a sense of urgency to fix the learning crisis that exists today in many public schools. It is hoped that this book will help political and community leaders, administrators, and teachers who must bring fundamental change to urban and rural school districts.

# ACKNOWLEDGMENTS

Although I have been employed in the fields of education and training for more than 30 years, this book is based on my experiences of the past 14 years, during which I have participated in the education reform movement. During those years, I had the opportunity to work with hundreds of educators who were state school officers, district superintendents, directors of curriculum, principals, union leaders, and teachers. All of this happened because IBM's senior management team asked me to become involved with school reform issues because the company was receiving many grant requests from school districts for funds and equipment. Ursula Fairbairn was the senior executive who urged me to meet with school reform movement leaders. Based on their input, I developed a seminar that became the basis for my first book, *Educating America: Lessons Learned in the Nation's Corporations*, which was published in 1989.

The late Al Shanker, former president of the American Federation of Teachers, provided me with great insights into school reform issues through his presentations, writings, and personal conversations when we would meet on the New York–Washington shuttle and at various education conferences. David Kearns, former chief executive officer of the Xerox Corporation and Deputy Secretary of Education, also counseled me over the years. Various speakers at education reform conferences, including the series of Education Summits sponsored by *Fortune Magazine*, were extremely informative in my early years about ways to fix our public school system. Many publications by the Business Roundtable, the Committee for Economic Development, the National Alliance of Business, The Conference Board, and the New American Schools Development Corporation were also most helpful.

Both Dr. Bob Morgan and Dr. Bob Branson at Florida State University greatly influenced my thinking because they successfully applied the instructional design methods that I had learned from Dr. Herb Miller in corporate education to K–12 schools. Dr. Miller, who is a former school teacher and one of the leading practitioners of instructional design methods, provided many suggestions to enhance this document. I owe a special thank you to Dr. Hines Cronin, former district superintendent at Moss Point, Mississippi, and his faculty, who showed me the first districtwide school system based on instructional design methods, learning systems, tutoring systems, and assessments that were based on an integrated curriculum. All of this was possible because of the creative work of Dr. Bob Corrigan and his wife, Betty, who developed the learning ladder of instruction.

Woody Klein, editor-in-chief of the *Westport News* in Connecticut, gave me a great opportunity to write a monthly newspaper column on "Education Breakthroughs" for more than three years. This experience enabled me to successfully communicate with the general public on key school reform issues.

In recent years, I have had the privilege to be an education consultant to Price Charities. This opportunity allowed me to work with the College of Education at San Diego State University on the City Heights Pilot Project involving administrators and teachers at an elementary school, a middle school, and a high school. Dr. Ian Pumpian, executive director for the project, added to my thinking on many of the key issues. Dr. Lionel Meno, dean of the College of Education, and his faculty, including Dr. Allison Rossett and Dr. William Streshly, enhanced my knowledge. The superintendent of the San Diego Unified School District, Alan Bersin, provided a case study on education reform and several suggestions for the book, which also influenced my thinking. All my knowledge of the San Diego area comes from the generous support of Vice Admiral, U.S. Navy (Retired) Ray Peet, who introduced me to the key players, including the San Diego Dialogue, with whom I had many informative discussions. He also introduced me to Sol and Robert Price, who provided great encouragement of my efforts. Most important, he introduced me to Yvonne Larsen, who agreed to write the Foreword to this book and who added great insight into the overall history of education reform programs.

Articles in *Education Week, ASCD* (Association for Supervision and Curriculum Development) *Educational Leadership, American School Board Journal, Technology and Learning, Phi Delta Kappan, Harvard Education Journal*, and many other education journals have been a great source of knowledge. Most important, the authors of the books in the Suggested Reading section of this book have greatly shaped my decisions and messages.

Several educators read an early draft of this book and provided many helpful suggestions. One person in particular made this book more readable than it would otherwise have been: Rob Bowsher, who did an outstanding job editing both the proposal for this book and the first draft. My brother, Charles A. Bowsher, a former Comptroller General of the United States, provided many helpful suggestions for the manuscript. Dan Hunt, a chief financial officer of a major tutoring company, also spent considerable time reviewing the manuscript, which enabled him to suggest several enhancements.

This book would not exist without an invitation that was extended to me by Ray Fox to make a presentation at the SALT (Society for Applied Learning Technology) Conference in July 1999 on technology in urban schools. At that meeting, Michael Abshire, a senior editor at Aspen Publishers, recommended to Jo Gulledge, an acquisition editor, that they request a book proposal from me. Jo offered me a contract and provided me with the able services of Monica Hincken, their development editor, and Ruth Bloom, managing editor for books, who were most helpful over the months it took to create this book. The Aspen marketing department, under the direction of Jennifer Barnes Eliot, has also done a creative job of promoting this book.

I also thank my mother and father, Ella and Matthew Bowsher, who believed so strongly in the value of education and who sacrificed to enable my brother and me to have the benefit of a college and graduate school education. Finally, I owe a big thank you to all my teachers over the years who gave me the knowledge and skills to achieve a leadership position in the fields of education and training.

# INTRODUCTION

In 1989, Al Shanker, former president of the American Federation of Teachers, endorsed my first book, *Educating America*, with this message:

> Mr. Bowsher covers a lot of ground in his book, and he is correct in arguing there is much we can learn from the business world . . . [H]e managed to meet the needs of both IBM and its employees. I hope one day to see a similar success in our public schools.

Although there are some successful public schools, there are many schools in our cities and rural communities where most students are not successful learners. Even in the top-performing schools, there are too many failures in the bottom quartile of the class.

Many corporations, religious groups, not-for-profit organizations, and even countries that were once great have gone into decline because they could not move beyond the paradigm that made them successful. Their leaders remained committed to fine-tuning the existing paradigm with the hope that somehow the institution would return to greatness, but the goals and objectives were never achieved. Joel Barker, the expert on paradigms, makes the following comments:[1]

1. Our perceptions of an institution are strongly influenced by paradigms.
2. Because we become so good at using our present paradigms, we resist changing them.
3. It is the outsider who usually creates the new paradigm.

The public schools need a new paradigm that achieves the goal of making all students successful learners. This goal will never be achieved using the existing paradigms, no matter how much money is invested or how many "patches" are made to the current teaching methods and management systems of schools. In most paradigm shifts, practitioners who choose to adopt the new paradigm must do so as an act of faith rather than as the result of factual proof because there usually is not enough proof in the early stages of change to be convincing. Fortunately, the vision and management systems offered in this book enable school districts to move forward with factual proof of the value of change, so the risk of change is quite small, but the rewards are far reaching.

Many books on school reform issues have been written by nationally known educators. Most of them discuss one or two subjects, whereas others inventory various reform programs. Usually, 95 percent of these books tell us what is wrong with public schools, and then in the last chapter, the author leaps to a quick-fix solution such as smaller schools, smaller classes, or choice. In this book, I do the opposite. I have used only the first three chapters to define the root causes of poor student learning. Then I devoted 80 percent of the book to providing answers about what programs have worked in the past and what is required to achieve the new learning standards established by the state departments of education and local school districts.

Today, many school districts within the United States have a third-class education system compared to leading European and Asian countries. The United States has more poverty, more hard-core welfare cases, and more citizens in jail, on parole, or labeled "ex-con" than any other industrialized nation. The downtowns of our large cities are often surrounded by ghettos. All of these problems can be changed if Americans set a priority to fix schools first. Our schools should be the envy of the world, given the enormous amount of taxpayer dollars invested each year by federal, state, and local governments.

Fortunately, institutions of higher learning and our workplace training centers enable most Americans to possess the knowledge and skills required to enjoy a high standard of living. Our nation is the world's most powerful military country and a great economic leader; however, millions of Americans do not share in our wealth and success because they do not have the knowledge and skills associated with a good, solid kindergarten through high school (K-12) education. This intolerable situation must change.

The important pieces of the puzzle required for fixing public schools are discussed in this book. Part I starts with educators ringing the alarm bell after the famous *A Nation At Risk* report was published in 1983. In Chapter 1, the definition of a successful school is presented, which has been missing in most of the education reform discussions during the past 18 years. In Chapter 2, a second alarm bell is rung for the explosive growth in the cost of public school education. Chapter 3 explains what the root causes of poor performance are in student learning, a subject rarely discussed in other books and studies. Part II reviews nearly 50 quick-fixes and other programs such as vouchers and charter schools.

These three chapters also explain why these programs have raised student performance by only a few percentage points.

If readers already know why these 50 programs haven't fixed schools and fully understand the causes of why most students are not at grade level, they can go directly to Part III, which provides an exciting new vision that must be realized in order to have more than 90 percent of all students at grade level. Part IV shows how solutions for success can be implemented and who is responsible for fixing the American public school system. The book concludes with Chapter 15, which poses key questions for district superintendents and state school officers. Appendix A provides a summary of systems that must exist in successful school districts and in the schools.

Each chapter, and even some subheadings within certain chapters, could warrant an entire book. In fact, this book could be several thousand pages, but only a few people would read such a lengthy document. Therefore, my intent in this book is to discuss, in a reasonable number of pages, every piece of the puzzle that forms a successful school system. Suggested readings at the back of the book enable readers to obtain more in-depth information on each subject. No book on school reform can be the final word on this important subject. Research in this field will be a "work in progress" for many years, but it is time to focus on how to fix the fundamental causes of student learning problems rather than just trying to improve student performance by a few percentage points.

Today, education reform is a top-priority concern of parents, business executives, political leaders, and taxpayers. Thousands of people want to read about the "big picture" on how to fix our public school system. Millions of Americans are disgusted with schools that blame society and parents for poor student performance. They want solutions built not on good intentions, but rather on solid education research, sound management systems, and new education systems.

Many readers will ask, "Why has it taken so long for this solution to be documented?" The initial reaction in every organization with serious performance problems is to try to "patch" existing methods. Quick-fix solutions are always implemented, and only after years of "tuning up" the system do leaders get serious about reengineering the troubled organization with a total systems approach. Until situations are intolerable, people are reluctant to make wholesale changes. Winston Churchill once said, "Americans always do the right thing—after they have tried everything else." Simple solutions have been tried in our schools. Now is the time to do the right thing: institute comprehensive, systemic change. This overhaul will affect schools, teachers, administrators, local school districts, superintendents, state departments of education, chief state school officers, the federal Department of Education, and the Secretary of Education. This process must also result in the development of new learning systems, administrative systems that support those learning systems, and management (governance) systems.

Many assumptions about how to fix an organization turn out to be myths. And, too often, one myth leads to others, taking people with good intentions down wrong roads that have little or no impact. One reason that the Wright brothers were the first to fly was their investigation of all the existing aeronautical assumptions. They learned that most of these "accepted" theories were myths. Many of the so-called cures in the school reform efforts have also been myths, but it has taken many years and millions of dollars to prove them wrong.

***The following stakeholders in the education system should read this book:***

- The Secretary of Education and the professional staff in the federal Department of Education
- Political officials at the federal, state, and local levels
- Business executives involved in school reform
- District superintendents and the district staff
- Board of education members
- School administrators
- Teachers
- Union leaders
- Deans and faculty members at colleges of education
- Officials at accreditation agencies
- Leaders of advocacy groups for minorities
- Parents
- Taxpayers

All of these stakeholders need to share the vision that will ultimately fix the American public school system.

Some people will criticize the writing style of this book because it differs from traditional education research documents that use pedagogical terms and numerous footnotes. With such a wide audience, I decided to follow the plain-language movement that is currently experiencing a resurgence. After all, if people can't quickly discern information, they quickly lose interest and/or miss vital messages. Fixing our schools is a great challenge that requires outstanding communications skills in addition to great leadership.

A few years ago, the former governor of New Jersey said, "We have become masters of measuring poor performance and spending money, but we have had little impact on the improvement of student learning." Everyone in the room nodded in agreement. At last, a growing consensus exists that the primary problems interfering with student learning are in the classroom itself. Therefore, many people are now saying that we need better teaching. They place the blame on teachers and colleges of education who train teachers. Teachers and colleges of education *do* need to change many of their methods, but they are not the primary cause of inadequate student performance. The overall education system needs to change in order to enable both students and teachers to be successful. It is a systems problem. Administrators must become leaders of learning and change. School reform is an exciting story about necessary changes and how they can be implemented.

When he took office, the dean at one of the nation's leading colleges of education said, "President Kennedy didn't say we will improve the space program, which was in real trouble in 1960. The President said we would land a man on the moon before the end of the decade." In this book, I don't say we will improve student learning by a few percentage points. With failure rates between 25 and 75 percent in our schools, this nation must commit to fixing its public schools. If we are to maintain our great standard of living and our economic leadership role in the world community, "fix schools first" must become a unifying effort involving political leaders, business executives, community leaders, parents, taxpayers, and educators. This is why the title *Fix Schools First* was selected for this book. The good news in this book is that the education reform movement can achieve success if school districts decide to take two giant steps forward into a new paradigm. New learning systems and a new management system are essential to achieving the goal that all students can be successful learners. Many new messages and thoughts are included in this book.

*As educators read this text, they should constantly ask themselves three questions that are based on having a school achieve the goal that all students should be successful learners:*

1. What messages and facts do you agree with?
2. What messages do you disagree with and why?
3. What changes are necessary to modify the blueprint at your school to achieve the learning standards that have been established by the local school district and the state department of education?

---

**NOTE**

1. J. Barker, *Future Edge* (New York: William Morrow and Co., 1992).

# PART I

# Overpowering Reasons for Change

In 1983, educators once again rang the alarm bell with a famous government report that claimed that our country had serious quality problems within the American public school system. Although some improvements have been made, student learning continues to be far below the level that is acceptable by institutions of higher education, political leaders, employers, and parents. During the past 18 years, billions of incremental dollars have been invested in local school districts, with only a slight improvement in student learning. Many educators want to give up on education reform, but our nation must move ahead until the goal of all children being successful learners is realized. This section of the book identifies the real problems within the education system that cause more than 50 percent of the students to not perform at grade-level expectations and too many students to not have learned essential knowledge and skills required to enjoy a successful life in our country.

# CHAPTER 1

# Educators Ring Alarm Bell on Quality

Toward the end of the 1970s, President Carter elevated the stature of the federal Department of Education by creating a full cabinet-level position for a Secretary of Education. In 1980, Ronald Reagan defeated President Carter with a platform that government had grown too large and required too many taxpayer dollars. President Reagan stated that he would close some major government agencies. The federal Department of Education was a candidate for closure. The new Secretary of Education, Terrel H. Bell, convinced President Reagan that a study should be conducted on the overall health of public education before any major changes were made in the federal government's role. In August 1981, a National Commission on Excellence in Education was created.

On April 26, 1983, the commission published its famous 41-page book, *A Nation At Risk: The Imperative For Education Reform*. This publication highlighted the education system's serious quality problems and marked the beginning of the current education reform movement. This revolution has lasted 18 years and will likely continue at least another 12 years. It may even turn into a 50-year effort.

The report featured unusually sensational language for an education document:

> "Our Nation is at risk. Our once unchallenged preeminence in commerce, industry, science, and technological innovation is being overtaken by competitors throughout the world. This report is concerned with only one of the many causes and dimensions of the problem, but it is the one that undergirds American prosperity, security and civility. We report to the American people that while we can take justifiable pride in what our schools and colleges have historically accomplished and contributed to the United States and the well-being of its people, the education foundations of our society are presently being eroded by a rising tide of mediocrity that threatens our very future as a Nation and a people. What

3

was unimaginable a generation ago has begun to occur—others are matching and surpassing our education attainments. If an unfriendly foreign power had attempted to impose on America the mediocre education performance that exists today, we might well have viewed it as an act of war. As it stands, we have allowed this to happen to ourselves."

The Secretary of Education, Dr. Bell, almost refused to issue this report because of its emotional tone. Fortunately, the document was printed, and it initiated the education reform movement that is absolutely essential for our children and our country.

## HOW SERIOUS ARE THE QUALITY ISSUES?

At first, dozens of anecdotal stories were published about how many applicants for employment couldn't read or write. In addition, U.S. students' Scholastic Aptitude Test (SAT) scores had been declining for years. David Kearns, the former Chief Executive Officer of Xerox Corporation and former Deputy Secretary of Education, once stated that 700,000 functionally illiterate students graduated from high school each year.[1] Functionally illiterate meant that they could not read or write at the fourth-grade level. The *A Nation At Risk* report estimated functionally illiteracy as high as 40 percent among minority youth and stated that 23 million Americans were in this category.[2] Four of five young adults surveyed couldn't summarize the main point of a newspaper article, read a bus schedule, or calculate their change from a restaurant bill.[3] According to the most recent evidence, 78 percent of higher education institutions offer remedial courses in reading, writing, and mathematics.[4] And 29 percent of all first-time freshmen enroll in at least one of these courses each fall. Considering that this 29 percent of first-year students is from the top half of their high school classes who go on to college, the implications are shocking.[5] The high school diploma had become almost meaningless because, across the country, schools had lowered their standards for what a high school graduate should know or be able to do.

At international competitions, American students finished last or near last. When the United States was in a recession, the school system received considerable blame. In years of prosperity, it became evident that the United States could continue to be an economic leader because of the existing superior institutions of higher education and the world-class workforce-training programs. Even then, though, enormous costs were associated with students needing to take remedial courses after high school.

As cities and states became more concerned about student achievement, a series of examinations was implemented to determine how much students know at the end of the fourth, eighth, and eleventh grades. The results were unbelievable. Across the nation, it appears that only 50 percent of the students tested are at grade level. This means our schools tolerate a 50-percent failure rate, which is simply an unacceptable statistic. In fact, this failure number may be conservative because the National Assessment of Education Progress, which is produced by the U.S. Department of Education, has recorded that 70 percent of fourth-graders and eighth-graders are reading below grade level. In addition, 80 percent of fourth-graders and twelfth-graders are not at grade level in mathematics and 75 percent of fourth-, eighth-, and twelfth-graders are writing below the level of proficiency.[6]

In our best schools, where all students speak English, parents are supportive, budgets exceed $10,000 per student, the finest teachers and administrators are employed, and good facilities and adequate books abound, the failure rate is usually around 25 percent. In other words, 25 of 100 students are not at grade level.[7] That is why David Kearns stated, "There is a misplaced smugness and complacency about the quality of suburban schools. They look pretty good compared with their urban and rural counterparts. But they are a pale imitation of a real school compared with schools abroad."[8]

It's just the opposite within urban school districts. There the failure rate is approximately 75 percent.[9] Only 25 of 100 students are at grade level. In some high schools, only 5 percent[10] of students are at grade level because most of the good students have transferred to magnet schools. In a few magnet and charter schools, where the very best teachers and students have been relocated, the success rate can reach 95 percent.[11] This situation occurs when the best students have been carefully selected from other schools.

In 1998, Mibrey W. McLauglin from the Stanford University Department of Education and Robert B. Schwartz from the Graduate School of Education at Harvard University asked Ron Wolk, a former publisher and editor of *Education Week*, to develop a short essay reflecting his analysis and conclusions based on the Pew Forum on Standards-Based Reform, which was a meeting of two dozen leading policy makers, researchers, and education practitioners. He wrote the following statement concerning low-performing schools:[12]

> Often, fewer than 20 percent of the students score at grade level on standardized tests. It is not unusual for 75 percent of them to be several grades behind in reading, mathematics, and science. On any given day, one out of five high school students may be absent, and, on average, a student in the worst secondary schools may be absent a quarter or more of the school year. When they come to school, they are likely to sleep in class or roam the halls creating disciplinary problems. Suspensions and expulsions tend to be much higher than average. Many students change schools at least once during the year—nearly always moving from one bad school to another. More than half drop out before they reach 12th grade. Some of those who graduate cannot read or calculate well enough to hold a job or succeed in college without remedial education.

Overall, the 1983 *A Nation At Risk* report did not overstate the problem. A crisis clearly exists within the American public school system because more than half the students are not at grade level. The root problem to be solved is student learning.

## WHAT IS THE DEFINITION FOR SUCCESS?

An entire school district needs to have 90 percent or more of its students at grade level.[13] A defined and documented curriculum of lessons must be learned over 13 years (kindergarten through high school) by at least 90 percent of all students who speak the English language and who have lived in the school district for a reasonable length of time. The curriculum should be based on the standards established by the state department of education and the local school district. Unfortunately, most of our schools do not have or teach an integrated curriculum for K–12, and they do not even measure if students are at grade level.

For generations, schools have utilized the famous bell curve, which assumes that there are smart, average, and dumb children. Current education research informs us that more than 90 percent of students can be successful learners during the K–12 years. In other words, they can achieve A and B work in all subjects. Therefore, schools need to move beyond the bell curve in order to turn most students into successful learners. The traditional wide bell curve must be eliminated because it is the basis for the select-and-sort model that has helped create the crisis in student learning.

*With grade inflation occurring in nearly every school today, the current grading system actually means the following:*

*A.* Learned all of the lessons
*B.* Learned almost all of the lessons
*C.* Learned some of the lessons
*D.* Learned a few lessons
*F.* Learned almost no lessons

Only students with grades A and B are usually at grade level in most schools. *In the future, more than 90 percent of the students should earn A's or B's, and grades would mean the following:*

*A.* Learned all of the lessons as well as some enrichment lessons
*B.* Learned all of the lessons

Students would receive tutoring and additional assignments until they achieved at least a B in every lesson. No social promotions would take place. Students would become successful learners in the new paradigm. A few students would not be able to earn a B because of a serious impairment that prevented them from learning even if given special attention and resources, but these students would be very few. Figure 1–1 presents a picture of "The Great Transition" for learning.

Why is 90 percent the goal for success? Every school district and every school can establish its own target of how many students should be at grade level. Some will aim for 75 percent because that is what the top schools seem to achieve on mastery tests. Some may be able to reach only 60 percent because 40 percent of their students just enrolled at their school in the current year. A few may strive for 95 percent because they already exceed 90 percent. Now, more educators claim that all students can be successful learners in the K–12 years. If that is true, it seems as if 90 percent is a reasonable goal because it allows for 10 percent of the students to be in transit or in special education or language classes. For the remainder of this book, 90 percent is used as the objective as a general benchmark. In the past, the lack of a specific percent of successful students that is easily

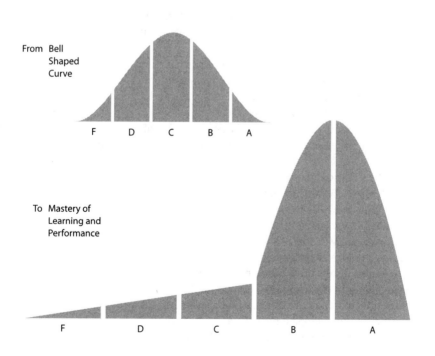

**Figure 1–1** The Great Transition

understood by educators, political leaders, community leaders, business leaders, taxpayers, parents, and students severely hurt the education reform movement.

Keep in mind that with a 90-percent objective for having students at grade level, more than 5 million students will still not be at grade level. If the objective is 75 percent, then 13 million students will be falling behind, and with the current 50 percent, more than 25 million students struggle to learn, with many unable to have any hope of achieving a real K–12 education.

Why is grade-level measurement so important? Everyone agrees that a 13-year process must be broken into measurable elements because it makes no sense to merely measure the effectiveness of learning at the end of a 13-year effort. Hence, educators created grade levels many years ago. In addition, if a student is not at grade level, it is difficult to learn the next lesson. For example, if a student in the fourth grade did not learn how to multiply or divide numbers in lower grades, it is almost impossible for that student to learn how to multiply and divide fractions. When children are not at grade level, they fall behind, get lost, and give up, which is exactly what is happening to millions of children in the public schools. The alternative is to adopt an individual learning plan for each student that requires outstanding learning systems, which are described in Chapter 9, and smaller classes, which most public schools do not have today.

Too often, people assume that the goal of making all students successful learners can be accomplished only by "dumbing down" the curriculum, but this is not true. The current bell curve has resulted in a curriculum with fewer expectations because millions of students are behind in grade level. Within inner-city schools, many educators believe that students can learn only half the lessons.[14] This means that inner-city fourth graders might only be capable of doing second-grade work, eighth graders may only be able to handle fourth-grade lessons, and high school seniors could really be at the sixth-grade level. The reader will learn later in this book how the American public school system can, instead, have a world-class curriculum in which all students succeed.

Dr. Renfro C. Manning, Superintendent of Schools in Orange County, Virginia, wrote a book in 1994 called *Schools for All Learners: Beyond the Bell Curve*. This book provides great insight into the issue that all students can be successful learners. In his book, Dr. Manning stated that a new paradigm must be developed to achieve significant improvement in student learning.[15] The old paradigm was developed for the "select-and-sort" model, which ensures a high failure rate. He further stated that education reform requires a new vision. Several school superintendents have stated in numerous presentations that all students can be successful learners. Fortunately, this belief is being adopted by more and more school districts. The new paradigm based on a new vision is documented in Part III of this book.

## WHERE DO YOU FIND SUCCESSFUL SCHOOL DISTRICTS?

It's easy to find a few successful teachers in almost every school. Contrary to what some educators believe, though, there is a bell curve for teachers as well. Some are outstanding, most are average, and, unfortunately, some need to improve or leave the teaching profession. This wide bell curve exists in all major job categories in all industries for which performance objectives have not been documented for mastery of the job. Sadly, it's almost impossible to find an entire school district that has 90 percent of its students at grade level because so many districts accept the wide bell curve for both teachers and students.

Today, however, major school reform efforts are taking place in almost every large city. Some famous superintendents at the forefront of this movement are and have been General John Stanford (and his successor Joseph Alchefske) in Seattle, Alan Bersin (former U. S. Attorney) in San Diego, David Hornbeck (leader of school reform) in Philadelphia, and Paul G. Vallas in Chicago. Unfortunately, though, not a single urban school district has achieved real breakthroughs in student learning. Some improvements have been made, but with a failure rate still hovering around 75 percent, urban superintendents need to identify the fundamental learning problems and fix their schools, not just improve student learning in small increments.

It is estimated that nearly one-quarter of the nation's public school students are enrolled in rural areas or small towns. Some of these schools are outstanding, but many have failure rates that are similar to urban school districts. Schools in Texas, Connecticut, Kentucky, and North Carolina are showing some improvement, but they have a long way to go before 90 percent of their students are at grade level. Rich suburban schools have also made some modest improvements in student learning, but 20 to 25 percent of their students remain below grade level. Therefore, copying suburban school methods is not necessarily a successful strategy for inner-city schools.

In the February 16, 2000 issue of *Education Week*, the article "Reality Check" stated that employers and college professors remain broadly dissatisfied with the skills of young people entering the job market and higher education.[16] These people are the ultimate consumers of high school graduates and drop-outs. For the third year in a row, three of four employers and college professors stated that today's high school graduates have just fair or poor skills in grammar, spelling, and the ability to write clearly.[17] Clear majorities give similarly lackluster ratings for basic math skills. Input from teachers and students suggests that many schools have not begun to adopt the standards, testing, and accountability policies being urged by political leaders, business executives, and state departments of education.[18]

## WHAT ARE THE MAJOR EXCUSES FOR FAILURE?

*A long list of excuses has been adopted by the education community to justify why more than 50 percent of the students are not at grade level,[19] including the following:*

- Poverty
- Breakdown of the family
- Minorities
- Mobility of students
- Crime and violence
- Too much television
- English as a second language
- Insufficient funds, which is discussed in the next chapter

Let's look briefly at each excuse to determine how it impacts quality and student learning.

### Poverty

The U.S. Census Bureau has defined poverty as an annual income less than $16,600 for a family of four.[20] This means that 11.8 percent of our citizens (34.5 million) are below the poverty line, which entitles them to special social programs for health care, food stamps, fuel grants, welfare payments, low-cost housing, and special attention from charitable organizations. Numerous rewards are provided for being listed below the poverty line, and, not surprisingly, rewarding failure creates more failure. In addition, other reports state that somewhere between 17 and 25 percent of school-age children are from families that live below the poverty line. In many urban schools, most students live below the poverty line.

How much does poverty affect the ability of a child to learn? First, children who are living below the poverty line are entitled to a free breakfast and lunch. They are not hungry. In most communities, they are entitled to free vaccines and medical services. Often, various charities and churches provide clothing for school for these children, if necessary. Children either live within walking distance of their schools or free transportation is provided for them. Their books are free. Simply put, they have the basic necessities of life. So, the opportunity to learn is available.

There are other interesting details about being poor in the United States, according to the U.S. Census Bureau. About 41 percent of the poor own a home (with a mortgage), which on average has three bedrooms, one and one-half baths, a garage, either a porch or a patio, and a backyard. It is estimated that 72 percent of poor households have a car. Eighty-four percent of the poor say their families have enough to eat; the average intake of protein, minerals, and vitamins is practically the same for poor children as for middle-class youngsters.[21] All of these statistics suggest that poverty by itself should not cause such a high level of failure in the urban and rural school systems. These facts are not meant to suggest, however, that the poor are well-off or that they do not have serious problems. They often are laid off from their work. They constantly worry about trying to meet their daily requirements. They have few or no special vacations or events in their lives, other than television and various sporting events.

Compared to Americans living during the Great Depression years, when unemployment levels reached 25 percent and employees took salary reductions of up to 60 percent to keep a job, most people who live below the poverty line today are in much better shape. Between 1930 and 1933, more than 9,000 banks failed, taking the life savings of hard-working people. Homes had to be returned to banks. Both mothers and fathers stood in long lines for food hand-outs. That situation was poverty like this country had never seen before or since.

Today, children living below the poverty line often have parents who work long hours at two or three jobs and sometimes lack good parenting and academic skills. These parents often do not provide the same support for education as their middle-class counterparts, which is the next excuse to be reviewed.

### Breakdown of the Family

Many people point to being poor and having a single parent as the root causes of poor student learning. This may be the case in some situations, but many single parents actually spend more time with their children on homework and other school issues because they have no requirements to spend time on activities with their spouse. Their children are the center of their lives. Many of these children are successful students who are at grade level.

One successful superintendent stated that too many children in his inner-city school district had parents who were failures in school. They were functionally illiterate, which meant that they did not have the knowledge or the skills to help their children with schoolwork. As a result, this superintendent designed his learning systems on the basis that children must be successful learners even if they receive no help from their parents. In his schools, a lack of parental involvement could not be used as an excuse for a high rate of students being below grade level.

An increasing number of schools offer after-school programs that enable students to do all of their homework before they go home. Then they are free to watch television, play videogames, or do anything else they need to when they go home. If parents want to help with homework, they may do so, but the success of student learning is not delegated to parents in these inner-city homes.

Fortunately, many city schools have social workers and psychologists to help children who have major family problems. Children are resilient. If they are successful students, they rarely let the day-to-day problems of poverty or family get in the way of their continued success at school. On the other hand, if they fall behind in grade level, they usually hate school and use the excuses related to poverty and family problems for their poor performance, which are too often accepted by educators. Parental involvement and breakdown of the family could be used as an excuse if schools were operated like they were in the 1940s and 1950s, but the new vision in Chapter 11 presents a more realistic model for parental involvement.

## Minorities

Today, the United States consists of five major groups of people. Latin Americans (Latinos or Hispanics) are the fastest-growing segment. By 2020, they are forecasted to be the majority population in California and Texas. Soon after that date, they will be the majority in New York, New Jersey, Arizona, Florida, Virginia, and Illinois.[22] African Americans are already the majority population in many major cities, where they often hold key leadership positions, including the Superintendent of Schools. In Hawaii, Asian Americans are in the majority. Asian Americans have become very successful students throughout the entire American school system. Their current success at institutions of higher learning ensures that their race will be well represented in leadership positions within government, business, and education in future years. European Americans (Whites) and other Caucasians constitute the majority in rural and suburban schools. On average, they do well in school, but 25 percent of students in these schools are behind in grade level. Native Americans have often struggled in reservation schools, but many of these schools have been less than optimal institutions of learning.

Saying that African American or Latin American children can only be successful learners if they are seated next to white children in suburban schools is racist and ridiculous. Inner-city schools can and must achieve 90 percent successful learners no matter who is sitting in the classrooms. Schools must be like airplanes: they all must be successful. Schools must work for all races and genders. Institutions of higher learning, corporate training programs, and military training do not have separate courses for minorities and different genders. Minorities can learn as well as majorities. The American public school system must stop using the percent of minorities in their schools as an excuse for poor performance in student learning. Too often, educators have set unnecessarily low expectations for Native Americans, Latin Americans, and African Americans, and then they act surprised when they get what they expect.

## Mobility of Students

Some teachers and administrators proclaim that inner-city schools are really child care centers where a little learning takes place.[23] This mindset stems from the high student mobility caused by frequent job and home changes in families who live below the poverty line. Mobility is a fact of life in a free society. In fact, 43 million Americans move each year.[24] Children could cope better with mobility if every school had a similar curriculum of lessons based on standards established by the state board of education. In today's educational world, very little standardization exists. Therefore, poor children are hurt by the lack of standards. This problem could be fixed quickly by large-city school districts and state boards of education. Mobility is a valid excuse under the current system, but the education community can reduce or even eliminate this disadvantage.

Children who are homeless have a serious and unique challenge. It should be no surprise that they score lower on test scores and are less likely to be promoted to the next grade. When both home and school disappear simultaneously, these children face a traumatic situation. They lose their friends, teachers, and schoolwork. They are stigmatized as homeless in their new environment, which is often a noisy shelter. In most situations, they move several times per year. The Stewart B. McKinney Homeless Assistance Act of 1987 requires states to ensure that local education agencies do not create a separate education system for homeless children. On the other hand, homeless students usually require special tutoring systems because they have missed so many school days. Homeless children and children in foster care represent about 1 percent of all students.

## Crime and Violence

Too many people accept the excuse that city children don't need to worry about being good students because they can become rich by being drug dealers. The number of students who are behind two or more grade levels is in the millions. They cannot all possibly become drug dealers any more than all the unsuccessful students in the 1930s could have become bank robbers. Besides, almost every bank robber and drug dealer eventually ends up dead or in prison. Numerous role models besides drug dealers are available for inner-city children. Children need to know how they can become successful students and working adults. Weak excuses are not helpful in building student self-esteem.

In recent years, accounts of students killing teachers and other students on school property have been well-publicized. Despite these tragic events, children are safer at school today than at almost any other location within a city. With a new emphasis on security systems, additional police, more uniforms, and the identification of potentially violent students, the number of violent incidents has declined. In fact, most problems occur in rural and suburban schools where security has not been taken seriously.

Class management is a real challenge within inner-city schools that have only a small minority of their students at grade level. In this situation, students are kept in the classroom by hall monitors who carry walkie-talkies and are stationed in every hallway. Once in the classroom, some teachers are not able to conduct classes successfully because of disruptions by students. Typically, these students are far behind in grade level and have given up on school. Their only enjoyment and satisfaction is to cause trouble. Teachers are reluctant to discipline them because they fear that they will be labeled as a racist or a child abuser. Such incidents can be a valid excuse for ineffective teaching and poor learning, but this situation exists usually when students are not successful learners.

All schools need to have a behavior and dress code that is agreed to by parents and students, as well as teachers and administrators. The school becomes the secondary parent as "in loco parentis." Going to school and being with their classmates is a privilege granted to those students who adhere to the behavior and dress codes. If students' behavior disrupts the orderly process of learning, an alternative organization must handle their education.

## Too Much Television

Television is both educational and entertaining. Although many people criticize what is offered by the networks and cable systems, people can learn a great deal by carefully selecting the programs they watch. Unfortunately, the education community did not embrace television as an education delivery system, blaming it instead as an excuse for poor school performance.

Too many classes are dull and boring. Education should be motivational and entertaining. Children should want to learn. Television has established new standards for excellence in learning, with a few outstanding educational programs. The education community should work with the television industry for more and better educational programs because almost every household has a television set. Broadcasters use the airwaves free and are required by law to serve the public interest. Educational programming is defined as programming designed with specific educational or informational goals, set forth in advance, and produced with cooperation from educators. Each station should offer some hours of educational television each week.

Many students do watch television in the evening hours or on weekends rather than completing their homework assignments, but these students are usually behind in their lessons and constantly lost in their academic subjects. The education system has failed them, and they have turned to television for something to do.

## English As a Second Language

In 1994, the General Accounting Office (GAO) wrote a report to Senator Edward Kennedy indicating that the number of limited English proficient (LEP) students increased by almost 26 percent in the last decade. More than 2.3 million

LEP students (5 percent of all students) live in the United States, representing many different linguistic and cultural backgrounds. The GAO estimated that 72 percent of LEP students are concentrated in six states: California, Florida, Illinois, New Jersey, New York, and Texas. Arizona and New Mexico also have a high percentage of LEP students. More than 40 percent of all LEP students are immigrants.[25]

Immigrant students provide a real challenge to school districts because many have significant health and emotional needs, especially those who have experienced the trauma of war and life in refugee camps. They are also highly transient, and often their parents think they cannot help them because they do not have a good command of English. Extra effort and programs must be mounted because the federal civil rights laws require that districts provide assistance to help LEP students participate in education programs.

The Bilingual Education Act of 1965 provides several hundred million dollars for school districts, and the Emergency Immigrant Education Act provides additional millions to address this problem.[26] State governments also contribute millions of dollars. There appear to be three major strategies currently in use to teach LEP students:

1. *Transitional Bilingual Education.* This is an instructional program in which subjects are taught in two languages: English and the native language. The goal is to have LEP students evolve to an all-English program of instruction. In theory, this program makes sense, but in practice, it has not been successful. Many schools do not have a sufficient number of bilingual instructors for the various languages. Too often, an insufficient number of LEP students transferred to an all-English program of instruction. Leaders of minority groups are split on the issue of bilingual education, but many have now concluded that it is a failed system because it keeps too many minorities in a second-class status. Every high school graduate must be proficient in English. In some school districts, 10 to 50 different languages are spoken by students. The bilingual strategy was only able to handle a few languages, which was a severe limitation.

2. *Immersion Into English Language.* In California and other states, children are expected to learn English first in an immersion class over a one- to two-year period. Then they are transferred to an all-English program of instruction. This strategy ensures that they will be able to read, write, and compute in the English language.

3. *Submersion.* This program involves placing LEP students in ordinary classrooms in which English is the language of instruction. Also called "sink or swim," this method was used for immigrants at the beginning of the century, and it still works for some students; however, it is unacceptable for most LEP students today.

California has almost 50 percent of the LEP students, and their voters adopted an immersion system.[27] Because of the problems of finding good bilingual learning materials and a sufficient number of well-qualified bilingual teachers, the future strategy appears to be immersion into English language, which upsets the bilingual teachers. Educators have had decades to prove that their methods would work, and now voters in several states want to try immersion because it's more affordable, measurable, and accepted by the overall population. Early indications suggest that the immersion programs are succeeding in California.

Immigration will always be an issue in our country. One to two percent of students on a national basis will always be LEP students. The goal must be to develop learning systems for immigrants to master the English language. A great deal more can be done in this area. In the meantime, LEP students should be tested separately for two to three years until they have mastered the English language.

## TIME TO DO AWAY WITH EXCUSES

Every profession is measured on results, not good intentions. Accountants must be able to balance their books and issue certified financial statements. Engineers must be able to construct buildings and roads that last for more than 50 years. Software engineers must create electronic systems that last for decades. Salespeople must achieve 100 percent of their quota. They are measured on actual sales, not good intentions such as outstanding presentations, great proposals, and motivational demonstrations. Accordingly, the job of teaching is not completed until students have learned their lessons and can perform the necessary skills. In the future, teachers and administrators will be measured on the quality of their curriculum and on how many of their students are doing grade-level work.

The trend toward offering excuses for student learning deficiencies accelerated in the 1960s when the government released a report called "On Equality of Education Opportunity," which stated that a child's family background and the school's socioeconomic makeup are the best predictors of student learning.[28] This report is commonly called the Coleman Report because Dr. James S. Coleman of Johns Hopkins University wrote the document. He later moved to the University of Chicago. Many educators and public policy experts used this study as well as other research papers to promote school integration and welfare programs. During the past 40 years, many schools were allowed to become child care centers where only a little learning took place. The Coleman and similar research studies are accurate based on the current paradigm for teaching, learning, and management of schools. If no systemic change occurs, then poverty, minorities, and language are valid predictors of low performance. With the new paradigm that is discussed in Parts III and IV of this book, however, more than 90 percent of all children can be successful learners. Educators must accept the fact that students will come from a wide variety of backgrounds, and the education system must enable most students to be successful.

Students who come from a low socioeconomic environment undoubtedly have a greater challenge to become successful learners. Dozens of research studies prove this statement. In many situations, these students' parents, brothers, sisters, aunts, uncles, cousins, and friends have disliked school because they fell behind, became lost, and gave up. They hated school for 13 years. Failure at school is accepted in some neighborhoods as a way of life. It is much easier to teach in a school where children are expected to be successful students because their parents, brothers, sisters, and other family members have been good learners. Special tutoring is often provided if necessary. Failure at those schools is not tolerated. All of this means that fundamental change is required in almost all schools for the bottom quartile in high-performing schools and for the bottom three quartiles in low-performing schools.

The Director of the Education Trust, Kati Haycock, has produced a counterargument to the Coleman Report. Based on both research and extensive experience in classrooms all over the country, she claims that poor and minority youngsters can achieve at the same high levels as other students if they are taught at those levels. Therefore, it is time to develop successful schools for all American children. Parents are tired of hearing excuses from schools. A brave African American mother stood at an education reform meeting and told the educators to fix the learning and teaching problems in the schools and to stop blaming parents.

No other major institution in the United States has failure rates like the public school system. Failure is not an acceptable outcome in this country. Schools must be fixed. Today, finding a solution to the crisis in student learning is one of the nation's top priorities based on the incremental money being invested and the talent being applied to this challenge. The following chapters explain how our school system will eventually achieve breakthroughs in student learning.

Now let's move on to Chapter 2 to see if schools have sufficient resources to achieve the educational standards being established by the state departments of education.

---

**NOTES**

1. D. Kearns and D. Doyle, *Winning the Brain Race* (San Francisco: ICS Press, 1988), 1.

2. National Commission on Excellence in Education, *A Nation At Risk* (Washington, DC: U.S. Department of Education, 1983).

3. J. Bowsher, *Educating America* (New York: John Wiley & Sons, 1989), 165.

4. D. Breneman, "Remediation in Higher Education: Its Extent and Cost," in *Brookings Papers on Education Policy*, ed. Diane Ravich (Washington, DC: Brookings Institute Press, 1998).

5. Breneman, "Remediation."

6. Estimation by author based on a series of articles about the drop-out rate and actual drop-out rates at some urban high schools. R.A. Kittle, "Making the Grade," *San Diego Union-Tribune*, 18 October, 2000, B8.

7. Estimation by author based on mastery tests in states, achievement tests, and various articles discussing results on classroom examinations. For example, HUD State of the Cities report based on NAEP data that in suburban schools 63 percent of the students achieved "basic skill levels in reading," 66 percent in mathematics, and 65 percent in science.

8. D. Kearns and J. Harvey, *A Legacy of Learning* (Washington, DC: Brookings Institute Press, 2000), 4.

9. Estimation by author based on mastery tests in states, achievement tests, and various articles discussing results on classroom examinations. For example: J. Kronhez, "Baltimore Public School Struggles to Improve Its Scores," *Wall Street Journal*, 16 June, 2000, A16, where the percent of students passing state tests was 0 to 12 percent.

10. Estimation by author.

11. Estimation by author.

12. R. Wolk, "Strategies for Fixing Failing Public Schools," *Education Week*, 4 November, 1998, 44.

13. Author is the source.

14. Interviews by author.

15. R.C. Manning, *School for All Learners: Beyond the Bell Curve* (Princeton Junction, NJ: Eye On Education, 1994), 1–26.

16. Public Agenda, "Reality Check 2000," *Education Week*, 16 February, 2000, 51–58.

17. Public Agenda, "Reality Check."

18. Public Agenda, "Reality Check."

19. Numerous books and articles read by the author.

20. L. Uchitelle, "Census Bureau Set To Sharply Increase Nation's Poverty Line," *New York Times* News Service, in *San Diego Union-Tribune*, 18 October, 1999, A1, A14 and *Education Week*, 4 October, 2000, 4.

21. Uchitelle, "Census Bureau."

22. D. Lindquist, "The Minority Majority," *San Diego Union-Tribune*, 10 October, 1999, C1, C3; based on a 1999 U. S. Commerce Department report written by Ruth Sandoval, Deputy Director of Minority Business Development.

23. Interviews by author.

24. C. Gewerty, "Demographic Challenges Ahead for Schools," *Education Week*, 19 April, 2000, 10.

25. General Accounting Report, *Limited English Proficiency* (Washington, DC: General Accounting Office, January 1994), 1–86.

26. General Accounting Report, *Limited English Proficiency*.

27. R. Porter, *Education Leadership* (Alexandria, VA: Association for Supervision and Curriculum Development, December 1999 and January 2000), 52–56.

28. D. Hoff, "Echoes of the Coleman Report," *Education Week*, 24 March, 1999, 33.

# CHAPTER 2

# Ring Another Alarm Bell for Escalating Costs

*A Nation At Risk* only addressed the quality problems that exist in the American public school system. The second major problem is the explosive growth in the system's cost.

**FIRST OR SECOND LARGEST LINE ITEM OF GOVERNMENT EXPENSE**

If all of the government budgets (federal, state, and local) were consolidated into a single package, the largest expense would be social security payments at more than $400 billion.[1] The second largest taxpayer expense would be the public school system, which costs far more than the entire defense budget, or the interest on the national debt, or Medicare.[2] This fact may surprise many people because they've heard that health care costs annually exceed more than $1 trillion; however, most health care funds come from private citizens, insurance companies, corporations, and not-for-profit organizations. In fact, the public school budget would be the largest expense if income tax on social security payments were deducted from the total payments, which is the net expense to the federal government for social security.

How much have public school costs risen? In 1959–1960, the cost of funding public schools was $15.6 billion.[3] This cost included the expansion for the "baby boomer" generation that started in 1946. By 1983, when *A Nation At Risk* was published, the cost had grown to $130 billion because of the rapid inflation that occurred during the 1970s and early 1980s.[4]

When *A Nation At Risk* was published, the business community and political leaders responded immediately to the educators' claim that schools were underfunded. Many tax increases were approved at both the state and local levels with the hope—and it was only a hope—that student learning would improve. This famous 41-page booklet may be the greatest fund-raising document of all time because the annual public school operating budgets grew by $200 billion from 1983 to 2000.[5] In addition, billions of dollars are being invested in new schools and renovated school buildings.

Almost every political leader claims that he or she will fix the public schools with a variety of expensive new programs. The forecasted cost of operating our schools could be close to $400 billion[6] by 2003, the 20th anniversary of *A Nation At Risk*. Thus the growth in spending from 1983 to 2003 will be close to $270 billion, the cost of the entire defense organization in recent years.[7] Hence, the term "explosive" growth is used to describe the second major problem in our schools.

The Defense Department can report that, for $270 billion, the United States has the most powerful military organization in the world. Our Air Force can win a war in weeks without losing any personnel; our Army won the Gulf War within a few days; and our Navy is vastly superior to any other. In other words, our country has an expensive, but world-class military organization.

On the other hand, even if costs escalate to $400 billion, the United States will continue to have, in many communities, a third-class public school system that is inferior to schools in the leading countries of Europe and Asia unless major changes are implemented. Institutions of higher learning will continue to spend billions of dollars on remedial courses for high school graduates who do not have adequate reading, writing, and mathematics skills. Corporations, government agencies, and not-for-profit organizations must also continue to spend a few billion dollars annually on remedial courses for their entry-level employees because more than 50 percent of students do not obtain a real high school education.

Surprisingly enough, most educators still claim that they are short of funds. In fact, many school districts claim they haven't received any part of this explosive growth in funding. Many educators have a difficult time believing that schools have two to three times more money than they had in 1983 because their salaries are not two to three times their 1983 compensation. And, most of the schools are operating in old buildings. So why is there so much more money in the public school budgets? The primary reason is the increase in the number of people working within the schools. For example, in a 700-student inner-city elementary school, it is not uncommon to find 75 to 100 paid employees.[8] Fifty years ago, a city high school of 2,100 students had only 82 paid employees.[9] The second reason is that both compensation and benefits of this enlarged workforce have increased. For example, *A Nation At Risk* reported that the average teacher's salary in 1983 was $17,000. Now it is over $40,000 and on the way to becoming $50,000. In addition, most schools use many unpaid volunteers in the classrooms as aides and tutors. The ratio of students per classroom teacher is a misleading figure in most schools today. In most classrooms, there are usually two or more adults working with students. For every four classroom teachers in the United States, there are nearly six other school employees, indicating that teachers make up only 43 percent of the total school employment. Conversely, teaching staffs in other countries constitute 60 to 80 percent of school employment.[10] Often, the growth in spending is attributed to inflation. In reality, the years 1983–2000 have had low inflation.[11]

The United States Department of Education claims that large increases in expenditures per pupil have occurred in every decade since World War II, even after adjusting for inflation. There was a 45-percent increase in the 1950s and a 69-percent jump in the 1960s.[12] These figures are surprising because costs per student should go down during a period of rising enrollments because central administration and fixed costs can be allocated over a larger number of students. During the 1970s and 1980s, the rate of increase in expenditures per student slowed to a more moderate rate of 35 percent and 33 percent, respectively.[13] Only during the Depression and in the years 1978–1981 did the costs decrease. In the 1990s, per-student annual costs have risen from $5,000 to approximately $7,000, a 40-percent increase.[14]

Where else did the money go? Very few dollars have been invested in the elements of learning systems such as new books, workbooks, computer courseware, tutoring systems, and so forth. By all reports, the money did not go to building maintenance. Some money was needed to handle the increase in the number of students because schools have reached an enrollment level of more than 50 million students;[15] however, when school enrollments declined in the late 1970s and 1980s, budgets did not decrease in most communities. For example, in Westport, Connecticut, 50 percent of the schools were closed, but budgets did not decrease. In fact, Westport's school budget has grown from $7.9 million in 1968–1969 (baby boom years) to almost $64 million in school year 2000–2001, with about the same number of students.[16] School officials say that the latest budget has no excess funds in it—only essential expenses. A growth of 800 percent far exceeds the rate of inflation. Every school district staff should look at its 1968–1969 budget, its 1983 budget, and the current year's budget. They will also find major growth over the years.

## INEQUALITIES OF RICH AND POOR DISTRICTS

In his 1991 book *Savage Inequalities*, Jonathan Kozol stated that in the schools of East St. Louis, New York City, San Antonio, Chicago, Washington, D.C., and New Jersey, children are being starved in body and mind. He described vividly how poor the conditions were in many major American cities. He also explained how wealthy suburban districts invested more money in their schools than their urban counterparts did. He then concluded that money makes the difference between a successful school system and an unsuccessful one.[17]

Over the past 25 years, more than half the states have been taken to court on the issue that the financing of school districts violates the state constitution, which guarantees an equal education for all children. Their fundamental argument is that geography should not determine educational opportunity, which is great for some children and insufficient for others. More than 20 states have had their education systems struck down as unconstitutional because of spending inequities among school districts.[18] In almost every situation, a large tax increase was proposed to allocate more money to the poorer school districts with the hope of leaving the wealthier and successful systems untouched. In these cases, there was a call for dramatic new education reform measures to convince taxpayers that schools will improve with this new investment of taxes. For example, mastery tests were implemented in Connecticut to help justify a major increase in taxes there. Kentucky touted a well-publicized series of education reform programs to justify its tax increase.

In other states, such as Michigan, Wyoming, Montana, Utah, Texas, New Hampshire, and Vermont, an attempt has been made to take local tax dollars from the more affluent communities and redistribute the funds to poorer districts, a policy known as the "Robin Hood" strategy. The concept of equality has few, if any, success stories to prove that merely giving more money to poor school districts results in major breakthroughs in student learning.

In fact, some of the lowest-performing school districts have some of the higher per-pupil spending. Cost per student is among the highest in the nation, and often 75 percent of the students are below grade level in the following cities: Hartford, Connecticut; Newark, New Jersey; Washington, D.C.; New York City; and Chicago.

In 1991, Kentucky entered the school reform arena with the best of intentions. The governor and legislature passed a whopping tax increase. A new state law mandated that all school districts would be financially equal. Cash poured into the less affluent areas. Unlike other states that adopted reforms in small pieces, Kentucky created a coherent policy for restructuring its schools. Successful schools would receive cash bonuses. State "experts" would help schools that could not improve. Statewide performance tests would be implemented. Each school would have a site-based management council consisting of three teachers, two parents, and an administrator. The council could make decisions on curriculum, budgeting, staffing, and extracurricular activities. Kentucky's 176 school districts would be led by a new education commissioner. The focus of the Kentucky reform was clear: to improve student learning.

Where is Kentucky after 10 years of effort? Few Kentucky students have reached the learning level that the Kentucky Education Reform Act (KERA) projected. Some students have moved out of the lowest category called "novice" to the next level, "apprentice." At the novice level, a student has a minimal grasp of the lessons, which translates to being far below grade level. The apprentice level means that students have a limited understanding of the subject matter, but again they are not at grade level. The next level is "proficient," and the goal is to have at least 80 percent of the students at this level. There was also a hope that 10 percent would be at the highest level called "distinguished." Most Kentucky schools are a long way from achieving these goals, but student learning did improve in many schools.[19]

Once again, good intentions and a great deal of money were not sufficient. Money was spent, but major increases in student learning were not achieved. Kentucky tried the method where the state department of education would set goals and measure students. Then it was up to local schools to determine how to get students at grade level with an A or B performance. Unfortunately, this method doesn't seem to work, but it continues to be implemented in almost every state.

New Jersey is also following the "share the wealth" policy being mandated by the courts. Several times within the past 25 years, the state courts have forced governors and state legislatures to make substantial changes in public school funding. In 1990, the new governor of New Jersey convinced the legislature to pass a $1.1 billion tax increase for incremental funding.[20] Once again, there was a good name for the tax increase: Quality Education Act. But, the tax increase was a bitter pill to swallow, so taxpayers threw out the reigning legislative party and defeated the governor in the next election. Today, major cities in New Jersey continue to confront high drop-out rates and poor performance by inner-city students.

The courts are now shifting funding and governance from local governments to state governments. Unfortunately, socialistic allocation of funds simply has not achieved breakthroughs in learning. This shift has undoubtedly supplied some poor school districts with more adequate budgets; however, the courts are beginning to understand that funding is not the sole answer to fixing schools. The Pennsylvania Supreme Court has decided not to hear any more lawsuits that challenge the school funding system. The poorest districts receive $4,500 per student from the state, whereas the wealthiest schools receive only $380 per student.[21] As the governor put it, "Pennsylvania needs education reform, not more lawsuits."

## WHAT ARE THE REALISTIC COSTS FOR OPERATING SCHOOLS?

This question is simple, but the answer is complex. First, experienced teachers cost twice as much as new teachers. This is one reason why the cost per student is often lower within inner-city schools than in suburban schools. Inner-city schools usually have many new and inexperienced teachers who cost less. To make a more valid comparison among schools, the number of people by job category must be examined as well as the overall costs. Salary scales vary widely. In some school districts, new teachers start at $20,000 and finish at $40,000, assuming they obtain a master's degree and acquire 15 to 20 years of experience.[22] In other school districts, teachers start at $32,000 and finish at $75,000.[23] Benefits, including a pension, usually cost between 25 to 30 percent in addition to their annual salary. In a few years, some experienced teachers in selected cities and states will earn close to $100,000 in salary and benefits.[24] In most schools, teachers and other staff members account for nearly 75 percent of the budget. Maintenance and utilities average 11 percent. Business operations are near 2 percent. Administrators and schools office personnel are about 6 percent of the budget. The district office is about 3 percent, and transportation is usually 2 percent. This leaves about 1 percent for instructional materials.[25] These figures vary, though, based on how a school district allocates various expenses to their accounts.

Accountants need to build standard cost models for what student costs should be within a school district. What cost factors are necessary for a student to be at grade level from kindergarten through high school? The current average cost in the United States is close to $7,000 annually per student.[26] New Jersey's per-student cost is almost $11,000, Connecticut is close to $10,000, and Mississippi is only $5,000.[27] The cost of living in a state or city significantly affects the cost per student. Every child, on average, costs taxpayers $91,000 for a K–12 education. By the year 2003, that figure will be nearly $100,000.

In the September 19, 1999 issue of *Education Week*, there was an interesting article entitled "How Much Is Enough?" A University of Wisconsin (Madison) professor, Allan R. Odden, performed a cost study by adding the components a school needs in order to implement the Modern Red Schoolhouse, one of the eight schoolwide models underwritten by the New American Schools. This cost study included 1 principal and 20 teachers (25 students per teacher) for a school containing 500 students. The design also included a full-time technology coordinator, one art teacher, and one music teacher. The annual budget included $125,000 for computer technology and $70,000 for staff development. Professor Odden also included the cost of a librarian and routine educational expenses, as well as the expenses for substitute teachers. The cost came to $4,270 per student, but this did not include expenses such as utilities, insurance, and so forth, which could add 30 percent.[28] The study showed that most schools are not underfunded. More such studies will be conducted as the state departments of education try to determine which resources are necessary for school districts to reach the new state standards for student learning.

## SCHOOLS ARE A BUSINESS

Many people believe that schools are not at all like businesses. That viewpoint is simply not true. One governor stated that education is to the state and local governments what defense is to the federal government. Military organizations are a business and are managed like a business, except that they have no profit objectives. Schools are exactly the same.

***All schools have the following components:***

- Operating, funding, and capital budgets
- Financial and accounting control systems
- Human resource/personnel systems
- Information systems
- Management systems for facilities
- Organization charts
- Assessment and measurement systems
- Major processes such as learning systems
- Management systems for operating schools

Government agencies, corporations, and not-for-profit organizations have all of these components. Schools also have a product: successful students learning at grade level who receive a real K–12 education. Too often, though, schools do not have a quality control system, but they will in the future. Schools must be managed like any other successful organization. They require structure and measurements.

Sometimes people say that schools lack motivation because they do not have to earn a profit. Most of these people do not understand how corporations work. Most employees in business are measured against budgets and performance objectives. Senior and line executives, as well as senior financial executives, are greatly concerned about profit, but they represent a small percentage of the workforce. Employees and the management team of government agencies and not-for-profit organizations are also focused on budgets and performance objectives. Therefore, the school administrator's role is not much different.

One area of schools that will require more management in future years is facilities. In 1995, the General Accounting Office (GAO) released a report on the "Condition of America's Schools." This report stated that only two-thirds of the schools are in adequate condition. About 14 million students attend the remaining one-third that need extensive repair or replacement. In addition, new schools need to be built in order to handle the explosive growth in new students. The projected cost was $112 billion.[29] The National Education Association (NEA) issued a report in 2000 estimating $322 billion for school facilities maintenance and construction.[30] The deferred maintenance practices of school districts have caused thousands of local and state tax increases in recent years. Every school district should publish its annual maintenance plan and long-range facilities plan.

Fortunately, the country is in a period of prosperity. Taxpayers are approving bond issues across the country, but many taxpayers are asking a fundamental question: With a national education budget of more than $300 billion, why didn't the school districts in years past allocate adequate funds to maintain their buildings like church schools have? It's a reasonable question. Deferred maintenance will be hard to sell when enrollments start to decline at the end of this decade.

## FEDERAL ROLE IN FUNDING SCHOOLS

The federal government, which pays for about 6 to 7 percent of school budgets, is helping to fix the facilities crisis.[31] Once again, when government rewards failure, it gets a lot of failure. For example, the federal government's main program for increasing learning is Title I, which provides aid to students with disadvantages who are behind in grade level. This well-intentioned program, which has cost taxpayers $118 billion over 30 years, has not enabled disadvantaged students to be equal to other students on achievement tests, although disadvantaged students are improving their test scores each year.[32]

Special education also requires more management and funding. It is not unusual for a school district to spend several times the amount per child on special education. Recently, the courts have made a series of decisions that force schools to shift more funds to special education. In 1999, the U.S. Supreme Court ruled that school boards in some situations must fund one-on-one nursing care for students with severe medical disabilities. In extreme cases, the cost of special education for an individual student can exceed $50,000 per year. Everyone wants special education children to be educated up to their potential, but the expense is getting out of hand. In addition, there is the cost of defending numerous lawsuits and the ensuing paperwork. Many special education teachers are simply burned out from all of the conflicts and demands.

The United States spends approximately $60 billion annually on special education programs, which is close to 20 percent of the total public school budget.[33] The average cost of a special education student is almost twice that of a general education student.[34] Our country has 10 times the number of special education students as Britain, Japan, and Korea. Many of our special education children only have reading problems. Students with real physical and mental handicaps must have special attention, but is that 11 percent of all American students? In some city schools, the number is 25 percent or more. Clearly, too many students are being assigned to special education classes. It may be that too many rewards are given for classifying a student as special education. Schools receive more money, additional teachers are hired, parents receive federal dollars from social security for disabled kids, and these students' test scores often do not count in state rankings.

In 1975, Congress passed the Education for All Handicapped Children Act, which is now known as the Individuals with Disabilities Education Act (IDEA). Tremendous progress has been made in educating the disabled since the passage of IDEA. Disabled students are receiving a free, appropriate public education based on an individualized education plan (IEP), which is developed by a team of psychologists and educators in cooperation with the student's parents. IDEA was envisioned as a federal-state partnership in which Congress would provide 40 percent of the cost and states would provide 60 percent.[35] In fact, during the 25 years of IDEA, Congress has provided only 8 percent of the cost of special education.[36] If Congress eventually does provide the 40 percent originally envisioned, the federal budget for education will grow by billions of dollars.

## OTHER SOURCES OF INVESTMENT

Foundations have invested more than $1 billion in various programs to achieve breakthroughs in student learning. One such donor is Walter Annenberg, who has given more than $500 million to various school districts and to innovative programs.[37] Annenberg was also the major donor to the New American Schools Development Corporation. Dozens of companies and individuals donated approximately $110 million to this multiyear effort to improve schools.[38]

The Dewitt Wallace–Reader's Digest Fund has given out several hundred grants and hundreds of millions of dollars since 1983 to improve elementary and secondary schools. Mike Milken, the famous investment executive, and his brother Lowell have donated millions of dollars to various education programs.

In 1997, Sol Price, founder of Price Clubs, funded an $18-million grant to San Diego State University to improve student performance in an elementary, middle, and senior high school.[39] In 1998, Barbara and Roger Rossier made the largest donation ($20 million) to a school of education, the University of Southern California.[40] The Gates Foundation has contributed $350 million to help improve K–12 education.

The business community has also contributed hundreds of millions of dollars in grants, awards, seminars, computers, and so on during the past 15 years. Marshall Loeb, former Managing Editor of *Fortune* magazine, and Jim Hayes, its publisher, sponsored a series of education summits in the late 1980s and early 1990s. The summit's leaders included Brad Butler, former chairman of Procter & Gamble; David Kearns, Chief Executive Officer of Xerox; and Louis Gerstner, Chief Executive Officer of IBM. At that time, approximately 70 percent of the top executives of more than 100 companies were involved in school reform programs.[41] Later, 200 large corporations in the Business Roundtable adopted schools in numerous states and cities. Unfortunately, most of those retired senior executives are disappointed in the results that were achieved with their money and time.

A new source of revenue for schools is some part of the $206-billion settlement from the tobacco industry, which will be flowing into state treasuries over the next 25 years.[42] At least 18 states have decided to use part of the money for education. Some, such as Michigan, are using it for scholarships.[43] Others, such as Ohio and New Jersey, will use the new funds for building and repairing school facilities.[44] Kentucky is investing some of the funds into early-childhood education.[45] Maryland will raise teacher salaries.[46] Colorado plans to issue grants for before-school, after-school, and summer programs for second, third, and fourth graders who read below grade level.[47]

In recent years, thousands of schools have established foundations asking parents and local businesspeople to donate what government cannot fund.[48] In California, a Consortium of Education Foundations helps local organizations throughout the state. One foundation raised $540,000 to put computers in the school.[49] Another foundation raised close to $2 million in just over two years.[50] Funds have also been raised for band uniforms, athletic teams, various clubs, school newspapers, and arts programs.

Finally, for generations, teachers have spent their own money on items for their classrooms, such as books, magic markers, bulletin board trim, posters, and magazines. As a result, teacher supply stores have sprung up in many cities. The NEA claims that their members spend nearly $502 per year, whereas the American Federation of Teachers (AFT) stated that their members spend nearly $1,000.[51]

Amazingly, though, no matter how many billions of dollars are allocated to schools, they always claim to be short of funds. In San Diego county, increases in school revenues over the past five years have amounted to nearly $1 billion, which is almost a 50-percent increase.[52] Part of this growth was the increase in the number of students. Despite this huge increase, educators claim they need more money because their spending is below the national average.

## ADDITIONAL COSTS FOR FAILURE

The United States has almost 2 million people in local jails, state penitentiaries, and federal prisons.[53] Two million people is essentially the population of a large city. In fact, this number equals the 10th largest city in the United States. The cost of housing these people amounts to $35 billion annually, or $17,500 per prisoner, which is equivalent to the cost of a first-class college education at a state university.[54] Billions more dollars are spent on parole systems. The United States has millions and millions of ex-convicts. Too many ex-convicts, who are often functionally illiterate and who possess almost no social skills, return to prison because no one wants to hire them. Even the prison guard associations are beginning to support more literacy classes, job training, and vocational programs to help prisoners successfully return to society.

Billions of dollars are spent annually on various forms of welfare, such as food stamps, aid to dependent children, Medicaid, fuel assistance, public housing projects, and so on. A 1996 law greatly reduced the number of welfare recipients, but 6 million Americans have remained on the welfare payroll.[55]

Why are these issues being linked to our education problems? Almost every person on welfare or in the prison system is a drop-out or poor performer from the schools. Very few people with a real high school education go to prison or receive welfare payments. Educators blame society, not the schools. On the other hand, every one of these failures had somewhere between 1,800 to 2,100 days of schooling, depending on when they left the system. In that length of time, they should have obtained the basics of reading, writing, and mathematics to the level where they could earn a living in our country. In the best of times, our nation has millions of "unemployables," who again amount to the equivalent of the size of a very large city. All of the services for these "problem" people, and the loss of tax revenues because they do not work, amounts to about $200 billion each year.

After spending trillions of dollars for the "War On Poverty" programs during the past 35 years (the equivalent of many Marshall Plans), the United States has learned that society cannot be fixed until schools are fixed. The long-term mayors in our major cities have certainly reached this conclusion, which is why they want the superintendent and school boards to report to them.

## HOW HIGH WILL THE COSTS GO?

Every corporation, government agency, and not-for-profit organization competes for funds. Competition within government programs is also increasing because taxpayers are telling their elected representatives to make do with fewer dollars. Voters want lower taxes, not tax increases.

Politicians have given up on welfare programs solving our country's social ills by putting a financial cap on these expenditures. They're also engineering a major drive to move people from welfare to work through literacy classes, job training, employment training, dressing for success classes, and even seminars on how to change people's attitudes about the workplace. Such programs work during periods of prosperity and low unemployment.

Mayors are now hiring police commissioners who are using the latest technology and "best practices" to reduce crime. For years, they threw their hands up at the ever-increasing number of crimes and offered excuses why additional crimes would be perpetrated each year. Now police forces have been told that they are in the business of reducing crime. Thanks to new measurements and new methods, crime is decreasing.

Government leaders are also trying to put a financial cap on Medicaid. Poor people in this country are going to live with reduced services. Taxpayers, it seems, are satisfied with a second-rate medical system for the inner-city populations. But education continues to receive large increases in funding because most taxpayers (rich, middle class, and poor alike) want good schools. How high will the costs go? As stated previously, it appears that costs will be about $400 billion by 2003. Assuming 5- to 10-percent budget increases annually in future years, costs could be $500 billion by the year 2008, the 25th anniversary of *A Nation At Risk*.[56] Remember that costs were $15.9 billion in 1959–1960, so by 2009–2010, the annual costs for public schools will have grown almost by $500 billion.[57]

The United States won the Cold War by outspending the Soviet Union on new weapon systems. Similarly, some educators want the government to invest unlimited funds into education until all students are successful learners. Using the traditional teaching and school management methods, that amount could approach $1 trillion from taxpayers annually, with the cost of both the K–12 years and higher education years combined.[58] Unless fundamental change occurs, that is where this nation is headed. If $1 trillion seems unbelievable, be assured that no one in 1983 would have believed that public school spending would have grown from $130 to $400 billion in the next 20 years during a low-inflation period.

Some citizens in other countries pay higher taxes for their socialized systems. Americans pay, on average, more than 40 cents from every dollar to various taxes such as the following:

- Federal income taxes
- Federal excise taxes
- Federal Social Security taxes
- Federal Medicare taxes
- State income taxes
- State sales taxes
- State personal property taxes
- State taxes on special items such as boats and automobiles
- Local property taxes

Average American workers contribute all of their earnings from January to sometime in May to pay for the services and programs of government.[59] Taxpayers today are looking for tax reductions rather than tax increases because of the surplus that now exists in most government budgets.

Before World War II, local property taxes paid for the public school system in most districts. Now state governments supply most of the funds. The federal government supplies almost 7 percent of the funds. On average, nearly 50 percent of the funds come from the state, but in many states, all funds are allocated by the state government.[60] The primary reason for state income tax is the funding requirements for schools.

Many people believe that not much has changed in the classroom during the past 100 years, but costs have certainly changed. The amount of money flowing into state treasuries in the last few years is unbelievable. Spending in the general fund will be close to $500 billion in the year 2000, which is a 49-percent increase over the past five years.[61] Education accounts for nearly half of all state spending.[62] In fact, state spending on education is growing faster than any other category. Now there is no recession in sight, so spending will increase next year, but if a mild recession similar to that of 1990–1991 occurred, current spending could not be sustained without large income and/or sales tax increases. A severe recession would require massive tax increases or major reductions in school budgets. Tax hikes could undoubtedly fuel a taxpayer revolt over education. Voters could conclude that schools are not going to improve, so why invest more money? In California today, some taxpayers believe that Proposition 13 was a major success because California went from being a leader in the cost of education to being below average in cost. Although some people think student performance suffered because of less growth in budgets, others believe that California schools were not great before Proposition 13, and they are no better now, which is debatable. Now they're just costing the taxpayers less money compared to other states.[63]

Is there any hope for cost containment? Not much these days. Unlike the medical field, which tries to eliminate disease through innovative and cost-effective methods for treatment, the public school systems have almost no cost containment efforts in effect. Too many educators believe that Americans will accept an annual increase in state and local funds for "good schools." The reality is that the cost of reinvention is enormous in our nationwide system. Every school is involved in the development of curriculum, lesson plans, administrative processes, and learning systems. There are no economies of scale in most states. At the head of this local effort is a large state department of education in each of our 50 states. In most state capitals, the largest department is for education.

The primary long-term threat to the quality of education in our public schools is the continuous increase in the cost of education. New methods must be developed that result in both breakthroughs in learning and cost containment. The alternative is to watch the taxpayers vote to limit school spending at some year in the future. When that happens, costs will decrease and the quality of education will plummet. Many educators believe this situation will never happen, but remember that few people predicted the impact that health maintenance organizations (HMOs) would have on costs and quality in the medical field.

Members of Congress and state legislatures are always looking for a quick-fix that will enable them to be viewed as an active supporter of school reform. What bill do you want me to pass? How much money will it take to fix a specific problem? What regulations or mandates should be enacted? They rarely become involved in the overall issues of school reform, which leads to an ever-growing budget for public education. Unfortunately, there is no simple solution for fixing the crisis of student learning.

If increased spending could improve schools and student learning, then the crisis in the American system would have been solved years ago. The current strategies of hiring more people and spending more money to try to fix the current education system will eventually be the downfall of education reform. Money is an important factor for having successful schools, but throwing millions of dollars at schools by itself will not create breakthroughs in student learning. In Parts III and IV of this book, the reader will learn about a vision in which almost all students can be successful learners without a major increase in operating expenses. Therefore, there is a need for systemic change, which is the subject of the next chapter.

---

## NOTES

1. U. S. Federal, State, and Local Budgets (Washington, DC: General Accounting Office), HRD-89-44, Social Security Report.
2. U. S. Federal Budget, 2000.
3. U. S. Department of Education, Office of Educational Research and Improvement.
4. U. S. Department of Education, Office of Educational Research and Improvement.
5. U. S. Department of Education, Office of Educational Research and Improvement.
6. Author's estimate.
7. U. S. Federal Budget, 2000.
8. Author's visits to schools.
9. 1949 Hirch High School Yearbook, Chicago, Illinois.
10. *American School Board Journal*, April 1999, 52.
11. Institute for Policy Innovation, "The Longest Boom," *San Diego Union-Tribune*, 26 March, 2000, G1.
12. U.S. Department of Education, Office of Educational Research and Improvement.
13. U.S. Department of Education, Office of Educational Research and Improvement.
14. U.S. Department of Education, Office of Educational Research and Improvement.
15. U.S. Department of Education, Office of Educational Research and Improvement.

16. W. Klein, *Westport News*, Westport, Connecticut, 9 December, 1998, editorial page; C. Hennessy, *Westport News*, Westport, Connecticut, 5 May, 2000, 1, A6.

17. J. Kozol, *Savage Inequalities: Children in American Schools* (New York: Crown, 1991), 1–6, 236–237.

18. "School Shell Games," *Wall Street Journal*, 21 May, 1998, editorial page (A16); S. Forest, "True or False: More Money Buys Better Schools?" *Business Week*, 2 August, 1993, 62–66.

19. D. Kearns and J. Harvey, *A Legacy of Learning* (Washington, DC: The Brookings Institute Press, 2000), 109–113.

20. J. Preston, "School Financing Is Whitman's Battle Now," *New York Times*, 26 November, 1996, A3.

21. R. Johnson, "PA High Court Throws Out 2 School Funding Lawsuits," *Education Week*, 13 October, 1999, 22.

22. "Education Vital Signs," *American School Board Journal*, December 1999, A22–A27.

23. "Education Vital Signs."

24. "Education Vital Signs."

25. D. Thompson and R. Wood, *Money and Schools* (Larchmont, NY: Eye On Education, 1998), 186–208.

26. "Education Vital Signs."

27. "Education Vital Signs."

28. A. Odden, "How Much Is Enough?" *Education Week*, 19 September, 1999, 28–30.

29. *School Facilities: Condition of America's Schools* (Washington, DC: General Accounting Office, February 1995), 2.

30. A. Richard, "NEA Pegs School Building Needs at $332 Billion," *Education Week*, 10 May, 2000, 3.

31. U. S. Department of Education, Office of Educational Research and Improvement.

32. J. Jennings, "Title I: Its Legislative History and Its Promise," *Phi Delta Kappan*, March 2000, 515–522; "Is Federal Intervention Really the Answer?" *San Diego Union-Tribune*, 20 January, 1999, editorial page.

33. U. S. Department of Education, Office of Educational Research and Improvement.

34. R. Wenkart, "Where's the Funding?" *American School Board Journal*, August 2000, 46–47.

35. Wenkart, "Where's the Funding?"

36. Wenkart, "Where's the Funding?"

37. S. Stecklow, "Man with Millions Is Seeking Schools Worth Spending It on," *Wall Street Journal*, 26 July, 1994, B1, B9.

38. New American Schools Annual Report, *Financial Highlights*, 1997, 28–29.

39. Author's interview with Sol Price.

40. J. Archer, "Teacher Education in California Lands 3 Windfalls," *Education Week*, 23 September, 1998, 6.

41. N. Perry, "What We Need To Fix U.S. Schools," *Fortune*, 16 November, 1992, 132–174; Education Summits by *Fortune* in 1988–1992.
42. J. Sandham, "States Devoting Tobacco Money to Education," *Education Week*, 21 June, 2000, 22, 28.
43. Sandham, "States Devoting."
44. Sandham, "States Devoting."
45. Sandham, "States Devoting."
46. Sandham, "States Devoting."
47. Sandham, "States Devoting."
48. C. Moran, "School Foundations," *San Diego Union-Tribune*, 9 April, 1999, A1, A18.
49. S. Parmet, "From Parents Pockets," *San Diego Union-Tribune*, 17 April, 2000, B1, B6.
50. Parmet, "From Parents Pockets."
51. C. Moran, "Class Struggle," *San Diego Union-Tribune*, 16 August, 1999, C1.
52. Rose Institute's Fourth Annual Analysis of San Diego County Public Schools District's Budgets, April 2000, 19.
53. N. Pierce, "Two Million: Couldn't We Do Better?" *San Diego Union-Tribune*, 7 February, 2000, editorial page.
54. Pierce, "Two Million."
55. C. Snow, "Is Welfare Working?" *University of Chicago Magazine*, April 1999, 24–28.
56. Author's estimate.
57. U. S. Department of Education, Office of Educational Research and Improvement; author's estimate.
58. "Education," *Business Week*, 10 January, 2000, 138.
59. "Federal Income Tax Has On-Again, Off-Again History," *San Diego Union-Tribune*, 14 March, 1998, E3.
60. U. S. Department of Education, Office of Educational Research and Improvement.
61. H. Gleckman, "Fat City for the States," *Business Week*, 19 June, 2000, 246, 250.
62. Gleckman, "Fat City."
63. "Keeping Schools Local," *Wall Street Journal*, 24 August, 1998, editorial page.

# CHAPTER 3

# Why Systemic Change Is the Only Alternative

Everyone is tired of hearing about fundamental and systemic change, but that is exactly what must happen in the United States if we are to have a first-class public school system. This chapter reviews what has happened over the past 100 years in our schools.

## ARE SCHOOLS BETTER THAN EVER?

Almost every American shares Thomas Jefferson's vision to have an educated population in order to "exercise the rights and responsibilities of citizenship." The federal Department of Education was created in 1867 to help state governments carry out their constitutional responsibility of offering public education.[1] In 1870, the new Commissioner of Education proudly reported that nearly 7 million children were enrolled in elementary schools, and 80,000 were enrolled in secondary schools.[2]

During the last half of the 19th century, only half of the 5- to 19-year-olds were enrolled in school.[3] To the surprise of many, enrollment rates for males and females were about the same, but only about 30 percent of African American students were enrolled despite the conclusion of the War between the States.[4] The beginning of the 20th century brought an increase in enrollments for all children. According to the U.S. Department of Education, overall enrollment rates for 5- to 19-year-olds rose from 51 percent in 1900 to 75 percent by 1940.[5] By the early 1970s, enrollment rates reached 90 percent for all races, and today that figure stands close to 95 percent.[6] Therefore, enrollment rates have improved dramatically over the years.

In the early part of the 20th century, many students limited their education to completion of the eighth grade, but they had a real eighth-grade education. They

35

could read, write, and compute at the level required by most jobs at the time. By 1940, only half of the U. S. population had more than an eighth-grade education. This situation changed for the better after World War II. By the end of the 20th century, 90 percent of European Americans and more than 75 percent of African American and other races had a high school education.[7] Today, more Americans are in school for a longer period.

Illiteracy was common in the late 19th century and early 20th century. In the last half of the 20th century, the illiteracy rate plunged to 4 percent for all Americans, which is a significant improvement.[8] Now, the focus is on "functional literacy," which addresses the issue of whether a person's reading and writing abilities are sufficient for functioning in a modern society. People who can read and write only at the fourth-grade level or below are considered to be "functionally illiterate." These people constitute 15 percent of today's American population, which is unacceptable.[9] That percentage, however, is lower than in previous decades.

Students are taking more challenging courses. The number of students taking Advanced Placement examinations has increased dramatically, and the drop-out rate has been reduced.[10] The United States leads the world in the number of college-age students who attend institutions of higher education. More than 60 percent of high school graduates enroll in some form of higher education.[11] About 25 percent receive a college degree, which is also higher than most countries.[12]

Some education convention motivational speakers receive standing ovations by citing all of these positive statistics and stating to education reformers, "Get off our backs. Schools are better than ever. Leave teachers alone. They are doing a great job considering how poor society is and how many broken families have emerged."

In 1997, Dr. Gerald Bracey wrote *Setting the Record Straight*, which was published by the Association for Supervision and Curriculum Development (ASCD). Dr. Bracey cites 18 common criticisms of schools and provides an in-depth rebuttal. He then admits that the public school system is not perfect and that he does not want the education reform movement to end. Serious problems must be fixed. David Berliner's *Manufactured Crisis* and the Sandia Report also state that our schools have no major problems based on the fact that schools are doing better now than in previous years.

Some educators have become masters at offering excuses for poor performance, whereas others have mastered covering up poor performance. The only way poor performance is corrected is with good facts that clearly show there is a significant problem.

That is why in 1983 a distinguished group of educators wrote *A Nation At Risk*. Today, Americans must compete in a global society where jobs can be sent overseas in a matter of days. Employees and citizens are expected to know more and do more. When the United States was losing market share to European and Asian companies, a new emphasis on quality was implemented. A company could no longer make a product or offer a service that had problems. "First time right" became the slogan. "Quality is free" meant that if you did a task right the first time, the overall cost of the process would decrease because costs of scrap and rework would be eliminated. The business community and political leaders responded, and the United States once again leads the world in business and economics.

Educators, like other people, do not enjoy hearing criticism of themselves or their institutions. This reaction is natural and understandable. General Motors personnel do not enjoy being reminded that they have lost nearly 50 percent of their market share to competitors. IBM employees and executives were embarrassed when their company had serious problems and experienced a major loss of market share. But, recognition of a problem or problems within an organization is the only road back to respect and recognition. Everyone wants to be proud of the public school system. Systemic change is required to earn the respect that everyone desires.

School performance that would have been acceptable in the middle of the 20th century can no longer be tolerated because a 25-percent failure rate in good schools and a 75-percent failure rate within inner-city schools are far below what all other areas of American society use as a benchmark of success. Other organizations aim for "six sigma" quality, which is 99.99966% defect free.[13] When people fly from one city to another on a jet plane, for instance, they are traveling with a six sigma company. Why can't schools be like airplanes and all be required to be successful? Why can't all students be successful students? Why can't more than 90 percent of all students be at grade level? These figures need to become the new standards for performance. The job of teaching is not complete until students learn their lessons and can apply those lessons. Enforcement of these standards would result in a giant leap forward from the current public schools' performance. Schools may be better in some respects today than they were earlier in the prior century, but they're simply not good enough for the 21st century. Our country now requires an education system where all students receive a real high school education.

Dr. Diane Ravitch, who was a distinguished academic at Columbia University before she served as the Assistant Secretary of Education Research and Improvement in the U.S. Department of Education, explained progressive education with these words:

> Progressive educators dismissed as nonsense the theory of improving functioning by studying specific subjects. Instead progressives argued that what is learned is not nearly as important as the process of learning how to learn. Their position was that a student should not study content to learn how to do a thing, but should learn how to think and then select the content he or she wants to learn. All this resulted in a pronounced shift away from obtaining mastery of a subject area.[14]

This approach led to the decline of student performance that created the need for *A Nation At Risk*. Lessons came in all shapes and sizes. Academic freedom was great, but soon "traditional" educators were saying that students were not receiving a basic education. The Scholastic Aptitude Test (SAT) and the American College Testing (ACT) were embraced by institutions of higher education because almost no standards were used to evaluate applicants. SAT scores between 1962 and 1980 dropped from an average of 478 (of a possible 800) to only 424 for the verbal test, and from 502 to 466 for math.[15] Employers quit looking at high school diplomas or transcripts because grades tended to be inflated, and some high school graduates could barely read and write. Social promotion meant that all students were promoted whether or not they learned the lessons.

After the alarm bell was sounded again by *A Nation At Risk*, political leaders and the business community insisted on mastery and achievement tests to determine if student learning was benefiting from the billions of dollars being invested in education reform programs. These tests uncovered the shocking numbers of 25 to 75 percent of students not being at grade level. When top students competed against the finest students of other countries, Americans often finished last or near last.[16] Drop-out rates at inner-city schools ranged from 10 to 50 percent.[17] Thousands of students in major cities were taking five and six years to complete high school. Several states implemented "exit" exams for high school graduates, which were similar to the Regents exam in New York state. Once again, the results were shocking. Our public schools continue to be "a nation at risk," and it is time to fix the problems of student learning.

## WHAT ARE THE ALTERNATIVES FOR FUTURE EDUCATION REFORM PROGRAMS?

The education reform movement has to select one of the following three strategic roads for its future course:

**1. *Give Up and Accept Schools As They Are.*** No one really wants to admit it, but two educational groups of learners are operating in the United States. In the first group, less than 50 percent of students go to school on a regular basis, work hard, and maintain themselves at grade level. The public schools work for them. Unfortunately, in the second group, more than 50 percent of students are not at grade level. They may be one, two, three, or more grades behind. Many of these students are often behind in grade level even at successful public schools. The worst case is high school seniors who are functionally illiterate, meaning that they are eight grades behind. In many situations, these students are attending schools that are essentially child care centers where a little learning takes place. The public schools currently do not work for millions of students. Dozens of new students arrive each month, and dozens of students transfer to another school. Attendance is terrible because the students are not learning very much. This failure rate continues to feed the ghettos in every major city where people live below the poverty line. Many of these failures end up in prisons or as hard-core welfare cases in areas where the literacy rate is very low.

Evan Keliher, a retired Detroit public school teacher, wrote an article in the June 17, 1998 issue of *Education Week* entitled "If It Wasn't Around in the Middle Ages, It's a Fad."[18] This cleverly titled article simply states that the current education model cannot be improved. One piece of evidence he pointed to was the failure of the much-touted reform effort funded by a $500 million grant from Walter H. Annenberg.[19] *The Los Angeles Times* reported no elevated reading scores, no improved achievement level, and no visible success of any kind as a result of the money received from the grant. Money was also given to Boston, Chicago, Detroit, Los Angeles, New York City, Philadelphia, and San Francisco city public schools. The programs failed across the nation.

Keliher went on to list other failed programs such as New Math, Movies, Television, Whole-Language, Team Teaching, Block Schedules, Single Sex Schools, and so forth. He concluded that we should stop all school reform because no one can come up with an idea that works better than the current system. He urged schools to resume traditional methods: a classroom teacher with a chalk-board, a piece of chalk, textbooks, and a room full of willing students. He pointed out that this successful process currently operates in all well-run parochial schools.

Secretly, many educators believe that Keliher is right on target. If he is right, then more than $1 trillion has been wasted in the past 18 years. Chief executive officers of the nation's largest companies have wasted both their time and money. Political leaders have approved billions of dollars in useless programs—a costly blow to taxpayers. Philanthropists have donated millions of dollars for a cause that has no hope.

**2. *Continue Looking for "Silver Bullets."*** Whenever an organization fails to meet its goals and objectives, senior executives look for a quick-fix. "Will a 'silver bullet' solve performance problems?" they ask. For 18 years, the education reform movement has tried one quick-fix program after another. A recent "silver bullet" is pay for performance. The school theme becomes: "Let's try this." If "silver bullet" programs were the answer, then all children would be at grade level. In Part II of this book, each of these quick-fix programs is examined to see what impact, if any, it had on solving the severe performance problems in public schools. Unfortunately, it now appears that a new generation of leaders working on education reform could recycle many of the programs that had little or no influence on student learning.

**3. *Adopt a New Approach for Systemic Change.*** When an organization invests large sums of incremental funds in quick-fix programs over an extended period that fail to fix its serious performance problems, it must determine if the problems are being caused by its management and/or employees, or if the problems stem from the basic processes within the organization, which are referred to as systems problems. With close to 5 million teachers and administrators, there are bound to be some performance problems, but probably no more than are found in most other large and complex organizations. Almost every teacher and administrator goes to work each day with a positive attitude and good intentions. They want students to learn. They are shocked to find that so many students are behind in grade level, but they believe that the reasons are beyond their control. In a teacher survey conducted by Louis Harris and Associates, the question of what problems constitute serious obstacles to learning elicited the following responses:[20]

65%: Lack of support or help from parents
41%: Poverty
32%: Parents' drug or alcohol problems
22%: Physical or psychological abuse
21%: Poor nutrition
13%: Student's own alcohol problems
11%: Violence in school
11%: Problems with English language
9%: Student's own drug problems
7%: Poor health

In this survey, teachers clearly blame society and parents for poor student performance. But remember that even the best schools with good parents and good neighborhoods have on average a 25-percent failure rate.

Should the education reform movement continue to strive for breakthroughs in student learning? The answer is simple: Yes. The other two choices simply do not make sense. The good news is that American public schools can be fixed with the recommendations and programs outlined in Parts III and IV of this book. The school reform movement needs to focus more on the basic learning systems that exist in schools today. Clearly, there is a serious problem with the current process of learning in our schools today, and systemic change is the only feasible decision. A new paradigm for student learning is required.

## THEORY OF UPPER LIMITS

Florida State University's Dr. Robert K. Branson published a 1987 paper entitled "Why The Schools Can't Improve: The Upper Limit Hypothesis."[21] In 1998, an updated paper on the same subject was published by Cambridge University Press.[22] Following are some of Dr. Branson's conclusions:

Learning was not studied empirically until the 1870s in Wundts' laboratory, long after the traditional model of teaching was in place. In applied science, valid knowledge flows from the laboratory into practice, and there is continuous interaction between the field and the laboratory. Thus, the teaching hospital concept. This knowledge based on research does not now happen in education. Current job responsibilities for teachers provide little discretionary time to plan and think. As a consequence, teachers must ignore significant psychological research literatures including the literatures on assessment, behavior analysis, learning and cognitive development, transfer, simulation, expertise, learner strategies, and organizational psychology.

In the traditional model of education (called teaching-centered model), the individual teachers develop lesson plans, deliver instruction to classes of students, make the majority of decisions regarding methods and means, and conduct assessments. The success of today's schools depends totally on individual teachers' abilities to develop valid lessons and to deliver and assess them so that they cause learning in students.

In my view, the basic teaching-centered model, used predominantly in American schools, has reached the *upper limit* or asymptote, of its potential capability around 1960. (See Figure 3–1.)

Because a process cannot exceed 100 percent of its design capability, it is estimated that the teaching-centered model is now performing at about 97 percent of its potential. Therefore, it will not get any better than it is.

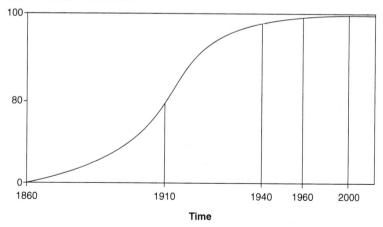

**Figure 3–1** Upper Limit Hypothesis. Copyright © Dr. Robert K. Branson.

In Branson's original 1987 paper, he stated that trying to make the current model 100 percent efficient, which would only be a 2 or 3 percent improvement, would require years of effort and a 50- to 100-percent increase in the cost of schools. This is exactly what has happened during the past 18 years.

Dr. Branson's "upper limits" theory is supported by Paul Hill, a University of Washington political scientist, and his colleagues James Guthrie at Vanderbilt and Larry Pierce, also at the University of Washington, when they stated in their book *Reinventing Public Education* (1997) that the United States has gone as far as it can go in perfecting a bad system.[23] Even if the current system is polished to its maximum efficiency, it cannot do what is required of it in the modern world.

To fully understand the concept of upper limits, think of the desire to fly from Boston to San Diego in six hours. If that objective had been established in 1940, many people would have tried to improve the internal combustion engine, the diesel engine, the electric motor, and the steam engine. At that time, these engines were all working near their upper limits as far as speed and range were concerned. A new power plant or system would be necessary to fly across the country in six hours. The jet engine had to be invented to reach the six-hour goal. Similarly, educators now need to find the jet engine that will achieve breakthroughs in student learning so that more than 90 percent of all students will be successful learners.

Dr. Branson agrees with Evan Keliher, who said that all recent programs have amounted to nothing more than a fad; however, Dr. Branson proposes an alternative solution: a new learning-centered school model.

> He claims that the learning-centered processes developed in the laboratory, based on research from a variety of disciplines, prove to be equal to or more effective than conventional instruction even in their early state of development and they are incrementally improvable.

The vision and learning systems described in Part III of this book are directly correlated to Dr. Branson's research and other projects. Dr. Branson's paper also had some other major findings, including these views on the effects of individual teachers:

> When children enroll in school, they have a 50-50 chance of getting a below-average teacher. The following year, they again have a 50-50 chance, resulting in a 25 percent chance for two bad years in a row. So 25% of the children will have below-average teachers two consecutive years, and 12.5 percent will suffer three years in a row. Moreover, three bad years does not ensure getting a good teacher the next year.

Rural and inner-city schools have a high percentage of new and inexperienced teachers, and a high number of teachers who have not been selected by the better schools in the wealthier communities. In other words, these schools do not have many long-term, outstanding teachers. Dr. Branson has some additional insights on this subject:

> Lay people and insiders alike pursue the hero model exemplified by movies such as "Stand and Deliver" and "Mr. Holland's Opus." This fiction or isolated examples dramatize single cases that cannot be replicated elsewhere. Jaime Escalante, the hero of "Stand and Deliver," had little success in getting his Sacramento students to Advanced Placement examinations after he moved from Los Angeles, where he had outstanding success. Repeatedly, for 50 years we have read and heard that the right principal can turn things around, yet we have not found many such heroes. Like the teachers they supervise, only 20 percent of principals are in the upper quintile. Poor education performance is a systems problem; rarely is it a simple people problem. Principals and teachers are not to blame.
>
> Although critics and insiders blame most school problems on individuals rather than the work process, Dr. Deming, who was internationally famous for implementing statistical quality control systems, demonstrated that performance problems in organizations are caused by badly organized work procedures 85 percent of the time and by people errors only 15 percent of the time.
>
> Deming's work suggests that 85 percent of the problem in the American school system stems from the work process—the teaching-centered model—not the teachers who meet all the requirements of their job descriptions and follow the processes required by their schools. Even if we tried to replace "bad" teachers, we could expect to find about the same capabilities in the pool of applicants.

Too many people in the education reform movement believe that replacing experienced teachers with new teachers is the answer. Frankly, this strategy will only reduce the effectiveness of the teaching-centered model unless changes are made to the curriculum at the colleges of education and to the learning systems within schools. If it is a systems problem rather than a people problem, schools need a "rising tide" of new administrative and learning systems, like the ones described in Part III of this book.

## WHAT ARE THE REAL EDUCATIONAL PROBLEMS THAT MUST BE ADDRESSED?

Undoubtedly, the challenges for the teaching profession have grown significantly because of the poverty level, influx of immigrants, and the break-up of the traditional family structure; however, the following problems are in the schools themselves:

## Lack of Integrated Curriculum

With a decentralized school system, few schools have an integrated curriculum designed to meet the learning standards established by the school district and the state department of education. An integrated curriculum answers the fundamental question: What do you want students to know and be able to do after 13 years (K–12) of schooling? Once that question is answered, learning standards must be devised for each of the 13 grades. Then each grade's lessons must become the foundation for the next grade. In such a system, students who come from several elementary schools will be at the same grade level in knowledge and skills when they enter middle school.

In reality, though, middle school teachers have only a vague idea of what has been covered in previous grades, so weeks of duplicate effort and boring lessons are usually presented to bring most students up to the same level of knowledge and skills. This process repeats itself when students arrive from several middle schools to begin high school.

An integrated curriculum means not only that the grades are integrated but also that lessons learned in one subject (such as grammar) are reinforced in other classes such as history and science. Too often, teachers within the same grade in a given school are teaching different lessons with varied teaching methods and assessment systems. Although teachers may work in the same school, they know very little about what is being taught in other classrooms. In many schools, the system is at best a collection of one-room schoolhouses.

## Lack of Grade-Level Measurements

If there is no integrated curriculum, there is usually no learning objectives list for each grade and subject within the school. In other words, schools operate without a detailed list of lessons to be taught. Schools have to be measured by mastery tests and achievement tests because there is no grade-level assessment system. With social promotion being accepted for decades, the schools did not need any assessments by grade level.

## Lack of Instructional System Design Methods

The United States military organization developed instructional systems design (ISD) methods in the 1950s. Much of this work was based on the research of

Robert Gagné, who started his work in the 1940s. Gagné took what was known about human learning and organized it into a useful model for teachers, trainers, and instructional designers. His book, *The Conditions of Learning*, which was published by Holt, Reinhart & Winston in 1965, 1970, 1977, and 1985, has been the foundation for a series of texts by other well-known educators such as Dr. David Merrill, Dr. Robert Mager, and Dr. Robert Morgan. Dr. Branson has also worked closely with Dr. Gagné.

The systemic design of instruction involves a six-phase process, as follows:[24]

1. Define the learning and performance objectives that are required to achieve the standards.
2. Document the prerequisites for learning.
3. Determine what lessons are required.
4. Develop the instructional strategy by deciding on what motivational methods of teaching and learning should be utilized.
5. Develop and/or select the instructional materials as well as the delivery system.
6. Determine how a teacher will decide whether students have learned the lessons (assessment documents).

This method is far different from expecting teachers to create lesson plans in the evening or over the weekend. The goal of ISD is simple: To enable the vast majority of all students to be successful learners.

ISD methods are used throughout the military because students must master the lessons in order to survive life-and-death situations. Interestingly, young people serving in the military were once the same bell-curve graduates of our nation's high schools. Some were great students and others ranked in the bottom half of their class, but more than 90 percent became successful learners in the military services. Corporations and government agencies are now using ISD methods to ensure mastery of learning and performance, but most teachers and administrators in public schools have never even heard of ISD.

## Lack of Effective Lesson Plans

Numerous teachers have ineffective lesson plans that violate all of the ISD principles. Their lesson plans have never been validated or tested by a third party. Such is too often the case with new and inexperienced teachers. It takes several years for most teachers to develop outstanding lesson plans. The colleges of education do not spend nearly enough time on this important task. Also, most lesson plans are developed by teachers during evening hours, on weekends, or between other tasks. Some teachers make a great investment in their lesson plans, whereas others do not even have such plans. Some teachers expend a little effort in developing lesson plans but never use them in the classroom.

### Lack of Class Management Skills

This subject should be taught at every college of education using television modules showing the right way and the wrong way to handle classes. Most teachers learn their class management skills "on the job." Many experienced teachers do an outstanding job of keeping students on track with few interruptions or distractions. Unfortunately, class management is a common weakness among new and inexperienced teachers. Students quickly pick up on this weakness, and the amount of learning for a grade can decrease by 25 to 50 percent as a result.

### Lack of Adequate Course Materials

Television and newspaper reporters enjoy showing outdated books, videos, movies, and other course materials being used in today's classrooms. In inner-city schools, such examples are usually readily available. Too often, the lowest priority in a budget cycle is new course materials, when it should be either the first or second most important line item. For example, research has shown that literacy development can be facilitated by classroom libraries with a careful selection of books. Yet most classrooms have books that were either donated, were inexpensive, or they have very few books at all. Worse yet, course materials often do not tie into lesson plans; teachers use whatever is available. It is almost a given that most course materials were never designed for the state's new learning standards.

### Lack of Adequate Assessment Systems

Developing a test or other assessment instruments requires specialized knowledge and experience. The typical classroom does not have tests to determine the number of students who have learned the lessons being taught to meet the district and state learning standards. Most districts do administer annual achievement and mastery tests, but the school year is almost over when these "mega-tests" are taken. The assessment goal should be to keep students at grade level throughout the year, not just at the end of it.

### Lack of Tutoring Systems

When students fail to learn a lesson and begin to fall behind, they need tutoring with a volunteer, teacher, or a personal computer. Everyone realizes that tutoring is the most effective way to teach and learn. Teachers are expensive, so many schools use volunteers or courseware on an interactive personal computer. If a school has few or no tutoring systems, chances are that students will not be at grade level.

## Lack of Time To Learn

Research tells us that students have various learning styles that require different teaching methods. Students also require different lengths of time to learn. The current teacher-centered model allocates a specific amount of time to teach a given subject. When the teacher has finished teaching the lesson, he or she asks the class, "Do you understand what I just taught?" Good students say yes or nod their heads. Those who don't understand keep a low profile and hope no one notices them. Sadly, the class moves on while many students fall behind, get lost, and give up.

## Lack of an Embraceable Responsibility

Schools are still run like a series of one-room schoolhouses under a large roof. If a consulting firm conducted a task analysis for teachers and principals, it would find that these jobs do not have an embraceable responsibility. There is simply too much work to do within a given day, week, or semester. This is especially true when teachers work a second job. In all situations where an employee has too much to do, the person makes decisions on what tasks must be done just to survive on the job. (This issue is addressed further in Chapter 12, Need for a New Management System.)

The reader should compare the 10 problems within schools that were listed previously to the survey of teachers about reasons for poor student performance presented earlier in this chapter and the excuses in Chapter 1 to realize why the education reform movement has not focused on the real problems for the past 18 years.

The 10 classroom deficiencies explain why the work that The Education Trust accomplished a few years ago is right on target. Kati Haycock, in her 1998 article "Good Teaching Matters . . . A Lot," displayed many charts showing studies that proved students learned very little from least-effective teachers and two or three times more from most-effective teachers.[25] She wrote that two years after the fact, performance of fifth-grade students was still affected by the quality of their third-grade teacher. She also said that content knowledge alone was not sufficient for effective teaching. Inconsistent teaching creates inconsistent learning which is the fundamental reason for poor performance by students. Inconsistent teaching has been standard practice in our schools for decades and this problem must be solved to achieve the goal that almost all students can be successful learners.

Teachers must have the tools that are necessary for students to learn the lessons. Course materials must be designed to teach the learning standards established by the state department of education and the local school district. Learning and tutoring systems must be utilized in the classroom. New professional development sessions must be designed based on the new integrated curriculum. All of this is discussed in Part III of this book.

## WHY SUPERINTENDENTS AND PRINCIPALS ARE NOT LEADERS OF LEARNING

In recent years, almost everyone has agreed that a superintendent and principals must be leaders of learning if a school district is going to have a high percentage of successful learners. This will not happen unless the following conditions exist:

1.  Integrated curriculum is implemented.
2.  Grade-level measurements are documented.
3.  Learning systems are utilized.
4.  High-quality course materials that are aligned to learning objectives are purchased.
5.  Tutoring systems are available.
6.  Formal schoolwide assessment system is in place that provides frequent reports to the principal on student learning.

These conditions do not exist in most schools today. Most superintendents and principals have the best of intentions, but current methods of managing schools do not enable them to be leaders of learning.

## NEW ATTITUDE FOR EDUCATION REFORM IS REQUIRED IN SCHOOLS

When employees in corporate America first heard of Dr. Deming's "quality" program, they arrogantly dismissed it as a "fad" applicable only to companies with a low-wage workforce. Eventually, though, all the leading companies embraced the "quality" principles, which espoused that world-class corporations performed work correctly the first time. The quality program required a major attitude shift by everyone, from chief executive officers to mail room clerks.

Education reform will not succeed until it is embraced by superintendents, principals, guidance counselors, teachers, and aides. What a wonderful working environment schools would be if students learned their lessons the first time and if more than 90 percent of all students were at grade level. Time could be spent on developing an enhanced world-class curriculum, and the teaching profession would achieve a much higher level of respect.

Salespeople would all love to have a perfect territory with pleasant customers and no competition. Unfortunately, this "perfect world" is totally unrealistic. Salespeople must accept competition, product problems, and difficult customers. Educators have to accept an imperfect world as well. All students are not going to be 100 percent motivated as they enter school. Nor will every parent do everything that teachers would like them to do to help their children learn. Despite these barriers, though, the number of successful students must exceed 90 percent in future years.

Educators must accept the fact that schools will need to make major changes in order to create a breakthrough in student learning. David Kearns, retired Chief Executive Officer of Xerox Corporation and the Deputy Secretary of Education under President Bush, declared that we must stop tinkering around the edges like we've been doing the past 18 years.[26] Now the heavy lifting begins. Just improving schools is not enough. Current teaching and learning processes simply do not work for more than 50 percent of the students across the nation. Schools must be fixed and restructured. Part III of this book shows how Americans can adequately restructure their public school system.

## WHAT HAPPENS IF EDUCATORS DO NOT SUPPORT SYSTEMIC CHANGE?

Not long ago, the United States was in the midst of a medical care crisis. Costs were skyrocketing. Doctors and hospital administrators simply said that, in order for the United States to maintain its world-class medical system, corporations and government had to pay the costs even if they rose 5 to 10 percent annually. Instead of complying with this demand, government and corporations decided to support health maintenance organizations (HMOs) and Medicare, which dictated costs to doctors and hospital administrators. Today, doctors are receiving less income and working longer hours. Many hospitals can barely break even. Insurance companies, government agencies, and corporations now make most of the key decisions in our national health care system. The lesson is simple: When costs and/or quality are out of control, another group takes over and rewrites the rules.

American taxpayers are not going to accept explosive costs and a third-class education system forever. Taxpayers are already upset with the frequent increases in state and local taxes. They are also beginning to realize that the thousands of students who fail in public school wind up feeding the prison and welfare systems, which increases the need for more taxes. Most important, Americans are discovering that current learning and teaching processes damage many students. Students' self-esteem is lowered when they are labeled "slow learners" by teachers and "dumb" by their peers. Americans have never accepted being in second or third place for an extended period, and education will be no exception.

## TIME TO FOCUS ON THE REAL PROBLEMS IN LEARNING

During the past 18 years, thousands of well-intentioned community leaders, educators, business executives, and political leaders have served on education task forces. As a result, more than one thousand reports have been written on how to improve our schools. Each group spends nearly 90 percent of its time studying the problems. At the end of each study, the task force makes a leap of faith to a few highly publicized, quick-fix, and sound-good solutions that add millions of dollars to the cost of education. Lower class size is the latest example of these solutions. At best, this program will slightly improve student learning, but it will add billions to the cost of education.

Few business executives and political leaders have reviewed the current learning and teaching methods because, frankly, they do not have the knowledge or experience to do so. Education reformers should ask themselves what they are doing to address the 10 major problems that are listed in this chapter. If they are not working on these issues, then they are still tinkering around the edges and driving up the cost of education.

American students and teachers are not inferior to their Asian and European counterparts. Most Americans fare well in the world once they leave their K–12 years of schooling. Our schools can still be the envy of the world. Restructuring the public school system could become a unifying experience for the country.

Before we review this new vision for successful schools in Chapter 11, we need to understand the history of education reform programs that have not achieved great breakthroughs in learning. Part II of this book deals with this subject.

---

## NOTES

1. S. Sniegoski, *Know Your Government: Department of Education* (Washington, DC: Chelsea House Publishers, 1988), 26.
2. National Center For Education Statistics, *120 Years of American Education* (Washington, DC: U.S. Department of Education, 1993), 5–9.
3. National Center, *120 Years.*
4. National Center, *120 Years.*
5. National Center, *120 Years.*
6. National Center, *120 Years.*

7. National Center, *120 Years.*

8. D. Wagner, "To Read or Not To Read," *Education Week*, 25 October, 1995, 33, 34.

9. Wagner, "To Read or Not To Read."

10. D. Kearns and J. Harvey, *A Legacy of Learning* (Washington, DC: The Brookings Institute Press, 2000), 26–27.

11. National Center for Education Statistics, *The Condition of Education* (Washington, DC: U.S. Department of Education, 2000), 148–149.

12. National Center, *The Condition of Education.*

13. W. Wiggenhorn, "When Training Becomes an Education," *Harvard Business Review*, July–August 1990, 71–83.

14. Kearns and Harvey, *A Legacy of Learning*, 40–41.

15. Sniegoski, *Know Your Government*, 51.

16. Kearns and Harvey, *A Legacy of Learning*, 28–33.

17. The National Education Goals Report, *Building A Nation* (Washington, DC: National Education Goals Panel, 1997), 39.

18. E. Keliher, "If It Wasn't Around in the Middle Ages, It's a Fad!" *Education Week*, 17 June, 1998, 47–49.

19. P. Reilly, "Annenberg's 'Challenge' Is a Bust," *Los Angeles Times*, 7 April, 1998, B7.

20. Louis Harris and Associates, "What Hinders Learning? Here's What Teachers Say," *American School Board Journal*, 1998, 15.

21. R. Branson, "Why the Schools Can't Improve: The Upper Limit Hypothesis," *Journal of Instructional Development*, 1987, 7–12.

22. R. Branson, *Teaching-Centered Schooling Has Reached Its Upper Limit: It Doesn't Get Any Better Than This* (Cambridge, MA: Cambridge University Press, 1998), 126–135.

23. P. Hill et al., *Reinventing Public Education: How Contracting Can Transform America's Schools* (Chicago: University of Chicago Press, 1997).

24. W. Dick and L. Carey, *The Systematic Design of Instruction* (Glenview, IL: Scott, Foresman and Company, 1990), 2–11.

25. K. Haycock, *Good Teaching Matters: How Well-Qualified Teachers Can Close the Gap* (Washington, DC: The Education Trust, Summer 1998), 1–14.

26. D. Kearns, Washington, DC: Address to American Society for Training and Development Conference, Spring 1992.

# Good Intentions for Almost Two Decades

Now that the fundamental problems of student learning have been identified in Part I, it would seem appropriate to go directly to the solutions that are in Part III. To avoid the mistake of repeating history with many easy-to-do programs that have been tried during the past 18 years, it is important to understand what has worked and what programs have had little impact on student learning.

Part II reviews nearly 50 programs that have been implemented in past years. Most of them have been a waste of time and money because they were not focused on the process of learning. A few have enabled our schools to achieve a slight improvement in student performance. Some are myths that will never be successful. A few have taken on a life of their own, requiring years of effort, billions of dollars, and great frustration, when a careful analysis would have revealed that they never had any hope of success.

CHAPTER 4

# Low-Cost, Quick-Fix, and Sound-Good Programs

After *A Nation At Risk* was published in 1983, many governors carried out their constitutional responsibility for overseeing the public schools by assembling task forces to study the system's problems and to recommend quick-fixes. If good intentions alone could fix the problems in American schools, the education crisis would be over.

Except for defense issues during the Cold War years, no subject has had more talent and money invested in it than school performance. The next three chapters summarize these efforts and discuss the impact that each program has had on student learning. People who are going to be involved in education reform in future years should not merely repeat history, which is exactly what's currently happening in many cities and states. The education reform movement needs to learn from the first two decades and move on to programs that will achieve major breakthroughs in student learning. This chapter examines the low-cost, quick-fix, and sound-good solutions that have consumed enormous amounts of time, effort, and resources for nearly 20 years.

## ADOPT-A-SCHOOL

Thousands of companies adopted schools and made great statements such as the following:

> For as long as it takes, we're ready to work in partnership with others to help build a world-class education system. Together, we ought to agree that all students can learn at high levels and that we can teach all students successfully. We can instill in our children a love of learning that will last a lifetime.[1]

These adoption programs included long-range planning seminars, change management seminars, quality courses, management development programs, guest speakers, tutors, guest instructors, training on technology, free computers, career seminars, mentors, support on public policy issues, technical support, loaned executives, television sponsorship of education-related programming, support for exhibitions, drop-out prevention programs, school-to-work transition programs, sporting events, and community service programs. Even more important, businesses provided millions of dollars in grants and supported billions of dollars in tax increases to provide additional resources that school districts requested. Almost any school that wanted to be adopted by a company could find a willing partner. Many schools, though, believed that these programs were too commercial, so they declined adoption.

Most of these programs succeeded in terms of school administrators' and teachers' happiness. They relished the extra money, special attention, awards, and gifts. Business executives and employees gained numerous friends in the education community. But at the sixth annual Education Summit sponsored by *Fortune* magazine, two key questions were asked: "Is the education reform movement making any progress, and is business making a difference?" "Painfully little," said David Kearns, a former Deputy Secretary of Education and retired Chief Executive Officer of Xerox Corporation. He went on to state: "That doesn't mean all the business efforts have been to no avail. There are programs out there that work and make a difference." One summit participant added, "I am staggered by the lack of progress."[2] Unfortunately, most of these quick-fix programs had little or no impact on teaching and learning within the classroom. Businesspeople and political leaders were too concerned about upsetting a teacher or administrator—they didn't want to risk bad publicity.

## SITE-BASED MANAGEMENT

Almost every organization holds the belief that the local operating unit and employees closest to the clients know more about how to manage the business than do the headquarter personnel. Such is the case in businesses, churches, YMCAs, and government agencies, and it's true in schools as well. Most teachers believe that they would be better off if they were completely disassociated from the state department of education and district office. Many teachers also believe that a principal is not necessary. Administrators, too, blame most of their problems on district personnel and "those people" in the state capitol.

Not surprisingly, then, educators quickly bought into the concept of site-based management, which assumes that teachers and principals alone can run a successful school. It is estimated that 80 percent of schools have some form of a site-based management committee.[3] This concept sounded good, but when mastery and achievement test results were measured, cities that had implemented site-based management showed little or no improvement in student learning.

In their book *Research on School Restructuring*, Professors Ellis and Fouts reported the following findings:

> Thus far, researchers have identified no direct link—positive or negative—between school-based management and student achievement or other student outcomes, such as attendance. In some settings, student scores (on standardized or local tests) have improved slightly, in others they have declined slightly, and in most settings, no differences have been noted.[4]

Many well-intentioned people want to help fix the public school system, but, unfortunately, many unqualified people are now sitting on various school management committees. Most people would think it preposterous to form a committee of automobile drivers to improve the overall performance of General Motors, but that's exactly what's happening today in these school management committees. Often, the only qualification these committee members have is that they attended school as a student. Some were even poor students, and now they are evaluating teachers and principals. In some cases, they even help select the principal. These committees operate on the false assumption that anyone can manage a school.

Site-based management enables a lot of tinkering to take place, but, in most cases, it maintains the status quo because these committees rarely make the major decisions needed to restructure a school. Chicago city schools hoped that site-based management would make a difference, but instead it has impeded the progress of true reform strategies. In New York City schools, decentralization has also failed.

In order to achieve breakthroughs in student learning, full accountability must be returned to administrators at the state, district, and school levels. Split responsibility results in no responsibility. Today, many administrators hide behind the fact that the school governance committee won't allow them to make major changes in curriculum, learning systems, teaching methods, schedules, and assessment systems. Governance teams enable school administrators to say: "Don't blame me. I am just one member of the team." The message is clear: Do not expect breakthroughs in learning from schools with site-based management programs.

## CREATE SMALLER SCHOOLS

Many years ago, our country moved from the one-room schoolhouse to centralized schools. These new schools grouped children into 13 grades (K–12), with a teacher in charge of each grade. Everyone agreed that centralized schools were a step forward for both teaching and learning. When the population grew, several classes of each grade formed within a school. High schools started to specialize by subject; students moved each hour to a classroom where a teacher specialized in a subject such as English, history, or mathematics. These reforms seemed reasonable and appropriate at the time.

But now, some researchers claim that large inner-city schools have more behavior problems, lower academic performance, greater attendance problems, more supervision problems, and lower student participation in extracurricular activities.[5] Numerous studies have shown that poor student performance in large urban schools relates directly to teachers and administrators not being able to establish a personal relationship with their students.[6] It's unfortunate that more research has not been conducted on large, successful suburban schools. Why do their students do so well? School size doesn't seem to be a problem there.

If you really investigate this issue, it does not seem to have much merit. In the early grades, the teacher in the classroom knows each student well. Class size might be a factor, but having one first-grade class compared to five first-grade classes is not the issue. In the middle schools, many principals and teachers have adopted the high school model of changing classes. If this model is wrong, schools should go back to having students stay in one classroom most of the day. Smaller schools are often not able to have as many electives, or as successful music/arts programs, and may not field successful athletic teams.

In larger schools, there are vice-principals, so the ratio of administrators to students is about the same as in a small high school. The ratio of counselors to students is also about the same in a small or large school. The number of students per teacher is also similar. Schools can break up into schools within a school, but do not expect a big breakthrough in learning. Some studies show that they have confused grouping better students into small magnet schools as proof that smaller schools provide more individual student attention.[7] The increase in student learning, however, is often so small that it's hardly measurable. By the way, if smaller schools are better, why did educators support larger schools for decades? Since the middle of the past century, the number of schools has declined by two-thirds.[8] School size should not be accepted as an excuse for high failure rates.

## TEST THE TEACHERS

The professions of law, medicine, and accounting test students to certify that they have acquired the knowledge to practice in the profession. Some education reformers are convinced that the colleges of education are allowing unqualified students to graduate, so they now support a certification test. Overall, the picture does not seem nearly as grim as it has sometimes been suggested. A study conducted by the Association For Supervision and Curriculum Development (ASCD) found that students who pass teacher licensure tests have academic skills that are comparable to or even slightly better than the skills of the overall number of students who take the Scholastic Aptitude Test (SAT). The passing rates on the Praxis I examination for females and males were also comparable.[9]

Most of these examinations test subject standards. Do students have in-depth knowledge of the subject that they will teach? Fortunately, most teachers know their subject. These tests often show that many new teachers, like other college graduates, have weak writing skills. In California, 15 percent of the teacher candidates failed a rather easy test even when they took the test several times, proving that low standards exist for passing throughout the K–16 years.[10] The test can also catch a few (and it is hoped that there are only very few) graduates who are illiterate. One gentleman wrote a book after he learned how to read and write about how he graduated with a teaching degree and taught for 17 years without being able to read or write. It is a fascinating (albeit somewhat disturbing) story.[11]

Most teachers, however, do not fail on the job because they lack subject matter knowledge. They often fail because they have poor class management skills and almost no knowledge of instructional design methods. Their lesson plans are ineffective, and their assessment methods fail to tell them which students did not learn the lessons. Their tutoring skills are below average. Tests rarely examine these skills, which are critical to teacher success.

New tests are now being developed that are aligned to the state standards for teachers, which is a step in the right direction. These new tests are called the National Council for Accreditation of Teacher Education 2000.[12] Adopting new teacher licensing tests is a controversial decision for states during a teacher shortage, but testing is currently taking place in 44 states.[13] These tests alone will probably not achieve breakthroughs in student learning, but they will enhance the quality control system in our schools. Testing will also help rebuild the quality image of our schools, and it probably is necessary as long as social promotion exists in the K–16 education system.

Many people attack the tests' validity rather than the issue of why so many potential teachers fail these tests.[14] Teachers like to test students, but they do not want to take tests themselves. The teaching profession's image will be enhanced if everyone can agree on how to develop valid assessments for future teachers.

## HIRE NONCERTIFIED TEACHERS

Hiring noncertified teachers is now a big issue in the education community because the school districts must hire more than 2 million teachers over the next decade.[15] Some education reformers want to allow anyone to teach. They believe that any college graduate can be a teacher by Monday morning as long as a person has proper subject matter knowledge. This argument would hold true if the delivery of information were the only requirement of teaching. If students must learn their lessons, then it is most helpful if the teacher has been taught class management skills, instructional design methods, lesson plan preparation skills, teaching methods, and assessment techniques. Unfortunately, many states and colleges of education have made certification a costly and lengthy process, which discourages college students from entering the education field. This situation, in turn, has helped to create a teacher shortage. For example, in one of our largest states, a student must earn a four-year college degree, then take a fifth year to earn a certificate to teach, and then take two additional years to earn a Masters of Education degree. In other states, a four-year degree from a college of education enables a student to become a certified teacher.

In Texas, education reformers want parents to be notified if their child is being taught by a noncertified or inappropriately certified teacher, but this proposal was rejected by the state school board. Some education experts want to blame all public school problems on this issue, including the fact that our finest students have poor performance at international competitions. In almost every school, however, our top students are taught by well-qualified teachers. Out-of-field teaching is a problem that defies simple solutions. For example, 28 percent of high school mathematics teachers have neither a major nor a minor in math; for science teachers, 18 percent were not science majors or minors. Much of the blame for out-of-field teaching can be attributed to state certification rules and to the way schools are being managed and operated. Principals will assign a teacher to a class whether they have a degree in that subject or not because they are confident that these people can teach successfully in the subject based on additional study and experience.

Out-of-field teaching is another excuse used to justify poor student performance, but this situation could be greatly improved if educators would establish more reasonable certification requirements. Distance learning may be a breakthrough in this area. California will soon be introducing a new delivery system called CalStateTeach, which is a hybrid of traditional instruction and distance learning.[16] The curriculum will be covered on a strict schedule in four phases over an 18-month period. The programs will use traditional textbooks and written materials, as well as lessons and communications over the Internet. The goal is simple: California wants to make it easier for emergency teachers to become professionally competent and fully credentialed.

An interesting case study was conducted on the issue of using outstanding college graduates as teachers who do not have teaching certificates and are not graduates from colleges of education. Teach For America is an organization that is now 10 years old. Only one in five applicants from 200 colleges are accepted. Their combined SAT scores average 1248, and their average grade point average is 3.4. They are trained during the summer months (seven weeks) to become teachers, and they have a two-year commitment to teach in urban and rural public schools. Despite challenging working conditions and difficult adjustments to new communities, about 90 percent of these teachers finish the two-year commitment, and about one-third continue teaching afterward. Another one-third have taken jobs in administration, public policy organizations, or colleges of education. The program has provided 5,000 teachers over a 10-year period, but only one-third remained as teachers. The overall program has been a good effort, but it has not provided a large volume of qualified teachers.[17]

## OBTAIN MORE PARENTAL INVOLVEMENT AND SUPPORT

Almost every educator claims that parental involvement will improve student learning. Private and church schools believe that parental support is one of the major reasons why their schools are successful. A 1998 study by the Brookings Institute states that one-third of students believe their parents have no idea how they are doing in school, and two-fifths of the parents never attend school programs.[18] There are three key reasons why schools today do not have adequate parental support and involvement.[19]

1. At inner-city schools, some parents work two or more jobs in order to feed, house, and clothe their families. These parents are extremely tired when they get home, or they are often not at home when their children do homework. These parents mean well, but they do not have the time or the energy to help their children with schoolwork.
2. Some parents are illiterate. Either they were failures in school or the school system failed them. They hated school and never felt comfortable there. In fact, many of these people can barely carry on a conversation with a teacher.
3. At some schools, teachers do not invest the time it takes to build a working partnership with parents. They invest the minimum amount of time and effort possible into "back-to-school" or parent/teacher conference nights. When these teachers do meet with parents, the teachers usually tell the parents that their children are doing fairly well or will probably do better as they mature. These teachers never send any information home to tell parents how they can help. Secretly, these teachers hope that they never see the parents except at required back-to-school nights.

At other schools, teachers send e-mail messages to parents on homework assignments. Real growth has taken place in the creation of Internet services designed to help foster communications between schools and parents. The Internet provides "anytime" and "anywhere" communications for parents who have unusual schedules and family demands. In some communities, more than 90 percent of the homes have computers and e-mail. In inner-city neighborhoods, only 10 percent of families may have the ability to use electronic communications. In some communities, parent centers at schools enable mothers and fathers to work with teachers and administrators on site.

The chief executive officer of the Chicago public schools system has decided to try a new approach to obtain parent involvement. In the fall semester of 2000, checklists will be provided by teachers to parents on how well students are prepared for school. Some people claim that these checklists are report cards on parent performance. Time will tell if this program builds teamwork or an adversarial relationship between teachers and parents.[20]

One giant step forward for parental involvement would be a documented and integrated curriculum, with the key lessons written out by grade and subject. Guidelines on how parents could help would be included in the curriculum, which could be distributed through computers or through handouts at back-to-school nights. Schools can do a great deal more to encourage a meaningful working partnership between teachers and parents. It is hoped that these efforts will not overburden teachers and busy parents, which has sometimes happened in the past.

As parents become more educated on the issues of school reform, they may emerge as a strong voice for systemic change. Parents could be vocal and demanding. Therefore, it is important that schools develop a positive working partnership with parents.

## VOLUNTEER PROGRAMS

Years ago, there were almost no volunteers in schools, even though most mothers did not work outside the home. Today, millions of community volunteers work in schools across our country. Senior citizens, who have years of retirement ahead of them, are one major source of volunteer support. Business and government organizations that are trying to help their local schools are another, and parents are a third major contingent of school volunteers.

Many schools have a full-time, paid coordinator of volunteers. The National Association of Partners in Education (NAPE) promotes volunteerism in schools. The local media often write positive stories about volunteers. Recognition is a large part of the process. The Williamsen County School District in Franklin, Tennessee, presents a "Shiny Apple Award" to their top volunteers at an annual dinner.[21]

What do the volunteers do? Almost every task in the school. Tutoring is one of the most effective programs if volunteers are properly trained. Many volunteers serve as teacher aides, which enables every classroom to have two or three adults for small group lessons. Supervision of students at recess or in the cafeteria or helping students get on and off school buses are other volunteer tasks. Some volunteers even ride the school buses to ensure students' safety. Library and study hall assistants are two more volunteer positions.

How much does this volunteerism help student learning? The answer is almost zero if the program is small and not well managed, which is the case in many schools; but volunteerism is a real contribution in many other schools that have formal volunteer training programs. As would be expected, the top-performing schools often have an above-average volunteer program, and the low-performing schools offer an ineffective volunteer program.

## UNIFORMS FOR STUDENTS

Years ago, only students who attended church or private schools wore uniforms. Overseas, children usually wear school uniforms. Now uniforms are becoming a national phenomenon in our public schools. Little evidence supports the notion that uniforms improve students' learning levels, but they do have a positive effect on student attitudes and behavior. Uniforms help students believe that they are part of a team. Uniforms also help eliminate the "baggy gang" look that enables students to smuggle weapons, drugs, and other banned items into schools. Dress codes also make it simpler to spot intruders.

Students wear uniforms in most major cities today, especially in elementary and middle schools. Philadelphia is the largest school system (212,000 students) to require school uniforms. Chicago, New York, and other cities have moved in this direction, but the decision rests with the local school.[22] President Clinton supported uniforms, and numerous political leaders have agreed with him. Some schools offer uniforms to children for free. In other communities, charities donate uniforms. Uniforms level the playing field between the haves and the have-nots. Most educators also believe that uniforms contribute to a better learning environment in classrooms. Although uniforms can improve attendance and behavior, the practice simply is not a panacea for achieving breakthroughs in student learning.

## LEARNING CONTRACT

Under the terms of the contract, students promise to attend school regularly, talk about school programs with their families, do homework, prepare for tests, and observe home rules about study time.

Parents agree to see that the children attend school, keep track of what is happening at school, set aside a quiet time and place for homework, help with assignments, and attend school-related events.

Teachers promise to do a good job of instructing, answer home queries, be sensitive to the students' needs, evaluate the students' work promptly, and keep parents informed about rules.

This program is an example of good intentions by all parties, but there are no specific measurements of performance such as being at grade level or earning A's or B's or teaching to the learning standards. It is another example of a quick-fix and sound-good program that was tried 15 years ago which has had a small impact on student learning.

## IMPLEMENT TOTAL QUALITY MANAGEMENT

Total Quality Management (TQM) was conceived by three management experts, including W. Edwards Deming, who revitalized the Japanese industry with his 14-point methodology. At that time, the United States was losing market share to Japan. Deming said that the only way that the United States could regain its leadership position was to make "Made In America" a guarantee of quality again.

Business executives immediately adopted this strategy. Some companies succeeded, whereas others accomplished very little. Some thought that a few announcements by senior executives and some posters on the walls would inspire employees to rally around the quality drive. They made the same mistake that so many education reformers have made with quick-fix, sound-good tactical programs. A performance system must be devised for every major job category within a corporation in order to make TQM a reality. Most companies and government agencies failed to invest in such performance systems.

TQM must be a long-term, new strategic direction in order for quality to reign in business, government, or schools. The chief executive officer or superintendent must visibly and wholeheartedly support this new strategic direction. A few speeches will not suffice. The vision must be made clear and shared by all levels within the organization. For example, "first time right" in a manufacturing or administrative organization is a goal that all employees can understand. Similarly, "learn the first time" is a goal that all educators can understand. "Students at grade level" is another goal that must be implemented by schools adopting TQM. But goals alone do not guarantee a successful quality program. Goals must be translated into the vision and the action programs outlined in Part III of this book.

TQM has been successfully implemented in some administrative departments, but most classrooms are nowhere near TQM with the failure rates that exist today. The principles of TQM can help achieve breakthroughs in learning, but it is not going to happen under current school management practices. Learning systems, which are described in Chapter 9, are also essential to achieve the TQM goals. The new Baldrige Award in Education, which is under the direction of the National Alliance for Business and which has the support of the Business Roundtable, may move schools in the right direction.

## INSTRUCTIONAL GROUPING

*For decades, schools have classified students into various groups (called tracking), and the following list illustrates the most common groups:*

- Gifted or advanced students
- High-performing students
- Medium- or average-performing students
- Low-performing students
- Remedial or "at-risk" students

Students may be tracked in one group all the time or placed into another group for a subject such as reading. Grouping is based on the concept that a few children will be ahead of their grade level, some will be at grade level, others will be one grade behind, still others will be two or more grades behind, and some students will be totally lost. This approach coincides with the current bell-curve model that is used in almost all schools today. Current teaching methods have made grouping necessary because of the high failure rates and the constant use of social promotion. Except for those students in advanced and high-performing classes, almost all other students do not receive grade-level instruction. As a result, they perform poorly on achievement and mastery tests. Parents often don't realize that their children are not being taught at grade level. Their children are earning B's and C's, so they think all is well.

Another problem is that students labeled as "slow learners" in early grades rarely, if ever, get back to grade level. The intent of such labeling may be to help students at their perceived learning level, but children rank their learning groups from inferior to superior. This labeling hurts children's self-esteem, aspirations, and ability to gain entrance into good jobs or institutions of higher learning.[23]

Several alternative grouping methods have been tried. At the same time, educators state that all children can be successful learners during their K–12 years. Rather than look for more creative grouping methods, educators need to adopt teaching and learning methods that enable more than 90 percent of the students to be at grade level. Grouping hides failure and below-grade-level students in the schools. First-time learning should be the goal instead of another student grouping method.

## SINGLE-SEX SCHOOLS

Often, quick-fix and sound-good programs are old ideas being tried once again with the hope of improving student learning. They fit the category of "willing to try new programs." Single-sex schools fall into this category. Almost no research proves that single-sex schools offer any unique academic benefits. The few remaining female colleges emphasize that girls learn better when they are not distracted by boys. The American Association of University Women (AAUW) conducted a study trying to prove that teachers favor boys in a classroom, but many experts have refuted that study.[24] Today, almost no male-only institutions of higher learning remain, including military academies. Even most single-sex church schools have transformed into coeducational institutions.

Undoubtedly, boys receive lower grades on average and have higher suspension rates than girls. Boys get into more trouble with the law and are more likely to drop out of school at age 16 or 17. They also get more involved in substance abuse. On the other hand, girls receive higher grades in almost every subject, except science and math, where they are only slightly lower than boys. Girls are now the majority population at institutions of higher learning, where they earn about half the professional degrees.

Federal law prohibits public schools from practices that discriminate on the basis of sex or race.[25] As a result, single-sex schools now have high legal expenses. Most judges have concluded that public school problems are not the result of having both sexes in the same classroom.

Most single-sex schools receive extra funds so they can afford to have smaller class sizes. Teachers are hand-picked for these schools. At the same time, students are selected because they are not successful learners in regular classrooms. Such an environment makes it almost impossible to prove that single-sex classrooms or schools achieve breakthroughs in learning.

## SCHEDULING ADJUSTMENTS

One new approach to scheduling is block scheduling, which provides 90-minute rather than 45- or 50-minute periods. Some teachers like this approach because it enables students to learn a subject in greater depth. This approach also results in less student movement in the building. Some educators believe this schedule also reduces discipline problems and improves teacher morale. Block scheduling is great for science courses because it provides adequate time for laboratory experiments. There also appears to be a small improvement in student learning at some schools.

In their book, *Block Scheduling: A Catalyst for Change in High Schools*, Robert Lynn Canady and Michael Rettig made the following comment:[26]

> Simply altering the manner in which we schedule schools will not ensure better instruction by teachers or increase learning by students. We

strongly believe, however, that a well-designed school schedule can be a catalyst for critical changes needed in high schools across America.

What teachers do with their class time is the critical issue. In the same book, the authors wrote the following:

> The argument that educators should become more efficient in their use of currently allocated time was supported by research in the early 1980s. For example, Rossmiller (1983) reported that observations by a number of researchers suggest that only about 60 percent of the school day is actually available for instruction. Dr. Justiz (1984) reported that 16 percent, or approximately one hour of instruction time each school day, was lost on the average in the process of organizing the class and by distractions resulting from student conduct, interruptions, and administrative processes. Other researchers have said that students only engage in productive academic activities during 38 percent of the school day.[27]

In addition, public schools have held class time constant even though the amount of learning varies by student. This inflexibility forces students to learn what they can during the fixed period allocated for a lesson. Some students learn the lesson, but others are confused or totally lost. Everyone knows by now that if a major breakthrough in learning is to occur, the time must be flexible to ensure that the lessons are learned by all students. This common-sense approach, unfortunately, is not common practice despite the great efforts being made by education reformers to change school schedules. Instead, most of the focus on scheduling has been to please teachers rather than to achieve breakthroughs in learning.

## STANDARDIZED LESSON PLANS

Standardized lesson plans is a new program being tried by the Chicago school system.[28] Teachers in some schools have volunteered to receive their daily lesson plans from the central office. This is the same city school system that, a few years ago, believed that local control and site-based management would significantly improve student learning. The improvement never happened, so now the schools are turning to headquarters for more structure.

A team of 100 of Chicago's top teachers developed the current K–12 lesson plans.[29] The lesson plans also need to conform to the district and state standards. One principal said in an October 13, 1999 article in *Education Week* that the lessons plans are "a godsend." She reported that the lessons in the structured curriculum enable teachers to cover information that students need to learn in order to be at grade level. This step away from the hit-and-miss methods of the past has been especially beneficial for new, inexperienced teachers. These lesson plans are currently optional, so perhaps a study will be needed to compare students who learned under the standardized lesson plans with those who received the old, teacher-specific plans. Some teachers, however, are completely against this intrusion into their academic freedom. This new approach to lesson plans also helps inner-city students who frequently change schools. Over the past five years, Chicago has had a 30-percent new-teacher-attrition rate. Lesson plans may reduce this rate.

## MOVE THE MOST EFFECTIVE TEACHERS TO INNER-CITY SCHOOLS

Ministers seek out churches in good communities. Sales personnel look for the most profitable territories. Teachers are just like these other professionals: they move to schools that have good administrators, above-average students, and parental support.

Experienced and top-performing teachers who work in good schools are not going to volunteer in great numbers to move to inner-city schools where 75 percent of the students are behind in grade level. Even if they are offered a bonus, most teachers will not accept positions in those schools because they will be labeled failures each year when the rankings come out for achievement and mastery tests. Attrition rates would quickly escalate if effective teachers from good schools were forced to relocate to inner-city schools.

## HIRE MORE MINORITY TEACHERS

The theory that hiring more minority teachers will improve learning is the old "role model" solution. Some people believe that African American children learn better from African American teachers who have grown up within inner-city neighborhoods. There may be a slight increase in learning, but there is no evidence of major learning breakthroughs. After all, when a person boards an airplane, the individual rarely looks into the cockpit to see the race of the pilots. Everyone just wants a well-trained and capable pilot. The same is true of teachers.

With all the job opportunities available to minorities as a result of equal opportunity and affirmative action programs, most minorities who are college graduates are not going to select teaching as a career. They know, all too well, the problems within inner-city schools. Why join a failed institution and be labeled a failure? Minorities will only sign up to be teachers at inner-city schools when the process of learning is fixed and most students are already at grade level.

## WARRANTY PLEDGES FOR NEW TEACHERS

A few colleges of education have agreed to aid stranded and struggling teachers during their first year on the job by shuttling education professors to school districts for one-on-one advice. In some warranties, the university agrees only to offer more classes or tutoring on the campus. Georgia has such a plan, but few schools have asked for help from the college of education.[30] Needless to say, many professors and deans are skeptical of this program.

This concept is a step in the right direction when colleges of education work closely with school districts that hire their graduates, but it doesn't translate into a big improvement for student learning. It is hoped that the warranty will reduce the high attrition rates of teachers during their first few years on the job.

## ELIMINATE TENURE

This solution is often proposed by business executives who do not have tenure in their own organizations. In fact, many people believe that improving schools is a hopeless cause as long as teachers have tenure, but this is not true. Undoubtedly, some teachers do take advantage of tenure just as partners do in accounting firms, management consulting companies, and law firms. Even in marriage, some partners take advantage of the lifetime contract. Fortunately, though, most people are hard workers with positive attitudes.

Tenure is a problem in schools when an integrated curriculum, learning objectives, documented and approved lesson plans, standard assessment systems, and adequate supervision are not in place. The schools lack documents and facts to fire a teacher, so most tenure terminations end in long court battles. As long as schools continue to be managed as they are today, below-average and nonperforming teachers will remain on the payroll. There are strict labor laws in the United States. Corporations, government agencies, and not-for-profit organizations must have good job descriptions, good performance plans, good training programs, adequate supervision, and improvement programs before they can fire someone. Tenure protects competent teachers by giving them the right to due process. It takes a great deal of effort, time, and expense to terminate an employee in any organization. That's why most organizations carefully select who they hire. They also invest more funds in training their new hires to ensure their success. Unfortunately, most of these human resource development programs are missing or are woefully inadequate in schools. Remember, no one dislikes an ineffective teacher more than a peer teacher who has to spend weeks teaching lessons that should have been successfully taught in a prior grade.

## RAISE THE BAR FOR ACADEMIC PERFORMANCE

Undoubtedly, the curriculum in most schools has been "dumbed down" as the number of students who are not at grade level has risen. Many students who are in the top half of their class, even in the best schools, need more challenging lessons. Therefore, raising the bar for the top scholars is a good strategy. On the other hand, raising the bar for the bottom half who are already one, two, three, or more grade levels behind is like playing a cruel joke on inner-city teachers, administrators, and students. Inner-city schools need systemic changes to enable them to achieve new heights. Educators who raise the bar have not, except in a few situations, provided new learning systems or anything else to solve this great challenge. Some inner-city students have succeeded with the new standards, but in almost every situation, the students were already at grade level. High academic standards are needed, but there must be a means to achieve the higher standards, which is described in Part III of this book.

## RECOGNITION AND REWARDS

When the business community allied itself with educators in the reform movement, one program that was quickly implemented was more recognition and rewards. At first, some teachers and administrators were concerned that "Teacher of the Year" and "Principal of the Year" awards would imply that all school workers were not outstanding employees. For decades, salary scales were based on the fact that all teachers are equal performers, so meritorious systems were avoided. But as time went by and awards became larger in status, money, and publicity, the education community grew to accept various awards based on merit. In fact, the annual awards dinner in many school districts is now a formal event that rivals any athletic banquet. This program has been a low-risk and highly publicized one for companies to sponsor. Firms receive great publicity and make numerous friends within the education community as a result of these programs.

The awards need to mean something. Everyone remembers the days when the school valedictorian was one outstanding student. In some schools, that honor now goes to 42 students because of grade inflation and demand for more recognition. The Superintendent of Schools in San Diego recently invited students from middle schools and high schools to debate the issue of how many valedictorians a school should have. The students voted for one valedictorian per school.[31]

Recognition events require time, effort, and money. Some education reform task forces have even proposed a recognition event as their only major change to the system. Recognition is important, but once again, it will not create a great breakthrough in student learning.

## MORE MALE TEACHERS IN ELEMENTARY SCHOOLS

According to the National Education Association (NEA), the largest teachers' union, currently only 9.1 percent of elementary teachers are males, which is a decrease from 17.7 percent in 1981. Some educators believe that good male role models can motivate young boys to have a positive attitude toward learning. Others say having more males would help all children who have only a single mother at home. This information is interesting, but it does not translate into major breakthroughs for student learning.[32]

Other educators have pointed out that if young boys saw more men as teachers in elementary schools, they would be more inclined to select primary education as a college major. Today, men have a difficult time explaining to their friends and family why they selected such a career.

## SUMMARY OF LOW-COST, QUICK-FIX, AND SOUND-GOOD SOLUTIONS

This chapter has reviewed 21 programs. At least a half-dozen more are currently being tried in various schools. Management and consultants often try to fix performance problems with low-cost and quick-fix programs during a one- or two-year period. If the quick-fix does not work, however, management must move on to more systemic changes. In the school reform movement, people have spent nearly two decades looking for the "silver bullet." This search has consumed a great deal of time, effort, and money, but in the end, student learning improved only slightly.

In the future, all quick-fix programs must have a direct bearing on improving student performance. Standardized lessons in Chicago is a good example of how a tactical program within a grand strategy can achieve improvements in student learning. Educators have been fine-tuning the system and tinkering around the edges for more than 100 years. If the goal were to increase student learning by just a few percentage points, then fine-tuning would be an acceptable strategy. But now that more than 50 percent of students are not at grade level, the goal must be to increase student learning by 80 percent. The American public school system needs to be fixed.

## NOTES

1. J. Akers, *Improving Our Schools* (Armonk, NY: IBM Corporation, 1990), 3.

2. "School Reform," *Fortune*, 29 November, 1993, 130–160.

3. J. Holloway, *The Promise and Pitfalls of Site-Based Management*, (Alexandria, VA: Association For Supervision and Curriculum Development, April 2000), 81–82.

4. A. Ellis and J. Fouts, *Research on School Restructuring* (Princeton, NJ: Eye On Education, 1994), 67–81.

5. E. Wynne and H.Walberg, *The Virtues of Intimacy in Education* (Alexandria, VA: Association For Supervision and Curriculum Development, November 1995), 53–54.

6. T.J. Sergiovanni, *Small Schools, Great Expectations* (Alexandria, VA: Association For Supervision and Curriculum Development, November 1995), 48–52.

7. A. Rotherham, "When It Comes to School Size, Smaller Is Better," *Education Week*, 24 February, 1999, 52, 76.

8. M. Raywid, *Small Schools: A Reform That Works* (Alexandria, VA: Association For Supervision and Curriculum Development, January 1998), 34–37.

9. A. Latham et al., *What the Tests Tell Us about New Teachers* (Alexandria, VA: Association For Supervision and Curriculum Development, May 1999), 23–26.

10. B. Egelko, "Court Upholds State's Teacher-Licensing Test," *San Diego Union-Tribune*, 13 July, 1999, A3, A4.

11. B. Owens, "Why John Can Read," *San Diego Magazine*, August 2000, 40.

12. A. Bradley, "Tests To Reflect New Teachers' Subject Savvy," *Education Week*, 29 October, 1999, 1, 18.

13. A. McQueen, "Emergency Teaching Credential Defended," *San Diego Union-Tribune*, 15 July, 1999, A6.

14. Teacher Skills, "Court Rules Competency Test Does Not Discriminate," *San Diego Union-Tribune*, 16 July, 1999, editorial page.

15. A. Bradley, "Crackdown on Emergency Licenses Begin As Teacher Shortages Loom," *Education Week*, 7 April, 1999, 1, 4.

16. R. Johnson, "Program To Let Teachers Log on for Licensing," *Education Week*, 2 June, 1999, 3.

17. W. Kopp, "Ten Years of Teach for America: What We Have Learned," *Education Week*, 21 June, 2000, 48, 52, 53.

18. L. Steinberg, *Standards Outside the Classroom* (Washington, DC: Brookings Institute Papers on Education Policy, 1998), 130.

19. A. Fege, *New Roles for Parents* (Alexandria, VA: Association For Supervision and Curriculum Development, April 2000), 39–43.

20. M. Galley, "Chicago To Size Up Parents with Checklists," *Education Week*, 31 May, 2000, 18.

21. J. Butler, "Community Involvement," *American School Board Journal*, August 2000, 41–43.

22. R. Johnson, "Philadelphia To Require Students To Wear Uniforms," *Education Week*, 17 May, 2000, 3.

23. D. Viadero, "On the Wrong Track?" *Education Week*, 14 October, 1998, 27–32.

24. S. Black, "Boys and Girls Together," *American School Board Journal*, December 1998, 30–33.

25. Black, "Boys and Girls Together."

26. R. Canady and M. Rettig, *Block Scheduling: A Catalyst for Change in High Schools* (Princeton, NJ:Eye on Education, 1995).

27. Canady and Rettig, *Block Scheduling*.

28. R. Johnston, "In Chicago, Every Day Brings a New Lesson Plan," *Education Week*, 13 October, 1999, 1, 10, 11.

29. Johnston, "In Chicago."

30. J. Blair, "Warranty Pledges Help for Struggling Teacher Graduates," *Education Week*, 3 March, 1999, 5.

31. M. Magee, "Valedictorian Policies Don't Make Grade: Kids Want One per School," *San Diego Union-Tribune*, 17 November, 1999, B1, B4.

32. D. Harrington-Lueker, "Elementary School Students Need More Male Teachers," *USA Today*, 11 September, 2000, 23A.

# CHAPTER 5

# High-Cost and
# Long-Term Programs

Not all of the school reform movement efforts during the past 18 years have focused on quick-fix and sound-good programs. Many political leaders, business executives, and educators have also invested in long-term programs that required substantial incremental funding. The success or failure of these programs should greatly influence the education reform movement's third decade of trying to achieve breakthroughs in student learning. Therefore, it was important to review and understand these programs before the new vision was developed in Part III.

## BUSING STUDENTS TO INTEGRATED SCHOOLS

Busing came long before the 1983 *A Nation At Risk* report, but this solution continues to be promoted by a few educators. This controversial and expensive solution grew out of the historic 1954 Supreme Court ruling, which stated that segregated schools for African Americans were no longer legal. The court was declaring that all American children deserve a first-class education. The doctrine of "separate but equal" has no place in our country; separate education facilities are inherently unequal. The court went on to say that schools should be integrated with "all deliberate speed."[1]

In the 21 states that allowed or required segregated schools, the reactions were a mixture of alarm and grudging compliance. Many private schools were created for white children. A great showdown took place in Little Rock, Arkansas, in 1957, when the governor sent in the National Guard to prevent a handful of black students from enrolling at Central High School. President Eisenhower federalized the National Guard and sent in troops to protect these new students.[2] Later in the 1960s, courts endorsed cross-county busing, redrew attendance zones, and established partnerships between city and suburban schools.[3] Busing helped to end racial segregation but came up short in its intent to provide a better education for minority children.

An unfortunate by-product of busing was that white people fled to the suburbs of major cities so that their children could have a first-class education in what they perceived to be better public schools. City tax bases declined, and minorities became the majority population in most major cities with a second-class school system.

In the 1990s, the tide began to change. After major turmoil in Boston, the courts ruled that busing was not the answer. The great American metropolitan areas had divided into two communities: one white, the other African American or Hispanic. Many educators as well as citizens began to realize that it was racist to believe that minorities learned better when sitting next to white children in school, where African Americans and Hispanics would always be a minority. Now the goal is to fix schools in the inner-cities so that all children can be at grade level. It's a shame this goal was not pursued during the past 40 years because a great deal of pain and suffering could have been avoided. Perhaps the major cities would have achieved more integration if the busing solution had never been implemented, and student learning could have been overhauled during this period at less cost to taxpayers.

## BUSINESS ROUNDTABLE ADOPTS STATES

The Business Roundtable (BRT) is an organization consisting of the 200 chief executive officers of the United States' largest companies. Responding to a challenge from President Bush in 1990, these chief executive officers made a 10-year commitment to work in partnership with the nation's governors, educators, and other interested parties to achieve systemic change in K–12 education in all 50 states and the District of Columbia. Through this program, thousands of companies adopted schools and major corporations adopted states.

*Nine components of the BRT's public policy agenda were as follows:*[4]

1. The new system is committed to four operating assumptions:
   - All students can learn at significantly higher levels.
   - We know how to teach all students successfully.
   - Curriculum content must reflect high expectations for all students, but instructional time and strategies may vary to ensure success.
   - Every child must have an advocate.
2. The new system is performance or outcome-based.
3. Assessment strategies must be as strong and rich as the outcomes.
4. Schools should receive rewards for success, assistance to improve, and penalties for failure.

5. School-based staff have a major role in making instructional decisions.
6. Major emphasis is placed on staff development.
7. A high-quality pre-kindergarten program is established, at least for all disadvantaged students.
8. Health and other social services are sufficient to reduce significant barriers to learning.
9. Technology is used to raise productivity and to expand access to learning.

These nine components are still on target 10 years later, but student learning has not improved as a result of this well-thought-out public policy agenda. Why? First, the assumption that we know how to teach all students successfully is simply not proven. Second, the business executives believed that changing public policy was the key to success, when actually systemic change within each school and school district is the key to fixing schools. Most of these executives didn't realize that most students were not at grade level, nor did they understand that the learning process was not working for more than 50 percent of the students.

Some BRT executives did a great job of creating task forces, performing in-depth studies, and documenting outstanding solutions that were never implemented. The business community did not understand the principles of change management as they applied to schools. Chief executive officers and their companies invested a great deal of time, effort, and funds into school reform, but they rarely achieved breakthroughs in learning; however, they did have a major impact on creating academic standards in most states. They also deserve a lot of credit for supporting tax increases to fund various education reform programs.

## EDUCATION RESEARCH

For years, the federal government has annually invested nearly $200 million for education research projects.[5] If the funds for education research from the National Institute for Child Health and Human Development and the National Science Foundation are added, the investment amounts to nearly $300 million per year. Most of the state departments of education have budgets for various education research projects. Colleges of education are conducting many research studies. Foundations have contributed millions of dollars to a variety of education research studies. The overall total is probably between $400 and $500 million per year.[6] This means that $5 to $7 billion in research projects have been funded since 1983.

What impact has billions of dollars invested in research since 1983 had on improving student learning? The sad answer is little or nothing. Therefore, it is hard to justify another $50 to $100 million investment. The challenge to the many dedicated professors and researchers is to be able to transfer the lessons from their research to the day-to-day operations of a school district. That achievement will happen only when new learning systems, tutoring systems, and management systems, which are discussed in Part III of this book, are implemented. School reform needs applied research projects, not more basic research programs.

## SOCIAL PROMOTION

This quick-fix policy of ending social promotion has enormous costs. The logic is correct in that students cannot succeed in the next grade if they haven't learned the lessons of their current grade. They fall behind more each year until they are completely lost. At that point, they give up on learning. This situation is especially true in cumulative subjects such as reading, writing, spelling, and mathematics. Some of these students sit quietly and hope that the teacher never calls on them, whereas others become troublemakers. Social promotion results in students graduating with far less than a real high school education. Thousands leave as functional illiterates with barely a fourth grade education. Promoting students so they can fail in the next grade is fundamentally wrong.

The primary problem with this concept is that millions of students would be held back if schools truly ended social promotion. This move would lead to large tax increases to fund the students needing one to six additional years to complete high school. On the other hand, keeping students back two, three, four, or perhaps eight grades is equally wrong. No one wants several hulking 16-year-olds sitting in the back row of the third or fourth grade. To prevent this situation, schools must implement "at-risk" programs that combine excellent in-class instruction with frequent diagnostic tests and daily tutoring sessions. Implementing new learning systems in all classrooms to ensure that 90 percent of all students learn the first time and stay at grade level would end the need for social promotion.

Retaining students in a grade means that they must repeat an entire year in school when they probably learned at least one-quarter or half of the lessons. To go back to the first day almost ensures that the student will be bored as well as a potential behavioral problem. The drop-out rate for children who have repeated a grade is much higher, and when it is two or more grades of retention, the student usually becomes a drop-out at age 16.[7]

Louisiana will be one of the first states to hold back elementary and middle school students who fail to pass (40 percent is passing) a statewide test administered at the end of the fourth and eighth grades. Nearly one-third of the fourth and eighth graders in this state (38,000 students) failed the test in the spring of 2000. Those students who fail will have an opportunity to learn in summer school and to retake the test in July, which requires millions of dollars in incremental funds. The 7,600 special education students are exempt from the test. In the previous year,

44,000 failed the test, so "tough learning" is working.[8] A new emphasis is being placed on teaching and learning in this state.

Numerous cities are investing millions of dollars into expanded summer school programs to help the thousands of students who didn't learn their lessons. New York City raised their number of students from 35,000 to 250,000.[9] San Diego, which has a drop-out rate of approximately 30 percent with students in the 9th to 12th grades, has implemented a major new "blueprint" that will cost $49 million in the first year. The plan hinges on the prevention, intervention, and retention measures that have been designed to improve the performance of their 141,000 students.[10] Students needing extra help and time will take expanded blocks of study and/or summer school. The plan is being implemented by the new "education reform" superintendent. Many teachers, administrators, and union members are skeptical, but others in the community are supporting the strong leadership being provided to improve student learning. It's too early to tell if taxpayers are just funding more "seat time" or if students are truly learning their lessons the second time around. Once again, why not have children learn their lessons the first time? As long as schools operate under "education as usual" practices, social promotion will continue.

Several educators want to give up on grade-level measurements because students learn at different rates. Dr. Stephen E. Rubin, who was the principal of Center School in New Canaan, Connecticut, designed a "ski school" method.[11] He eliminated the diversity in learning that takes place in most classrooms by grouping students based on their readiness to learn the next set of lessons. For example, a math class could have students from the first, second, and third grades to learn the lessons that would usually be taught in the third grade. The class could also have fourth and fifth graders who were behind one or two grades. The standards-based curriculum moved successful learners to new material as fast as they completed a lesson. Individual learning programs sound easy, but the challenge is to bring all students through a successful K–12 curriculum over a 13-year period, which is a major logistical effort that most schools are not equipped to handle.

## LONGER SCHOOL DAYS

This expensive program makes sense because some children simply cannot do their homework at home. They need to do their school work and studying on school property. This realization led some forward-thinking educators to have "six-to-six" schools.[12] Parents can bring their children to school as early as 6:00 AM and pick them up as late as 6:00 PM, which means that schools provide all-day child care. Extra school hours are dedicated to homework, supervised recreation, or extracurricular activities.

This program appeals to families who are below the poverty line and to wealthy two-income parents who work long hours. It has succeeded at many schools across our nation.[13] San Diego has implemented the program in 171 schools. Sometimes the cost is paid for by the working parents, but within inner-cities, the cost is usually funded by taxpayers.[14] Numerous studies have stressed the importance of involving students in adult-supervised activities after schools, rather than letting them roam the streets. In other words, it's better to spend money on preventive programs than on the costly criminal justice system. In 1998, both President Clinton and the Secretary of Education endorsed this new program.[15]

Other schools offer an "extended-day" program that enables students to do their homework before going home. At some schools, students must attend extended-day activities if they have a record of not doing homework or if they're falling behind in their studies. Students who do their homework and are at grade level may enjoy recreation or extracurricular activities. When they reach 16 years of age, the successful students can even hold a part-time job. Unfortunately, some programs tend to operate just as babysitting programs.[16] Schools need to supervise their "extended-day" programs, but they don't have to hire certified teachers to perform this duty.

## MORE DAYS PER YEAR

For years, some people have suggested that the school year be extended. The late Al Shanker, former president of the American Federation of Teachers (AFT), told this story that the author used at a 1988 seminar on school reform:

> If a company were manufacturing radios, automobiles, computers, or TVs, and only 25 percent of the units coming off the production line were in perfect working order, another 25 percent required minor rework, another 25 percent required major rework, and the final 25 percent had to be warehoused for 50 to 70 years, the company would immediately shut down the production line to fix the problems. There would be no talk of running the production line for a longer period of time to create more rework and problems.[17]

Accordingly, the cost of additional days per year should not be approved until 90 percent of the students can learn their lessons in the average 180 days that most schools fund today. When their students learn the first time, teachers will have sufficient time to teach all the required lessons. Under current teaching methods, numerous days are devoted to review and remedial lessons because many students need to hear each lesson two to three times.

Some schools are trying a year-round schedule because educators have known for years that a "summer slide" or loss of retention occurs when students are away from school for two or three months. More vacations are scheduled so that the total number of days in school is about the same; however, many people and organizations (e.g., camps, amusement parks, and parents) oppose the year-round schedule because they don't want to lose the long summer vacation.

## BREAKFASTS AND LUNCHES

For years, teachers would see many students at inner-city schools looking tired and listless because of hunger. One of the most successful government programs has been free or subsidized breakfast and lunches for students who live in poverty. There is no way to measure the exact impact on student learning, but teachers agree that two solid meals per day are essential for student learning and good behavior. The National School Lunch Program serves nearly 25 million students daily, which is about 50 percent of all students. Five million students receive a free breakfast.[18]

Now, some citizens are against these programs because, once again, the government is being forced to do what parents did years ago, even during the Great Depression. During the depression years, one parent (and in many cases, two parents) was usually home as a result of unemployment. Times have changed, and millions of taxpayer dollars are now required to be certain that children are ready to learn because studies have shown that students perform better in school if they are properly fed.[19]

## SCHOOL-BASED HEALTH CENTERS

For decades, schools have employed a school nurse who is either available on site or on call. In many school systems, this is sufficient because parents have health insurance for their children, who receive an annual physical examination and all the necessary preventive medicines.

A school nurse is not adequate for many inner-city schools where children have never been to a doctor unless they were involved in an accident. Some parents have no health insurance, which means they try to avoid any contact with the medical system. Because of this situation, more than 1,300 school-based health centers have been established within urban and rural schools.[20] These centers treat accident victims, asthma patients, common colds, fevers, child abuse, drug abuse, depression, sexually transmitted diseases, and every other medical problem that can befall children from ages 5 to 19 years.

A typical school-based health center is sponsored and operated by an established hospital, health department, or community health center in a facility provided by the school district. Services are usually provided by a nurse practitioner, physician assistant, or a clinical social worker, aided by administrative personnel. Outside medical and psychiatric specialists are also available for referrals and visitations. The median operating costs are running more than $200,000 per center annually.[21] Funding is provided by a variety of sources, which is a major challenge.

School-based health centers are located in 45 states and the District of Columbia.[22] High schools and middle schools house more than half of these centers, whereas elementary schools account for less than one-third. School-based health centers reduce barriers to learning and help keep students in school. They allow teachers to concentrate on their students' academic performance and help parents who cannot afford to miss work for their children's doctors' appointments. They also reduce the number of hospital emergency room visits and 911 calls.

School-based health centers were first established in the early 1970s. Organized opposition to birth control counseling and the dispensing of contraceptives slowed their progress in the 1980s, but since then, efforts to raise public awareness, use of parental consent forms, and fear of acquired immunodeficiency syndrome (AIDS) and other sexually transmitted diseases have counteracted most concerns. Each school-based health center requires an advisory board of concerned parents and health care workers.

This program is similar to the free breakfasts and lunches program. It will not increase student learning by itself, but inner-city schools must have these extra support programs to have any hope of reaching the goal of having most students become successful learners.

## MORE YEARS OF SCHOOLING FOR HIGH SCHOOL GRADUATES

A former United States President stated that all children should have a college education or at least two years of community college. This multi-billion-dollar proposal is not necessary in the United States because millions of jobs are available that require only a high school education.[23] Most retail clerks, fast food restaurant personnel, hotel employees, domestic help, truck drivers, medical support staff, administrative clerks, production line employees, and maintenance workers need only a real high school education in order to do their jobs. Many companies today recruit for some jobs from community colleges because the high school diploma has become meaningless; however, these companies are really looking for the equivalent of good high school graduates.

With the new exit examinations and the trend toward ending social promotion, many school districts are adding one, two, or three years of schooling for some students as they struggle to pass the final test. Rochester, New York, has just developed a plan that will enable high school students to have either three, four, or five years of schooling to pass the New York state Regents' examination (exit test).[24] Top students, who could pass the examination at the end of their junior year, could go on to college if they have taken all of the required courses or remain in high school for enrichment programs or college-level courses during a fourth year. In the class of 2000, only one-third of the 1996 freshman class completed high school on time and passed the New York state Regents' examination. By 2003, all Rochester students will have to pass the New York state Regents' examination to receive a high school diploma.[25] Chicago is adopting a similar five-year plan to reduce its high level of drop-outs. All of this requires major increases in school budgets.

Only the most motivated and successful students should go on to institutions of higher learning. For economic reasons, colleges and universities must keep all of their seats full. Thus many schools take almost anyone who can afford the tuition. These same schools offer remedial classes in reading, writing, and mathematics, which are really the equivalent of middle and high school courses. It is hoped that, rather than expanding their capacity during the next surge of students, institutions of higher learning will raise standards and eliminate remedial classes. Every American is not entitled to a college education, and taxpayers should not have to pay for university students who cannot read, write, and compute at a 12th-grade level.

## UNIVERSAL PRESCHOOL FOR FOUR-YEAR-OLD STUDENTS

In the recent Presidential election, there was great debate on the issue of the federal government providing funds for a universal preschool for all four-year-olds in the country. One candidate said it would require $50 billion and another candidate estimated the cost to be at least $100 billion. The numbers must include both the operating costs and capital funds because the average cost of a student in our public schools is a little over $7,000. With over 4 million potential preschool students, the operating costs should be around $30 billion with billions more in capital funds to build over 200,000 additional classrooms which is the equivalent of 10,000 school buildings. One consistent factor in education is that whenever a major program is added, the cost is in the billions of dollars due to the number of students. Of course, this program would reduce the costs of Head Start.

All of this supports the accepted belief that four- and five-year-old children can be successful learners in several subjects. This is covered in more detail in Chapter 8 when the world-wide curriculum is discussed.

## COMPUTERS

For decades, educators have known that high-quality, self-study courses motivate students to learn. Computers enable students to learn at their own pace with an interactive tutor. Students cannot go on to Lesson 2 until they have mastered Lesson 1, thus eliminating social promotion. Students love to learn on computers. Today, with multimedia video, audio, voice, touch screens, keyboards, and outstanding graphic features, computers have become marvelous learning machines. Unfortunately, most computers are still not being used as interactive tutors. Instead, they are used for drill-and-practice sessions or word processing. Like so many other technological breakthroughs, educators are using computers as a supplement rather than as an integrated part of new learning systems. One attendee at an education convention remarked that public schools have accepted only two new classroom technologies during the past 100 years: electricity and ballpoint pens. Audiotapes, radio, television, overhead projectors, videotapes, and now computers are used only occasionally to teach a lesson. Along the same lines, school districts are the only organization still studying the effectiveness of seat belts for use on school buses, even though they've been accepted by everyone else for the past 40 years.

Almost every classroom today has one or more computers in it, many of which have Internet access. In too many schools, classroom computers have become "hobby shops" for teachers and volunteers who enjoy using computers.[26] Students who are at grade level are allowed to have some "computer time," but computers are not used as interactive tutors. Nor are computers used for assessment because the old tests used in the old lesson plans are still being administered. Once again, costs rise by billions of dollars and student learning remains the same. Schools brag about how many computers they have, but the question remains: How do they use these computers to increase student learning? Colleges of education rarely teach how computer technology can achieve learning breakthroughs, a topic which is discussed further in Part III.

## COOPERATIVE LEARNING

A typical classroom features a teacher doing most of the talking as students listen. Research tells us that very little time is allotted for student-to-student interaction. In fact, some studies report that such interaction occurs only a few minutes each day. Cooperative learning involves students working in groups or teams to achieve certain education goals. Students learn from and depend on each other.

*Five major models are currently being offered by well-known educators:*[27]

1. *Learning Together* by David and Roger Johnson

2. *Student Team Learning* by Robert Slavin
3. *Group Investigation* by ShiomoYael Sharan
4. *Structural Approach* by Spencer Kagan
5. *Jigsaw* by Elliot Aronson

Cooperative learning is utilized in Israel, New Zealand, Sweden, Japan, and the United States. This method could help restructure education, but it needs to be integrated into the learning systems that are discussed in Chapter 9. Cooperative learning's impact is diminished when it is used with existing lesson plans and evaluation methods. Too often, cooperative learning is mandated by an administrator and presented in a three-hour inservice session that convinces a few teachers to try it for awhile. It then becomes another example of the "we already tried that method" way of thinking. Dr. Robert Slavin of Johns Hopkins University summed it up this way:[28]

> Another danger inherent in the success of cooperative learning is that the methods will be oversold and undertrained. It is being promoted as an alternative to tracking and within class grouping, as a means of mainstreaming academically handicapped students, as a means of improving race relations in desegregated schools, as a solution to the problems of students at risk, as a means of increasing prosocial behavior among children, as well as a method for simply increasing the achievement of all students. Cooperative learning can in fact accomplish this staggering array of objectives, but not as a result of a single three-hour inservice session.

In their book *Research on School Restructuring*, Arthur K. Ellis and Jeffrey Fonts made the following comments on the research base for cooperative learning:[29]

> A long tradition of research in social psychology has established that group discussion, particularly when group members must publicly commit themselves, is far more effective at changing individuals' attitudes and behaviors than even the most persuasive lecturer. At Level 2 research, the sheer amount of empirical evidence which has accumulated from research studies in cooperative learning is staggering. Of all the educational trends we have reviewed for this book, cooperative learning has the best, largest empirical base.

Cooperative learning clearly works when it is implemented and used properly, but with current school management systems, new learning method breakthroughs are just not implemented or used consistently. They're used haphazardly by a few teachers for a few years. When student learning is not the goal, new teaching and learning methods are difficult to implement.Therefore, even new methods that are successful rarely survive in today's schools.


## SCHOOLWIDE REFORM

Ten years ago, the business community, with the leadership of David Kearns (Deputy Secretary of Education under President George Bush), decided to try an entirely new approach to school reform. They asked hundreds of people working on various school reform projects to devise "Designs for a New Generation of American Schools."[30] It was a noble effort aimed to create schoolwide reform.

In October 1991, President Bush issued the following request for proposals:[31]

> Think about every problem, every challenge we face. The solution to each starts with education. For the sake of the future—of our children and the nation—we must transform America's schools. The days of the status quo are over.

This speech launched a new education strategy—AMERICA 2000. The strategy was the linchpin of a nine-year effort to close the gap between where our schools were at that time and the vision of where public schools should be by the year 2000. Benchmarked by six national goals, the independent nonprofit organization called the New American Schools Development Corporation (NASDC) became the new catalyst for educational change.

Nearly 700 individuals and organizations responded with proposals. With the help of the RAND Corporation, 11 design teams were selected. All 11 teams were not-for-profit organizations, which upset many for-profit firms that had invested thousands of dollars and months of effort in forming their proposals. The designs were intended to succeed in rural, urban, suburban, small, and large schools.[32]

Only three constraints were imposed on the design teams:

1. that the design help *all* students achieve world-class standards in at least five core subjects (i.e., English, mathematics, science, history, and geography)
2. that young people graduate prepared for responsible citizenship, further learning, and productive employment
3. that, after initial investment costs, the new school operate at costs comparable to conventional schools.

The following three phases were planned for the development program:[33]

**Phase 1**: Spring 1992 to Spring 1993, Develop the Design

**Phase 2**: Spring 1993 to Spring 1995, Implement, Test, and Refine the Design

**Phase 3**: Spring 1995 to Spring 1997, Assist Many Communities to Adapt and Use the Design

The business communities donated nearly $100 million to this program. The Annenberg Foundation, AT&T, Boeing, Exxon, Ford, General Motors, IBM, and Xerox each gave $3 million or more. Eight approved designs resulted from all of this money, time, and effort.[34]

What happened to this 10-year investment? At the end of 1997, the designs were being used in more than 700 schools in 26 states. In his 1998 booklet entitled "New American Schools After Six Years," Thomas K. Glennan, Jr. from RAND Corporation discussed how the design teams, who were selected to develop "mold-breaking" schools, had to eventually become professional service organizations with management, marketing, and product-refinement skills. This transition was difficult because these teams were selected on the basis of designing a new approach for education rather than on their skills to implement the design. Glennan pointed out that many schools and districts participating in the project never intended to use the designs throughout their schools. He concluded that "district-wide school reform with design-based assistance as a cornerstone is clearly not likely on a wide scale in the near future." In other words, design implementation had become a greater challenge than the NASDC had anticipated. They had created more "hobby shops" for testing pet projects instead of the schoolwide reform they wanted originally.[35]

In fall 1998, the NASDC went out of business, but a successor organization named New American Schools continued to provide reform models for schools. Their work is supported by a $145-million grant through federal funding for whole-school reforms that provides money to 2,500 schools and 1.25 million students.[36]

In 1998, the Education Research Service (ERS) published a manual called *Blueprints for School Success: A Guide to New American Schools Designs*.[37] This document helps school districts decide on which designs should be tested and adopted in their schools.

In 1999, the American Institutes for Research included all eight of the New American Schools designs and 16 other schoolwide reforms in its publication *An Educator's Guide to Schoolwide Reform*.[38] The American Institutes for Research performs its work under contract to the following organizations:

American Association of School Administrators
American Federation of Teachers
National Association of Elementary School Principals

National Association of Secondary School Principals
National Education Association

The publication's purpose was to enable schools and districts across the country to decide how to use their Title I funds and the $145 million allocated by Congress to encourage low-performing schools to raise student achievement. The report highlighted the fact that only 3 of the 24 programs had a proven impact on student achievement. Two of these programs, Success For All and Direct Instruction, apply only to the K–6 grades, and the third program, High Schools That Work, applies only to grades 9–12.[39]

Why did the various programs score so low? In the late 1980s and early 1990s, numerous programs devoted a great deal of effort to setting standards because states had not established standards at that time. Standards are important, but schools need methods to achieve these standards. Most schoolwide programs were weak on how to achieve standards. In too many cases, programs required more work than administrators or teachers were willing to invest. No schoolwide commitment to implementing these programs was made. Most schoolwide programs lacked instructional systems design (ISD) methods, so lesson plans were developed by teachers who had almost no training in ISD. The focus on these programs was, too often, on teacher morale and acceptance rather than on an increase in student learning. Some of these designs were not "mold-breaking" programs; instead, they only "tinkered around the edges." Only a few of these programs attempted to create complete learning systems that would lead to learning breakthroughs.

Numerous educators took great delight in the fact that all of this time, money, and effort showed less than successful results. Their delight will be short-lived, though, because political leaders and the business community will eventually agree with Dr. Branson that the current education system has reached its upper limits. They won't invest more money unless real systemic change takes place.

The leaders of the 24 schoolwide reform programs were unhappy with the American Institutes of Research report. Once again, their effort has shown how hard it is to judge the effectiveness of various education reform programs because so few agreed-upon evaluation standards exist. It is hoped that organizations will continue to work on schoolwide reform programs so that the American public school system can achieve learning breakthroughs.

## ENHANCED PROFESSIONAL DEVELOPMENT PROGRAMS

Recently, people have demanded more professional development programs to improve teacher effectiveness. These programs underscore the belief by many people that school conditions indicate a performance problem by teachers and principals rather than a systems problem stemming from traditional teaching and learning methods. No one says outright that teachers are to blame for the low test scores, but the implied message still upsets unions and teachers. No one wants to be against improving teacher performance, but the results from this strategy over the past 50 years have been unimpressive.

In the past, too many school districts have wasted time and money on professional development. For example, Boston's school system is in the midst of overhauling the way it organizes and finances professional development because a report on that subject stated that the district spent $23.5 million (almost $5,600 per teacher and administrator) in school year 1998–1999, but most of the programs were not focused on student learning standards.[40] Such sessions consist of talks and videotapes intended to entertain teachers and to provide some useful, but negligible information. With the new emphasis on student learning, today's professional development seminars are more focused, but they rarely involve system implementation or the review of "best practices" in lesson plans. Teachers need an intellectually rigorous study of what they must teach and how to teach a subject for a standards-based curriculum, including lessons on ISD methods.[41]

Research tells us that student learning is greatly influenced by the quality of teaching. Staff development must be results-driven and embedded into the education system based on learning systems that are implemented to achieve the standards established by the state department of education and the school district. Accordingly, professional development seminars must also be realistic. They can no longer be theoretical and out-of-touch with what is really being done in the classroom.[42] The superintendent, director of curriculum, and principals must be involved in the overall plan for professional development.

## ADDITIONAL COMPENSATION

At one time in our country, both teachers and administrators were clearly underpaid. Women, who were the majority of teachers, had only a few career choices (e.g., domestic help, retail clerking, food service, secretaries, administrative positions, nursing, and teaching). Teaching was considered the most professional career for women, and for decades, it attracted "the best and the brightest."

In early education reform years, the issue was raised that thousands of teachers would be retiring in the 1990s. These teachers were hired in the 1950s to handle the "baby boom" generation. Numerous states and cities passed sizable tax increases to raise teacher compensation. The goal was simple: To attract better people into the teaching field to replace one million teachers leaving the profession in the 1990s.

Connecticut was one state that increased teacher salaries substantially. In many communities, the starting salary is now close to $35,000, and an experienced teacher with a Master's degree can earn close to $75,000 plus benefits. The average salary in Connecticut is $52,503, according to "Education Vital Signs," which is an annual publication by the *American School Board Journal*. Average teacher salaries across the nation are now close to $43,000. New Jersey and New York average more than $50,000. Lower wages ($35,000) are found in Utah, New Mexico, Arizona, Wyoming, Idaho, Montana, and Nebraska, where student learning is often much higher than in states that have large urban school districts. The lowest salaries ($30,000) are found in North and South Dakota, where students also achieve high test scores. Mississippi averages $30,000 as well.

Little evidence supports the notion that higher teacher salaries produce more successful students or higher test scores. There is also little evidence that outstanding teachers in New Mexico or Mississippi will move to Connecticut to double their income. Although some states have reciprocal agreements, the fact that teachers need to be certified by each state on the subject or subjects they teach may be one reason why they do not leave low-wage states to obtain higher salaries.

Ten years ago, everyone predicted that a teacher shortage would occur in the 1990s—a fear that was blown out of proportion.[43] The same tactics are now being used for this decade. Recent estimates indicate that the nation will need to hire 2.2 million additional teachers in this decade.[44] That number is shocking because it means that a majority of existing teachers will leave their jobs within 10 years.

Even if the need to hire 2.2 million teachers were real, there still would not be a teacher shortage. E. Emily Feistritzer's new report "The Making of a Teacher," published by the Center for Education Information, informs us that the number of new teacher graduates jumped 40 percent from 134,870 in 1983 to 200,545 in 1998.[45] Indications are that even more graduates are on the way. For example, the number of California State University teaching graduates will increase by 25 percent.[46] Although a few famous universities, such as University of Chicago, closed their colleges of education, the number of institutions preparing new teachers increased from 1,287 in 1984 to 1,354 in 1999.[47]

Many positions (about 40 percent) will also be filled by former teachers coming back into the profession, teachers moving from district to district, and teachers who work in private schools moving to public schools.[48] Projections show that the number of public school students will start to decline after 2010 when the "baby boom" generation moves past its child-bearing years. With all the new teachers hired between 1990 and 2010, there could well be a serious teacher surplus, not shortage, by the end of this decade.

There has never been a shortage of qualified teachers for schools where 75 percent of the students are at grade level. Many communities do, however, have a shortage of math and science teachers. Teacher shortages also exist in rural communities and urban school districts. Very few teachers want to teach in a school where 75 percent or more of the students are not at grade level, where the neighborhood is not safe, and where the school and faculty are deemed failures each year by the state department of education. Learning problems within inner-city schools must be fixed in order to attract new teachers. Many new teachers at inner-city schools drop out of teaching or relocate to suburban schools or better schools within the district.

Attrition is a big problem in the teaching profession. Between 25 and 30 percent of graduates from the colleges of education never take a teaching position. In his October 6, 1999, *Education Week* article, "The Teacher Shortage: Wrong Diagnosis, Phony Cures," John Merrow stated, "Simply put, we train teachers poorly, then treat them badly, so they leave in droves. The teacher shortage is a problem of retention rather than recruitment."[49] He also reported that an estimated 30 percent of new teachers leave the teaching profession within five years. In some city schools, the exit rate is an astonishing 50 percent or more.[50]

The education reform years have helped teachers and administrators earn better wages. In many situations, their incomes have more than doubled since 1983. Unfortunately, student performance has remained about the same. Political leaders, business executives, and taxpayers should not increase teachers' salaries with only the hope that student learning will improve. In the future, school districts may consider a practice where teachers and administrators must implement new administrative and learning systems that enable more than 90 percent of the students to be successful learners before there are significant increases in salaries.

## HIRE BETTER TEACHERS

This suggestion implies that the current teacher population is second class, which is not true in most schools. Some extreme proposals suggest that inner-city teachers be hired at $50,000 and paid $90,000 if they have 10 years of experience.[51] Once again, some people believe that all of the problems in our schools can be solved with more money.[52]

Top students who graduate from high school are looking for jobs that have good working conditions, exciting opportunities to create new products and/or services, the latest technologies, and growth in job enrichment and real recognition for a job well done. Then, they look at the compensation plan. Teaching at inner-city schools under the current methods and management systems simply will not attract better personnel until systemic change is implemented. The education system must be fixed first.

## PAY FOR PERFORMANCE

Pay for performance has been utilized for years in the business world. Chief executive officers favor incentive plans because they have been made rich by stock options that have rewarded them far beyond their wildest dreams. Some people believe that these executives have been rewarded far beyond their contribution to their organizations. A "super bull" stock market has increased rewards to the point where compensation for senior executives seems excessive to many people. Everyone agrees, though, that the top-performing executives should be well paid because their leadership rewards stockholders, customers, and employees.

Salespeople also like incentive plans that make them rich, but they dislike plans that control their earnings. One salesperson said it well at a January meeting of the sales force: "If they use a multimedia presentation to explain the new pay-for-performance plan to me, I know they are reducing the commissions." Only those few people who have created incentive pay programs know how difficult it is to have a fair plan.

The business community wants to put teachers and administrators on a pay-for-performance plan. Denver public schools are trying such a plan. Under this plan, teachers' pay will be tied to student outcomes using three approaches: standardized tests, teacher-created tests and projects, and increases in teachers' knowledge and skills. In reality, this plan is a bonus system on top of the teachers' regular salary scale, but the hope is that it will eliminate pay increases that are given solely for additional years of service and education.[53] Cincinnati is another city that is trying an interesting pay-for-performance system which is really a career ladder of five jobs for teaching.

One private school had teachers on a payment plan that consisted of 70 percent salary, a 10-percent bonus for parent satisfaction, a 10-percent bonus for student learning, and a final 10-percent bonus for overall evaluation by the principal.[54] Other pay-for-performance plans are being tested in 10 states.[55]

Bob Chase, president of the National Education Association (NEA), has praised the Denver experiment, but he has reservations about it. He stated, "People are assuming that pay for performance will enhance student achievement, but nobody really knows whether that's true." At the NEA annual meeting in 2000, the largest teacher's union refused to allow merit pay and pay-for-performance plans.[56] Many education reformers will claim that this stance is a great defeat for change, but it may be a blessing that this distraction to improving student learning is no longer a big issue.

The defeat of pay for performance does signal that most teachers still do not want to be evaluated or paid based on students learning the lessons. Taxpayers will pay a great deal more for teachers if pay for performance succeeds because people on incentive plans always earn above the salary scale. It is always dangerous to implement a pay-for-performance system when major performance problems exist because someone fixes the fundamental barriers to success and the workforce gets rich for something they really did not accomplish. Paying a bonus for success rather than failure is a new approach for the education reform movement, and only time will tell if it encourages teachers and administrators to focus on student learning. Socialized pay systems that avoid merit increases or bonuses usually result in lower compensation for all employees, which may be one of the major problems in attracting and retaining outstanding young people to the teaching profession.

## TUTORING

Since the time of Socrates, we have known that one or two students per teacher is the most effective way to teach new subjects and skills. Yet, in most schools, almost no professional tutors are available because the average teacher earns more than $40,000 plus benefits, so the cost is prohibitive.

American companies, such as Sylvan Learning Systems, with revenues of more than $300 million, are offering tutoring systems to parents who can afford extra help for their children.[57] These companies serve students who are behind in grade level, who are frustrated with school, or who lack confidence and motivation. Sylvan and other companies, such as Huntington Learning Centers, have millions of prospects because of our poor public school performance. These companies have more than 1,000 centers where many former and part-time teachers become tutors for a professional fee. These tutors have proven learning systems and reward systems that return students to grade level.

Most people believe that if a person has knowledge about a subject, then he or she can become a tutor right away, but this is not true. Professional tutors, trained tutors, and tutoring systems working in public schools are far superior to amateurs trying to be tutors. One company with an impressive record in this field is Help One Student To Succeed (HOSTS). With more than 100,000 trained personnel, these mentors have a proven system for tutoring students to keep them at grade level. Their structured mentoring is research-based and is recognized as a nationally validated program for reading, writing, mathematics, and Spanish language arts. Their learning system is based on individual lesson plans that have received awards from many national organizations, including the U.S. Department of Education.

In Ohio, Governor Bob Taft launched a major educational initiative aimed at improving the reading skills of Ohio's kindergarten through fourth-grade students. "OhioReads" will funnel $40 million in state funding over the next two years into classroom and community reading grants for programs to help children pass the state-mandated fourth-grade reading proficiency test and advance to the fifth grade.[58] The fourth graders cannot be promoted to fifth grade unless they pass this test.

A unique component of "OhioReads" is the call for 20,000 volunteer reading tutors who will be carefully selected and trained. The Limited, Inc. (a women's retail fashion company) has agreed to underwrite the training for the tutors and is providing 400 tutors in the Columbus area alone. Many other companies are involved because this program has structure and measurements. Books alone will not do the job. A formal tutoring program is required to achieve a significant increase in reading scores. Structured and measured programs, such as HOSTS and Reading Recovery, often succeed in returning students to grade level. One has to wonder why structured and measured learning systems are not used in the first place. Tutoring is clearly a successful education strategy, and one that will be discussed further in Chapter 9.

## NUMBER OF STUDENTS IN THE CLASS

The average class size in American schools has dropped from 30 in 1961 to 23, and it appears to be heading toward 20.[59] This decrease is one reason why the cost of public school education has more than doubled, even though little improvement in student learning has occurred.

Reducing class size is a strategy receiving a great deal of debate and research. In 1999, the U. S. Secretary of Education stated that smaller classes will translate into more individual student attention, more orderly classrooms for teachers, and a better learning environment for all. The President and Vice President of the United States at that time and numerous state governors were convinced that this strategy would improve student performance.[60]

Smaller class sizes undoubtedly drive up the cost of education. A study conducted by the American Institutes for Research and the RAND Corporation concluded that the annual cost would be about $6 billion to reduce the number of students in primary grades to 18.[61] The cost increases significantly as the number of students per classroom decreases. For example, if you have 10,000 students in a school district that serves a town of 50,000, the cost to reduce classroom size by 10 percent is approximately $5 million in annual operating expenses and $30 million in capital expenses for new school buildings with 50 additional classrooms. That's a lot of money just to reduce the number of students from 20 to 18.[62]

With only 18 students per class, will teachers use different lesson plans? Probably not. Teaching time will remain the same. Time on task by students will also stay the same. One fundamental change is that tutoring time will be divided by 18 students rather than 20. Unfortunately, in most classes, tutoring time amounts to only a few minutes per week per student. For example, if a teacher uses 20 percent of the learning time each day for tutoring, that translates into 15 minutes of tutoring per student per week. By reducing the class size from 20 to 18, each student now has 17 minutes of tutoring time each week. Two more minutes will not create a breakthrough in learning.[63]

Is it any wonder that reports are now beginning to appear in newspapers, journals, and education research publications stating that small class sizes provide only a small increase in student learning? California is investing $4 billion to reduce class sizes for K–3 students.[64] Education research over the years tells us that unless class size is 10 or less, only small improvements in student learning will be made. To reduce the class size to 10 students would require more than $100 billion annually in operating expenses and billions more for new schools.[65] Education experts are now saying that class size reductions alone will not raise test scores. They want more teacher training, additional books in the libraries, and a greater emphasis on reading. Class size is not a "silver bullet" because it must approach the tutoring level to be effective.

A California report tells us that smaller classes can have negative impacts.[66] There are not enough classrooms in most schools to handle a major reduction in class size. More important, there aren't enough qualified teachers to handle such a growth in classrooms. The average education experience and teacher credentials in the primary grades declined sharply when class sizes were reduced. Decline in teacher qualifications was worst within inner-city schools, which should not be a big surprise.[67]

Other classroom programs (e.g., special education, art, music, computer labs, and even libraries) were reduced to free up classroom space. Many parents began to say, "I would rather have my child in a classroom with a well-qualified, high-performing teacher even if the number of students exceeded 20." Simply put, these parents want better teachers, not more classrooms.

Reduction in class size from 20 to 18 or from 25 to 20 is a long way from tutoring. The one bright spot for class size reduction has been the Student/Teacher Achievement Ratio (STAR) research project in Tennessee. This study collected 14 years of data based on 11,000 children in 42 school districts who were participating in a special class size study. Students were randomly assigned to classes of 15 students or 25 students during the K–3 grades. At the end of the third grade, the children from the smaller classes were four months ahead of the other children;[68] however, the study did not determine if any of these children were at grade level. The study did prove, though, that children in smaller classes did better in their remaining nine years of schooling.

On the other hand, Professor Eric Hanushek from the University of Rochester examined 277 separate studies on class size reduction. He stated that "only 15 percent suggested that there is a 'statistically significant' improvement in achievement, 72 percent found no improvement, and 13 percent found a negative effect."[69]

Students in Japan and Europe often sit in classes with 30 or 40 students, and Korea averages over 40 students per class. Many parochial school classrooms have 25 to 35 students. Children in these schools outperform American students who learn in classrooms of 18 to 25.[70] Can the United States afford to have class sizes of 10 to 15 students? Absolutely not.[71]

## ECONOMIC SCHOOL DESEGREGATION

As stated previously in this chapter, court-ordered racial desegregation programs are coming to an end because they have failed to improve student learning. Similar policy makers who promoted busing as a great solution over the past several decades are now urging communities to bus children who are below the poverty line to "middle-class" schools.[72] After all, across the nation, schools with middle-class students appear to have higher test scores than schools where students are on free lunch and breakfast programs. These policy makers also see this strategy as a way to continue to integrate the races of our country.

Fortunately, many leaders and parents in the minority communities are discouraged with the busing programs. They want good neighborhood schools where their children can be successful learners. Their request is not unreasonable, and the reader of this book will learn in Parts III and IV that every neighborhood school can be a successful learning institution with more than 90 percent of the children achieving as successful learners. Therefore, no one should support another busing program. Policy makers who constantly believe that there must be a simple "quick-fix" solution to student learning need to conduct an in-depth study on what the real problems are in the classroom and what required systemic changes will fix the American public school system. Once again, it is a racist belief that minority children must be bused to white middle-class schools for them to be successful learners. North Carolina's second-largest school system is committed to this new policy of busing to middle-class schools, so it will be interesting to see what success they achieve during the next few years.[73] It does allow a school district to spread performance problems around to all schools, but that is no real fix for student learning.

## BUILD FIRST-CLASS FACILITIES

For more than two decades, Kansas City tried to fix its city school district by investing $2 billion to improve the physical plants of area schools. With a magnet school concept, the goal was to attract white middle-class and wealthy students back into the city school system. Once again, there was a misguided belief that minority students would become successful learners if they were placed in classes with successful white children.[74]

Not only did student learning not improve, but the performance of the city schools was so low in the areas of student test scores, drop-outs, and attendance rates that their accreditation was revoked as well. Kansas City now realizes that their simple but expensive programs could not compare to inexpensive, daunting changes such as reforming the way students learn and how teachers teach.[75]

## OVERHAUL GOVERNANCE

In the year 2000, there appears to be a new focus on how schools are managed, which is termed *governance*. Foundations, state departments of education, and colleges of education are forming task forces, studies, grant requests, and the other types of action programs that are implemented when a new area is to be studied.[76]

The initial reaction to much of this work appears to be that it amounts to nothing more than "tinkering around the edges" rather than a real, in-depth study on why the current management systems and organization structures are a major part of the problem. Chapter 12 explains why major changes in governance must be made if there is going to be any hope of raising student learning to more than 90 percent. This is an important new area to be studied and systemic change is absolutely necessary in the area of governance.

## SUMMARY OF HIGH-COST AND LONG-TERM PROGRAMS

Over the past 18 years, the number of "show-and-tell" events where companies who adopted schools tell audiences how great their programs are have decreased. After several years of these events, the stories began to sound alike, and it became evident that student achievement was improving only slightly. Europeans have been known to comment that Americans confuse spending money and implementing a series of new action programs with solving serious performance problems.[77] This confusion has certainly happened in the education reform movement.

This chapter discussed 22 programs that, while adding many billions of dollars to the overall cost of the American public school system, have had only a minimal impact on student learning. Tutoring, meal plans, health centers, longer school days, and cooperative learning are a few programs that have positively impacted on student learning. Eventually, schoolwide reform should make a difference. Head Start and Title I programs were discussed in Chapter 2, and they are two more examples of high-cost, long-term programs that nevertheless have some positive attributes. In the future, all programs should be evaluated through pilot tests before billions of additional dollars are committed to them.

---

### NOTES

1. *Education Week* staff, "Lessons of a Century: Struggle for Integration," *Education Week*, 2000, 60–91.
2. *Education Week* staff, "Lessons of a Century."
3. *Education Week* staff, "Lessons of a Century."

4. *Essential Components of a Successful Education System* (Washington, DC: Business Roundtable, 1990), 1–8.

5. E. Robelen, "President Seeks Bigger Budget for Research," *Education Week*, 8 March, 2000, 30.

6. Robelen, "President Seeks Bigger Budget for Research."

7. W. Romey, "A Note on Social Promotion," *Phi Delta Kappan*, April 2000, 632–633.

8. E. Robelen, "Louisiana Set To Retain 4th, 8th Graders Based On State Exams," *Education Week*, 24 May, 2000, 24.

9. R. Johnston, "New York City Alters Summer Program," *Education Week*, 19 April, 2000, 5.

10. C. Gewerty, "'Blueprint' for San Diego Schools Draws Mixed Reactions," *Education Week*, 26 April, 2000, 5.

11. S. Rubin, *Public Schools Should Learn To Ski: A Systems Approach to Education* (Milwaukee, WI: American Society for Quality Control, Quality Press, 1994), 1–169.

12. A. MacMillan and D. Curran, "Despite Risks, Schools Play New Role: All-Day Child Care," *The Hour*, 2 January, 1994, 1.

13. "The 6 to 6 Program: Expanded School Plan Works for Kids and Parents," *San Diego Union-Tribune*, 30 May, 2000, B8.

14. R. Huard, "San Diego's 6 to 6 Program To Add 107 Schools," *San Diego Union-Tribune*, 14 June, 2000, B5.

15. D. Riley, "Building Extended Learning Opportunities," *Teaching K-8*, March 1998, 8.

16. L. Jacobson, "After-School Programs Not All They Could Be," *Education Week*, 2 June, 1999, 12.

17. Presentation by Al Shanker, former president of the American Federation of Teachers.

18. P. Wolfe et al., *The Science of Nutrition* (Alexandria, VA: Association for Supervision and Curriculum Development, March 2000), 54–59.

19. Wolfe et al., *The Science of Nutrition*.

20. N. Hurwitz and S. Hurwitz, "The Case for School-Based Health Centers," *American School Board Journal*, August 2000, 24–27.

21. Hurwitz and Hurwitz, "The Case."

22. Hurwitz and Hurwitz, "The Case."

23. R. Murnane and F. Levy, "Clinton Is Half-Right on Schools," *The New York Times*, 17 February, 1997, Editorial page.

24. R. Johnston, "Rochester Plan Adds Flexibility to High School," *Education Week*, 2 August, 2000, 1, 18–19.

25. C. Janey, "Pathways to High School Success," *Education Week*, 2 August, 2000, 45, 68.

26. J. Bowsher, "Hobby Shops or Enhanced Learning," *Westport News*, 13 August, 1993, A19.

27. A. Ellis and J. Fouts, *Research on School Restructuring* (Princeton, NJ: Eye On Education, 1994), 193–204.

28. Ellis and Fouts, *Research*, 196.

29. Ellis and Fouts, *Research*, 201–202.

30. *Designs for a New Generation of American Schools* (Arlington, VA: New American Schools Development Corporation, October 1991), 1–59.

31. G. Bush, *America 2000: An Education Strategy* (Washington, DC: U.S. Department of Education, 1991), 2.

32. T. Glennan, *New American Schools After Six Years* (Santa Monica, CA: RAND Education, 1998), 2–7.

33. *Designs for a New Generation of American Schools.*

34. *Stellar Schools for a New Century* (Arlington, VA: New American Schools Development, 2000).

35. Glennan, *New American Schools*, 1–85.

36. *An Educators' Guide to Schoolwide Reform* (Arlington, VA: Education Research Services, 1999), 1.

37. *Blueprints for School Success* (Arlington, VA: Education Research Services, 1998), 1–107.

38. *An Educators' Guide*, 1–141.

39. *An Educators' Guide*, 1–141.

40. "Teaching and Learning: Boston To Revamp Staff Development," *Education Week*, 8 March, 2000, 17.

41. D. Sparks and S. Hirsh, "Strengthening Professional Development: A National Strategy," *Education Week*, 24 May, 2000, 42, 45.

42. N. Oelklaus, "In Touch with Teachers," *American School Board Journal*, March 1999, 37–38.

43. J. Bowsher, "Teachers: Shortage or Surplus?" *Westport News*, March 1992, 17.

44. C. Feistritzer, *The Making of a Teacher: A Report on Teacher Preparation in the United States* (Washington, DC: Center For Education Information, 1999), 3.

45. Feistritzer, *The Making of a Teacher*, 5.

46. C. Reed, "Now It's Time To Focus On CSU's Future," *San Diego Union-Tribune*, 9 June, 1999, Editorial page.

47. Feistritzer, *The Making of a Teacher*, 5.

48. Feistritzer, *The Making of a Teacher*, 3.

49. J. Merrow, "The Teacher Shortage: Wrong Diagnosis, Phony Cures," *Education Week*, 6 October, 1999, 48, 64.

50. Merrow, "The Teacher Shortage."

51. L. Finkelstein, "Building a Powerful Team of Teachers for the Nation's Big City Schools," *Education Week*, 8 December, 1999, 29, 31.

52. B. Keller, "States Move To Improve Teacher Pool," *Education Week*, 14 June, 2000, 1, 20.

53. A. Bradley, "Denver Teachers To Pilot Pay-for-Performance Plan," *Education Week*, 22 September, 1999, 5.

54. Interview with John Golle, Education Alternatives.

55. T. Henry, "States To Tie Teacher Pay to Results," *USA Today*, 30 September, 1999, 1.

56. J. Archer, "NEA Delegates Take Hard Line Against Pay for Performance," *Education Week*, 12 July, 2000, 21.

57. A. Trotter, "Sylvan's Founder Rolling Out New Tutoring Company," *Education Week*, 28 October, 1998, 15.

58. "State Initiatives: Ohio," *Help One Student To Succeed (HOSTS) Newsletter*, Fall 1999, 2.

59. C. Lartigue, "Politicizing Class Size," *Education Week*, 19 September, 1999, Editorial page.

60. Lartigue, "Politicizing Class Size."

61. D. Viadero, "Federal Study Will Put Price Tag on Class-Size Reduction," *Education Week*, 28 April, 1999, Reporter's Notebook page.

62. Calculations and estimates by author.

63. Calculations and conclusion by author.

64. B. Keller, "Smaller Class Sizes Get Mixed Review," *Education Week*, 12 July, 2000, 25.

65. Calculation and conclusion by author.

66. R. Ross, "How Class-Size Reduction Harms Kids in Poor Neighborhoods," *Education Week*, 26 May, 1999, 30, 32.

67. *Evaluation Findings, 1998–99* (Santa Monica, CA: RAND Corporation, 1999).

68. C. Ochilles, *Students Achieve More in Smaller Classes* (Alexandria, VA: Association for Supervision and Curriculum Development, February 1996), 76, 78.

69. Lartique, "Politicizing Class Size."

70. R. McAdams, *Lessons from Abroad: How Other Countries Educate Their Children* (Lancaster, PA: Technomic Publishing, 1993), 1–326.

71. S. Black, "Less Is More—Don't Expect Miracles Just by Reducing Class Size," *American School Board Journal*, February 1999, 38–41.

72. R. Kahlenberg, *The New Economic School Desegregation* (Alexandria, VA: Association for Supervision and Curriculum Development, April 2000), 16–19.

73. R. Johnston, "North Carolina District To Integrate by Income," *Education Week*, 26 April, 2000, 1, 19.

74. C. Gewertz, "A Hard Lesson For Kansas City's Troubled Schools," *Education Week*, 26 April, 2000, 1, 20–21.

75. Gewertz, "A Hard Lesson," 21.

76. K. Reid, "Governance Report Calls for Overhaul," *Education Week*, 20 September, 2000, 1, 20.

77. Comment to author at European Meeting, 1996.

# CHAPTER 6

# Move the Educators and Students

After years of education reform programs that have failed to achieve break-throughs in learning, numerous political leaders and some education experts are now advocating the concept of moving teachers and students, instead of fixing fundamental student learning problems. Much of the business community has rallied around this easy solution of choice because it brings competition to a government agency that is essentially a monopoly.

It's not surprising that the business community would support reorganization because that is exactly what happens in most corporations when serious problems arise with operating expenses, revenues, market share, and earnings. If a company is centralized, it usually decentralizes to push decision making to a lower level. If the troubled corporation is decentralized, it centralizes so that the focus shifts to decision making by the senior management team. Companies often go through a series of these reorganizations until they realize that they have fundamental problems within their basic processes.

## CHOICE

The simple definition for choice is allowing parents to decide what school their children will attend. The emotional discussion often starts with the statement that wealthy families have always had the choice to send their children to private schools. About 10 years ago, the choice movement decided that all parents should have this opportunity

*To completely understand the issue of choice, the following subjects need to be reviewed:*

- Vouchers
- Magnet schools

- Charter schools
- Privatization of schools
- Home schooling

## VOUCHERS

Vouchers are grants of money by a government (federal, state, or local) agency from taxpayer funds to parents who are able to select another school and pay at least part of the tuition. They certainly lead in the number of articles written about a school reform solution. It's an easy program to sell, but a very difficult one to implement. First, teacher unions have always fought vouchers in the legislature and courts. Their lawsuits are usually supported by political leaders who want to appeal to voters by saying that they will not reduce public school funding. Lawsuits are pending in almost every state and city that has adopted vouchers.[1]

A greater obstacle to vouchers is the fact that most vouchers do not pay the entire private school tuition cost. Some vouchers consist of state funds that go to the local school. This amount is usually a few thousand dollars, which is less than half the tuition charged by private schools. Sometimes, vouchers consist of the funds provided by the local school district, which is also several thousand dollars short of a private school tuition. Most middle-income families simply cannot afford to pay taxes and thousands of additional dollars for the right to send their children to private schools. The one school system that vouchers can usually fund is an education at a church school because of lower tuition at these institutions. Such funding raises the issue of public taxes supporting church schools.

In addition, parents incur transportation costs to a school that's not located in their neighborhood. Vouchers are essentially the busing program for the 1990s and this century. They undermine the concept of neighborhood schools. In Cleveland, some students had to go to school by taxi at a daily cost of $15 per child. Taxi fares in Cleveland reached almost $2 million before the state legislature appropriated $2.9 million in additional state aid for transportation costs associated with the city's small voucher program.[2] Children going to school by taxi creates negative headlines in local newspapers and sometimes even in the national press. When children are driven to religious schools, the stories become even more sensational.

To avoid reimbursing all students who attend parochial and private schools, most voucher laws are written so that only children of poor families are eligible for vouchers. Such laws breed the same type of cheating that takes place in financial aid programs at institutions of higher learning. Too many families create the appearance of being poor. Sooner or later, the press finds families with incomes of $50,000 to $90,000 receiving a voucher. It takes a great deal of effort and numerous forms to ensure that only poor families receive vouchers. To solve this problem, many voucher opponents maintain that eventually all students in religious schools will receive a voucher, which means that the cost of church schools will be paid by taxpayer funds. This situation will almost certainly lead to more lawsuits.

In Cleveland, about 25 percent of the new vouchers each year go to students who are already attending private schools, and a law allows that proportion to rise to 50 percent.[3] Milwaukee students in grades 1 through 3 may obtain vouchers if they're already enrolled in private schools.[4] Vouchers will not achieve breakthroughs in student learning for students who are already attending private or parochial schools.[5] Critics will claim that vouchers merely allowed private and parochial schools to increase the tax burden on Americans.

The main problem with vouchers, however, is the lack of empty seats. If vouchers had started in the 1980s when there were thousands of empty classroom seats and empty schools being closed, the program would have been easier to implement. Today, almost every closed school has been reopened as a preschool building. Therefore, almost every school building is now running at near capacity. Choice is usually a myth. Political leaders act as if parents can select any school, but this is not true. If a school has 50 empty seats and those seats are filled with voucher students, what happens next year when 50 students show up from new families in the neighborhood? The choice is simple: The local school district either sends the 50 voucher students back to their neighborhood schools or denies admittance to its own neighborhood children.

Another alternative is to create more schools for voucher students. The typical cost to buy land and finance new schools is as follows:[6]

| | |
|---|---|
| *High School* | $50 million |
| *Middle School* | $25 million |
| *Elementary School* | $15 million |

Political leaders and voting taxpayers will never support extra school buildings for a voucher program. Members of Catholic parishes will not conduct multi-million-dollar fund-raising drives to build an alternative school system for voucher students. The vast majority of parochial schools are 50 to 80 years old, which is one reason more parochial schools close each year. Few new church schools have opened because of the high cost of construction. Remember that 80 percent of the private schools in the United States are run by the Catholic church.[7] Classroom seats in this system have declined each year. At one time, the number of American children in private or church schools was as high as 15 percent, but now it's less than 12 percent.[8]

The National Catholic Education Association helped set standards for curriculum and courses in their schools. Catholic schools were also innovators in the use of learning systems, which helped nuns become above-average teachers with large class sizes. Most Catholic schools had a college preparatory curriculum, with a few vocational high schools in large cities. Hundreds of new Catholic schools were built in the 1920s and 1950s. In these new buildings, a typical class size ranged from 35 to 50 students.[9] For example, the New York archdiocese built approximately 200 schools in the 1950s, but the class size soared to 50 or more because of the "baby boom" generation. Then tens of thousands of nuns retired or left the order, creating a shortage of teachers. As a result, faculties changed from 90 percent nuns to more than 95 percent lay personnel.[10] Enrollment dropped from more than 5 million to less than 2.5 million students. Many Catholic schools closed because of a lack of nuns, rising costs, and a shortage of students. The remaining church schools now operate at a funding rate that is 25 to 50 percent lower than the public schools. Most of the schools have only one or two nuns on the faculty.[11] Catholic schools continue to prove that poor children can be successful learners and that the cost can easily be within existing public school budgets.

In the meantime, Christian schools have been established for more than 500,000 students as a reaction to the racial integration of the 1950s and these parents' perception of a moral decline in the United States.[12] Jews, Muslims, and other religious groups have also established church schools.

Most private (nonchurch) schools begin operations after a wealthy family donates an estate and/or building. Additional buildings are funded by donations from other wealthy families who have children attending private schools. The United States cannot double or triple the number of private schools for voucher students because there simply are not enough wealthy families to support such growth. Private schools are in such demand that parents are spending thousands of dollars on tutoring sessions to gain admittance and then incurring annual tuition fees from $10,000 to $15,000.[13] Private schools make it clear that they accept only the best students who work hard. If students do not succeed, they are quickly asked to leave.

Vouchers claim to give parents a choice. In the real world, however, vouchers merely allow private and parochial schools to select the best students out of the public school system. Parochial schools carefully control their admissions and quickly expel poor-performing students. These schools are not going to be willing to serve as the last resort for students who are several grades behind in academic performance. Therefore, public schools must be fixed. Vouchers are not a major solution to student learning problems. In 1999, Florida provided an interesting case study after the state passed a voucher program. Two schools in Pensacola were rated failures, so students there became eligible for $4,000 vouchers. One of these Pensacola schools was called Advanced Learning Academy, proving that names can be misleading. Of the 860 students in these two schools, only 92 asked for vouchers. Because fewer than 60 seats were available in private and church schools, a lottery system was implemented where 5 students were accepted at one private school and 53 students were enrolled at four church schools. Roughly 80 students transferred to other public schools, leaving 722, or almost 85 percent, still attending the same two Pensacola schools.[14]

Recognizing that vouchers were not a solution, Florida agreed to no staff cuts even with 15 percent fewer students. This decision permitted the Pensacola schools to have 20 students on average in each classroom. Florida is now spending about $500,000 more in these two schools to implement a series of changes, including a shift from a 180-day year to a 210-day school calendar. Students now wear uniforms, and teachers focus more on basic academic subjects and align their lessons with state standards. In addition, the schools have recruited 50 volunteer tutors.[15] All of these efforts reemphasize the point that schools need to be fixed rather than offering vouchers because only a few seats are available in other schools. In the meantime, the Florida voucher program was declared unconstitutional. In October 2000, the Court of Appeals reversed the unconstitutional decision. In the summer of 2000, Florida announced that they no longer had any failed schools, so the entire voucher program was no longer required. Florida declared victory by stating that the competition of vouchers had forced all schools to improve.[16] Political and community leaders in Florida have given school reform an "extra effort" to try to raise student learning grades.

Another problem with vouchers is parents' inability to select a better school. Very few parents can ask informed questions about integrated curriculum, instructional design methods, assessment systems, and learning systems. Consequently, they select a school that's near where they work, thus solving the transportation problem. Often, they decide on a school with the longest hours and most days because they need free child care service. Sometimes, they select the schools where their children's friends are going. Rarely do they select a school based on its teachers, administrators, or the quality of its curriculum. Parents are able to distinguish between a very low- and a very high-performing school system based on rankings that now exist in some cities and states.

For years, Chicago was a leader in poor performance when compared to other public school systems. Because teachers are able to evaluate the quality of a school, almost half of the teachers sent their children to private or parochial schools. In those years, only 19 of 66 public high schools graduated more than 50 percent of their students.[17] On the other hand, Chicago had one of the largest Catholic school systems in the country where almost every student graduated and most went on to college. There simply is no evidence that the Chicago public school system was influenced at all by the city's successful Catholic school system. In this case, competition did not fix the public schools.[18]

There's no evidence either that Cleveland and Milwaukee have achieved major breakthroughs in learning through the use of vouchers. Indiana University evaluated the Cleveland system and concluded: "Students using vouchers to attend established private or church schools are slightly outperforming their public school counterparts in language skills and science, and doing about the same in reading, math, and social studies."[19]

The same study also concluded that students attending private schools that sprang up specifically to serve voucher students are now performing worse in all subjects. This finding is not surprising because schools run by new teachers and new administrators tend to be ineffective. Inexperienced educators rarely outperform their experienced counterparts. Naturally, many voucher supporters deny the validity of these studies, but they offer little in the way of research or assessments that show that vouchers are achieving breakthroughs in learning. It's difficult to prove that vouchers are a "silver bullet" when students attend so many different schools with different teachers using different teaching methods and a wide variety of course materials.

After 10 years of vouchers, there appears to be no great student exodus from the public schools. Private and church schools accounted for 11.3 percent of the student population in 1990, and that number has declined slightly by the end of the decade because of the closing of parochial schools.[20] Thus, the great fear that vouchers would destroy the public school system failed to materialize.

Vouchers are hardly a closed issue, though. Some business executives and numerous political leaders are still selling the concept. Business executives are currently raising millions of dollars for 40,000 poor students, and 1.2 million parents across the nation showed an interest in vouchers because they're convinced that public schools are in trouble.[21]

Many education reform movement leaders have given up, so they've joined the fight for vouchers because they believe educators will not fix the public schools. The most famous statements may have come from Arthur Levine, president of Columbia University's Teachers College and lifelong advocate of public education. In the May 10, 1999 edition of *Business Week*, he stated that the situation is so dire that a rescue operation is needed to reclaim the lives of America's most disadvantaged children. He proposed a limited voucher program for the poor, urban children attending the bottom 10% of public schools. Parents would be reimbursed an amount equal to the average cost per student (about $7,000 nationally) so their children could attend a wide range of nonsectarian private schools or a wide range of suburban public schools.[22]

The Children's Scholarship Fund, another voucher program, is the brainchild of Ted Forstmann, the former chairman of Gulfstream Aerospace, and John Walton, a director of Wal-Mart stores.[23] These businessmen have raised almost $175 million for vouchers in 38 cities. The fund's board of directors includes Barbara Bush, Colin Powell, Martin Luther King III, Henry Cisneros, Joe Califano, Pat Riley, Roger Staubach, Senator Daniel Moynihan, and former Senator Sam Nunn. Most of these people were active in the education reform movement, but they saw so little progress that they decided to support vouchers.[24]

A Silicon Valley venture capitalist, Tim Draper, spent millions of dollars in 2000 to place a voucher initiative on the ballot in California. The California Teachers Association, with the governor as their spokesperson, spent millions of dollars to defeat the voucher plan. The plan was intended to give parents $4,000 to send their children to the public or private school of their choice. In most cases, however, $4,000 would provide only for education at a church school rather than an exclusive private school. Mr. Draper said there would be no increase in taxes, but he never said where the empty seats would be located. The governor and the union said this plan would waste millions of dollars sending students to schools that had no accountability to the taxpayers, no certification for teachers, and no standards for students. This plan went down to a major defeat and the Michigan voucher proposal was also defeated in the last election.

## MAGNET SCHOOLS

Magnet schools create choice within the public school district without the need for vouchers. Magnet schools are public schools that have been designed with a special academic or vocational emphasis. Some magnet schools major in a field such as communications, science, technology, foreign languages, fine arts, food service, health service, or business. It's too early to tell if magnet schools prepare students adequately for college, but their school-to-work programs certainly help prepare students to be good workers within various professions.

Typically, better students in an urban school district attend magnet schools, whereas the general education schools are populated with students who are far behind in grade level. Because of magnet schools, some city high schools have only 5 to 10 percent of their students at grade level. Thus, good students are being culled from general schools and sent to magnet schools. While the magnet school students may learn more, overall, city school systems do not seem to be achieving major improvements in mastery tests, achievement tests, exit tests, or Scholastic Aptitude Tests (SATs) based on the implementation of magnet schools. If an improvement is occuring, it is a small factor.

Career academies are one form of magnet schools. The concept of a career academy was developed 30 years ago, and there are more than 1,500 academies in high schools across the nation. The Manpower Demonstration Research Corporation (MDRC), a nonprofit social policy–research organization based in New York City, started an in-depth study in 1993.[25] Their conclusion is that career academies do not necessarily raise students' test scores for learning, but they do help at-risk students to stay in school. The study stated that this result was not unexpected because teachers in career academies used similar instructional methods to those of their counterparts in traditional schools. Once again, if the magnet schools do not implement systemic change inside the classroom, no breakthroughs in student learning will take place.

## CHARTER SCHOOLS

With vouchers off to such a slow start, the education reform community came up with a more effective idea—charter schools. A charter frees schools from numerous state and district regulations. In return, charter schools are held accountable for improving student performance and for achieving other goals stated in the charter. Charter schools are funded by taxpayer dollars just as public schools are. In some situations, a school district allows a building to be used by a charter school.

More than 2,000 charter schools are now operating in 36 states and the District of Columbia.[26] This number is an increase from 178 in 1996.[27] Their enrollment approaches 500,000 students, which is almost 1 percent of the total K–12 enrollment.[28] Charter schools have a median enrollment of 132 students compared to 486 students in public schools.[29] According to the U.S. Department of Education's *Third Year Report: The State of Charter Schools*, which was issued in 1999, students in charter schools have similar demographic characteristics to students in public schools; however, charter schools in some states serve significantly higher percentages of minority or economically disadvantaged students.

With millions of dollars available from state departments of education and school districts, people are bound to want to start a charter school. After all, many people believe that anyone who has knowledge in a subject can be a teacher with no training. These same people believe that business executives, retired military officers, and various well-meaning people can be school administrators with little or no training. Why not try to create a school within a few weeks or months if you will be paid for such a task? Several charter schools are only child care centers where a little learning takes place similar to some low-performing public schools. It takes knowledge, experience, and talent to create a new institute of learning, which is what a charter school must be. As with any other new enterprise, we must expect great failures and great successes from charter schools. The current primary measurement for charter schools is quantity (how many schools), with quality (student learning) being a distant second measurement. Quality should be equal to quantity when charter schools are evaluated.

### Four Types of Charter Schools

Let's examine four different types of charter schools. *The first type is run by proven educators who select outstanding students, hire above-average teachers, and appoint administrators who have a successful track record.* This process is often termed "creaming." Needless to say, this charter school type should always succeed. An example of this type of school is the Preuss School at the University of California at San Diego (UCSD). A UC regent, Peter Preuss, gave $5 million to build a new school building on the UCSD campus. The owner of the San Diego Padres and the publisher of *The San Diego Union-Tribune* each donated $1 million as well.[30] The goal of this venture was to raise $13.1 million for the school building, which was completed in 2000. Eventually, the objective is to educate 700 successful students, who will be the first members of their low-income families to receive a college degree. The school will be fully operational by the year 2003, serving the sixth to twelfth grades. The school will have a single, college-preparatory curriculum designed to help students achieve admission to the University of California or comparable institutions of higher education. The San Diego Board of Education has granted the charter for this school.

It would be wonderful if more universities within major cities would develop a similar school for top-performing inner-city school students. On the other hand, this type of charter school will not solve most students' learning problems within inner-city schools.

*Another group of charter schools are essentially "education-as-usual" institutions without the restriction of state department of education or school district regulations.* In fact, the main goal of many charter schools is to be independent of their school district, which is not a valid objective if no plans are in place to improve student learning. These schools are built on good intentions rather than on new, innovative learning and teaching methods. Simply put, they will not achieve breakthroughs in learning; however, with a new staff and with a better selection of students, these charter schools may produce some improvement in student learning. According to the Small Business Administration, however, 53 percent of small businesses fail within the first year, and almost 80 percent fail within 10 years.[31] Therefore, some failures in charter schools must be expected.

*The third group of charter schools have developed new "homegrown" management systems, learning systems, and assessment systems.* Some of these schools will be failures, whereas others will be real success stories. The challenge here is to close down the failures quickly and replicate the successful schools. The state departments of education should carefully review the methods of instruction used in successful charter schools to determine "best practices." There should be a formal program to transfer "best practices" to traditional public schools. Fixing one school at a time will take 100 years unless boards of education and superintendents copy the successful schools. The proponents of this type of charter school program take pride in the number of different schools that are created. With high student mobility, though, the last thing this country needs is 100,000 different schools with various curricula and lessons creating knowledge-transfer barriers for students. Individual charter schools also don't have economies of scale, which drives up the costs.

*The fourth charter school group consists of successful for-profit or not-for-profit school chains.* The Edison Schools, started in 1991 by Christopher Whittle, are the most successful example to date. Benno C. Schmidt, Jr., former president of Yale University, is now Edison's chairman. The Edison Schools are discussed next under the section on Privatization of Schools.

In summary, it is important for states to hold charter schools to high standards. Charter schools should be closed if most students are not performing at grade level. Fifty-nine charter schools have been closed so far, and more need to be closed.[32]

In August 1999, *The American School Board Journal* published an article entitled "A Mixed Report Card for Charter Schools." The article stated the following facts:[33]

- Recent test results in Minnesota, Michigan, and Chicago show that charter school students generally have not performed as well on this school year's standardized tests as have students in other public schools.
- In Minnesota, which pioneered charters in 1991, test scores for charter school students were widely variant, with a few outperforming the public schools and others appearing to do miserably.

Another study by the UCLA Graduate School of Education found that California charter schools lack the methods to gauge achievement.[34] They have not been able to tell a great story on student learning. Charter school educators explain that they are not surprised by these results because they are serving so many "at-risk" students. Other charter school teachers do not want to be measured by standardized tests. How quickly they forgot why charter schools were created: To improve student learning. There should be no excuses; charter schools need to achieve student learning breakthroughs or go out of business. It is important to remember that any type of school (e.g., public, private, church, charter) is capable of damaging children if a curriculum is not in place and aligned with state and district standards and/or instruction methods are not successful.

The state department of education and the local school district should develop a list of penetrating questions for educators who want to establish a new charter school by using the recommended programs in Part III for obtaining breakthroughs in learning and Part IV for institutionalizing change. This screening program will ensure a higher rate of success and minimize the damage done to children who attend charter schools that eventually fail to maintain students at grade level.

Chester E. Finn, Jr., former assistant secretary for education at the U.S. Department of Education, Bruno V. Manno, former assistant secretary of education for policy and planning, and Gregg Vanourek of the Thomas B. Fordham Foundation, have written a new book, *Charter Schools in Action* (Princeton University Press). They recommend an accountability system for charter schools which is akin to the Generally Accepted Accounting Principles (GAAP) with which private-sector firms (and many nonprofit organizations) report their fiscal activities and results using standardized formats and independent audits. They recommend a Generally Accepted Accountability Principles for Education (GAAPE) which verifies acceptable performance by charter schools. The school districts and state departments of education should review their methodology.

Another interesting challenge appears to be developing for charter schools: Many church schools want to close their doors as a church school and reopen them as a charter school. After all, some states are providing vouchers to parents who select church schools, meaning that taxpayer funds are going to church schools through vouchers. So why not fund a church school as a charter where most students are at grade level? Catholic schools in Chicago and New York City and private schools in Wisconsin are moving in this direction.[35] Forty-nine full-time Islamic schools certainly could use millions of dollars in taxpayer funds,[36] and African American church schools are asking the same questions.[37] If all church and private schools become charter schools, taxes will increase across our nation by approximately $25 billion.[38]

Charter schools have 37 percent of their students eligible for free or reduced-price school meals. Seven of ten charter schools have a student racial/ethnic composition that is similar to surrounding districts. About 16 percent of charter schools serve a higher percentage of students of color than their surrounding districts. The estimated percentage of limited English proficient (LEP) students in charter schools is 10.1 percent compared to 10.7 percent in the states that authorize charter schools. The reported percentage of students with disabilities at charter schools is 8 percent compared to 11 percent nationally.[39] Overall, it is a noble experiment.

The public school system continues to control 92 cents of every dollar spent on elementary and secondary education, but charter schools are now available to create change.[40] Unfortunately, these schools have produced very few new, exciting approaches to teaching and learning despite their smaller classes and freedom from many bureaucratic structures and rules. Charter schools need to achieve breakthroughs in student learning to survive.

Nevertheless, charter schools appear to have more potential than vouchers. Society has been sold on the need to take operating funds away from failing schools. Taxpayers want educators to be penalized for poor performance just like other Americans are when they cannot meet the goals and objectives of their organizations. Every state that plans to take over poor-performing schools will need to implement successful charter schools. Perhaps vouchers combined with charter schools will provide the competition that will ultimately contribute to rebuilding the public schools into a student-centered organization with effective learning processes.

## Will a Market-Based Education System Be Successful?

In the summer of 2000, Florida's governor and his cabinet made Volusia County schools the first public charter school district in the state and the largest in the country. This district has 66 schools and 60,500 students.[41] The superintendent claims that the purpose of the charter is to improve instruction and student learning. These charters include benchmarks for increasing students' scores on state tests, raising the district's graduation rate, and getting parents and the community more involved in school activities. In addition, no school should receive less than a C rating in 2002 and a B rating in 2003. Florida is preparing to convert two other large school districts into charter districts.

This program is leading to the concept that all schools and school districts should be charters, which means that the work performed by the state department of education will be duplicated in cost by 15,000 school districts or 90,000 schools. Some educators would like to eliminate the state department of education because they believe that their tasks are a waste of money.

Once again, there is no proof yet that charter schools can achieve major breakthroughs in learning. Before the state departments and federal department of education are eliminated, it might be wise to conduct a pilot test of the concept of charter schools to be certain that this is not just another education reform fad.[42] There are lots of stories about misuse of funds, lack of accountability, poor management, and even inadequate instructional methods. Yet, the real success stories need to be studied.

No state has more charters than Arizona, which has about 40,000 students or 5 percent of the public school enrollment in 357 schools. A report on Arizona schools in *Phi Delta Kappan* stated the following:[43]

> Clearly the Arizona experience shows that a free market in public education is viable, but whether market-based education is actually better than conventional models remains a matter of debate.
> *We find four conclusions about free-market education.*
> - *First*, school choice and charter schools depends on political support from the state and federal governments.
> - *Second,* free markets in education require a strong state government to provide information to parents through school report cards or similar mechanisms, to close failing schools, and to ensure options for students from those schools.

- **Third,** a free market in education unlocks enormous energy from entrepreneurial parents and teachers.
- **Fourth,** at least in the near term, charter schools will not replace district schools.

It is hard to see why the fourth conclusion is correct if charter schools develop innovative methods for teaching and learning, which has yet to happen. The second conclusion may be the most important. If a state is going to close low-performing (failing) charter schools, it should close low-performing schools in school districts. This means that states must establish the same standards and accountability systems for all schools in states that receive taxpayer funds.

This discussion leads to people such as Dr. Caroline Minter Hoxby, associate professor of economics at Harvard University, who supports an "ideal voucher system."[44] This means that every public school student in the country would receive a voucher to cover tuition costs at the school his or her parents chose. Some people call this the "GI Bill" for K–12 students.

Once again, some people believe that schools can be fixed through public policy, tax incentives, and quick-fix programs rather than addressing the 10 major problems in the classroom that are listed in Chapter 3. Economists have been interested in school vouchers since the early 1960s, when Milton Friedman from the University of Chicago published *Capitalism and Freedom*, in which he advocated a national system of tax-financed vouchers as a means of freeing the public school system from the control of state government.

This system is the "university" model. It is important to remember that institutions of higher learning in the United States have two major problems: First, explosive growth in costs at universities and colleges far exceed the explosive growth in costs at public schools. The second major problem is quality of instruction. Institutions of higher learning enroll the graduates from the top half of the K–12 school system. Fifty percent of these students drop out before they achieve a degree. If universities and colleges had the same accountability systems applied to their student performance, quality measurement would no doubt show major learning problems similar to public schools. Therefore, no evidence suggests that a competitive system such as the "university" model would contain costs and improve student learning.

Why is the quality level so low at universities and colleges? Professors are hired based on their subject matter knowledge and their research, which includes publications. Teaching ability is a low third priority at most universities. Professors have almost no training on instructional systems design (ISD) methods, lesson plan preparation, assessment systems, graphic design, communication skills, or class management skills. They learn how to teach by hit-and-miss methods over many years. Some never learn to be effective teachers. Students must make a far greater effort to learn after high school years, which happens because eventually only the top quartile is still in school. Al Shanker, the former president of the American Federation of Teachers, once said:

> Voucher supporters are correct in saying that competition would force schools to be sensitive to what customers want, but what most kids (and most adults) want is not to have to work very hard. In the free market of colleges and universities, students are more inclined to seek easy courses than excellent courses. Why wouldn't market forces do the same thing in public elementary and secondary schools?[45]

Remember, the goal in the K–12 years is to have almost all students be successful learners. That is not the goal at institutions of higher learning. Charter schools are a great vehicle for trying new methods of teaching and learning, which could lead to breakthroughs in student learning, but successful charter schools require more than enthusiasm, good intentions, and hard work. Sponsors of charter schools must address the 10 teaching and learning problems that exist in the classroom, which are documented in Chapter 3. Therefore, leaders and teachers of charter schools need to read Parts III and IV of this book to develop a realistic and affordable vision for breakthroughs in student learning. A market-based education system will not create superior learning institutions with just vouchers and charter schools.

## Residential Charter Schools

In the 19th century, the Bureau of Indian Affairs barged onto reservations and forced Indian children to attend residential boarding schools that were located many miles as well as hours away from the reservation. Some political leaders claimed that assimilation was crucial to the Indians' survival. At that time, no one had heard of the term "Native Americans." The children were forced to renounce their heritage and adopt the white man's customs; rebellious students were beaten. Overall, it was an educational failure.

Some people are now suggesting residential charter schools for children who are poor performers at inner-city schools. The theory is that a 24-hour, seven-day learning environment would help students become successful learners. In 1997, the nation's first public boarding school opened in Trenton, New Jersey. Boston University has opened a state-funded residential charter school in Granby, Massachusetts. Another school is being operated at the Capital Children's Museum in Washington, D.C. The Piney Woods Academy, a black preparatory school in rural Mississippi known for its academic rigor and strict discipline, is helping the Detroit school system's Paul Roberson Academy phase in a dormitory component.[46]

With millions of children not at grade level, this approach appears to be a last resort effort. It certainly is one of the costliest solutions. At least the students are volunteers to this program, which was not true of the Indians.

## PRIVATIZATION OF SCHOOLS

Most parents and taxpayers would like to see their neighborhood schools achieve breakthroughs in learning without using busing and vouchers. They ask, "Why not hire an education company that knows how to operate a local school or an entire school district, that has a world-class integrated curriculum, that knows how to implement proven learning systems, and that can achieve a successful learners rate of more than 90 percent?" This approach seems like such a simple answer to a national crisis, and it is the American way: if one organization cannot run a successful operating unit, you hire another company. This approach is called solution through competition.

Over the past years, many people and organizations have pioneered this concept of choice. It is never easy being a pioneer, and some of those who tried did not achieve the success they had hoped for, but they provided the school reform movement with valuable lessons. The Edison Schools learned from failures of earlier companies to take a giant step forward in the education field. Edison hires outstanding educators who work full-time on the development of an integrated K–12 curriculum and the selection of proven classroom learning systems. The goal is simple: To achieve quantum gains in students' academic performance. Edison also uses computers for daily administration and for improvements in student learning. In fact, Edison spends roughly $500 per student per school year on technology.[47] Edison also spends nearly $500 per student on new instructional materials when the company takes over a school.[48] Many Edison schools are charter schools, which is an alternative that didn't exist when Education Alternatives and other school management companies were trying to get started.

Edison also spent four years and millions of dollars developing their systems before opening their first schools in 1995. About 75 percent of its curriculum is standardized across the nation, and the other 25 percent is devoted to local lessons on laws, history, traditions, and cultural differences.[49] Edison's objective is to turn all students into successful learners.

How successful has the Edison Project become? The company now manages more than 100 schools across the country in 21 states serving more than 50,000 students, which is the equivalent of a large school district.[50] Edison is the first large chain of successful schools. Edison's management, learning, assessment, and administrative systems work in a wide variety of communities. The company knows how to take over a school, how to select a principal who is a leader of change and learning, and how to manage a school on a daily basis. More important, student learning is improving in Edison schools. Students have made average annual gains of seven percentage points on criterion-referenced tests and five percentiles on norm-referenced tests.[51] Edison's secret to success is a systems approach to the overall design of managing schools. Students and teachers start school around August 15 and complete the school year with 200 to 205 days on the following June 30, which gives students a six-week summer vacation. The eight hours of learning in a school day can be covered during the time period from 8:00 AM to 6:00 PM.[52] With this extra time, students complete the basic high school courses by the end of the tenth grade and devote their final two years to Advanced Placement courses. On average, 140 children are on the waiting list at every Edison school, which is another indicator of success and community support.[53] Parents and children are committed to the schools, as evidenced by a low (7%) rate of mobility, whereas the rate is much higher at other inner-city schools.

Two dozen other companies are currently managing schools. Most of these companies only manage a few schools, however, so it's too early to tell how successful they will be. One thing is clear, though: Privatization will succeed only if schools are managed by educators who design integrated curricula, select and develop learning systems, and implement assessment systems. The corporate headquarters must also develop superior management and administrative systems that lower school operating costs. Economies of scale must be created in this new school management model. The charter school concept may provide great opportunities for national chains, but it's not easy to succeed in this business.

It is possible that two or three successful national chains will emerge that will have a great impact on the number of successful learners in the United States—an achievement that will ultimately reward these companies' investors. Continuous improvement through competition will be the reason for this success. Learning is measurable. The sales presentation to the Board of Education in communities will be a straightforward message: "We can manage your schools at no greater cost than you have today, and more than 90 percent of the students will be at grade level." Parents will like our education system, and taxpayers will, for the first time, see cost containment within their schools. The public will gladly pay a profit to achieve successful schools. If this happens, not-for-profit public schools will be in a state of shock, and church schools could suffer a major decrease in enrollments. Communities will insist on the for-profit chains taking over their poor-performing not-for-profit schools. Such situations will create a catalyst and the last chance for the traditional public school system to implement systemic change.

Many educators believe that the profit motive is evil, even though our country has emerged as the world's only superpower as a result of capitalism. These naysayers forget that the way most organizations make profit is by caring about and meeting people's needs. Our society wants schools to succeed, but if the not-for-profit schools cannot achieve the simple goal of more than 90 percent successful learners, then taxpayers will turn to the traditional American method of creating success. People who build school buildings make a profit. Publishers have made profits on school textbooks for more than a century. Schools are surrounded and serviced by profit-making organizations. Learning is the only not-for-profit aspect, but that's where the problems lie. Not-for-profit public schools have had two decades to fix learning problems. Their progress has been so pitifully slow that many Americans are now demanding an alternative solution.

Christopher Whittle, founder of the Edison Schools, often uses the following analogy:

> [Seventy-five] years ago, most American towns and cities had locally managed banks, grocery stores, stationery shops, clothiers, restaurants, and hardware stores. Today, those industries are dominated by national chains such as Home Depot, Wal-Mart, Safeway, Staples, and McDonald's. Why? Because of the economies of scale in management systems, human resource programs, financial systems, administrative systems, computer systems, and performance systems.[54]

Mr. Whittle believes that the Edison Company could become the Wal-Mart of public school education. Edison has incurred major losses getting started, but economics of scale may turn them into a financial as well as an educational success. It has taken several hundred million dollars of investment to create the Edison Schools. Other for-profit chains will emerge as long as poor performance continues within not-for-profit schools. The profit motive creates change at a rate not known in the not-for-profit world. For example, 40 years ago Wal-Mart had not opened their first store.[55] Today, they are the largest corporation in the United States, with more than 1 million employees.[56] They are five times larger than Sears, Kmart, or J.C. Penney, which were in business long before Wal-Mart, which proves that the first chain of operating units does not always emerge as the largest and most successful company.[57] The only way the public school system can stop the privatization movement is to fix schools first.

Another sign that the for-profit education industry is gaining greater recognition is that Harvard University has established the David T. Kearns Program on Business, Government and Education, which will be housed at Harvard's John F. Kennedy School of Government.[58] The program will research the advantages and disadvantages of business involvement in education. Columbia University has established a similar program called the National Center for the Study of Privatization in Education at Teachers College. It is hoped that they will also study why not-for-profit public school systems have failed to fix the crisis in student learning at inner-city schools.

*For-profit companies understand that to be successful they must reach three key objectives:*

1. Their students must be better as successful learners.
2. Their schools must be different and appeal to parents and taxpayers.
3. Their costs must be equal to or lower than other successful public schools.

## HOME SCHOOLING

As this chapter has indicated, choice has become a controversial issue within the education reform movement. Great arguments are given for and against choice, centering around vouchers, charter schools, magnet schools, and busing. Another emerging choice is home schooling.

In 1998, Dr. Lawrence M. Rudner, director of the ERIC Clearinghouse on Assessment and Evaluation (an information service sponsored by the National Library of Education at the U.S. Department of Education), conducted a study of 20,760 students in 11,930 families, using questionnaires and achievement tests. Dr. Rudner, who has worked with the U. S. Department of Education, has been involved in quantitative analysis for more than 30 years. A summary of his findings tell this story:[59]

- In every subject and at every grade level, home-schooled students scored significantly higher than their public and private school counterparts.
- Home schooling allows student[s] to progress at [their] own pace, [which is] a major factor in their academic success.
- [An estimated] 24.5 percent of home-schooled students are doing work at one grade level higher than their age.
- Only 5.1 percent of home-schooled students are behind in grade level, so almost 95 percent are at grade level, which should be the goal for our public schools.
- Students who have been home-schooled their entire academic lives have the highest scholastic achievement records.
- No meaningful difference was found among home-schooled students when classified by gender. Only 6 percent of the students are minorities, and they also do well in home schooling.
- Overall cost for home schooling is less than 10 percent [of] the cost of students in public schools. On the other hand, the median amount of money spent on education materials for home-schooled students was $400 per year, which is far more than the amount invested in public school children.

It is interesting to note that parents who plan the lessons for home schoolers do not have a college of education or a major education research center to design their lessons. They buy course materials (books, workbooks, etc.) and courseware (personal computer) programs that are available on the shelf in many stores to anyone, including schools. With these materials and common sense, their lessons enable home schoolers to be at grade level, which proves that educating children in their K–12 years is not an impossible or overly complicated task.

Home schooling appears to be a great success for middle-class and wealthy families when one parent is home most of the time. With a 90 percent cost reduction and with more than 95 percent of students at grade level, there simply is no better story in the field of K–12 education than home schooling.[60] Unfortunately, home schooling does not work in inner-city neighborhoods because parents either work during the day or actively look for work. Numerous estimates between 1 and 2 million have been made regarding the number of home-schooled children in this country. Home schooling will grow in the future as course materials and tutoring systems vastly improve.

Not too many years ago, learning at home meant reading a book and doing homework with tutoring from a parent or older sibling. Today, homes have an outstanding tutor available 24 hours a day, seven days a week. This tutor never loses its patience, becomes upset, turns critical, or scolds a child for poor performance. In fact, the new tutoring system constantly recognizes good performance and provides praise for progress in learning. This tutor, which best exemplifies the qualities of Socratic learning, is the multimedia personal computer. For decades, students have been learning via television programs. In recent years, K–12 students have learned how to use a personal computer. Now technology is bringing together the Internet, video, slides, CD-ROM, and the interactivity of a computer to create multimedia presentations that students enjoy.

The cost of this tutoring system is about $1,200. It can be used for at least six years, so the annual cost is $200. If there are two students in the family, the annual cost drops to $100 per student. In many households, the parents also use the computer, which reduces the annual cost even further.

The tutoring system allows home schoolers to explore subjects without a parent or teacher telling them what to do next. The computer also provides a safe environment for students to take risks. They see and hear immediate, positive reinforcement every time they learn something. Immediate, positive remediation also is available when the student doesn't fully understand the lesson. The computer is truly a breakthrough in student learning and in building self-esteem.

At first, courseware developers thought they had to sell their products to curriculum directors, teacher committees, and school boards. Their selling cost cycle was enormous. Now, these companies sell courseware directly to parents. For example, instead of buying a leather-bound edition of the Encyclopedia Britannica, working parents can purchase a computerized encyclopedia for $35 or less.

Courseware for preschool through high school subjects is produced with the latest authoring systems by teams of master teachers, subject matter experts, instructional designers, graphic experts, assessment specialists, and programmers. Courseware quality and course materials improve annually because parents and students buy only high-quality and motivational courses. With millions of home schoolers and other children using these materials, the price per subject now varies from $20 to $40.[61] In the early school years, one or two courseware systems are sufficient for the entire school year. The courseware market has become a multi-million-dollar industry in which quality increases and costs decrease constantly. Many people have heard of the famous geography course entitled "Where In The World Is Carmen Sandiego?" Its success and effectiveness have convinced teachers to use it in their classrooms even without the approval of their curriculum committees.

Studies have shown that interactive courseware speeds learning by 30 to 50 percent over conventional teaching methods. Lesson retention also improves. Many home schoolers need to study only three or four hours, leaving them more than enough time for extracurricular activities.

How will courseware impact the public schools? It can either be viewed as a sideshow that has no place in a school system, which would be a mistake, or public schools can study why courseware and home schooling have succeeded. Investing in outstanding course materials, learning systems, and tutoring systems have been home schooling's keys to success. This is exactly what most public schools do not do, even though they spend more than $300 billion in taxpayers' money. Instead, they claim they have no money for outstanding course materials, learning systems, and tutoring systems.

It should also be noted that most home-schooling parents are not former teachers. Many of them just have high school diplomas or have studied a year or two in community colleges. This information indicates that certified teachers within inner-city schools could be more successful if their classrooms had outstanding course materials, learning systems, and tutoring systems.

Home schooling will grow in response to the violence in schools and to the constant drone of messages about poor student performance, but it cannot replace our public school systems because most parents are simply not available to provide home schooling. It is hoped, however, that public schools will begin to adopt the successful aspects of home schooling. In some communities, school districts are working with home-schooling families on special classes and extracurricular activities. This partnership helps solve the problem of overcrowded schools and helps reduce the massive building costs associated with new school buildings.

Another interesting model is the combination of a charter school and the "best practices" of home schooling. A charter school can reduce its expenses significantly by designing an independent study program for each student that features high-quality course materials and an interactive tutoring system. Teachers become facilitators who help students work at learning. In some situations, the teachers are parents. In California, 49 of the 255 approved charter schools are home school charters. The state allocation for charter students is more than $4,000 per student, which is a real financial boost for the home-schooling community.[62]

## SUMMARY OF GOOD INTENTIONS FOR TWO DECADES

This section has reviewed nearly 50 different programs supported by the education reform movement in its sincere effort to fix the American public school system. As mentioned previously, some of these programs are important for inner-city schools to move toward a breakthrough in student learning, but most of them do not achieve major improvements in learning as a stand-alone program. Most of these programs have had little or no impact on student learning because the goal for breakthroughs in student performance just started to receive public support during the past few years. A great deal of time, effort, and money have been invested in these programs, but, unfortunately, hard work and good intentions by themselves cannot produce breakthroughs in student learning. It is clear that there are no shortcuts to improving student learning. Choice has been a real motivator for creating the demand to fix student learning problems, but choice alone does not fix the problems. Systemic change is the only way to achieve significant improvements. Only recently with tutoring, extended-day programs, cooperative learning, new technologies, and charter schools has the education reform movement started to move in the direction of significant breakthroughs in learning. Fixing the American public schools is becoming a more realistic goal.

Some people say that the various reform programs of the past 18 years are like pieces of a jigsaw puzzle being dumped from a box onto each school. The state department of education and the school districts must now invest the time and resources to connect the pieces into an exciting new vision and a new operating paradigm, which is the content of Part III. Let's proceed to read how the American public school system can be the envy of the world for the more than 20 million students who are not at grade level.[63]

## NOTES

1. M. Janofsky, "School Voucher Measures Face Uphill Battles," *New York Times* News Service, *San Diego Union-Tribune*, 31 January, 2000, A1, A11.

2. J. Archer, "Obstacle Course," *Education Week*, 9 June, 1999, 22–27.

3. Archer, "Obstacle Course."

4. J. Archer, "Positive Voucher Audit Still Raises Questions," *Education Week*, 16 February, 2000, 3.

5. L. Clemetson, "A Ticket To Private School," *Newsweek*, 27 March, 2000, 30, 32.

6. A. Ramirez, *Vouchers and Voodoo Economics* (Alexandria, VA: Association for Supervision and Curriculum Development, October 1998), 36, 39; and estimates by the author based on a series of school building projects.

7. J. Wilgoren, "Voucher Program Rules Unconstitutional," *New York Times* (cruise ship edition), 21 December, 1999, 1.

8. J. Archer, "Uncommon Values in Lessons of a Century," *Education Week*, 20 October, 1999, 206–215.

9. Archer, "Uncommon Values."

10. Archer, "Uncommon Values."

11. Archer, "Uncommon Values."

12. Archer, "Uncommon Values."

13. S. Parmet, "Playtime's Now Tutor Time," *San Diego Union-Tribune*, 12 June, 2000, A1, A13.

14. J. Sandham, "Schools Hit by Vouchers Fight Back," *Education Week*, 15 September, 1999, 1, 20.

15. Sandham, "Schools Hit."

16. J. Sandham, "Vouchers Stall As Florida Schools Up Their Scores," *Education Week*, 12 July, 2000, 1, 32–33.

17. J. Bowsher, "Choice Is a Quick-Fix, Feel-Good Program," *Westport News*, 14 May, 1993, Editorial page.

18. Bowsher, "Choice Is a Quick-Fix."

19. M. Walsh, "Vouchers Yield Mixed Results, Report Says," *Education Week*, 2 December, 1998, 18.

20. J. Newman, "Bribing Students Out of Public School," *Education Week*, 27 January, 1999, 53, 76.

21. Editorial Writer, "Choice Goes Mainstream," *Education Week*, 28 September, 1998, Editorial page.

22. Editorial Writer, "What Vouchers Can—and Can't—Solve," *Business Week*, 10 May, 1999, Editorial page.

23. Editorial Writer, "What Vouchers Can."

24. R. Melcher and A. Bernstein, "Itching To Get Out of Public School," *Business Week*, 10 May, 1999, 38, 40.

25. J. Gehring, "Fewer Dropouts from Career Academies," *Education Week*, 9 February, 2000, 6.

26. K. Jackson, "Charter Schools," *American School Board Journal*, March 2000, 48.

27. D. Bowman, "Billionaire Joins Drive for Charters in Washington," *Education Week*, 7 June, 2000, 18.

28. Bowman, "Billionaire Joins."

29. C. Pipho, "Stateline: Choice Options on the Increase," *Phi Delta Kappan*, April 2000, 565, 566.

30. Chancellor's Report, "Youngsters Break Ground for Model School," University of California at San Diego, May 1999, 2.

31. A. Shanker, American Federation of Teachers, "Risky Business," *New York Times*, 18 February, 1996, E7.

32. C. Pipho, "Choice Options on the Increase," *Phi Delta Kappan*, April 2000, 565.

33. "Before The Board: A Mixed Report Card for Charter Schools," *American School Board Journal*, August 1999, 6–7.

34. M. Magee and L. Leopold, "Study Finds Charter Schools Succeed No More Than Others," *San Diego Union-Tribune*, 4 December, 1998, A1, A15.

35. L. Schnaiberg, "Buildings in Hand, Church Leaders Float Charter Ideas," *Education Week*, 10 February, 1999, 1, 11.

36. M. Zehr, "Guardians of the Faith," *Education Week*, 20 January, 1999, 1, 26.

37. Zehr, "Guardians of the Faith."

38. Estimate by author.

39. J. Conaty, *The State of Charter Schools* (Washington, DC: Office of Educational Research and Development, U.S. Department of Education, 1999), 1–3.

40. P. Aupent, "At Least These Kids Have a Choice," *San Diego Union-Tribune*, 23 November, 1998, Editorial page.

41. "Across The Nation: Nation's Largest Charter District OK'd in Florida," *Education Week*, 2 August, 2000, 3.

42. T. Good and J. Braden, "Charter Schools: Another Reform Failure or a Worthwhile Investment?" *Phi Delta Kappan*, June 2000, 745–750.

43. A. Gresham et al., "Desert Bloom: Arizona's Free Market in Education," *Phi Delta Kappan*, June 2000, 751–755.

44. J. Cassidy, "Schools Are Her Business," *The New Yorker*, 18 October, 1999, 144–160.

45. A. Shanker, "Students As Customers," *New York Times*, 8 August, 1993, E7.

46. C. Weatherford, "An Overnight Solution," *Education Week*, 8 March, 2000, 42, 60.

47. M. Walsh, "Edison Schools Joins with IBM in Technology Alliance," *Education Week*, 21 June, 2000, 9.

48. Edison Schools, "Second Annual Report on School Performance," March 1999, 7.

49. Edison Schools, "Second Annual Report."

50. Walsh, "Edison Schools."

51. Walsh, "Edison Schools"; News Release on April 7, 1999.

52. Edison Schools, "Experience A Different Kind of School," 1999, 1–23.

53. Edison Schools, "Second Annual Report"; News Release on April 7, 1999.

54. M. Walsh, "All Eyes on Edison Schools As Company Goes Public," *Education Week*, 24 November, 1999, 17.

55. B. Ortega, *In Sam We Trust* (New York: New York Times Business, 1998), 35.

56. "500 Largest U. S. Corporations," *Fortune*, 17 April, 2000, F1.

57. "500 Largest U. S. Corporations."

58. M. Walsh, "Harvard To Study Rise of For-Profit Education," *Education Week*, 19 April, 2000, 14.
59. L. Rudner, *Home Schooling Works* (Purcellville, VA: Home School Legal Defense Association, 1999), 1–12.
60. L. Rudner, *Home Schooling Works*.
61. Estimate from The Edutainment Catalog, Winter 2000.
62. S. Gembrowski, "Charter Home Schools Begin Appearing Here," *San Diego Union-Tribune*, 12 September, 1999, B1–B2.
63. Estimate by author.

# PART III

# The Search for Breakthroughs in Learning

People are surprised to hear someone claim that the American public school system can be fixed to the level where all students will be successful learners. *To reach this goal, six important steps must be taken:*

1. Establish goals, standards, and accountability systems.
2. Create an exciting new vision.
3. Develop a world-class curriculum.
4. Select, modify, or develop learning systems that are validated to ensure that more than 90 percent of the students learn their lessons.
5. Implement tutoring systems.
6. Implement assessment systems that prevent students from falling behind.

These six action programs are all essential for success. After all, if a lesson is taught, all students should learn that lesson. School districts must either implement all six action programs or continue to live with a high level of failure and ever-increasing costs within their schools.

# CHAPTER 7

# Goals, Standards, and Accountability

The President of the United States set a goal that our country would land a man on the moon by the end of the decade. That goal was accomplished by 1969. At the beginning of the 1990s, the President of the United States established national goals for our public schools to be reached by the year 2000 that have yet to be achieved. Why was the investment in our space program such a success and our investment in school reform such a failure when, in each case, almost unlimited talent and resources were available to achieve the goals?

The space program was an incredible technical challenge because so much had to be researched and invented; however, engineers are systematic performers. They implemented a vision, detailed plans, systems design, systems integration, systems testing, project management, change management, communications, and financial control systems. Although a great deal of discussion, debate, disagreement, and even disappointments were encountered during the decade, the engineers' approach led them forward one step at a time. Today, the United States is the unquestioned leader in space exploration and technology.

## ESTABLISHING NATIONAL GOALS

On the other hand, in school reform, it took almost seven years to establish six national goals. Then came four more years of debate with two additional goals being established. Engineers had achieved their goal of landing a person on the moon in less time than it took educators and political leaders to agree on eight national education goals. Unfortunately, no real progress could be made in fixing our schools until the goals were established because everyone knows that the first step in achieving any objective is to establish goals.

127

Let's review the eight goals and see where the nation is after almost 18 years of school reform efforts.[1]

### Goal One: Ready To Learn When Children Begin School

Some progress has been made on this goal. An estimated 90 percent of children are fully immunized against preventable childhood diseases. The percentage of three- to five-year-olds whose parents read to them is up to 72 percent.[2] More children are in preschool and Head Start programs, but the quality of these programs could be better. Many eligible children continue to be placed on wait lists for local Head Start programs. Too many children who come from non–English-speaking homes receive inadequate training on the English language in their preschool and kindergarten years. Our nation should study Japan and France because they have excellent preschool programs.

### Goal Two: High School Graduation Rate Will Be 90 Percent

The graduation rate has remained at 86 percent for completion of high school by age 24 or through general education development (GED).[3] The drop-out rate is much higher at inner-city schools if the objective is to complete high school in four years. For example, in San Diego County, only two-thirds of the freshmen in the fall of 1994 graduated on time four years later.[4]

### Goal Three: Student Achievement and Citizenship

Under this goal, fourth, eighth, and twelfth graders are measured on core subjects. Only in mathematics has any improvement been made in all three grades. Reading has improved slightly at the fourth- and eighth-grade levels, but it has declined at the twelfth-grade level.[5] Writing scores are even lower than reading. The federal testing system has not been able to collect data in subjects such as science, history, and geography. The objective for goal three by year 2000 was that all students would leave grades 4, 8, and 12 having demonstrated competency over challenging subject matters, including English, mathematics, science, foreign languages, government (civics), economics, arts, history, and geography. Simply put, this goal has shown minimum progress, even though it may well be the most important goal.

### Goal Four: Teacher Education and Professional Development

The number of teachers who teach in their main subject area has declined. The investment in professional development programs has increased, but quality must improve in the future.

Teachers are not getting an opportunity to improve their skills. That is the conclusion of a 1999 study by the Educational Research Service in Arlington, Virginia, which provided the following facts:

Of those teachers who had spent more than eight hours in professional development to learn to integrate local or state performance standards into their teaching, only 20 percent said that the training helped them "a lot."

Less than 40 percent said the same for training in education technology, new teaching methods, student performance assessment, and addressing the need of immigrant students whose primary language is not English.

Less than half of the teachers said professional development helped them "a lot" in understanding their main subject area and maintaining discipline in the classroom.[6]

Like so many areas in our schools, the quantity of professional development has shown increases, and now the focus must be on the quality and effectiveness of the programs.

### Goal Five: First In Math and Science

At grades 8 and 12, the United States is far from being first in world competitions. According to the Third International Math and Science Study (TIMSS), American fourth graders scored above the international average in both math and science. As they progressed through school, however, American students' performance at the 12th-grade level were ranked near the bottom in both subjects. It is hoped that the new learning standards will turn this situation around in future years.[7]

### Goal Six: All Adults Will Be Literate

Millions of adults (20 percent of the population) continue to be functionally illiterate, which means that they read at the fourth-grade level or below.[8] This situation continues despite many literacy programs throughout the nation. Improvement will no doubt depend on breakthroughs in reading instruction during the K–12 school years.

### Goal Seven: Safe, Disciplined, Alcohol/Drug-Free Schools

Performance has actually worsened in some areas during recent years, but school safety is now higher on the education agenda than at any time in the past 15 years. The percentage of 10th graders who say someone offered to sell or give them illegal drugs at school increased from 18 to 33 percent between 1992 and 1997, according to the University of Michigan Survey Research Center. In addition, the percentage of 10th graders using illegal drugs has increased from 24 percent in 1991 to 40 percent in 1997, whereas the percentage who say they used alcohol has held steady at about 65 percent since 1993. The percentage of 10th graders who were threatened or injured at school declined from 40 percent in 1991 to 33 percent in 1997 despite some well-publicized incidents in which children were killed on school grounds.[9] Thefts, rapes, and assaults dropped almost 33 percent since 1992 and the proportion of high schoolers bringing in weapons dropped by 25 percent.

### Goal Eight: Parental Participation

With all of the available funds and programs for increased parental participation, you would think that significant progress has been made in this area, but measurements have not established that fact. Many parents do not participate in their children's education. Schools need to do more to achieve the goal set for parental involvement. The percentage of students in grades 3 through 12 whose parents say they have participated in two or more activities in their children's school has remained at about 62 percent for most of the previous decade.[10]

The National Education Goals Panel publishes an annual "Goals Report," which provides many details on the progress of achieving the national education goals. In summary, progress to date on the eight goals is dismal. Why has so little progress been made with so much money being invested and so much talent being applied to these goals? Primarily, the responsibility for achieving goals is not as clear as it was for NASA in the 1960s. Split responsibility has resulted in no one person or group being held accountable. The education community, in fact, is still debating whether the goals are essential and how to attain them.

Educators have not taken a systems approach to improving public school performance. They have tried to apply patches to an existing system that does not work for 50 percent of the students. Almost no real systems design, pilot testing, systems integration, project management, or change management systems have been implemented in most school districts to improve student learning. Rather, in most school districts, various education fads have been tried, with little or no impact on student performance. This book is one of the first attempts to document an overall vision and plan of action to achieve the eight national goals.

On the positive side, these eight national goals have unified the school improvement effort through the enlisted support of political leaders, business executives, parents, and educators. These groups have helped to secure billions of dollars in incremental funding. It is hoped that all of these stakeholders will recommit themselves to achieving the goals by 2010, which would be 27 years after the alarm bell rang with the *A Nation At Risk* report. One major strength of the national goals is that they are bipartisan, having transcended changes in the White House, Congress, and state houses.

Numerous educators ignore these goals because they believe the goals are meaningless until the country has better students, parents, school facilities, teachers, and administrators. In fact, many educators use the statement that policy makers have never supported the goals effort with the funds needed to produce radical change as their main excuse for unimproved education. This is absolutely not true (see Chapter 2). These educators want a perfect world before they will be held accountable for achieving national goals, but schools will never improve if we wait for such a perfect world and for all educators to accept standards and measurements.

Some people say that the goals were unrealistic, but this is not true. If the strategies and programs outlined in Parts III and IV of this book had been implemented over the past eight years, the goals could have been achieved by the year 2000. Unfortunately, no detailed plan was created to achieve the goals, but, it is hoped that a realistic plan will be formulated during this decade.

## STANDARDS TO ACHIEVE GOALS

If the establishment of national goals were the first step toward creating and maintaining a world-class education system, then the second step would be to establish learning standards; however, the standards movement has had a rough start. Denis Doyle made the following observations in an article entitled "De Facto National Standards" in the July 14, 1999 issue of *Education Week*:

> When then U.S. Secretary of Education Lamar Alexander, a Republican, proposed national standards earlier in this decade, Democrats were derisive. Republicans returned the favor several years later when Secretary of Education Richard W. Riley, a Democrat, endorsed them. Indeed, an unholy coalition of conservative Republicans and liberal, big-city Democrats defeated Secretary Riley's proposal. It fell to the education pundit Chester E. Finn, Jr. to offer a convincing explanation. "Republicans oppose any proposal with the word 'national' in it; Democrats oppose anything with the word 'standards' in it," he wryly observed. "It is clear that de jure national standards—that is to say, federal government standards—are not in the cards. But even if standards won't be federalized in the near future, they are quietly going national as the century draws to a close. They are doing so for two reasons: First, in the realm of education at least, there is more that unites Americans than divides them, congressional posturing not withstanding. Second, high-technology is playing a significant role."[11]*

In 1995, only 13 states had real academic standards. By 2000, 49 states had established such standards (Iowa is the exception). Denis Doyle reacted as follows to these new state standards:

---

*Source:* Reprinted with permission from *Education Week*, Vol. 18, Issue 42, July 14, 1999.

Do the 49 sets of standards differ much? Not surprisingly, the short answer is—not much. Truth be told, there is no Portland, Oregon math vs. Portland, Maine math, anymore than there is Arizona science vs. Pennsylvania science. And while there may be differences in emphasis (the story of the Alamo fails to capture the Virginia imagination as it does Texas), historical narratives are structurally similar.[12]*

In fact, at least 75 percent of the curriculum across our nation is the same, and some educators claim that the number actually approaches 90 percent. Local history, traditions, government, and laws impact the curriculum by only a few percentage points. Denis Doyle goes on to say the following:

How do we know this to be true? You can see for yourself when you visit www.achieve.org on the World Wide Web. Achieve, Inc. is the non-profit creation of a group of business CEOs and the National Governors' Association that is busily posting state standards in English, math, science, and social studies. Each state can be compared with another in a very useful, side-by-side screen presentation. This information can be used by schools of education, textbook publishers, school districts, directors of curriculum, and teachers.[13]*

Each school district and state department of education can be compared to the consensus standards. Common sense tells us that no state wants to be known for its low standards.

Business executives and governors deserve much of the initial credit for establishing standards in these 49 states. The second education summit in 1996 drove the states to establish further standards. The third summit in 1999 addressed how schools will achieve standards and which accountability programs they'll need.

*Several educators have the following five important comments to make about standards, which appear to have some validity:*

1. Standards in some states are not specific to the point where learning objectives can be documented for an integrated curriculum. The language is broad and confusing, not unlike the legal language used by lawyers.
2. Standards must be realistic for all students in the K–12 years to be successful learners. This does not mean that standards should be "dumbed down" to the lowest performing student. On the other hand, standards should not be written for the top 5 percent of successful learners either.
3. Standards need to include three types:
   • Content standards

---

*Source: Reprinted with permission from *Education Week*, Vol. 18, Issue 42, July 14, 1999.

- Performance standards
- Opportunity-to-learn standards

4. Assessments must be aligned to learning standards. Teachers should teach to the learning objectives that enable students to achieve the learning standards.
5. Educators who establish standards must be partnered with educators who develop assessment instruments to ensure that the standards are achievable. For example, in some states, there are too many standards, which should be highlighted by the assessment system.

Unfortunately, many school districts do not have an integrated curriculum to enable students and teachers to achieve these standards. Many textbooks are woefully inadequate for meeting the new standards, and teachers need more training. Too often, students are being tested on subject areas that were never taught in the school year.

Fortunately, though, the top school districts are developing lesson plans to achieve standards established by the state department of education and the local school district. The president of the National Education Association (NEA) stated: "Of course, we see these as transitional problems arising as we move swiftly from an old to a new order. If addressed, they can be corrected. Meanwhile, the progress achieved by public schools during this period of turbulence is cause for optimism. We know that the task of raising standards would be an arduous one—and everyone agrees there is no turning back now."[14]

Just like the national goals, many educators continue to resist standards until they find the elusive better students, parents, schools, teachers, and administrators that they wish for. In every profession, people are held to high standards long before they're working in a perfect environment. Some parents are going to be upset when they find out that their children are not at grade level. Students will also learn that standards create a new and better world of performance for them.

## ACCOUNTABILITY TO ACHIEVE STANDARDS

Standards and testing are undoubtedly the primary reason for the improvement that some states and school districts have achieved in the last few years. If student learning is measured, both teachers and principals become serious about raising test scores. They begin to teach the lessons that are going to be tested. This is not "teaching to the test," as some have suggested. Accountability is the glue that holds together standards, curriculum, lessons, and assessments, which enable students to be successful learners.

The second Education Summit in 1996 was attended by 41 governors, 49 corporate leaders, and 30 education experts. Louis V. Gerstner, Jr., Chief Executive Officer of IBM, said at that summit's opening session, "It's time to stop debating. It's time to stop making excuses. It's time to set standards and achieve them."[15] Now that the standards have been implemented, thousands of students may be denied a high school diploma, thousands more have been asked to repeat a grade, and thousands of schools have been listed as unsatisfactory. People are feeling great pain in this period of transition, but the President of the United States has urged the governors to proceed with implementing strict accountability systems for the standards. Mr. Gerstner represents the business leaders when he later stated at the third summit, "It's going to be tough. Institutionalizing change always is, but we have to bear the pain of transition. There can be no going back on the issue of world-class standards."[16]

Many educators are now writing and speaking out against standards. They question the quality of the accountability instruments being implemented. They want another 10 to 15 years to develop perfect tests, but political leaders, business executives, and taxpayers are fed up with the slow pace of school reform. These groups want accountability systems implemented during the next few years, and they are not interested in a lot of excuses that call for delays. District superintendents and state school officers know that they must have the support of political leaders and business executives in order to receive annual increases in funding. For that reason alone, testing and accountability systems have become a way of life today and will continue to be long into the future.

Accountability systems evolved because almost no standards or assessments were used at the national, state, and local levels until the past few years. Political leaders want to show taxpayers that student learning is taking place as a result of their investment in public schools. Government agencies, commercial companies, and not-for-profit organizations want to know what knowledge and skills their future employees will have. Institutions of higher education are interested in knowing which high school graduates will succeed at their schools. Last but certainly not least, most parents are anxious to know how well their children are doing in school.

For decades, educators had everyone believing that almost every school and every student was above average. This unrealistic picture of student performance was termed the "Lake Wobegon Effect" after a fictional town created in the 1980s by humorist and author Garrison Keillor in which all children were above average.[17] A researcher at the RAND Corporation, Daniel Koretz, found that test scores were exaggerated and the terms "average" and "above average" were often used when students were not even close to being at grade level. Some schools even had 32 valedictorians. That's why so many Americans were shocked to hear that the public school system had the serious problems that were described so vividly in the 1983 *A Nation At Risk* report.

Accountability systems will be even more essential during this critical transition period of school reform. Everyone wants to know which programs really improve student learning. Let's briefly define a few broad categories of account-ability because the terms are confusing to many people.

*Standardized Achievement Tests* tell us what knowledge and/or skills a given student possesses in a particular content (subject) area. Usually, these tests are based on a norm-referenced method, which allows an individual student's relative knowledge and/or skills to be compared to a national or statewide sample of students at the same grade or age level. In a norm-referenced test, 50 percent of the students are always above the average and 50 percent are below the average. One limitation to these standardized tests is that they're often not based on the learning standards set by the state department of education and the local school district. Therefore, it's difficult to evaluate the quality of a school's learning processes, lesson plans, and teaching or effect improvement because its students may never have received instruction in the academic content being tested. Nationally, there are five well-known standardized achievement tests: California Achievement Tests, Comprehensive Tests of Basic Skills, Iowa Tests of Basic Skills, Metropolitan Achievement Tests, and Stanford Achievement Tests.

*Mastery Tests* are based on the standards of a state and/or school district and identify the strengths and weaknesses of student learning. The goal of mastery tests is to achieve high scores by all students in each subject. These tests tell schools and parents if students are learning the lessons established in the standards and curriculum. They are sometimes referred to as criterion-based tests. They encourage administrators and teachers to improve their teaching methods and lesson plans or to implement learning systems that enable more than 90 percent of the students to be successful learners. The Texas (TAAS), Pennsylvania (PSAA), and Connecticut Mastery Tests are examples of criterion-based tests. Mastery tests help a school district evaluate student achievement through the learning systems, lesson plans, teaching methods, and curriculum. The goal, of course, is to improve student learning, not just to score well on a test.

*Formative Evaluation* involves assessing programs that are not yet completed or fully implemented. The primary purpose of formative evaluation is to obtain data to improve the process of instruction and/or learning systems.[18]

*Summative Evaluation* involves assessing fully implemented programs to determine the degree to which they are satisfying their objectives. The primary purpose of summative evaluation is to obtain data to guide decisions about program and learning system effectiveness. This method is sometimes called validation testing.[19]

*Performance Measures* assess students on what they know and are able to do, not just on what information they have learned. Such assessments typically require students to demonstrate learning on open-ended tasks by writing, present-ing, performing, demonstrating, explaining, and exhibiting.[20] Portfolios could also be considered performance measurements.

*Standardized Aptitude Tests* predict how well a student will perform at the next education level. The most famous aptitude tests are the Scholastic Aptitude Test (SAT) and American College Testing (ACT) programs that forecast how well high school students will perform at a college/university level.

Many groups want to prove that all children can achieve the learning standards. Therefore, billions of dollars are being invested by colleges of education, education research centers, testing companies, and school districts to improve test instruments. Unfortunately, there are too many examples today of invalid tests and errors in tests. Some examinations even cover areas of knowledge that have yet to be taught in most schools.

An attempt was made to implement national tests, but the lack of national standards or a national curriculum undermined this movement. Therefore, tests for the fourth, eighth, and twelfth grades are taken on a voluntary basis, but such tests do not enable one state to be ranked among all 50 states (the original intent of national tests). The National Assessment of Educational Progress (NAEP) was supposed to have been a nationwide report card for the public schools. Each state was supposed to provide a 2,500-student representative sample for the NAEP tests; however, great debate has sprung up over the games being played by various states regarding what comprises a representative sample.

What impact has all of this testing had on our school system? In one study published by the *Technology and Learning Journal*,[21] the following facts were stated:

- 76% Taught students to be better test-takers
- 66% Revamped the curriculum
- 20% Changed to better tests
- 21% Involved parents more directly
- 11% Educated the community.

Tests are certainly creating changes in the classrooms and at district offices.

In the meantime, many states and school districts are implementing new assessment programs. One approach that is rapidly expanding across the nation is the exit examination for high school seniors. For decades, New York has had a Regents' Examination, which certifies that a high school graduate has mastered the K–12 lessons and has met the statewide education standards. In recent years, far fewer than 50 percent of high school graduates have passed the Regents' Examination. Now New York has issued a ruling that all high school students must pass this examination in order to receive a high school diploma. More than 20 states, including North Carolina, California, and Texas, are implementing exit examinations.[22] These examinations are criterion-referenced tests to measure mastery of academic content and skills. The tests measure whether students learn and retain the lessons that were taught. If school districts had a curriculum that was aligned with the state learning standards and the state had mastery tests for each grade level, there would be no need to have exit exams at the end of high school.

Several states are also implementing mastery tests. Connecticut has shown that standards and mastery tests result in more learning. Colorado, Kentucky, and other states are following Connecticut's lead. Mastery tests for each grade level help implement statewide education standards. Some schools use these exams to determine if a student should move forward to the next grade level in middle school or high school.[23]

Tests at the end of the fourth, eighth, and twelfth grades are interesting snapshots, but they do not enable schools to make changes to improve their learning processes, lesson plans, and teaching methods when many students achieve poor results on the tests.

***Exit examinations administered at the end of each grade serve two purposes:***

1. They send a clear message to students and parents that learning must take place in order to receive a promotion to the next level of schooling.
2. They force schools to develop a curriculum of lessons that clearly spells out what must be learned at each grade level.

Many states, such as Florida, are grading and ranking school performance. Florida is using the familiar grades of A, B, C, D, and F to rank schools. Schools are ranked based on the results of the Florida Comprehensive Achievement Test, as well as a state writing examination. In addition, schools are measured on student absences, suspensions, and drop-out rates. Most of these schools are currently ranked C and D. Only 1 percent of Florida's middle and high schools failed in 1999, whereas 4 percent of its elementary schools (for a total of 78 involved schools) were deemed failures. According to state officials, schools are working very hard not to be labeled D or F. In July 2000, Florida reported that 20 percent of its elementary schools increased at least two grade levels, and 30 percent increased one grade level. Once again, measurements and structure resulted in improved schools. Most of Florida's schools are still ranked C and D, but they will improve in future years.[24] Cash awards are given for high-performing schools. For decades, report cards have motivated students. Now report cards for schools in Florida are motivating administrators and teachers.

Some states are using three grading categories: exemplary, average, and low-performing.[25] The positive side of grading and ranking schools within a school district or state is the ability to reorganize and reconstitute a failing school with new administrators and teachers. This way, states and school districts won't continue to send money to a school for poor performance year after year.

With standards comes an entirely new grading method: student progress must now be reported based on standards. The most important advantage of this new grading system is the alignment of standards, assessment, and instruction with a learner-centered focus. With this grading system, teachers will know how well each student is doing in relation to a standard. Additional help, such as tutoring, can be given before the student gets behind and gives up in a subject. This type of grading cannot be implemented, however, until realistic standards are in place, instruction and course materials are supporting the standards, and assessment is aligned with standards and instruction. In fact, the amount of testing could decline in future years if schools have a standards-based curriculum and a standards-based grading system. After all, the goal is to have successful students at all grade levels, regardless of the number of tests they've taken to reach that level.

Studies on international tests have been conducted to determine if standardized examinations and mastery tests influence school and student performance. John Bishop, an economist from Cornell University, analyzed the results of the Third International Mathematics and Science Study for seventh and eighth graders from 39 countries.[26] He found that students from the countries that had standardized mandatory examinations did significantly better than those from countries that lack such tests. Another study of students from Canadian provinces showed that provinces with mandated standard curriculum-based examinations did significantly better than the provinces that lacked such tests. Education is like athletics: if the game rules are clear and if there's a scoreboard, students will try harder to be winners. Even professors at the traditionally liberal University of California Santa Cruz campus have discarded one of their founding principles of "no required grades." This announcement ended a 30-year experiment with alternative narrative, essay-like evaluations. Assessment and grades are the common currency in education.[27]

## "BEATING THE SYSTEM" AND CHEATING

In every profession (e.g., medical, law, accounting), there are approved performance standards and codes of ethics because temptations are present in every job. Accountants are sometimes guilty of making false or misleading entries in accounting records. Doctors are sued for malpractice. Lawyers hide evidence or are guilty of actions that are against the law. Even sales personnel record orders that were not approved by customers.

When these unfortunate situations happen, an investigation is usually made by management or a panel of the guilty party's peers. In most organizations, cheating is a cause for job termination. Justice can be very swift. When the investigation is completed, word spreads fast among both management and employees. The usual reaction is that the guilty person should have been fired for stupidity because the gain for cheating is usually quite small compared to the penalty, a philosophy that is otherwise known as: "don't do the crime, if you don't want to do the time." Most important, though, the rules are kept in place, which prevents more employees from cheating.

The importance of this code of conduct makes it surprising that some educators suggest less accountability and testing, especially considering that several cheating scandals have been discovered across the United States. *Newsweek* published an article entitled "When Teachers Are Cheaters," which tells about an elementary school principal who had to resign.[28] In New York City, more than four dozen teachers and administrators from 30 schools stand accused of urging their students to cheat on various standardized city and state tests. Stories of cheating by teachers and administrators now appear frequently in the media.[29]

As the cheating scandals emerge from various schools, some educators want to abolish tests, standards, and accountability, but what an insult this proposition is to the vast majority of administrators and teachers who are honest. When the workforce consists of over 3 million, there are bound to be some dishonest people. The solution is not to eliminate tests and standards. Cheating problems can be quickly fixed by terminating the contracts of those few teachers and principals who cheat.

Again in *Newsweek*, Nicholas Lemann wrote an article entitled "Don't Let Scandal Scuttle Standards."[30] He states that the nationwide movement for educational standards and accountability is arguably the most significant domestic government intervention since the New Deal. Achieving the intended goals of testing means using good tests, administering them under fair, secure conditions, and using them as much as possible to encourage students and teachers to do better and as little as possible simply to punish these people. After all, tests are required to show how many students have learned the lessons and to determine what must be done to tutor or reteach students who failed to learn their lessons.

Because tests are being used to evaluate teachers, to rate principals, to award recognition, to provide bonuses, to determine if a student is promoted to the next class, and so forth, does not give anyone a valid excuse for cheating. This is the type of accountability that students and professionals in all other industries work under each day.

Besides clear-cut cheating situations, many other situations take place in which teachers and principals are trying to "beat the system." Using the same questions each year on a test makes its easy for teachers to signify that this lesson must be learned.[31] This tactic is often referred to as "teaching to the test." Teachers should teach to the learning objectives that are documented to meet state and local learning standards, which is not teaching to the test. If a learning objective is that students will learn how to multiply fractions, it is not teaching to the test to communicate this knowledge. It *is* teaching to the test, however, when a teacher provides the answers to questions that are on the test.

In some articles, people complain that teachers are spending almost all of their time preparing for the various tests. This is not possible because students have to learn the lessons of a school year before a teacher can prepare them for a test. Lawyers study old bar examinations and accountants study former CPA examinations as they prepare for their tests. Students learn by studying previous examinations, but this approach should be permitted only if the questions on the next examination are going to be different.

A good rule for educators to follow regarding ethics is that if you can satisfactorily explain your decisions and actions to your family, peers, friends, and the press, you are no doubt making good decisions. On the other hand, if the explanation is long and difficult, then you should think twice before making that decision. Many people want to blame cheating on the pressure to achieve standards. Others argue that cheating is a character issue and not the result of new assessment tests. It is unacceptable behavior, and no excuses should be tolerated. The American public school system needs high standards of ethical behavior by all educators as well as high standards for student learning.

## BACKLASH ON TESTING

In education, some groups of people always disagree with the new programs designed to enhance student learning. So it's not surprising that a backlash against testing and accountability has resulted. In Texas, where they are achieving significant improvements in student learning, some critics are claiming that the tests are not tough enough. On the other hand, the Texas Federation of Teachers claims that the tests are too difficult and complicated for students. Other Texas educators point to the fact that their students' attainment on the NAEP test is evidence that the state assessments are adequately rigorous.[32]

In other states, educators claim that the mastery tests are too difficult and are not fair to certain student segments. When a state first implements a test, taxpayers, parents, and educators must be prepared to accept results that are below expectations. The citizens of Virginia were shocked when they received their first statewide test results. Maryland, Massachusetts, Delaware, and other states have also had a difficult first year. Some Massachusetts students even refused to take the test during the second year, but their protests have not swayed state officials.

In Texas, several groups sued to set aside the Texas exit examination because only 70 percent of the high school students passed the test. A federal judge later rejected the claims that the examination discriminates against minorities.[33] The judge ruled that the state is using the test to identify and fix education disparities between whites and minorities. The system is not perfect, but the court would not deem it unconstitutional. With more than half of the states now planning to use exit examinations, this ruling was significant.

Evidence suggests that student learning is improving in Virginia and other states where mastery tests have been utilized for several years. Practical superintendents and principals quickly realized that the world of little or no accountability is over. They encourage teachers to align their lessons and classroom tests with state standards. Other administrators joined some teachers by criticizing the new standards and tests, but they soon had to explain to taxpayers, real estate boards, business leaders, and parents why their schools were ranked so low in the state. For example, 93 percent of Virginia schools administering the fifth-grade writing tests in 1999 improved their scores. Eighty-five percent of the schools improved scores on the algebra test. Tests force schools to eliminate time-wasting activities and focus on teaching and learning.[34]

Wisconsin appears to be taking a step backward for accountability by canceling its state graduation test. Its neighbor state, Minnesota, also has a vocal minority who want to stop the move to standards and accountability, but Governor Jesse Ventura is strongly in favor of higher standards. Many educators do not want accountability until there's a proven means to achieve new standards. Once again, business executives, political leaders, and taxpayers who fund schools are not going to wait for such a perfect world. Our children's education is too important to be left unmonitored by people who want to be measured only on their good intentions. Testing and accountability systems will help school systems achieve new statewide education standards.

## SMALL IMPROVEMENT IS NOT VICTORY

When a large, complex organization struggles for years to fix major performance problems, it is a great moment when positive results are achieved. That scenario is happening today in many schools and school districts because of the new focus on standards and accountability. Everyone should be proud that schools are beginning to move along a strategic tract that will improve student learning.

On the other hand, some of the standardized tests, such as the Stanford 9, used the same version of their test repeatedly over the last three years. Teachers remember the questions and are able to teach to the test. Standardized tests are sold to other states, and some educators obtain the questions from outside sources. In addition, students are learning how to be more successful when taking standardized tests.

Some educators recommend that if standardized tests are used, new questions should be asked each year. Previous years' tests should be released to all schools to provide a study guide for all students, which eliminates the potential that some schools have the tests and others do not. After all, as previously mentioned, bar and CPA examinations from other years are available to lawyers and accountants, who learn a great deal by studying these examinations. Test publishers, however, may not wish to release copies of previous tests.

All of these developments will undoubtedly accelerate the requirement for each state to develop its own mastery tests that are closely linked to state standards of learning. States such as New York, Connecticut, Texas, and Massachusetts have developed their own mastery tests and provide previous tests to schools and the public.

Most educators complain that standardized tests are not aligned to their standards of learning. Professor Fenwick W. English of Iowa State University made a clear statement when he said, "Without alignment of lessons to the curriculum and standards, there is nothing fair, open, or equitable."[35] Standardized tests, too often measure lessons that teachers did not teach which gives an unfair advantage to students who come from middle class and wealthy families. For the learning standards and accountability to survive in future years, mastery tests (criterion reference tests) should replace the standardized or norm-referenced tests. Then, the goal is simple: every student should aim for a high score on the mastery tests and the questions should be different each year. Mastery tests should be aligned to the learning standards and the integrated curriculum. When there is poor performance on the mastery tests, investigation will determine if the lesson was ever taught or whether it was not taught in an effective manner, or that the student made no effort to learn the lesson. Corrective action can then be taken. Each school and/or district then needs to establish a goal for what percentage of their students should pass the mastery tests. It is hoped that the goal will be near 90 percent. When the goal is achieved, then and only then should victory for student learning be declared.

The other challenge is to create an accountability system in which everyone is motivated to aim for best performance. For example, students must want to do their very best on the mastery tests because the scores will appear on their transcripts. Teachers and principals should have positive motivation because test scores will be part of their annual evaluations. The district staff, including the director of curriculum, should have a major part of their performance evaluations based on test scores. Finally, the state department of education should feel responsible for the overall performance of all their schools.

No test is a perfect indicator of what a student has learned. Political leaders, business executives, community leaders, school administrators, and parents are not going to tolerate the old system of measuring on good intentions until a perfect assessment system is developed. Top-performing schools, teachers, and students do not fear assessments. Teachers and administrators in low-performing schools will not be overly concerned about accountability if the systemic changes that are outlined in Part III are implemented because breakthroughs in student learning will occur.

On the other hand, if traditional methods of teaching and learning continue to be used at inner-city schools, the future will be grim because a small improvement in student learning will not be an acceptable solution to the crisis that exists today.

Tests are necessary to measure progress and to show teachers which students need help. Tests are an essential part of the reform that is now beginning to work. *Everyone realizes that too many tests are given today because the following five groups of educators want to know what students have learned:*

1. Institutions of higher education
2. National Advanced Placement courses
3. State Departments of Education
4. Local school districts
5. Local schools and teachers.

This price must be paid for two reasons: First, a decentralized school system without an approved integrated curriculum cannot certify what students have learned. Second, the grades, course descriptions, and so forth of a local school often have little or no meaning because of social promotion and grade inflation. Therefore, each group that must know what students have learned creates another test. This situation can only be fixed by implementing the vision in Chapter 11.

When political leaders say they do not expect to be reelected if schools do not improve, and when school officials vow to resign if student learning doesn't improve, then the period of accountability has arrived. On the other hand, educators who support high standards and accountability do not have an unlimited time to demonstrate how low-performing schools can be successful in achieving the new standards. That's why it is urgent to fix (not just improve) student learning in all schools, which is the subject of the next four chapters.

---

## NOTES

1. K. Bushweller, "Goals 2000: Does Our Reach Exceed Our Grasp? Education Vital Signs," *American School Board Journal*, December 1999, A6–A11.
2. Bushweller, "Goals 2000," A6–A7.
3. Bushweller, "Goals 2000," A7.
4. C. Moran, "Dropout Rate Puts State among the Worst," *San Diego Union-Tribune*, 8 September, 1999, A1, A15.
5. Bushweller, "Goals 2000," A7–A8.
6. Bushweller, "Goals 2000," A7–A8.
7. Bushweller, "Goals 2000," A8–A9.
8. Bushweller, "Goals 2000," A10.
9. Bushweller, "Goals 2000," A10–A11.
10. Bushweller, "Goals 2000," A11.
11. D. Doyle, "De Facto National Standards," *Education Week*, 14 July, 1999, 36, 56.
12. Doyle, "De Facto National Standards."

13. Doyle, "De Facto National Standards."

14. B. Chase, "An Academic Boost," *Education Week*, 10 November, 1999, 32.

15. P. Applebome, "Education Summit Calls for Tough Standards To Be Set by States and Local School Districts," *New York Times*, 27 March, 1996, B9.

16. L. Olsen and D. Hoff, "Teaching Tops Agenda at Summit," *Education Week*, 6 October, 1999, 1, 20.

17. D. Koretz, "Arriving in Lake Wobegon: Are Standardized Tests Exaggerating Achievement and Distorting Instruction?" *American Educator*, Summer 1988, 8–15.

18. S. Ross, *How To Evaluate Comprehensive School Reform Models* (Arlington, VA: New American Schools, 2000), 19.

19. S. Ross, *How To Evaluate.*

20. S. Ross, *How To Evaluate.*

21. J. Salpeter and K. Foster, "Playing the Testing Game," *Technology and Learning Journal*, June 2000, 26–34.

22. L. Olson, "States Ponder New Forms of Diploma," *Education Week*, 21 June, 2000, 1, 30–31.

23. D. Hoff and K. Manzo, "States Committed to Standards Reforms Reap NAEP Gains," *Education Week*, 10 March, 1999, 1, 12–13.

24. J. Sandham, "In First for States, Florida Releases Graded 'Report Cards' for Schools," *Education Week*, 14 July, 1999, 18.

25. E. Mendel, "Davis Tells Plan for Rankings of Schools," *San Diego Union-Tribune*, 20 January, 1999, A3.

26. P. Barton, *Too Much Testing of the Wrong Kind; Too Little of the Right Kind in K-12 Education* (Princeton, NJ: Education Testing Service, 1999), 28.

27. M. Mendoza, "After 3 Decades, UC Santa Cruz Professors Vote To Give Out Grades," *San Diego Union-Tribune*, 24 February, 2000, 8.

28. B. Kantrowitz and D. McGinn, "When Teachers Are Cheaters," *Newsweek*, 19 June, 2000, 48–51.

29. A. Gerber, "An Alarming Trend, Teachers Are the Cheaters," *USA Today*, 13 July, 2000, 10D.

30. N. Lemann, "Don't Let Scandal Scuttle Standards," *Newsweek*, 19 June, 2000, 54.

31. J. Betts, "The Secret about Student Testing," *San Diego Union-Tribune*, 19 July, 2000, Editorial page.

32. J. Sanham, "Report Says Texas Tests Aren't Tough Enough," *Education Week*, 18 November, 1998, 13.

33. Associated Press, "Texas School Exit Exam Upheld; Claims of Minority Bias Rejected," *San Diego Union-Tribune*, 8 January, 2000, 16.

34. J. Popham, *Education Quality* (Alexandria, VA: Association for Supervision and Curriculum Development, March 1999), 11.

35. F. English, *Deciding What To Teach and Test : Developing, Aligning and Auditing the Curriculum* (Corwin Press, Thousand Oaks, CA, 1999), xi, xii.

# CHAPTER 8

# Need for a World-Class Curriculum

Now that the United States has eight national education goals and learning standards in 49 of its 50 states, the next question is: How should teachers and principals in more than 90,000 schools across this country teach to the standards? And equally important, how will more than 50 million students learn their lessons, which will enable them to be successful learners and to be successful on all the tests that they must pass? These challenges are far greater than agreeing on eight goals or writing learning standards.

Remember that most teachers, principals, and district superintendents did not play a major role in the national goals debate or in writing learning standards. Neither did most schools pay much attention to the gradual acceptance by the political leaders, business executives, and superintendents that all students should be successful learners. They continued to operate schools on good intentions and hard work during the past 18 years. Only through the various tests that were linked with the accountability focus did local schools and their faculties take the school reform movement as a serious new strategic direction.

The initial reaction to tests was: What do we have to do to pass or improve on the test scores? Most faculty members viewed tests as a tactical program, not as an important new strategic way to measure and manage student learning. In reality, in order to achieve more than 90 percent successful learners, a revolution on how to measure and manage student learning needs to occur within almost every school and school district.

## DEFINITION OF STANDARDS, CURRICULUM, AND LESSONS

The next step in this new management system is to develop a world-class curriculum. Before this concept is discussed, all readers should have a common understanding of relevant terms because it is easy to become confused by various terminology used by educators.

*Learning Standards.* Standards define what students must know and be able to do. They should be written in jargon-free language so that superintendents, directors of curriculum, principals, teachers, parents, and students can all understand them and have a meaningful conversation about what they entail. Standards state what knowledge and skills are required to meet the learning goal. Standards must be specific, not generalized statements of good intentions.

*Curriculum.* Curriculum is the overall "big" picture of what students will learn during their K–12 years. The curriculum is broken into 13 curricula so that learning by grade can be documented. Think of the curriculum as a summary of all the lessons. The curriculum tells all the concerned parties when students will achieve each learning standard.

*Lessons.* Lessons are often called curriculum frameworks. Lessons tell directors of curriculum and teachers what should take place in the classroom in order for all students to be successful learners. Lessons involve teaching guides, lesson plans, student assignments, course materials (books, workbooks, etc.), courseware (on personal computers), tutoring sessions, tests (for the lesson), and the methods for instruction. To develop the lessons, a teacher or instructional designer should make a detailed list of learning and performance objectives that must be achieved in order for students to successfully pass the mastery test for the lesson.

These concepts can be made to sound extremely complicated, but it is important for the sake of effective communications to keep this process simple and understandable for all concerned parties.

## REQUIREMENT FOR INTEGRATED CURRICULUM

Too many schools lack an integrated curriculum that clearly articulates what students must know and be able to do at each grade level from kindergarten through high school. "Integrated" means that middle school teachers know what has been taught in the elementary schools, and high school teachers design their lesson plans based on what lessons have been taught in the elementary and middle schools. Integration is further enhanced when a history or science teacher reinforces grammar lessons taught in an English class. The lack of an integrated curriculum was one of the major factors contributing to serious learning problems in the classroom listed in Chapter 3. This defect in the education system is one reason why children in elementary schools do fairly well, students in middle school begin to have serious learning problems, and high school graduates are ranked low compared to other countries.[1]

Some schools have a curriculum document, but no one pays any attention to it. This is what happens to many strategic plans within the corporate world. Classroom time is filled with various lessons, projects, field trips, and so forth, but vital lessons are either not documented or not taught. It's a real hit-and-miss situation.

This unfocused approach can change in most schools over the next few years. With the state departments of education and school districts establishing standards within each school district, the next logical step will be to develop an integrated curriculum that helps students learn their lessons and do well on state mastery or achievement tests. In some states, the state department of education will develop the curriculum; in other states, school districts will develop the integrated curriculum; and in some districts, an individual school develops its own curriculum.

## DIRECTORS OF CURRICULUM ARE ESSENTIAL

With 180 days or more per year for 13 years, American students have between 12,000 and 15,000 hours in school to learn their lessons. With afterschool programs or "six by six" (6 AM to 6 PM) schools, the number of total hours students spend in school will increase in future years. Much of this precious time will be wasted if an integrated curriculum is not developed.

Most school districts now have a director of curriculum who reports to the District Superintendent. In large districts, the director supervises specialists who are responsible for every major subject area. These key administrators need to be responsible for determining what students should know and be able to do at the end of each grade level. These people are also responsible for designing lesson blueprints and professional development (training) programs for teachers. A director of curriculum is as important to a school district as an architect is to a major building project. They are the Chief Educational Officer or Chief Academic Officer of the school district.

Developing a curriculum has become more challenging over the years because it involves so many groups: parents, teachers, administrators, the federal Department of Education, governors, mayors, legislators, and special interest groups. Everyone is interested in what lessons will be taught to American children and how these lessons will be communicated. The core curriculum of reading, writing, and arithmetic has expanded significantly over the years. There is always pressure to add more subjects and lessons and reluctance to eliminate lessons that have been in the curriculum for decades. The current curriculum in most schools is a product of the past 100 years, during which great debates have taken place on every subject. The standard school curriculum is often described as "a mile wide and an inch deep."[2] As we begin the 21st century, great debate will ensue regarding what subjects should remain in the curriculum. The state departments of education will have a greater say in this matter because of new state standards and textbook adoption policies.[3]

The biggest challenge of this whole process will be to successfully teach each lesson in the minimum amount of time it takes for all students to learn the lesson. Such effectiveness will enable schools to teach all of the academic content and skills required by the state standards and still leave room for local elective lessons not required by these standards.

Directors of curriculum must set the pace for teaching and learning. They must eliminate "nice to do" lessons that have little or no impact on learning the core curriculum designed by the state and school district. The curriculum should move at a pace that enables students to learn the first time and demonstrate mastery, thus eliminating the need for so much remedial education. In the past, the pace often has been inconsistent—too slow in some classes and too fast in others.

When a school district adopts an integrated curriculum and lessons by grade level, the next step is to develop a library and Internet services that support the lessons. This support structure is sometimes called knowledge systems. Just filling a room with books does not create an effective library. Neither does a hook-up to the Internet achieve learning without effective planning. Directors of curriculum and lead teachers must determine what knowledge resources need to be on hand to service the lessons of the integrated curriculum.

## NEED FOR A WORLD-CLASS CURRICULUM

The famous *A Nation At Risk* report clearly states that our country has a mediocre education system, which is an indication of a weak curriculum. In fact, the curriculum has been "dumbed down" over the years for the many students who are not at grade level. Current lessons in public schools are not tough enough for the challenging assignments that high school graduates face in the workplace and at institutions of higher learning. Now most people are demanding a world-class curriculum because other countries have a richer set of lessons. If our future adults must compete in the global economy, they need to learn more during their K–12 years. Our country is currently the world economic leader. To maintain our high standard of living, public schools must be upgraded to world-class institutions.

What is a world-class curriculum? Numerous books and articles list four years of English (including literature), mathematics, and science, plus two years of language and history in addition to one year of government as the requisites for a world-class curriculum. This curriculum may be world-class, but it is also exactly what the Chicago public schools and some other districts used 50 years ago. The words and descriptions are more complex, such as "Physical Sciences Concepts" rather than "General Science," but one wonders if the lessons are different.

Several organizations within each subject area, such as the National Alliance for Civics Education, National Council of Teachers of Mathematics, National

Center for History in the Schools, National Reading Panel, and American Association for the Advancement of Science (Project 2061) are trying to improve the curriculum. According to the American Association for the Advancement of Science, the 20th century ended with virtually the same curriculum it started with, and many of the lessons are obsolete.[4] This group also claims that the curricula tend to cover too many topics—far more than can be taught effectively during the average school year.[5]

Therefore, the American public school system has two great challenges: One is to improve the curriculum, which is an ongoing process. This book will not address what lessons should be taught within each major subject area of the curriculum. Rather, this book addresses the second major challenge: how to improve the number of successful learners based on whatever lessons are in the curricula. Thus, this document focuses on how to fix the *process of learning* and the *management of schools*. Also, there must be a balance of subjects in the curriculum. Taking 13 years to teach reading, writing, and arithmetic is not going to be a world-class curriculum. Every subject area needs to be enhanced during this decade.

At the same time, the curriculum must be realistic. All English-speaking students must be able to keep up with the lessons. Students must remain at grade level so they have all of the prerequisites for the next lesson and the next grade. Students are not going to be able to learn how to multiply or divide fractions if they cannot do basic multiplication or division problems.

In future years, however, advancing technology will create the need for more changes in the curriculum. It will not be easy to eliminate lessons that teachers are accustomed to, but the directors of curriculum will need to prune the integrated curriculum to add new lessons as they are required. The task of developing and managing a sound curriculum has become more complicated than ever. Fortunately, several computer systems (listed as follows) are available to help experienced teachers and directors of curriculum accomplish this work.[6]

- Knowledge Adventure, Torrance, California (Class Works Gold)
- CompassLearning, San Diego, California (Compass Management Tools)
- NovaNET Learning, Inc., Tucson, Arizona (NovaNET)
- Tudor Publishing, San Diego, California (Curriculum Designer)
- Media Seek, Bellingham, Washington (Curriculum Orchestrator)
- Computer Curriculum Corporation, Sunnyvale, California (EdMAP).

All of these systems and others that will exist in future years are designed to help ensure that what is taught is in line with the growing body of expectations generated by the current standards movement. Now let's look at the curriculum taught within each major segment of the K–12 education years.

## Preschool and Day Care Centers

Before the 1960s, most mothers worked at home raising families and managing homes—an important full-time job. Only single-parent homes needed child care, which was often provided by grandparents or friends. In some upper middle-class and wealthy families, three- to four-year-old children attended half-day preschool centers.

This family structure changed during the past 40 years. Now most mothers work outside the home, and even those who are at home usually send their three- to four-year-olds to a half-day preschool center for two to five days per week or to a Head Start program. Some children from poor families are still on the waiting list for Head Start, but it appears that this program will be expanded. Education research tells us that children learn a great deal during these preschool years. In 1986, Robert L. Fulghum wrote a book entitled *All I Really Need To Know I Learned In Kindergarten* that remained on the bestseller list for 93 weeks.[7] This book communicated the message that the early school years are important.

Child care and preschool are two major subjects being discussed by all political leaders and millions of parents, who require this level of education because it has a direct impact on Goal One: By the year 2000, all children will start school ready to learn.

Although many critics claim that too little is being done, the federal budget reveals another story. In May 2000, the General Accounting Office (GAO) issued a report called *Early Education and Care: Overlap Indicates Need To Assess Crosscutting Programs*.[8] This report stated that 69 federal programs provided or supported education and care for children younger than age five in fiscal year 1999. The Department of Education and the Department of Health and Human Services (HHS) ran most of the programs. Twenty-nine of the 69 programs provided education and care as a primary purpose at a cost of at least $9 billion. Three HHS programs (i.e., Head Start, Child Care Development Fund, and Temporary Assistance to Needy Families) accounted for about $8 billion of the $9 billion.[9] In addition, state governments provide nearly $2 billion annually to support preschool programs.[10]

The Department of Education published the first report card on the nation's youngest students.[11] This report stated that most students can count to 10 and identify shapes when they start kindergarten. Two of three preschoolers know their alphabet, and more than 80 percent make friends, cooperate, and otherwise avoid bad behavior. All but three percent of these students are in good health.[12] But the news is not as good for children living in poverty, single-parent homes, and non–English-speaking families. Political leaders of both parties have promised to expand child care, preschool, and Head Start programs.

This change in early childhood preparation has created a major problem for schools: children now arrive for kindergarten with a wide range of knowledge and capabilities. Years ago, children were more similar: they knew their name and were ready to learn. Now some children are reading at the first-grade level, whereas others do not even recognize the letters of the alphabet.

*This situation raises a fundamental question: How do you bring all children up to grade level before they start first grade and not penalize the ones who are way ahead?*

First, a stronger partnership must be formed between the local school district and the local preschool institutions, as there is in France. The school districts should encourage these institutions to focus on subjects such as basic information on students and their family, social skills, and self-care skills, as well as language development. Children should also be interested in books and learning as they enter school. The school district should contact families of three-year-olds to educate them on what parents, and, in some cases, grandparents, should do for children who are not attending day care centers or preschools. For instance, the school districts could encourage the use of many good learning materials and computer courseware programs available for preschoolers. Such suggestions would help children arrive at kindergarten with similar capabilities. Japanese mothers are given a document when they become pregnant that provides guidelines on what they must do to raise healthy children who are ready to learn when they enter school. These mothers do an outstanding job of following the guidelines. Currently, too many school districts do nothing to promote early childhood education and merely use the differences in preschool-age children's learning levels as another excuse for not having all children at grade level during the elementary school years.

Another giant step forward would be to transfer the $5-billion Head Start Program to the federal Department of Education in order to enhance the program's educational value. Head Start was instituted in 1965 as a day care, health, and nutrition program for children living in poverty. It was a key component of the "War On Poverty" program carried out by the federal Department of Health and Human Services; however, a 1997 report by the GAO concluded that past research had not proven whether Head Start was making a positive difference.[13] Billions of taxpayer dollars (more than $5 billion per year) were thrown into the overall education system with the hope—and it was only a hope—that it would make a difference.[14] Split responsibility once again resulted in no responsibility. Congress has now authorized Head Start until year 2003, with the goal to cover 1 million children.

After 35 years, a first-class Head Start program should be operating throughout the country, with meaningful measurements proving that billions of dollars are being well spent. Head Start should be held responsible for preparing children to learn in public schools. The program should emphasize early reading skills and language development to the 1 million children it serves. Children living in poverty need to enter school ready to learn, rather than being labeled "slow learners" right from the start.

The country appears to be moving in the direction of more government funding for child care as well as preschool education. One catalyst of this strategy is the "welfare to work" program, which places a greater requirement on the existing child care services. Some people believe that if the government is going to force mothers (mostly single mothers) into jobs and their children into child care settings, then the government would be behooved to improve child care services. Many proposals have been made for government to help subsidize more child care services.[15] As government funds flow into child care centers, it is hoped that children will be properly prepared for school. High-quality child care not only prepares children for school, but it also helps them succeed once they get there.[16] The cost of child care and preschool education will rise by 25 to 75 percent if school districts take over the responsibilities of child care because K–12 teachers earn almost twice as much as child care workers.[17]

The primary void in preschool education today is the lack of English-language training for children who come from homes where English is not spoken or where it is spoken poorly. Head Start, day care, and preschool programs could teach the English language to these children. This training could be continued in kindergarten, providing these children with three years of instruction. Research proves that young children are capable of learning multiple languages.[18] If necessary, a fourth year could be added in "junior" first grade, which would provide four years for students who must learn the English language. Then all first-grade children would be fluent in English, and only older children of immigrant families would require special English-language classes. Other states are following the lead of California to curtail bilingual education classes to bring a greater focus on learning in English. The school district and the state departments of education need to do in-depth research on what is the most effective way to teach the English language to immigrant students. The current teaching methods for this important subject are too often inadequate. After schools are restructured to fix the current learning problems, it might be possible to teach a second language to all children in the lower grades. Such an addition would be a major enhancement to the American curriculum.

## Elementary Schools

Kindergarten is now part of the universal education system in the United States. In the 1998–99 school year, 4 million children were enrolled in kindergarten. More than half (55 percent) attended all-day programs, which are often driven by the need for free child care service as much as any education requirements because 75 percent of mothers with kindergarten-age children are in the workforce.[19]

Kindergarten lessons are becoming more sophisticated in most schools. In many schools, they are miniature first grades. In most schools, the kindergarten teacher must accept all children who have reached the age of 5 by a certain date (dates vary from August 1 to December 1), which is established by each school district or the state department of education. Then teachers must work with the strengths and weaknesses of all children to prepare them for first grade. This includes knowing their name, address, telephone number, the alphabet, how to use scissors, how to hop on one foot, basic vocabulary, and reading readiness.

Everyone agrees that learning to read is the most important objective for elementary school children, and reading is based on cumulative learning. If students are poor readers, they will be slow learners in almost every other subject. Arithmetic is another cumulative learning subject; a student who doesn't learn the basic lessons will struggle in advanced mathematics and science courses. Even in college, one can easily see the impact of poor performance in cumulative subjects. For example, if a student gets a C in Accounting 101 and a D in Accounting 102, he or she will most likely fail Accounting 201. Failure began in the first year for this student, who simply did not have the prerequisite knowledge to learn Accounting 201. He or she was not at grade level for the next course.

It's hard to believe that after 100 years of research and debate, as well as an estimated 100,000 published studies, no single method for teaching reading to children in the first three or four school grades has been agreed upon. Millions of adults are functionally illiterate because of this failure in our school system. Recently, the National Reading Panel recommended that phonics be used in kindergarten through sixth grade.[20] At present, a move is being made toward spending more time on learning to read, with a "dumbing down" of lessons in all of the other important subjects rather than fixing the methods for teaching reading. The argument of phonics versus whole language should end. Directors of curriculum, principals, and master teachers in elementary schools must instead identify and adopt the most effective method for teaching reading. Cost must be a secondary issue because the savings generated by eliminating remedial reading programs will more than justify the initial cost to teach the subject correctly the first time.

If learning to read is a problem in schools, then learning to write is an even greater crisis. Thousands of studies conducted on reading skills across the nation usually provide the same depressing information. If writing skills were measured the same way, the nation would plunge into a state of depression. Grammar lessons are weak in many schools, to say the least. The writing skills of American students are far below their reading skills. Schools need to focus more on how to improve writing skills because writing and reading are so interrelated.

Subjects such as history, geography, and mathematics will continue to suffer as long as extra hours are being spent on reading and writing. Directors of curriculum must design well-balanced curriculums that satisfy the overall learning standards established by the state departments of education and the school districts. Directors of curriculum should also not lose sight, however, of the fact that play time is a critically important part in the development of children from birth through the early school years. Children learn when they are playing.

## Middle Schools

Problems begin to be visible in middle schools and junior high schools. At inner-city schools and in the lowest quartile of suburban schools, students who are two or three grade levels behind no longer have the prerequisites for learning the next lessons. They either sit quietly and hope no one calls on them to participate in the current lesson or they become troublemakers. It is not uncommon for some students to be absent 20 percent or more of the time. If a student has a high number of absentee days, there usually is no hope for that student to be at grade level. The middle schools too often have an undemanding curriculum that fails to challenge students.

No consensus has been reached across our nation on how to divide the K–12 years among elementary, intermediate, middle, junior high, and senior high schools. Today, there are 16,000 middle schools and 2,000 junior high schools. Principals and superintendents must fit all students into a school district's existing buildings. Some towns send the fifth graders to middle school, whereas others send them to elementary schools. Ninth graders are sent to either junior high or senior high, depending on the school. Principals and superintendents claim these shifts are better for the students based on the latest education research, but the real reason for the shifts is to fit students into school buildings.

For decades, students in the K–8 grades remained in one room with one teacher except for art, music, and physical education. In recent years, students in many junior high schools and middle schools change classrooms every 40 to 50 minutes like high school students do so they have a teacher with specialized training in each subject. The current trend, however, is to have less student movement because teachers want to have fewer students. As a result, many middle school teachers now teach more than one subject.

There used to be a rule that students learned how to read in elementary school and read to learn in middle and high school. Various assessment tests have now shown that a large percentage of students did not learn to read in elementary school, and a movement is being made toward instituting reading classes in middle schools. In some inner-city schools, 80 percent or more of the students fail to meet grade-level reading standards.[21]

Students need to learn how to read more complex textbooks that have more challenging vocabulary and more charts, graphics, and statistics. Reading assignments must be given in social studies, science, and mathematics classes. This goal is not easy to accomplish because many mathematics, science, and social studies teachers have not been instructed on how to teach reading. Students often fake "silent reading" assignments by just turning pages. Thus, reading lessons cannot be merely "read Chapter 2 by yourselves."

Many schools have substituted English literature, computer literacy, and other elective classes for the more traditional reading classes. On the other hand, all electives cannot be eliminated to focus on reading, writing, and arithmetic. Physical education, music, art, and other electives must remain in the curriculum to develop well-rounded individuals.

Fortunately, the gender gap in mathematics has almost disappeared.[22] Mathematics is a key subject during middle school years. In too many cases, middle school students have not learned arithmetic basics in the first four grades. The curriculum is usually "dumbed down" because of these fundamental problems in the early grades. These years are often the period when many students claim school is boring. They accept the fact that they are slow learners, and they give up any hope of becoming good students. Instead, they start to cause trouble because their minds need something to do.

Remember, students must learn the lessons at every grade level in order to be successful students. The curriculum in most middle schools needs to be enhanced as soon as elementary schools start producing successful students. Several successful schools now teach algebra in the eighth grade and some early lessons in geometry. Debates on how to teach mathematics will continue to rage until schools adopt a mathematics learning system that enables all students to achieve the basic lessons set by state standards.

## High Schools

High school appears to be the greatest challenge because of the high drop-out rate and the large number of students who are two or more grade levels behind in learning. Magnet schools have enabled school districts to select and sort students on a voluntary basis. Students at grade level who are serious about learning attend the high schools that have solid college preparatory courses as well as Advanced Placement courses. The bottom half of the middle school students go to high schools that are actually child care centers where a little learning takes place.

Several cities have implemented charter schools for the better students, such as High Tech High in San Diego, but these charter schools are like the magnet schools that carefully select the best students.[23] They are good high schools for the top-performing students. Many innovative curricula are being developed by these new schools. It will be interesting to see how well these students perform on the accountability tests that are based on the state learning standards. If these students do well, these new, innovative curriculum and teaching methods should be implemented in the low-performing high schools.

By the time students have completed 10th grade, they must decide whether to go on to institutions of higher learning. If they choose to do so, then they need to continue in a precollege curriculum that emphasizes courses in English, mathematics, science, and social studies. Top students should also take advantage of Advanced Placement courses. One of the great inequities in the American public school system is the lack of Advanced Placement courses in every school. The Advanced Placement program gives high school students college-level courses and rigorous examinations through which they can earn college credit as well as a bonus point in their grade-point average. Only 50 percent of our high schools offer Advanced Placement courses. More than 1.1 million Advanced Placement tests were given in 1999.[24] State departments of education should develop Advanced Placement courses through the Internet and distance learning so every school within the state can offer such courses even if only a few students are eligible. Most high schools are geared for students who are continuing on to higher education, so the best teachers are assigned to the Advanced Placement courses. Many educators have concluded that encouraging students to take challenging high school courses produces students who can later succeed in college. More than 60 percent of high school students go on to higher education institutions, but that figure can be 99 percent in some schools and 10 percent in others.

The real challenge is what happens to students who want to enter the workplace after high school. Many educators have vehemently opposed vocational courses and schools. They would force every student to take advanced mathematics, physics, chemistry, and advanced English courses. For the 40 percent who want to go to work, a different and more practical set of courses should be available during the last year or two of high school.

Working students need "school-to-work" courses. They should learn how to write a good résumé, how to prepare letters for employment, and how to dress for and conduct themselves at an interview. Students should understand all of the various job opportunities in the state, enabling them to do some career planning. They need to know the good character traits of working, such as good attendance, arriving at work on time, persevering to complete a job, producing quality work, problem solving, teamwork, motivation, being responsible for tasks, and lifetime learning. Some researchers call these traits emotional intelligence or EQ, which refers to social and emotional skills that are as essential as an IQ (intelligence quotient).[25] Most people who do well in life have both a good IQ and EQ. Research tells us that learning these basic traits should not be left to chance; feeling good about yourself (self-esteem) is important. Schools should start working on EQ in preschool and develop EQ skills throughout the K–12 years for both college-bound students and those entering the workforce after high school.

The need for vocational courses and schools was debated throughout the 20th century. Vocational programs reached their highest popularity levels from the 1930s to 1980s, when woodworking, auto mechanics, building trades, clerical skills, and home economics tasks were taught in most high schools. With the reduction in manufacturing jobs, many schools have phased out vocational courses in favor of a more general education. The School-To-Work Opportunities Act of 1994 intended to expose students of all academic levels to experiences in the workplace, but it has been more successful in schools where students intend to enter the workplace after high school. New magnet schools in major cities have also succeeded in preparing students for careers in financial services, retailing, health services, and food service. European and Asian countries do an outstanding job of preparing students for the workplace.

All students need to learn how to use a personal computer. Every middle school graduate should be capable of "touch typing" on the keyboard. Students should also be able to do word processing, spreadsheets, presentations, and database applications. Computer literacy is as important to high school graduates in this century as penmanship was in the last century. Most high schools have an inadequate set of lessons in this subject area. High school students also need lessons on statistics as well as high-level mathematics courses.

In addition, every high school student needs a course on practical life matters, including how to pay bills, balance a checkbook, develop a household budget, understand the real cost of interest, interpret insurance requirements, learn some basic cooking, perform simple household repairs, and manage a house. Many educators oppose this course, but if they want their students to succeed in life, they should help them learn these important functional lessons as well. In September 2000, 29 panelists were named to a new national commission taking a critical look at the senior year of high school because there needs to be a well-structured transition into adulthood.

One important question for the directors of curriculum and school administrators is how much time should be allocated to school-based service-learning programs. To answer that inquiry, another question needs to be asked: What are students learning in their community service projects. In many programs, the answer is very little. Students prefer this assignment because school is too often boring, but that should not be the basis for having 13 million students leave the classroom to do some well-meaning tasks in the "outside" world.[26] Learning objectives must be assigned to this area of the curriculum. Of course, there is nothing wrong with having a Service Learning Club that does volunteer work after school.

Where would the time be found to teach these new courses? If students learn their lessons the first time, adequate time would be available for new courses. High school curricula should provide all students with good academic skills, marketable occupational skills, and appropriate workplace behavior skills. Our schools must prepare our youth for success in the workplace because that's where most students wind up eventually after completing their education.

## ALTERNATIVE CLASSROOM OR SCHOOL FOR "PROBLEM" STUDENTS

When the new vision and paradigm are implemented, most students should be successful learners and at grade level. In a free country, the opportunity exists to be either a successful individual or a failure. A small percentage of students—and it is hoped that it is a very small percentage—will not conform to the school environments and traditional learning methods. These students are labeled juvenile offenders, troublemakers, and truants. Rather than allow them to disrupt a productive classroom, they need to be placed in a special room or school where teachers have the training and resources to handle such problems. It appears that one-on-one interactive tutoring using a personal computer is one potential solution. These students need to be more productively engaged. Waldorf Schools has had success in this area. There are now 130 such schools in the United States and many special programs for so-called at-risk students.[27] It should be considered a privilege to attend traditional schools that require acceptable behavior, dress, attendance, and ethics.

Teachers and principals must be offered incentives to work with students who cause trouble in a classroom because the education system does not need another group of students designated as special education who cannot remain in the traditional classroom environment. On the other hand, an extremely disruptive student has to be removed from the classroom.

## WORKPLACE EDUCATION AND TRAINING

Not-for-profit organizations, government agencies, and commercial companies have an obligation to provide in-depth job training as they recruit new employees and as they promote experienced employees to greater responsibilities within their organizations. This type of training is not the responsibility of the public school system. Currently, these organizations spend more than $60 billion annually on job-training courses and events.

In this field, a bell-shaped curve is evident as well. Some organizations provide little or no training. They usually have higher costs because they need additional employees to correct errors. Their employees usually have low morale and higher attrition rates, driving up the cost of employee separation and recruitment. These companies also have higher supervision costs because their workforce was inadequately trained. These organizations have a difficult time implementing tactical decisions and new strategic directions because their employees cannot adapt to new methods and procedures. Too often, this type of organization leaps from crisis to crisis, resulting in massive downsizings whenever the competition achieves a larger market share.

On the other hand, successful organizations recognize the value of lifelong learning. They provide outstanding job-training programs as well as new performance systems for every key job within their organization.

*A performance system consists of the following elements:*

- Personal development courses
- On-the-job training/experience
- Performance-based training curriculum
- Basic support systems (i.e., job aids, knowledge systems)
- Electronic performance support system (if necessary).

These organizations provide all of the training and support necessary to do a job right the first time for all employees within a job category, without spending one dollar more than is necessary. This approach reduces costs, increases market share, raises revenues, and provides a strategic advantage that leads to higher earnings. Job satisfaction and employee morale is much higher, resulting in lower attrition rates. Details for this type of education and training are available in my 1998 book *Revolutionizing Workforce Performance* (Jossey-Bass, San Francisco).

## HIGH-POTENTIAL AND GIFTED STUDENTS

Too often, high-potential and gifted students have been short-changed because of the costs of providing special education and remedial programs to slower learners. In the past, gifted students were pulled out of their classes for special courses and tutoring in schools that could afford such programs and that had a sufficient number of these students. Today, most gifted students are learning in general education settings rather than in pull-out programs or ability-grouped classes. Although many educators oppose this general education practice, others believe this positive step can help fast learners (gifted students) teach other students within cooperative learning groups. It is important to understand that gifted students do not automatically succeed because they are gifted. Too often, gifted students become bored and drop out from learning.

With personal computers serving as low-cost interactive tutors, gifted children can also be given more challenging assignments, which can be accomplished in class, after school, or at home. They can be challenged on an intellectual basis through computerized study programs. Today, numerous course materials and courseware are designed for educating gifted children. The Internet is also an astounding new tool for gifted students. This extra instruction is affordable because no extra costs are accrued for special classrooms with special teachers. In a large school or school district, one teacher might be required to coordinate the extra assignments for gifted children.

The school districts and directors of curriculum should work with parents of gifted children to ensure that they are challenged, not bored, in school. Every school district can serve gifted students, but parent involvement is essential. The state departments of education could also develop an enrichment set of assignments, course materials, and courseware. Special recognition should also be provided to these outstanding students. The United States is not serving this talented group of students as well as it could. Better programs for our gifted students would raise the performance of American students who participate at international competitions. At least 2 million students in our nation are gifted learners. Their success has been and will always be a positive motivator within our schools.

## SPECIAL EDUCATION

Recent accounts of improved test scores and higher expectations for students with disabilities who are attending public schools are welcome news for educators attempting the reform known as "education inclusion."[28] For years, two separate systems have served general (mainstream) education and special education students. This structure was based on the belief that students with disabilities required a separate curriculum, different lessons, and specially trained teachers.

Like all well-intentioned programs, several unintended consequences resulted from this strategy. Students started to believe that they were less than capable, and so did society. More and more minorities were classified as slow learners and were assigned to special education classes. This view is changing, however, because of the 1997 amendments to the Individual With Disabilities Education Act, which required states to shift accountability to meet state standards and to raise the bar on expectations for students with disabilities. School districts must now document their efforts to educate all students to the same standards. Inclusion reform is under way in more than two-thirds of our school districts.[29] More important, national data now indicate that as a consequence of education inclusion, more than 95 percent of students with disabilities attend schools in regular classroom environments with their nondisabled peers.[30]

This change is not happening without considerable debate. For example, in Massachusetts, which has the second highest rate (17 percent) of students classified as needing special education, consideration is being given to adoption of new standards based on federal guidelines that reduce the number of special education students.[31] Rhode Island, which has an even higher percentage of special needs students, should also reconsider its standards. Some of the most structured and creative teaching and learning systems have been developed for special education students. This is one area of education where the process of learning is well understood.

## EDUCATION FOR IMMIGRANTS

Over the past decade, numerous studies have shown that children whose parents are immigrants or who are themselves immigrants do better in school on average than students whose families have been in the United States a generation or more. These newcomers score high grades despite language barriers, some poverty, and personal hardships.[32]

How can this be? Immigrants bring hope and optimism. They work hard in school. European immigration in the early 1900s became a great success story. Asian students are often academic leaders in public schools as well as institutions of higher learning. Indians from India are very good students, and Cubans have done well in American schools. Immigrant parents believe, for the most part, that it is absolutely critical for their children to do well in school. These children want to be successful learners because they strive to become "real" Americans.

The performance of Hispanic students needs to be raised, but that goal can only be accomplished if the programs outlined in Parts III and IV of this book are implemented. Once again, more than 90 percent of students at grade level is a realistic goal. Schools that have a high population of immigrants require better learning systems and an outstanding immersion program for the English language, but the curriculum does not need to be altered.

## CURRICULUM PLANNING IS THE FOUNDATION FOR
## STUDENT LEARNING

It is important for everyone to understand that a school or school district that does not have an integrated curriculum is aligned to the learning standards of the state department of education and local school district has very little chance of having 90 percent or more students as successful learners. Then the school district or school must have a series of lessons to achieve the curriculum for each grade level. Unfortunately, very few schools in this country have lessons and curriculum aligned to the learning standards. This work must be accomplished in the next few years to achieve the national education goals by the year 2010. Too often in the past, schools have designed a curriculum either for top performers or for the lowest performers. In the future, directors of curriculum, school administrators, and master teachers must collaborate to implement an integrated curriculum that will enable almost all students to be at grade level and to do well on state mastery or achievement tests. If readers wish to know more about curriculum planning, they should read *Mapping the Big Picture* by Heidi Hayes Jacobs, *Cultural Literacy* by E.D. Hirsch, Jr., and *The Educated Child* by William Bennett, Chester Finn, and John Cribb. They should also look at the books listed in this text's Suggested Reading section.

It is hoped that cities and states will work together to develop similar lessons in their curriculum because most American students will not grow up in one neighborhood. They'll attend schools in several communities as their parents move from job to job in this new world of intense competition and global economy. A citywide and/or statewide curriculum will help solve the educational problems associated with a mobile society. Once the curriculum is designed, however, the big challenge becomes how to achieve a consistent level of teaching so that all students can be successful learners. That answer is provided in the next several chapters.

---

## NOTES

1. D. Kearns and J. Harvey, *Ranking of Performance of American Students Relative to Their International Peers, by Subject and Grade Level* (Washington, DC: Brookings Institute Press, 2000), 31.

2. K. Manzo, "The Evolving Curriculum: Lessons of a Century," *Education Week*, 19 May, 1999, 1, 20–44.

3. Manzo, "The Evolving Curriculum."

4. 2061 Today, *Guiding K-12 Curriculum Reform* (Washington, DC: American Association for the Advancement of Science, Spring/Summer 2000), 1–2.

5. 2061 Today, *Guiding K-12 Curriculum Reform*.

6. S. Brooks and M. Simkins, "The Curriculum Management Creature," *Technology and Learning*, October 1999, 10–22.

7. R. Fulgham, *All I Really Need To Know I Learned in Kindergarten* (New York: Random House, 1988).

8. General Accounting Office, *Early Education and Care: Overlap Indicates Need To Assess Crosscutting Programs* (Washington, DC: U.S. Government Printing Office, May 2000), 3.

9. General Accounting Office, *Early Education and Care*.

10. General Accounting Office, *Early Education and Care*, 5.

11. A. McQueen, "Kindergartners Who Lag Classmates To Be Study's Focus," *San Diego Union-Tribune*, 18 February, 2000, A10.

12. McQueen, "Kindergartners Who Lag Classmates."

13. General Accounting Office, *Early Childhood Programs* (Washington, DC: U.S. Government Printing Office, May 1997), 1–5.

14. L. Jacobson, "Advocates Question Bush Plan To Revamp Head Start," *Education Week*, 1 December, 1999, 14.

15. L. Jacobson, "Problems in Child Care Found To Persist," *Education Week*, 9 February, 2000, 1, 15.

16. L. Jacobson, "Study: Effects of Child Care Linger in Early Grades," *Education Week*, 23 June, 1999, 10.

17. L. Jacobson, "Tensions Surface in Public-Private Preschool Plans," *Education Week*, 15 September, 1999, 7, 12.

18. J. Amselle, "Foreign Languages: The Scales Tip in Favor of Starting Early," *Education Week*, 1 March, 2000, 16.

19. A. Lewis, "Playing With Equity and Early Education," *Phi Delta Kappan*, April 2000, 563–564.

20. K. Manzo, "Reading Panel Urges Phonics for All in K-6," *Education Week*, April 19, 2000, 1, 14.

21. Curriculum Update, *Before It's Too Late: Giving Reading A Last Chance* (Alexandria, VA: Association of Supervision and Curriculum Development, Summer 2000), 1–3.

22. D. Baker, "Gender Gap in Math Is Disappearing," *Education Week*, 21 June, 2000, 12.

23. W. Symonds, "High School Will Never Be the Same," *Business Week*, 28 August, 2000, 190–191.

24. J. Mathews, "The 100 Best High Schools," *Newsweek*, 13 March, 2000, 50–53.

25. A. Farnham, "Are You Smart Enough To Keep Your Job," *Fortune*, 15 January, 1996, 34–48.

26. J. Westheimer and J. Kahne, "Service Learning Required," *Education Week*, 26 January, 2000, 32, 52.

27. T. Oppenheimer, "Schooling the Imagination," *The Atlantic Monthly*, September 1999, 71–83.

28. L. Ware, "Opening Our Schools to All," *University of Rochester Review*, Spring/Summer 2000, 11.

29. Ware, "Opening Our Schools."

30. Ware, "Opening Our Schools."

31. M. Galley, "Special Education Report Reignites Debate in Massachusetts," *Education Week*, 22 March, 2000, 28.

32. D. Viadero, "Research Yields Surprising Achievement Patterns among Recent Immigrants," *Education Week*, 7 June, 2000, 28–29.

# CHAPTER 9

# Why Learning Systems Are Essential in Classrooms

Whatever the design intent may have been, the current teaching methods and management procedures used in today's public schools are not achieving the necessary level of successful learners. Failure and mediocre performance have been tolerated for more than 100 years. When we look at the schools today, we see that:

- Some teachers are outstanding, most are average performers, and some are below average.
- Some students are above average, others are average, and too many are below average.

If the objective is to have more than 90 percent of all students become successful learners, then new concepts and new learning systems must be introduced to achieve more consistent performance in teaching and learning.

*Let's quickly review the 10 major problems that exist in the classroom as described in Chapter 3:*

1. Lack of integrated curriculum
2. Lack of grade-level measurements
3. Lack of instructional systems design methods
4. Lack of effective lesson plans
5. Lack of class management skills
6. Lack of adequate course materials
7. Lack of adequate assessment systems
8. Lack of tutoring systems
9. Lack of time to learn
10. Lack of an embraceable responsibility.

The first two problems were addressed in Chapter 8 with the need to have an integrated curriculum and learning measurements by grades. In this chapter, we'll see how outstanding learning systems can resolve the other eight problems.

## DEFINITION OF A LEARNING SYSTEM

A very successful southern California school superintendent tells parents of his students that: "We are in the business of student learning rather than just teaching."[1] He and other leading educators believe that the job of teaching isn't complete until students have learned their lessons. To them, communicating information to students is just one phase of teaching. Unfortunately, too many educators behave as if communicating information is the total teaching job, even if only half the students learn the lessons. Learning systems are based on the wider definition that the job of teaching is not complete until students have learned the lessons and can apply them as well.

*Therefore, the definition of a learning system is as follows:*

> A learning system integrates systems design principles and instructional design methods to produce a set of group learning sessions, individual learning models, interactive tutoring, and high-quality motivational course materials. All of these elements are essential to enable *all* students to become successful learners by achieving learning objectives derived from educational standards.

## CONCEPTS OF A LEARNING SYSTEM

Students, who are learners, are the central people within a learning system. Both research and common sense tell us that children must be actively involved in learning. Effort is often more important than other attributes. Students need challenging books and workbooks written by instructional designers. If students learn the lesson and provide correct answers, then they can go on to the next lesson. If the answers are wrong, students receive remedial lessons and explanations on why their answers were not the best ones. In other words, no one advances to the second lesson until the first lesson has been mastered. It is important that students feel responsible for their academic performance in school. Students quickly learn that if they give minimum effort, they will receive only minimum results. Students learn that they must achieve mastery of learning and performance with a grade of A or B.

Millions of public school students claim that their lessons are boring.[2] Well-designed, engaging learning systems will fix that problem. For example, students could learn about fractions by discussing how a pizza is sliced into halves, quarters, thirds, eighths, and so forth. Administrators and directors of curriculum know that their lessons and learning systems must meet the important criteria of being interesting and motivational. If they do meet these criteria, then no one will need to sit in the back of a classroom to determine if a teacher has interesting lessons. In other words, learning systems greatly reduce the amount of supervision required for teachers because the learning system provides structure for teacher performance. It almost ensures that teachers teach the lessons based on the "best methods," which are outlined in the system. The lessons are also aligned to the learning standards of the school district.

Children must like their schools, teachers, and course materials in order to be motivated to learn. School should be entertaining as well as hard work. Content of instruction must be as meaningful as possible. Lessons should be relevant to students' current and future lives. Learning systems increase the probability of success in all of these areas. Simply put, well-designed learning systems promote self-esteem and the other positive consequences associated with student accomplishment. Discipline problems decline, and absenteeism situations also decrease.

Learning systems within the K–12 schools require a dedicated classroom teacher who must be properly trained to implement all of the high-quality course materials. Teachers are in charge of the entire learning system. They not only teach group lessons, but they are also responsible for managing cooperative learning sessions and individual learning sessions. Teachers are the managers of learning.

Learning systems provide the "rising tide" for all teachers to be successful in their classrooms and for almost all students to be successful learners. Learning systems provide teachers with the necessary tools and support that are now missing from most traditional classrooms. As it now stands, only one in five teachers feels "very well prepared" to work in a classroom, according to a report released in January 1999 by the Education Department's National Center for Education Statistics (NCES).[3] It is unrealistic to think that colleges of education or more professional development seminars will fix this problem. All teachers must succeed with the learning system in order to achieve highly successful learning rates with students. The traditional bell-curve model moves to the right for both teachers and students when they use validated learning systems. Learning systems are based on the applied research by many educators, including Robert K. Branson, Robert E. Corrigan, Robert M. Gagne, John Henry Martin, Robert Kaufman, David Merrill, Robert M. Morgan, Robert Slavin, Seymour Papert, and other educators who want all students to be successful learners.

## BASE INFORMATION FOR GOOD LEARNING SYSTEMS

Readers should refer to Figure 9–1, Elements of a Learning System, as you read the next seven subsections of this chapter.

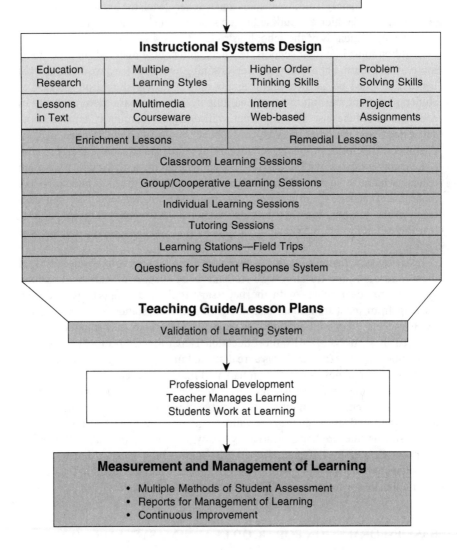

**Figure 9–1** Elements of a Learning System.

The overall design of a learning system starts with the learning standards established by the state departments of education and school districts. The integrated curriculum defines what students must know and be able to do within a subject area for a particular grade level. By reviewing the integrated curriculum, an instructional designer can determine when the prerequisites for this lesson were taught because a good learning system usually has a simple pretest exercise on the prerequisites. This pretest ensures that the lesson will not be taught to people who do not have the basic knowledge to learn the new lesson. For example, suppose a teacher is going to teach young children the use of "911" to call for emergency help. An instructional designer would step in and say, "First determine if the children can recognize a 9. Then be sure they can recognize a 1. Check to be sure they recognize and can say 911. Then and only then should the teacher start to explain how to dial 911 and what happens when the operator comes on the telephone." Then, the detailed teaching points or learning objectives must be documented for this learning system. When all of this knowledge is documented, an instructional designer is able to design the teaching guide and course materials.

## DESIGN OF TEACHING GUIDES AND COURSE MATERIALS

Using the latest information from various education research projects such as different learning styles and brain research, an instructional designer creates layouts for the lessons. As lessons are designed, requirements for higher-order thinking and problem-solving skills must be included.

The next step is to decide how information will be delivered to the students. If the lesson is very simple, the entire lesson may be communicated in a few pages of text. But, if the lesson is more challenging and the goal is to have more than 90 percent of the students learn the lesson, an instructional designer might use workbooks, multimedia (e.g., video, audio, text) courseware, information from the Internet that is now called Web-based activities, and project assignments.

The instructional designer's goal is to use as many instructional methods and delivery systems as is necessary to have more than 90 percent of the students become successful learners, but not to use any more methods than are absolutely necessary. Cost containment is a primary objective for learning systems. Lessons are to be delivered in a minimum amount of time and at a minimum expense, but only on the basis that more than 90 percent of the students will be successful learners. Quality is the first priority, but cost-effectiveness is a close second priority. Learning systems are expensive to develop but very affordable, which is explained in the next chapter.

Next, instructional methods must be determined, which could be any of the following methods or a combination of methods:

- Classroom learning sessions
- Group learning sessions with or without cooperative learning techniques
- Individual learning sessions (self-study with text or interactive multimedia personal computer)
- Tutoring sessions (volunteer tutor, teacher aide, personal computer, teacher)
- Learning stations or field trips.

Then an instructional designer develops questions for students that determine if they are learning each teaching point toward mastering the lesson. Questions can be delivered in text form, on the computer, or by the teacher. It is important to constantly check the students to ensure that they are learning each teaching point. In some classrooms, teachers use a deck of cards with the name of a student on each card so students never know when their name will be called. This technique is designed to keep all students involved in the lesson. In other classrooms, teachers keep their students' names on small wooden sticks in a can. They shake the can with the sticks and draw out one stick to determine which student must answer the questions. Both of these low-technology methods are more effective than merely asking for a show of hands. In this century, schools should consider investing in low-cost electronic student-response systems that enable all students to answer every question. These systems also communicate to the teacher which students could not answer the question correctly. This method is far more effective than having only one student answer each question.

The final document to be completed in the overall learning system is the teaching guide, which is far superior to traditional lesson plans. A teaching guide tells a teacher how to set up the room, what equipment is necessary, and what course materials are required. The guide provides "best practices" for managing the lesson and how to achieve maximum participation by all students. This approach reduces discipline problems. It also explains to a teacher how to deliver each teaching point within the lesson. Usually, there is a balance between individual sessions, group sessions, and full classroom teaching.

When this work is completed, which usually takes months for each learning system, a system is validated with a series of sessions that include every type of student that might be in the classroom. A learning system must be successful for European Americans, Native Americans, Asian Americans, African Americans, and Latin Americans, as well as both boys and girls. A learning system must work for students from wealthy families, middle-class families, and families living below the poverty line. A system must also work with students who have two parents, a single parent, a grandparent guardian, or who are in foster care. A system should also be successful whether there are supportive parents or almost no support at home. Remember, learning systems are only purchased if more than 90 percent of the students become successful learners. Marketplace pressures and competition will ensure that learning systems are subject to continuous improvement for decades.

Validation by assessment specialists takes months to complete. Each version of a system is enhanced after each validation session, which is how the goal of more than 90 percent successful learners is achieved. This validation process ensures that students will not be damaged by inadequate course materials or instructional methods. The validation process also enables students to do well on state achievement or mastery tests. Validation enables a principal or a department head to tell a new or inexperienced teacher that this learning system enables more than 90 percent of the students to be successful learners if properly implemented.

## WHY INSTRUCTIONAL SYSTEMS DESIGN METHODS ARE ESSENTIAL

In order to train millions of military personnel in a short period during World War II and the Korean War, the military had to develop a systematic, rule-guiding process that reliably achieved learning objectives. Later, the military used these same instructional systems design (ISD) methods to train people on sophisticated weapon systems. In life-or-death situations, all students must be successful learners; they cannot wait for a "gifted" teacher to come along.

ISD methods are also used to train employees in the corporate world and government agencies. With an emphasis on quality (first time right), all students had to be successful performers on the job. Therefore, all teachers had to be successful as well. Dr. Robert M. Gagné was a leader in the development of ISD. His methods and research are outlined in his 1965 book *The Conditions of Learning*. Ron Zemke, senior editor of *Training* magazine, wrote an article in July 1999 entitled "Toward a Science of Training."[4] In that article, M. David Merrill, a professor of technology at Utah State University, was quoted as saying, "Gagné's revised edition is as fresh and important today as when the first edition was written in 1965. Effective instruction needn't be mysterious or treated as an art form but can and should be based on the science of learning."

Today, many public school educators acknowledge that ISD is good for adults in military, government, and corporate organizations, but to them it doesn't really apply to the K–12 years. How wrong they are. Dr. Robert Morgan of Florida State University used ISD methods to restructure the Korean public school system and, as a result, students achieved breakthroughs in learning starting in the 1970s. In fact, Korea, which previously had a low performance like the United States at international competitions, rose to first or second place in most subjects. Korea restructured its school system over an eight-year period.[5] ISD methods are often used for lessons for special education and gifted students alike. In future years,

ISD needs to be the foundation of learning systems that are utilized in mainstream classrooms.

In the 1950s, Dr. Don H. Parker of Science Research Associates (SRA) reinvented similar concepts of instructional design when he produced the SRA Reading Laboratory Series. This program, which is used in many parochial and some public schools, successfully taught reading, arithmetic, and science. These high-quality, self-study materials enabled nuns and teachers to have 40 to 50 students in their classrooms with more than 90 percent successful learners. These course materials, an early version of a successful learning system, were later used by millions of students in 62 countries.

Dr. John Chubb is the Chief Education Officer of the Edison Schools. He has written that the hardest part of large-scale school improvement is not school design; it is systems design. He is referring to the selection, modification, and/or development of learning systems that are absolutely essential for every school district and every school management company. Systems design and systems integration are two important skills that must be mastered within the district offices and the schools. Our country needs outstanding learning systems in our schools in order to achieve the eight national education goals by the year 2010.

Learning systems are essential for both group and individual learning. They are even more essential for individual learning because each student is on a different plan for learning. Differentiating instruction sounds fine, but this method of teaching is easier to describe than it is to implement. Many educators are stressing the concept that "one size doesn't fit all students." This may be true, but most teachers struggle to practice differentiated instruction without a structured learning system. Flexible grouping is usually essential.[6]

After reviewing hundreds of courses, a simple conclusion emerges. Whenever an education program has a high drop-out rate or a large percentage of students not at grade level, there is close to a 100-percent chance that the principles of ISD have not been utilized. On the other hand, when students must learn a lesson that is a life-or-death situation (e.g., nuclear power employee, pilot training, or weapon systems), ISD methods were probably used to ensure that 100 percent of the students are successful learners and performers. Perhaps educating children is not a life-and-death situation, but it is fundamentally wrong to damage millions of K–12 students with inconsistent teaching and substandard course materials.

## INTERACTIVE TUTORING

For centuries, educators have known that a very effective way to teach a lesson is through "tutoring," the interaction between a teacher and a student. Tutoring also works well with two or three students per teacher, but it is very expensive to devote one teacher to just one to three students. Tutoring is essential, however, for students who fall behind in their lessons, which is a major problem in today's schools. Unfortunately, teachers simply do not have the time to be effective tutors.

As mentioned in Chapter 5, this problem has been solved by more than 1,000 schools in 41 states, thanks to a volunteer tutoring system developed in 1971 by William E. (Bill) Gibbons called Help One Student To Succeed (HOSTS). In this system, more than 100,000 volunteer tutors work with thousands of students to improve reading, writing, vocabulary, and mathematics skills. These tutors also help prepare preschool and kindergarten children for the first grade. The system even features a Spanish Readiness program. The learning system also includes highly structured tutoring guidelines, games, workbooks, audiotapes, videotapes, theme books, kits, and courseware on CD-ROMs. Each student has an individualized learning plan, and the time to learn is flexible. HOSTS has served more than 1 million students, so it is a proven system with excellent results.[7]

Other schools and home schooling sites use personal computers as a low-cost interactive tutoring system. Almost all K–12 lessons are now available on courseware CD-ROMs or on the Internet. Millions of children use these systems at home because the lessons are entertaining and educational. Unfortunately, students in inner-city schools rarely have a computer at home. Therefore, inner-city schools need multimedia computers, and these computers must be used as interactive tutoring systems. Children like to work with computer tutoring systems because they reward their successes and never criticize their mistakes. Again, no one proceeds to Lesson Two until they learn Lesson One. Therefore, no one gets behind, fears asking a "dumb" question, or feels lost. Learning becomes fun.

## MULTIPLE INTELLIGENCE IN LEARNING SYSTEMS

In 1985, the Harvard Graduate School of Education's Howard Gardner published a book called *Frames of Mind*, which concluded that humans learn by different methods because they have multiple intelligences. Originally, Gardner said there were seven intelligences, but he recently added an eighth.[8] Gardner tells us that, as individuals, we do not have the same strength in each intelligence area, so each of us learns differently.

*The eight intelligence areas are as follows:*

1. Linguistic
2. Logical-Mathematical
3. Spatial (graphics)
4. Bodily-Kinesthetic (physical)
5. Musical
6. Interpersonal (learning with others)

7. Intrapersonal (oneself)
8. Naturalist.

In addition, considerable work is being done on brain research. Dr. Mel Levine, a pediatrician, has done research in the area and he is training teachers to analyze how students learn. This important new information will help educators who develop curriculum, courses, courseware, textbooks, audiotapes, videotapes, workbooks, and learning systems. Needless to say, most classroom teachers struggle to keep up with all of the new information from various education research projects. It is even more challenging for them to design or modify lesson plans with these new teaching methods because they simply do not have the time. They often do some patching of their plans, but classroom teachers are rarely able to utilize all of this important information.

With funding from IBM, the late Dr. John Henry Martin, a former teacher, principal, and superintendent of schools in the New York City area, developed a learning system called "Writing To Read." It was used in more than 7,000 elementary schools in the United States as well as several other countries.[9] This learning system was also used by millions of students in many inner-city schools. Dr. Martin designed his program so that students would learn at five stations, which provided different learning methods. He knew that "one size" did not fit all students, so his learning system accommodated different learning styles. Two of the stations utilized personal computers as interactive tutors, with one focused on learning phonics. Like other learning systems, "Writing to Read" achieved its success by applying learning theory to the design of educational learning systems. It also effectively utilized the expanding research in the fields of artificial intelligence, cognitive psychology, and instructional design. The Sequoyah Literacy System is the follow-up work to the pioneering efforts that the late Dr. John Henry Martin developed.[10] This new learning system provides language arts instruction that integrates reading, writing (composition), spelling, speaking, listening, and keyboarding. It builds on the oral language skills (English or Spanish) that each child brings to the classroom. Learning systems in general are based on the accepted results of education research studies. Today, however, the gap is widening between research in learning and its application in the classroom.

Many outstanding learning systems use multimedia (videotapes and/or audiotapes with computers) to enliven certain lessons. Research tells instructional designers that pictures and graphics enhance the learning process and increase lesson retention. Videotapes are often more efficient and effective than field trips. Thousands of videotapes are available to help instructional designers and teachers communicate lessons. Courseware companies, which are often referred to as the "edutainment" industry, are using ISD methods and multimedia computer technology to enable millions of children to learn many of their K–12 lessons through the use of a personal computer. The Internet has also become an effective delivery system for lessons.

Research also tells instructional designers that children learn faster when they work in groups, a concept that is termed "cooperative learning." Children learn from each other when they work together on an exercise or question. This "positive interdependence" is a key characteristic of a learner-centered learning system. The learning system must allow some flexibility in the time students have to complete the lesson. After all, if all students must learn the lesson, the variable must be time. In the past, time was fixed and the number of students learning the lesson correctly was the variable.[11]

## PROFESSIONAL DEVELOPMENT FOR TEACHING

Remember that one great advantage of learning systems is their consistent delivery of lessons, which is a benefit that can ultimately help all teachers to perform successfully. When all teachers perform successfully, then, and only then, is it reasonable to expect all students to be successful, as previously stated. Teachers must be like airplane pilots in that they are all required to be successful.

A well-designed learning system has teaching guides based on input from master teachers, subject matter experts, and instructional designers. The standardized lesson plans are provided and tied directly into all of the new high-quality course materials and state standards. Teachers can add a layer of creativity to the lesson plan and teaching guide, but the essential lessons and messages to achieve learning standards must still be taught. The built-in assessment system will quickly identify inappropriate teaching methods as well as poor-performing students. The assessment system also highlights any essential lessons that were not taught, which is another major problem in schools today.

*A well-designed professional development program must have the following three important elements:*

1. *Content Knowledge.* Every teacher who utilizes the learning system must have subject matter knowledge that is clearly defined by a well-designed learning system. This eliminates the problem of whether a teacher has a degree or advanced course in a subject. The content can be delivered with reading assignments, exercises, assessments, and workshop sessions.
2. *Teaching and Class Management Skills.* Videotapes of experienced teachers actually using the learning system can be most effective to communicate "best practices." This instruction can be supplemented with real-life stories from experienced teachers. Well-constructed teaching guides also enable teachers to perform the complete job of teaching the lessons.

3. ***Integrated Curriculum Learning Standards.*** Teachers must understand that they are part of a K–12 team that educates a student over a 13-year period. If the learning system is not fully implemented, students cannot be successful on the end-of-year tests and state assessments, or be prepared to learn in the next grade. Therefore, teachers within a grade must be teaching the same lessons to the same learning objectives. All teachers in elementary schools that feed a middle school must have consistent teaching. Likewise, all teachers in the middle schools must achieve all of the learning objectives for students who will eventually go to a high school.

A mentor, principal, or representative from the office of the director of curriculum should carefully supervise the implementation of new learning systems and the new teachers using the learning systems for the first time.

## MEASUREMENT AND MANAGEMENT OF LEARNING

Throughout the K–12 years it is important for a school, teacher, and student to know that every lesson is being learned in sequence within the curriculum for each grade. Learning must not only be measured, but equally important, learning must be managed. If a student does not master the lesson, it is important to reteach the lesson or provide tutoring. This approach is the only way students are able to stay at grade level. Therefore, end-of-school assessments are appropriate only as a gateway to tell if a student is qualified to be promoted to the next grade. Assessments at the end of the fourth, eighth, and twelfth grades record only how well a student has done for four years but do not enable a teacher to maintain a student at grade level.

Learning systems use frequent assessments to ensure that students do not proceed to Lesson Two until they fully understand Lesson One. No social promotion is allowed with learning systems. Assessments are much like merit badge assessments in scouting. Students want to do the exercise and take tests to show how much they have learned. Assessments may consist of simple exercises in a workbook, questions at the end of a chapter, a portfolio of work, or a test at the end of a lesson.

Both teachers and students will feel good when they know that the goal in a class using a learning system is to have all students become successful learners. There is no intent to sort or select students into above average, average, or below average. Students also know that if they do not understand the key points of a lesson, they will receive immediate feedback and tutoring until they do learn the lesson. Dr. Robert Corrigan, an education consultant, described this process as climbing a learning ladder (on which each rung is a lesson) to achieve predictable success for the learners.

*Students develop positive self-esteem because they can say the following key statements:*

1. I can do it.
2. I did it successfully.
3. I can do it again.

Equally important is the fact that if students are able to complete the lesson ahead of time, they can either help other students through cooperative learning and/or be given enrichment lessons that result in an "A" grade.

Learning systems teach to the learning objectives of a lesson. There is no reason to "teach to the tests" in a well-designed learning system. Good curriculum-based tests, based on good content standards, will be part of good learning systems. This structure eliminates the need to use standardized achievement tests such as the Stanford Achievement Test. Measurement reports enable teachers to work with parents, the director of curriculum, and their principal when they encounter a difficult learning situation with a student. It is a team effort to maintain each student at grade level.

John Bishop of Cornell University has shown that educational systems that require content standards and use curriculum-based tests to determine whether the curriculum has been learned greatly improve achievement for all students, including those from less-advantaged backgrounds.[12] Curriculum-based tests should be approved by the state departments of education and the school districts that developed the learning standards.

Dr. Lauren Resnick, Director of Learning Research and Development at the University of Pittsburgh, wrote an article in *Education Week* on June 16, 1999, entitled "Making America Smarter: A Century's Assumptions About Innate Ability Give Way to a Belief in the Power of Effort." In the article, Dr. Resnick stated:

> In experimental programs and in practical school reforms, we are seeing that students who, over an extended period of time are treated as if they are intelligent, actually became so. If they are taught demanding content, and are expected to explain and find connections as well as memorize and repeat, they learn more and learn more quickly. They think of themselves as learners. Intelligence is incremental. People can get smart. When people think this way, they tend to invest energy to learn something new or to increase their understanding and mastery. As we approach a new century, it is increasingly evident that the educational methods we have been using for the past 70 years no longer suffice.[13]

Learning systems and curriculum-based tests that are aligned with learning standards are essential so that more than 90 percent of students will be at grade level in almost every public school.

## CLOSING THE ACHIEVEMENT GAP WITH MINORITIES

In a recent study conducted by the U. S. Department of Education, it was disclosed that test scores of black and white students that had narrowed throughout the 1980s had widened from 1990 to 1999. Shockingly, the average black 17-year-old reads only as well as the average white 13-year-old. A major reversal of the gains made over the past two decades appears to have occurred.[14] Many people are guessing about why this situation has happened, but it certainly cannot be because of a decline in funding or a lower number of students in Head Start or larger class sizes. All of these so-called deficiencies of the past have been corrected.

If educators would examine the deficiencies in the classroom that are outlined in Chapter 3 and at the beginning of this chapter, they would see that these issues are where the problem lies. Until the public schools implement an integrated curriculum aligned to the learning standards and utilize learning systems with curriculum-based assessments, the gap will not be closed because minorities simply do not have the type of schools they need to be successful.

Even in affluent suburbs such as Shaker Heights (outside of Cleveland), Evanston (outside of Chicago), and similar schools, children of successful college-educated, minority parents are not doing as well as would be expected. Once again, students and parents are being blamed for poor performance. Some people argue that a peer culture exists in which African Americans ridicule top-performing students as "acting white." Some researchers also believe that the difference may be in parenting. Anecdotal evidence suggests that white parents may interact with their young children in ways that support school success.[15] It is hard to believe that successful African American parents do not support school success.

Too many educators forget how well African Americans do in athletic contests when the rules of the game are the same for all players and a scoreboard is used. Consistent teaching through validated learning systems will close the gap. The same will happen with Latin Americans. The White House held a strategy session on June 15, 2000, to focus on closing the achievement gaps for Hispanic students. Five goals were established for this decade. Now students and teachers need the means to reach those goals.[16] It is hoped that educators will finally implement learning systems. Every other program has been tried over the years, but in this decade the focus should be on validated learning systems.

One piece of good news is that all races are taking more challenging courses, with Asian Americans serving as leaders in this area.[17] New programs are being implemented for gifted children of minorities. At inner-city schools, gifted children may require a separate curriculum, learning systems, and specialized teachers until the student learning problems in the urban school districts are resolved.

In 1999, Latin Americans, Asian Americans, and African Americans became the majority population in California, which is the largest state in the United States. With nearly 17 million people in the so-called minority populations of California, residents of the state will demand and vote for political leaders who will fix the California public school system. Their children are not going to attend low-performing schools for another decade. This situation will occur in most of our large states in the near future.

## WILL TEACHERS ACCEPT LEARNING SYSTEMS?

Some educators are concerned about the dangers of centralized school reform.[18] In the old paradigm of minimum structure and social promotion, no reasons or motivation were provided for teachers to accept learning systems. They had the academic freedom to teach any lesson using any method and with any course materials. Only a little concern was voiced in the community about whether the students learned the lessons because there were few assessments and no agreed-upon curriculum. Besides, every student was promoted to the next grade at year end.

Now teachers know that students learn very little in some classrooms. In other classrooms, students learn about half of what they should accomplish. And in some other classrooms, students receive all of the lessons and learn their lessons. Everyone knows that becoming a successful teacher requires a steep learning curve that takes several years of effort. Many mistakes are made by beginning teachers that damage millions of students, which is one reason why so many students are behind in grade level. Inconsistent teaching is one of the fundamental problems in schools today, and it is a very big problem in low-performing schools. How does this problem of inconsistent teaching get resolved? Good teachers know that more structure and measurements are needed. Teachers must be like professional musicians: They need to have the same sheet music (i.e., curriculum and lesson plans) if they want to have an integrated curriculum and lessons that enable their students to be successful learners in each grade. Good teachers also know how much time, effort, and funds must be invested in the development of a successful learning system. Therefore, they will accept learning systems if students arrive in their classroom at grade level, ready to work hard on the lessons required for another school year.

New teachers welcome learning systems because it makes them more success-ful in their first years of teaching compared to struggling several years to master the teaching of their subjects. It is inconceivable that new teachers are sent into inner-city school classrooms to "sink or swim" without learning systems. Many of these teachers fail within one or two years. Experienced teachers, who have many students in their classes who are behind in their lessons, will embrace learning systems because they will soon tire of being rated as low-performing teachers in low-performing schools.

Some teachers sincerely believe that their teaching methods are superior to the methods used in the learning system. In these situations, the principal and director of curriculum should observe these methods to determine if they are superior. If so, the learning system should be enhanced with the better methods. Every teacher should have the academic freedom to use any teaching methods as long as more than 90 percent of their students are successful learners based on the assessment systems that support the learning standards from the state department of education and the local school district. There is even greater inconsistency in teaching when the methods of experienced teachers are analyzed based on the evaluation made for candidates at the National Board for Professional Teaching Standards.

Learning systems have another big advantage for most teachers. The teaching guides (lesson plans), course materials, and student exercises are all developed. This approach is far different from expecting a classroom teacher to create outstanding lesson plans and course materials in the evenings and/or weekends. Teachers need to focus only on successful implementation of the learning system, not development. This structure enables teachers to have a reasonable workload and an embraceable responsibility. "Ease of use" is a common term used to describe successful learning systems.

An associate research scientist at the Education Testing Service, Harold H. Wenglinsky, published a report, "How Teaching Matters: Bringing the Classroom Back into Discussions of Teacher Quality." He studied 15,000 National Assessment of Educational Progress (NAEP) scores in the subjects of mathematics and science. Then he sent questionnaires to the student test-takers, their teachers, and principals to determine what methods of teaching were used. He stated that the study shows that not only do teachers matter most, but how they teach matters most.[19] What they did in the classroom had a major impact on student performance. Once again, inconsistent teaching is a big factor and the impact is greater on students who are only slightly motivated to learn or are turned off by school. The report made one strong recommendation: Improve teaching through high-quality professional development. To achieve a 90 percent goal of successful learners, teachers will need both high-quality learning systems and professional development.

Some teachers will evolve from being a classroom teacher to a developer of learning systems. These positions are like the composer of music. The jobs will provide great satisfaction as well as increased opportunities for additional compensation. The entire concept of learning systems will improve the career paths of teachers, as well as their compensation, because success brings rewards.

Some educators will still talk about the "good old days" when teachers could close the classroom door and teach anything they wanted and with any method.

Every profession talks about the "good old days," but we all live in a world today of high expectations and quality performance. A new paradigm of learning systems is essential if student learning is to be fixed rather than just improved a little.

The number of Advanced Placement tests taken by high school seniors is growing every year. Every high school in every state must offer Advanced Placement courses because the top-performing students can earn college credits and obtain admittance to good universities and colleges. Learning systems using distance-learning methods will be implemented in one-third to one-half of the high schools. When teachers see how successful learning systems are with top-performing students, they will soon conclude that similar programs could be successful within mainstream classrooms with local teachers.

Teachers are now receiving their master's degrees in education from a few leading-edge colleges of education through distance learning. It is only a matter of time until teachers accept learning systems as the most productive way to teach if the objective is for all students to be successful learners.

When teachers are asked today what is needed to improve student learning, they usually answer that more pay, more training, better parents, and more respect are needed.[20] Someday, they will also say that better learning systems are needed. In the future, teachers will not only accept learning systems, but they will also apply intense pressure on school administrators and boards of education to supply them with the finest learning systems available in the marketplace.

## WHAT ARE THE CONSEQUENCES FOR NOT USING LEARNING SYSTEMS?

New Jersey invests more money than almost any other state in their public schools. Researchers at Rutgers University found that the four-year-old academic standards have started to influence what is taught in mathematics and science classes throughout New Jersey, but they have yet to significantly alter how teachers teach the subjects. New Jersey officials say that the state is still in the early stages of its standards-based improvement program and that change will be incremental.[21] At this pace, change will take decades because no sense of urgency is present. Learning systems could greatly accelerate the pace.

States are trying to stop the large increases in resignation from teachers who give up. Some pundits go so far as to say that "education is a profession that eats its young teachers."[22] One teacher wrote that the two most practical ways experienced teachers can help new teachers are through chance meetings in the hallways and through scheduled discussion during common preparation times, which rarely occur.[23] No wonder new teachers leave the profession within a few years. They need learning systems to survive.

Many mathematics and science teachers are leaving the profession. The main reason for their leaving is job dissatisfaction. Thirty-two percent of teachers with one to three years of experience and 37 percent of those with four to six years in the classroom are thinking about leaving their teaching jobs.[24] Despite these facts, school systems only tinker with the existing teaching and learning methods. Teaching mathematics and science to students who often are one or several grades behind provides very little job satisfaction.

Job satisfaction will further decline if the means to reach the learning standards are not soon realized in most urban school districts. The entire standards movement is "at risk" because administrators cannot provide a vision to teachers on how they will eventually achieve success. People like Alfie Kohn want to enlist masses of teachers to help turn back the reform they claim is destroying great schools.[25] This movement will condemn teachers and administrators to the terrible working conditions that now exist and to a complete loss of respect as scores on accountability systems drop in future years. He should be asking teachers to have a mass protest to demand outstanding and validated learning systems.

Finally, if standards-based learning systems are not implemented, political and business leaders will cease to support annual increases in school budgets. And, perhaps most important, learning can be measured without learning systems, but it cannot be managed. This means that administrators cannot be real leaders of learning without learning systems, so inconsistent teaching will remain in the system no matter whether it is a small, intermediate, or large school district. At inner-city schools, the number of successful learners at grade level will rarely be above 50 percent, and top-performing schools will no doubt peak at 80 percent, which is a long way from the concept that all students can be successful learners.[26]

Management is often thought of as a negative term in education, but all successful organizations have outstanding management systems for their major processes. Student learning is a major process in schools, and management means being able to quickly identify students who are falling behind in learning so corrective action can be taken.

## LEARNING SYSTEMS ARE CRITICAL TO SUCCESS IN
## MOST CLASSROOMS

Some top-performing school districts can continue to match the "good" teachers with the "good" students because 60 to 75 percent of those students are successful learners who are at grade level. The successful teachers with the successful students may not have any desire to change their methods. Parents do not really want to see great change either in these public schools because their children are successful learners who go on to attend top institutions of higher learning. Later, these same children are offered the best entry-level jobs in government agencies, not-for-profit organizations, and commercial companies; however, even the best schools need learning systems for the 25 percent or more students who are turned off by school and who are not at grade level. The top-performing schools will improve by having all students achieving their learning objectives, which is the great benefit of this systems approach to learning.

It is important that educators use learning systems with the entire student body at inner-city schools, not just with special education and at-risk students. Inner-city schools will not achieve breakthroughs in student learning until outstanding learning systems are implemented. Superior teachers with motivated, superior students can do everything that a learning system does, but there are very few superior teachers and students at inner-city schools. New and inexperienced teachers need help, and merely asking for "better teaching" is not going to achieve a substantial increase in student learning. It is foolish to rely on "heroic" teachers or super principals when they simply are not the norm in urban schools. Teachers need new tools and support, which are provided in learning systems.

Learning systems also minimize the amount of time it takes to teach a lesson, which is a vital benefit when new lessons need to be inserted into the curriculum. Projects and field trips can also be incorporated into learning systems, as long as they achieve documented learning objectives. Child care activities must be replaced by learning sessions.

Several articles have appeared in education journals, *Education Week*, and business magazines concerning how E-Learning will transform education and the future wired classroom. What these articles fail to tell readers is that no real breakthroughs will occur in learning unless the latest developments in technology are combined with validated design methods. Some major improvements in learning can take place, but it takes the complete learning system to improve the entire school system.

Unfortunately, many educators want to continue living in the world of almost no structure and few assessments. They make speeches and write articles empha-sizing how each teacher must customize learning for each student based on the individual needs of a local school and students. This theory sounds well-meaning until one realizes that this lack of structure and little management results in failure rates between 25 and 75 percent. It means that teachers and administrators within inner-city schools must continue to work in a "no-win" situation. Frankly, it takes little talent to talk about the "good old days." Educators who want to maintain the status quo should remember the old saying, "If you keep doing what you have always done, you will keep getting the same results." It takes a lot of talent, knowledge, and experience to create an action plan for achieving the learning standards being established across our nation. It is time to move on to an education system that creates nothing but successful learners. Our schools must be learning institutions, not child care centers where a little learning takes place. More and more people are saying that good teaching makes the difference. How does the

American public school system greatly improve the effectiveness of teaching in a few short years? The answer lies in implementing learning systems.

In the 1930s, Dr. Robert Hutchins, president of the University of Chicago, said, "Perhaps the greatest idea America has given to the world is the idea of education for all children. The world is entitled to know whether this idea means that everybody can be educated, or that everybody must just sit in school. I believe that everybody can be educated."[27] Learning systems will enable Dr. Hutchins' vision to be realized nearly 80 years later.

In the next chapter, development and affordability of learning systems will be reviewed. Learning systems are not a quick-fix tactical solution. They are a new strategic direction that will achieve breakthroughs in student learning. Together with an integrated curriculum, they can eliminate the 10 major learning problems that exist in today's classroom, which were discussed in Chapter 3 and listed again at the beginning of this chapter.

---

**NOTES**

1. R. Reeves, Presentation at Rancho Bernardo to the Conservation Order of Good Environment (COGE) organization, San Diego, CA, June 2000.

2. Before the Board, "Kids Find School Boring," *American School Board Journal*, March 2000, 12.

3. S. Black, "Building a Better Teacher," *American School Board Journal*, April 1999, 51.

4. R. Zemke, "Toward a Science of Training," *Training*, July 1999, 28, 32–36.

5. R. Branson, *Robert Marion Morgan* (Tallahassee, FL: 30th Anniversary FSU Learning Systems Institute, June 1999), 5–12.

6. S. Willis and Z. Mann, "Differentiating Instruction," *ASCD Curriculum*, Winter 2000, 1–7.

7. B. Gibbons, *How HOSTS Works* (Dallas, TX: Help One Student To Succeed, June 1999), 3.

8. K. Checkly, *The First Seven and the Eighth* (Alexandria, VA: Association of Supervision and Curriculum Development, September 1997), 8–13.

9. S. Chaap, "Writing To Read: A Program for Literacy," *Technology In Education Journal*, May 1989, 56–59.

10. D. Winter, Interview Sequoyah, August 2000.

11. L. Easton, "If Standards Are Absolute, Time Must Be a Variable," *Education Week*, 12 April, 2000, 50, 52.

12. E. Hirsch, "The Tests We Need: And Why We Don't Quite Have Them," *Education Week*, 2 February, 2000, 41, 64.

13. L. Resnick, "Making America Smarter: A Century's Assumptions about Innate Ability Give Way to a Belief in the Power of Effort," *Education Week*, 16 June, 1999, 38–40.

14. K. Zernike, "Gap Grows between Test Scores of White, Black Kids," *New York Times News Service, San Diego Union-Tribune,* 25 August, 2000, A1, A22.

15. D. Viadero, "Even in Well-Off Suburbs, Minority Achievement Lags," *Education Week,* 15 March, 2000, 20–22.

16. J. Rosenthal, "White House Strategy Session Focuses on Hispanic Student Achievement," *Technology and Learning Journal,* August 2000, 18.

17. U. S. Department of Education, "High School Students Are Taking More Challenging Courses," *American School Board Journal,* March 2000, 12.

18. The Editor's Page, "First Do No Harm," *Phi Delta Kappan,* June 2000, 722.

19. J. Blair, "ETS Study Links Effective Teaching Methods to Test Score Gains," *Education Week,* 25 October 2000, 24-25.

20. A. McQueen, "Teacher of Year Urges More Pay, More Training, More Respect," *San Diego Union-Tribune,* 10 May, 2000, A3.

21. McQueen, "Teacher of Year."

22. M. Delgado, "Lifesaving 101: How a Veteran Teacher Can Help a Beginner," *ASCD Educational Leadership,* May 1999, 27–28.

23. Delgado, "Lifesaving 101."

24. D. Hoff, "Science Teachers' Turnover, Dissatisfaction High, Survey Finds," *Education Week,* 19 April, 2000, 5.

25. D. Lindsay, "Contest," *Education Week,* 5 April, 2000, 30–37.

26. Estimate by author.

27. D. Kearns and J. Harvey, *A Legacy of Learning* (Washington, DC: Brookings Institute Press, 2000), 20.

# CHAPTER 10

# Development and Affordability of Learning Systems

Irving Harris, the well-known business executive, philanthropist, and child advocate, tells a parable about people picnicking beside a river.[1] Suddenly, they see several children being carried down the river by the swift current. People jump into the river and try to save as many of the children as they can, but many drowning children keep being carried with the current, and the rescuers can save only a few. Finally, a couple of people decide to go up the river to see why so many children are falling into the river. Only then, by fixing the problem at the top of the river, could the crisis be eliminated.

In the school reform movement, almost everyone is involved in the process of saving students at the bottom of the river—the ones who are one or more grades behind in learning their lessons. Students are lost and drowning. Very few educators are working full time at the top of the river to ensure that students will not fall behind, get lost, and give up on their schooling. In the past, when most school districts lacked goals, integrated curricula, and assessment systems tied to the state and local learning standards, there was no great motivation to investigate the concept of using learning systems. It is astonishing how much research and development has been conducted since 1983 with schools having so few learning standards. In the next few years, a flurry of activity will ensue as more educators focus on the design, development, validation, and selection of learning systems to eliminate the large number of students failing during their K–12 years.

## PERSONNEL REQUIRED FOR LEARNING SYSTEM DEVELOPMENT

It's important to remember that secretaries did not invent or develop word processing systems; sailors and junior officers did not invent nuclear submarines; pilots did not invent the jet engine or the 747; and accountants did not create software for spreadsheets. Therefore, it's no surprise that classroom teachers do not develop most learning systems. As stated previously, the development of learning systems requires months and sometimes years of full-time effort by many talented people. Decades ago, an inventor working alone would sometimes make a great discovery such as the telephone, a personal computer, or even a better razor. But in today's complex world, nearly all great inventions require a team of people who have specialized knowledge and skills. This need for a team effort is also true of learning systems. Years ago, a single individual (e.g., a teacher, instructional designer, professor of education, or retired administrator) would create a learning system that was a giant step forward for student learning. In future years, most learning systems will be developed by a team of people.

*The following roles are associated with a typical development team (keep in mind that one individual may perform two or three roles):*

- Project Director
- Master Teachers (experts in teaching methods)
- Subject Matter Experts
- Instructional Designers
- Professional Writers
- Graphic Specialists
- Programmers (using authoring systems)
- Assessment Experts.

Clearly, one teacher should not be expected to have all the knowledge, experience, and skills required to fulfill all of these roles. Even if one teacher did have all of the knowledge for developing learning systems, the task cannot be accomplished in evening hours or on weekends. Remember, the challenge is to develop a high-quality learning system that will enable more than 90 percent of all students from a variety of backgrounds to learn the lessons and acquire the skills.

Some "homegrown" learning systems developed by groups of experienced teachers over the summer months are a major improvement compared to the traditional lesson plans. These local learning systems should be compared to the commercially available systems on the basis of student learning, price, teacher acceptance, and student reaction. If the local learning system has more than 90 percent of the students as successful learners, and it is well accepted by both teachers and learners, then the school or school district should continue to use the learning system.

## WHO WILL DEVELOP LEARNING SYSTEMS?

Many companies and organizations devote their time and resources exclusively to developing learning systems for K–12 schools. One of the first companies to develop professional K–12 learning systems was a group of educators from Provo, Utah, called Wicat Systems, Inc. They were bought by Jostens Learning of San Diego in the late 1980s, which provided Jostens with 60 percent of the market share for integrated learning systems.[2] Recently, Jostens has changed its name to CompassLearning, and they employ more than 500 people to develop and implement learning systems in thousands of schools across the country. This company has a curriculum planning program that integrates standards-based curriculum with assessments that are based on the lessons in the courses. The subject matter learning systems are based on the input of numerous teachers over many years. More than 20,000 schools serving nearly 14 million students use the more than 7,000 hours of instruction in CompassLearning's various learning systems.[3]

The Computer Curriculum Corporation (CCC), which was established in 1967 by Stanford University's Dr. Patrick Suppes and Dr. Richard Atkinson, created a product in 1970 for mathematics that ran on mainframe computers. At about the same time, the Chief Executive Officer of Control Data Corporation (CDC) funded the development of the Plato system using CDC mainframe computers. Mainframes and national network costs proved to be too expensive, but they validated the concept of interactive tutoring. The Plato system with 37 years of experience has been redesigned for personal computers and modern networks.

In the 1980s and 1990s, color graphics and low-cost personal computers provided a significant breakthrough in both quality and costs. CD-ROMs were another breakthrough in that decade. CCC now has more than 900 employees, many of whom are former teachers. Their learning systems have been used by more than 10 million students, and their revenues exceed $200 million. CCC learning systems have been installed in more than 20,000 schools around the world, including the United States, Canada, Japan, the United Kingdom, Australia, and New Zealand. They have trained more than 100,000 teachers in a single year on how to implement their learning systems successfully. They now offer more than 50 courses/titles in reading/language arts, mathematics, science, life skills, and English as a Second Language (ESL)/bilingual. Last but not least, their learning systems have been approved by such groups as the National Council of Teachers of Mathematics (NCTM), the International Reading Association (IRA), the National Council of Teachers of English (NCTE), and the National Science Teachers Association (NSTA).[4]

Other companies, such as NovaNet, SkillsBank, Wasatch, Accelerated Math, and Curriculum Associates, also develop learning systems. Riverdeep Interactive Learning has emerged in recent years. They claim to have a world-class curricula with powerful assessment tools that serve more than 1 million students in more than 500 schools.[5]

All of the learning system companies have a long list of success stories about how their systems have increased student learning and test results. Many of them also have conducted some research showing why their learning systems are effective. This applied research is worth reading.

Another source for basic learning systems is the Edutainment Catalog, which lists more than 20 companies that are producing hundreds of courses for home computers. This multi-million-dollar business once again validates the concept that tutoring with interactive personal computers is a successful practice.

*Prominent names in this field include:*

- Broderbrund (a branch of Learning Company)
- Cognitive Technologies Corporation
- Creative Wonders
- DK Multimedia
- Edmark/IBM (Crayola series)
- Havas Interactive
- Knowledge Adventure
- The Learning Company
- Learning Curve (Jump Start Series)
- Microsoft
- National Geographic Society
- Ohio Distinctive Software
- Scholastic.

The Association for Supervision and Curriculum Development (ASCD) publishes an annual report on the highest-rated software and multimedia courseware with the addresses of all the vendors. The ASCD also provides many documents and videotapes that can be utilized in the classroom.

The Jump Start series (preschool to sixth grade) has succeeded because of the continuity it gives students and the way it packages lessons by grade. The Learning Company and other corporations are also using this strategy. Most of these programs are aimed at a certain age level and a specific subject. As mentioned previously, one of this field's early successes was "Where in the World is Carmen Sandiego?" a program used by many parents and geography teachers. Several outstanding encyclopedia programs are also available. Edutainment companies could quickly shift their efforts to produce learning systems for public schools once a real market for such a product opened up. In the meantime, they'll serve parents and grandparents of successful learners who study at home in order to improve their performance at school and the home schooling market.

## NEW AMERICAN SCHOOLS

The New American Schools Corporation (NAS) is another learning systems source that was discussed in Chapter 5. NAS is a not-for-profit, nonpartisan organization that was founded in 1991 by business leaders who wanted to improve the quality of this country's public schools. They were driven by one powerful mission: To assist schools in helping large numbers of students achieve at high levels. NAS invested more than $100 million into several Design Teams during the 1990s. These teams were selected from nearly 700 proposals that featured innovative, cost-effective, and academically rigorous ideas for improving American schools.[6]

NAS Design Teams operate under the principle that no school should have to start from scratch when it comes to improving teaching and learning. These teams package the best research and practices in usable and practical ways and then combine the results with concrete assistance, tools, and materials to help teachers and administrators strengthen their schools. NAS calls this process "designed-based assistance." NAS designs have been implemented in more than 2,000 schools.[7] Since 1991, the RAND Corporation, serving as the independent evaluator of the NAS effort, has released periodic summaries of its findings on the initiative's implementation and effectiveness. For more information on NAS designs, school district personnel should read the 1998 publication "Blueprints for School Success: A Guide to New American Schools Designs" by the Education Research Service (ERS)[8] and the 1999 publication "Working Toward Excellence" by NAS.[9]

One of the NAS designs is called "Roots and Wings." The "roots" portion is derived from the widely used "Success for All" program, which focuses on language arts for elementary grades and features tutoring, family support, and other program elements. "Wings" components include a mathematics program and an integrated social studies/science program. Roots and Wings guarantees that every child will progress successfully through the elementary grades. This "off-the-shelf" program has comprehensively restructured children's education from pre-kindergarten to age 11. Its goal is to ensure that every child has a firm foundation in the knowledge and skills needed to succeed in today's world and to progress to higher-order learning and knowledge integration. Roots and Wings enables every student to meet world-class standards. This learning system is being used now in nearly 2,000 schools. Most of these schools are Title I institutions, which means they serve disadvantaged students with the help of federal funding.[10]

Success for All was originally developed in 1986 by Dr. Robert Slavin at Johns Hopkins University in Baltimore. More than 270 employees now work at the not-for-profit Success for All Foundation. Like other successful learning systems,

Success for All course materials are custom designed to achieve learning objectives. Tutoring is applied as soon as a student fails an assessment. Students also learn in teams because Dr. Slavin believes positive peer pressure is as potent as teacher approval. The program proves that students learn if the learning system is properly implemented. Some teachers believe they lose their academic freedom because these programs clearly define how to teach; however, these programs eliminate the problems of inconsistent teaching.

In a front-page article in the July 19, 1999 *Wall Street Journal*, Dr. Slavin spoke bluntly about the failure of other programs. He believes the problem with most of them is that they depend on the whims of individual teachers who may have received their training any time in the past 40 years and who've been influenced by too many pedagogical ideas. In most cases, he stated, "Teachers just layer on different interventions," making it hard to see what actually works. It's essentially Christmas tree reform. He believes his program has disproved the widely held belief that every school has to develop its own homegrown reform.[11]

Once again, all teachers must be successful if all students are going to be successful learners. Teacher discretion has produced generations of failures in the public schools. Allowing every teacher to decide how and what to teach was feasible when there were no standards and accountability systems. Now that students must achieve state standards, learning systems like Roots and Wings need to be adopted by schools.

## SCHOOLWIDE REFORM MODELS

In 1999, the American Institutes for Research published *An Educator's Guide To Schoolwide Reform*, which evaluated 24 whole-school reform models based on whether they improved student learning. Three of the models were identified as the top performers for improving student learning; Success for All (Roots and Wings) was one of those three successful models.[12] Direct Instruction, which emphasizes the use of carefully planned lessons, designed around a highly specified knowledge base and a well-defined set of skills for each subject, was also recognized as a superior system. This program's original focus was on reading, language, and mathematics, but it has been expanded to include social science, physical science, fact learning, and handwriting. The program serves students from kindergarten through the sixth grade. It has been widely used among low-performing schools in high-poverty areas, and it works for all students. Direct Instruction grew from Dr. Siegfried Engelmann's work on teacher-directed instruction, which he began at the University of Illinois in the late 1960s and later continued at the University of Oregon.[13]

The third program that was recognized for solid improvement in student learning was the Atlanta-based High Schools That Work, which is used in about

1,000 schools across 25 states.[14] This program is an initiative of the Southern Regional Education Board, which provides an enriched curriculum of courses to students who are not planning to attend college, but who want to work in meaningful jobs after graduating from high school. Like Success For All and Direct Instruction, High Schools That Work features customized professional development sessions, special course materials, and frequent assessments that verify whether students are learning the lessons.

Why were the other 21 programs not rated as high on student achievement? In the early 1990s, the goal was to improve schools, which was often translated into making teachers and students feel better about their work. Some schoolwide reform programs simply did not focus on improving student learning, which is clearly the objective today. As a result, some of these programs should be terminated, but other programs just need to be enhanced so they focus more on improving student learning. The concept of schoolwide reform is right on target; the federal government has allocated $145 million to support comprehensive school reform, and the U.S. Department of Education now recognizes that learning systems based on schoolwide reform are the most practical way to achieve breakthroughs in student learning.[15]

NAS estimates that school reform services now total $460 million per year and are growing by as much as 50 percent annually.[16] But this is a slow pace that needs to be accelerated. In 1999, the New Jersey supreme court handed down a ruling that required hundreds of urban schools to implement schoolwide change no later than in school year 2000–2001.[17] This court ruling was a shock to educators.

This pressure from the courts may be far more effective than school busing or decrees on equalized spending. New Jersey has tried busing and socialized budgets without fixing student learning problems in urban schools. Now the focus is on whole-school reform. Many of the schools are implementing the Success for All/Roots and Wings program and other learning systems. Although the selection of learning systems should be a local school district decision, educators must realize that if the pace is too slow, the state and courts may make decisions for them.

## SCHOOL REFORM MODELS THAT ARE AVAILABLE

The Catalog of School Reform Models Web site content as of July 5, 2000 is shown as follows. This list was developed to support schools, districts, states, and others as they proceed with their work under the Obey-Porter Comprehensive School Reform Demonstration program (CSRD), which was passed by the U. S. Congress in 1997.[18] It contains descriptions of 64 models, including 33 whole-school–based models (reading, mathematics, science, and other areas). The list was prepared by the Northwest Regional Education Laboratory (NWREL) with the assistance of the other nine regional educational laboratories and the Education Commission of the States. It presents information as prescribed by the U.S. Department of Education.

**Whole-School Reform Models:**
- Accelerated Schools Project (K–8)
- America's Choice School Design (K–12)
- ATLAS Communities (PreK–12)
- Audrey Cohen College: Purpose-Centered Education (K–12)
- Center for Effective Schools (K–12)
- Child Development Project (K–6)
- Coalition of Essential Schools (formerly 9–12, now K–12)
- Community for Learning (K–12)
- Community Learning Centers (PreK–12)
- Co-NECT Schools (K–12)
- Core Knowledge (K–8)
- Different Ways of Knowing (K–7)
- Direct Instruction (K–6)
- Edison Project (K–12)
- Expeditionary Learning Outward Bound (K–12)
- Foxfire Fund (K–12)
- High Schools That Work (9–12)
- High/Scope Primary Grades Approach to Education (K–3)
- Integrated Thematic Instruction (K–12)
- League of Professional Schools (K–12)
- MicroSociety R (K–8)
- Modern Red Schoolhouse (K–12)
- Montessori (PreK–8)
- Onward to Excellence (K–12)
- Paideia (K–12) ·
- QuESt (K–12)
- Roots and Wings (PreK–6)
- School Development Program (K–12)
- Success for All (PreK–6)
- Talent Development High School with Career Academics (9–12)
- The Learning Network (K–8)

- Urban Learning Centers (PreK–12)
- Ventures Initiative and Focus R System (K–12)

**Skills- and Content-Based Reform Models:**
*Reading/Language Arts*
- Breakthrough to Literacy (K–2)
- Carbo Reading Styles Program (K–8)
- Cooperative Integrated Reading and Composition (2–8)
- Early Intervention in Reading (K–4)
- Exemplary Center for Reading Instruction (K–12)
- First Steps (K–10)
- Junior Great Books (K–12)
- National Writing Project (K–16)
- Reading Recovery (1)
- Strategic Teaching and Reading Project (K–12)

*Mathematics*
- Comprehensive School Mathematics Program (K–6)
- Connected Mathematics Project (6–8)
- Core Plus Mathematics Project/Contemporary Mathematics in Context (9–12)
- Growing with Mathematics (K–5)
- Interactive Mathematics Program (9–12)
- MATH *Connections* (9–12)
- University of Chicago School Mathematics Project (K–12)

*Science*
- Developmental Approaches in Science, Health and Technology (K–6)
- Foundational Approaches in Science Teaching (middle school)
- GALAXY Classroom Science (K–5)
- Iowa Chautauqua Program (K–12)

*Other*
- ACCESS (PreK–1)
- Basic Skill Builders (K–6)
- COMP: Creating Conditions for Learning (K–12)
- Feuerstein's Instrumental Enrichment (4–12)
- HOSTS (Help One Student To Succeed) (K–12)
- HOTS (Higher Order Thinking Skills) (4–8)

- Lightspan Achieve Now (K–6)
- Positive Action (K–12)
- Responsive Classroom R (K–8)
- Success-in-the-Making (K–9).

It is important to remember that the foregoing list is not a "recommended" or "approved" catalog of reform models. Schools and school districts are encouraged to look at other schoolwide programs and learning systems. This list will grow to cover 100 programs because funds are available and there is pressure to fix student learning problems. For example, the Accelerated reader program by Renaissance Learning in Wisconsin Rapids, Wisconsin, is used in 51,000 schools where a test of 5 to 20 questions must be passed after a book is read. In Tiftin, Georgia, this learning system has helped students to be successful readers. Over time, the list will no doubt be consolidated to contain less than 50 programs as the marketplace decides what are the most effective programs.

This list highlights how challenging it is for a school and even a school district to keep up-to-date with all of the research projects and available programs. No teacher would have the time to do this type of work and teach a full class load. The director of curriculum on the district staff should be the executive in charge of researching all available programs. A principal and committee of lead (experienced) teachers could then select from a recommended list of two or three programs.

Several of these organizations do not qualify as having validated learning systems with a proven record of improving student learning. Therefore, a school district must conduct a thorough review of any proposed system. Too many organizations just have a list of "good intentions" for the existing paradigm, which will not be sufficient to achieve real breakthroughs in student learning. Many school districts are carefully selecting parts of various systems to develop their own customized list of learning systems.

NAS has established a blue-ribbon panel with 16 members to help schools evaluate various systems. The goal is to help schools decide which designs and providers would be right for their schools and which are most likely to succeed. Dr. Joe B. Wyatt, Chancellor of Vanderbilt University, is the panel's chairman. The marketplace will ultimately determine success or failure of the learning system, but school districts will learn quickly how to evaluate various models, designs, and learning systems because their success or failure will determine the ranking of the school within a state.

## OTHER SOURCES FOR LEARNING SYSTEMS

What other organizations could develop successful learning systems for preschool and K–12 schools? Book publishers are clearly one source. Learning systems need outstanding workbooks. McGraw-Hill recently purchased Science Research Associates (SRA), and Simon & Schuster purchased CCC in 1990. Prentice Hall and Houghton Mifflin are two other publishers that are doing some development work for learning systems. Textbooks that are not part of validated learning systems may not survive in future years. Decisions such as how much color should be in a textbook will give way to how much instructional design talent has been invested. Publishers have the advantage of a long-term, continuous relationship with public schools, but there's no guarantee that they'll become leaders in the development of proven learning systems.

Colleges of education that have strong programs in education research, instructional design, education technology, and student teaching could create learning systems and provide a steady flow of income to their institutions. This work would enable graduate students to earn funds for college expenses and, at the same time, learn valuable practical lessons on how to develop learning systems. State departments of education could also enter this field. They have large budgets and hundreds of educators working in various programs. Developing learning systems could easily become one of their responsibilities.

Venture capitalists and foundations could fund both not-for-profit and for-profit organizations to create outstanding learning systems. The millions of dollars now being invested in vouchers and campaigns to establish voucher programs would be better spent producing learning systems that enabled more than 90 percent of students to be successful learners in their neighborhood schools.

## PROOF-OF-CONCEPT CASE STUDY

Moss Point, Mississippi has a population of approximately 20,000 people. Located on the Gulf Coast in southern Mississippi, this small town has nearly 6,000 students in nine schools. About 65 percent of the students are African American and 35 percent are European American. More than 40 percent of the parents were high school drop-outs. Approximately 65 percent qualify for free or reduced-price lunches, which is an indication of the community's low socioeconomic level. Moss Point's average per-pupil expenditure is far below the national average; however, the local property tax rate for schools is one of the highest in the state because the town has almost no industry. There is moderate mobility in this community because of construction jobs and economic factors. The town has been severely damaged numerous time by hurricanes and floods. Overall, Moss Point would not be considered an ideal place in which to launch a major schoolwide reform effort, but that's exactly what happened there in the 1980s.[19]

The reform process began in the late 1970s when the town hired Dr. C. Hines Cronin, a man familiar with instructional design methods, as the new superintendent. In 1978, the school board approved the installation of the Systematic Approach for Effectiveness (SAFE), a learner-centered program with components that included instructional design methods and a management system for learning. SAFE was developed by Dr. Robert E. Corrigan and his wife, Betty (a former school teacher), at the Institute for Effective Learning in New Orleans, Louisiana.

Experienced teachers worked with Dr. and Mrs. Corrigan on the systems integration by using successful learning systems and materials that ultimately created Functional Learning Paths (integrated curriculum) for all grades in the K–12 schools. Most of their learning systems were homegrown, but they used existing course materials such as the SAXON mathematics textbooks. For other grades, the development team used the IBM learning systems called Writing to Read and Writing to Write. Computers were used as an instructional tool and for interactive tutoring. Students were tested every two to three weeks with short skill mastery tests. Test results were graded electronically and returned to teachers quickly so they could determine whether each student had mastered the skills. For students who had not achieved this goal, teachers provided further attention to those skills. Principals also received test results, and they met with teachers to develop approaches that would improve student performance. The goal was to ensure that no student would fall behind, get lost, or give up during the K–12 years.

Drop-out rates fell to less than 5 percent in Moss Point. Attendance stopped being a problem because students liked school and succeeded at learning. Discipline problems also decreased. All teachers (i.e., new teachers, those with a few years of experience, and long-term instructors) liked the system because students were successful learners. In this case, administrators were leaders of learning and change. Upon entering a classroom, one quickly determined that the teacher and all students were active participants in the learning process. The principal could describe in detail the lessons and the Functional Learning Path, which demonstrated the working partnership between teachers and principal. From 1978 to 1992, students more than doubled their scores on the standardized achievement tests.

The Mississippi Education Reform Act of 1982 created a State Board of Education, which later established a state mastery test. By the end of the 1980s, Moss Point students were scoring above 90 percent on this test. Please note that this means that more than 90 percent of their students were successful learners.[20] African Americans were as successful as white students, and boys were as successful as girls.

In 1993, the U.S. General Accounting Office (GAO) was asked by the Chairman of the Committee on Education and Labor to conduct a report on systemwide reform.[21] Moss Point was one of the four districts evaluated. In all four situations, a new superintendent was the leader of change, which reinforces the concept that, even in schools, change rolls down from the top. A well-meaning desire to do better is not sufficient; a new paradigm must be created.

Moss Point set an objective to eliminate the two bell curves; all teachers and all students were to be successful. The new paradigm would not only be schoolwide but also systemwide (throughout all schools within the district). The reforms took about eight years, so they were strategic ones, not quick fixes. An integrated curriculum was designed based on what students should know and be able to do at the end of each grade. Learning systems were developed by integrating the best course materials with the best instructional design methods. When teachers were confident that most, if not all, students had learned a lesson, they administered a test on the lesson's learning objectives. Students who had learned the lesson worked on enrichment activities, while the others received corrective instruction and tutoring. The Moss Point school district evolved from a teacher-centered paradigm to a learning-centered paradigm.

Dr. Roger Kaufman, a professor at Florida State University's Learning Systems Institute, made the following comment:

> Since Deming's work, first in Japan and now returned home to the United States, on total quality management and continuous improvement, the sense of defining everything we do and deliver on the chart seems to be getting proper attention. The new paradigm for learning at Moss Point exemplifies total quality management. First, the client is the learner—what the student will have to know and be able to contribute in school and life. Second, everyone, including the learner, is focused on performance, success and quality. Third, a team of educators is built which works together for results, not a splintered, non-integrated fashion. Also, evaluation is used for continuous improvement, not for blaming. Sensible, rational and cost-effective education will and does use the principles of total quality management.[22]

Moss Point received no big grants from foundations. Instead, the superintendent reserved 1 percent of his budget each year to create change. No political leaders or business executives were involved other than the few businesspeople who served on the local board of education. Except for the important instructional design work contributed by Dr. Robert and Betty Corrigan, the entire restructuring was developed and implemented by local administrators and teachers dedicated to achieving breakthroughs in learning. As mentioned previously, leadership by the superintendent, Dr. C. Hines Cronin (now a professor at Delta State University in Mississippi), was absolutely essential. Unfortunately, when outstanding leaders of change leave the office of superintendent, most school districts regress to traditional education methods and practices. This situation happened too often in the past because state school officers were not communicating "best practices" throughout the state. Now that there are standards and accountability systems at the state level, the hope is that state school officers will become leaders of learning and change.

In 1992, the Governor's Council on Education Reform and Funding in the state of Washington implemented a vision and plan of action to reach the goal that all students could be successful learners. The program put in place plans to develop learning standards for students, goals for student learning, assessments based on student performance and mastery, major new professional development opportunities, and significant efforts to encourage school-site planning. To quote David Kearns in his book *A Legacy of Learning*, "In a nutshell, this program revealed that successful teachers and schools have stopped 'doing their own thing' and begun to orient teaching and the curriculum around standards."[23] Researchers concluded that reading and mathematics scores increased dramatically when the entire school focused on changing teaching methods to develop core skills. This is a combination of top-down support from the state for whole-school reform at the district and school level.

## OPPORTUNITY FOR FEDERAL DEPARTMENT OF EDUCATION

Most people are not aware that the 185 schools on Indian reservations are the responsibility of the federal government. In the last presidential race, one candidate said he would spend $800 million to repair the crumbling schools and $126 million to replace six schools that are in the worst condition.[24]

Responsibility for these reservation schools should be transferred from the Bureau of Indian Affairs to the United States Department of Education. This would give the federal government a set of schools to try out the latest findings in education research, learning systems, assessment methods, and management systems. The Bureau of Indian Affairs has done an inadequate job for decades. Why not ask the Department of Education to take over this area of our public schools and make it a role model for how to manage a large school district. Native Americans deserve no less than an outstanding school system to improve their standard of living. They need not only good school buildings but also outstanding learning systems within the schools.

Another set of schools that should be managed by the U. S. Department of Education are those on military bases that are operated by the federal government. Much could be learned that could later be transferred as "best practices" to other school districts. The defense department schools need a worldwide integrated curriculum that enables children to move from one school to another every two or three years without being behind or ahead in lessons. Once this concept is proven, our 50 states should adopt a statewide curriculum. These large-group trials would justify the research and "best practices" role for the Department of Education. As a practical matter, whichever group funds education research and development projects, should benefit from the results.

For example, Ireland has an outstanding school system with a 98 percent literacy rate.[25] In the past 20 years, the country's economic growth has been just short of miraculous because of the emphasis placed on education. In fact, several learning systems used in the United States were developed in Ireland. The federal government could make a major contribution to the development and implementation of new learning and management systems for public schools. The federal government of Korea created the Korean Educational Development Institute, which had impressive results in student learning.

## AFFORDABILITY OF LEARNING SYSTEMS

According to the 1999 Education Vital Signs report in the *American School Board Journal*, the average per-pupil expenditure ranges from as low as $3,732 in Utah and $4,528 in Mississippi to as high as $9,427 in Connecticut and $10,153 in New Jersey. The national average is $6,407.[26] The average expenditure is much higher in inner-city schools than in rural schools. Thus, $7,000 is a reasonable, if not conservative, figure for inner-city schools.

What accounts for the more than 100-percent difference between the high-cost states and the lower ones? Teacher and administrator salaries are the primary factor. Teachers and principals in Connecticut and New Jersey earn twice as much as their counterparts in the low-cost states.[27] The other major cost driver is the number of employees in a school in excess of one teacher per classroom and one principal per school. These positions include vice-principals, deans, department heads, teacher aides, counselors, nurses, attendance personnel, security guards, bus drivers, secretaries, and clerical personnel. In fact, it's not uncommon in high-cost school districts to have twice as many employees as the number of teachers who carry a full teaching load. Salary increases, benefits increases, and the addition of many new employment positions in schools have driven up public school budgets since 1983. At the same time, school districts have invested little in learning systems or course materials. In fact, new course materials are seldom considered until all other line items (e.g., salaries, benefit, utilities) have been resolved.Therefore, most schools have outdated and poorly designed course materials.

If a breakthrough in student learning is going to occur, the purchase or development of new learning systems, tutoring systems, and high-quality course materials must be considered a priority item in all school budgets. How much do these systems and materials cost? In the *1999 Educators' Guide to Schoolwide Reform*, the following expenses and per-pupil costs were associated with the three learning systems that had the greatest impact on student learning:[28]

| Program | First-Year Costs | First-Year Costs with Current Staff Reassigned |
|---------|------------------|------------------------------------------------|
| Roots and Wings (Success for All) | $270,000 | $70,000 ($140/student) |
| High Schools That Work | $48,000 | No Change ($96/student) |
| Direct Instruction | $244,000 | $194,000 ($388/student) |

The costs are based on school size of 500 students.

Compared to the aforementioned $7,000 per-pupil costs for inner-city schools, these numbers are more than reasonable. Most of the other schoolwide reforms varied from less than $100,000 to $250,000; only one was more than $500,000. Other studies claim that the cost of change to structured learning systems varies from 1 to 5 percent. The costs often decline by 50 percent in years two and three.[29] Remember, however, that Moss Point achieved breakthroughs in learning by utilizing 1 percent of its budget annually. If changes are phased in over five years, schools could expect 1 percent incremental growth in each of the five years, which is a very affordable cost to achieve breakthroughs in student learning.

Courseware programs for interactive tutoring systems using personal computers at home that are being sold to parents and grandparents now average $25 per grade or course. Schools can purchase these programs with quantity discounts and provide a rich set of lessons that motivate students to learn at a very low cost. Courseware is like software: it costs a great deal to develop the product, but the cost to reproduce it is much smaller. With almost 4 million students per grade, schools can now purchase courseware at very reasonable prices.

Then there's the big question about buying multimedia personal computers that are used as interactive tutoring systems. Schools can purchase computers with education and quantity discounts for approximately $1,000. If two students use a computer at the same time and at least two groups of students use the same computer, the cost would be $250 per student. New computers last at least five years, so the annual cost per student would be $50. Compare $50 to the $25,000 price of a new tutor or teacher's salary and benefits, and it is clear that the cost of tutoring by teachers is simply not affordable. Schools need to use either volunteers or interactive personal computers, the more affordable option.

Parents of inner-city children often cannot afford a personal computer at home; however, all inner-city schools must have tutoring systems if they are going to meet the learning standards established by the state departments of education and the local school districts. Interactive tutoring is a bargain compared to having a child who's an underachiever and who dislikes school. The American public school system spends $330 billion annually, but educators insist that no funds are available for new learning and tutoring systems that utilize high-quality course materials. This claim should not be accepted by parents, taxpayers, business executives, or political leaders in the future.

In 1999, the Milken Foundation provided a grant to *Education Week* to study the use of technology in schools, resulting in the publication of "Technology Counts '99." Here are a few facts from that document:[30]

- Schools have an average of one instructional computer for every 5.7 students. (The ideal situation is one instructional computer for 4 students.)
- Computers are in 80 percent of the classrooms.
- There is certainly no lack of digital content available to teachers. Thousands of CD-ROMs and Web sites have been created specifically for educators and students. Many general-purpose software tools, such as word processing, spreadsheets, and desk-top-publishing packages, can also be adapted for the classroom.
- There are many courseware packages to teach keyboarding and computer use.
- Ninety-seven percent of all teachers use a computer at home and/ or at school.
- Fifty-three percent of all teachers surveyed use software for classroom instruction, and 61 percent use the Internet.
- The nation's schools spent $571.3 million on stand-alone software, comprehensive courseware (integrated learning systems), and online courseware. The rate of growth is about $50 million annually.

Why hasn't this large investment in computers, software, and courseware resulted in major improvements in student learning? As stated in Chapter 4, the answer is quite clear: Most teachers are using technology to entertain their students in a child care setting rather than adopting learning systems that ensure that more than 90 percent of the students learn their lessons. Computers are used merely as supplementary resources in more than 80 percent of classrooms. Most computers are used in a hobby shop environment rather than in a learning environment. Most schools do not have an integrated curriculum, and almost every school has social promotion. With more than half the class not at grade level in inner-city schools, computers have become just another expense rather than an effective tutor for proven learning systems.

The subheadline in the "Technology Counts '99" report read: "Now that most classrooms have at least one computer, educators are focusing on what 'digital content' they should put on them."[31] Teachers, who did not have time to create outstanding lesson plans in the precomputer world, are now expected to research dozens of courseware choices to determine what they want to merge into their old lesson plans. Directors of curriculum should take a leadership role here instead and ensure that the school system utilizes computers and courseware to improve student learning. Directors of curriculum should review carefully all of the courseware and learning systems that are available.

Only 12 percent of teachers in the *Education Week* survey said that their state or district provides lists of courseware titles that match curriculum standards. Even more surprising is that only 18 percent of teachers receive lists of approved courseware.[32] In essence, students are attending schools that operate like one-room schoolhouses in which the teacher is expected to know everything and to do everything. It's wrong to expect teachers with a full class load to be experts on computers and courseware. In fact, if individual teachers make learning systems and courseware decisions for each classroom, the problem of inconsistent teaching and learning will continue with the same low performance of students, but with greater expense. Teachers need approved learning systems that meet state and local standards and that utilize interactive tutoring systems to achieve breakthroughs in learning. The key question in future surveys should be: Do you as a teacher use courseware and tutoring systems that are part of a proven learning system?

## COST OF FAILURE AND RETENTION

In 1996, Irving B. Harris, one of the education reform movement's pioneers, wrote *Children In Jeopardy*. Here are some key facts from this book:[33]

- Several hundred thousand students drop out or graduate with less than a fourth grade education each year. In 1984, it cost taxpayers, on average, $300,000 for various support programs over the lifetime of a child who becomes an unemployable and who gets involved in teenage pregnancy, drug abuse, welfare, crime, or alcohol abuse. That cost would be at least $400,000 today and climbing to $500,000.
- Over a million babies are born each year to unmarried women who usually end up on welfare. The vast majority of these women are failures in school and their children become failures one generation later.
- To figure the cost of failure, add all the costs associated with support services, prisons, and loss of tax revenues (close to $200 billion per year). An investment in learning systems would be a minor expense compared to the continued expense of warehousing our school system failures.

In the past few years, there has been a public outcry to end social promotion, which exists in almost every American school. A major city with inner-city schools developed this plan to combat the problem:

- No promotion to the next grade without proven ability in reading, writing, and mathematics. Report card grades would no longer determine which students failed or passed. Test scores on district examinations would be used to show proven ability in literacy and mathematics.
- Students who did not meet academic standards would be placed in a special accelerated class. In accelerated classes, students would focus in small groups on literacy and mathematics during an 11-month school year.
- There would be summer school for failures and five years of high school for freshmen held back for poor academic performance.

This plan makes sense for schools in which most students learn only 50 percent of their lessons. In other words, if they're in the eighth grade, the students can accomplish only fourth-grade work. The plan required a complete reorganization of the billion-dollar annual school budget and many millions of incremental dollars. The plan is designed to end social promotion and to stop rewarding students for "seat time." The goal is to have the vast majority of the students achieve as successful learners.[34]

One can understand why Phillip Crosby entitled his book *Quality Is Free.*[35] When students learn the first time, a school system can increase its spending by 5 percent over a five-year period for the most outstanding learning systems on the market. Remediation and review costs are now in the billions of dollars. Colleges and universities could reduce the cost of higher education if they could eliminate all remedial courses. Remember, 78 percent of colleges offer remedial courses, and 29 percent of entering freshmen are enrolled in these courses.[36]

Another program to end social promotion is a mandate of summer school for students who failed to learn their lessons during the school year. In Washington, D.C., 30,000 students (40 percent of the total enrollment) were sent to summer school; in New York City, it was 250,000 students (25 percent); and Los Angeles had 35,000 students in summer school. This extra schooling costs millions of incremental funds, but it is absolutely essential if social promotion is to end in schools in which more than 50 percent of the students fail to learn their lessons. Summer school provides a second chance for lagging students to learn and remain with their age-group class.[37]

Now the question is whether the students learn the lessons in summer school or if the program just adds extra weeks of "seat time." In one major city, less than 40 percent of the students identified for summer school appeared.[38] Many students view summer school as punishment. Many students do not improve their test scores at the end of summer school. By using traditional teaching methods and learning, the success rate is often under 50 percent.[39]

Learning the first time is even more important for students, according to Dr. Robert E. Slavin, creator of Success for All learning systems. He states that:

> Remediating learning deficits after they are already well established is extremely difficult. Clearly, the time to provide additional help to children who are at risk is early, when these children are still motivated and confident and when any learning deficits are small. Schools must shift the emphasis on remediation to an emphasis on prevention and early intervention. Programs must be built around the idea that every child can and must succeed in the early grades, no matter what this takes.[40]

Schools should change, Dr. Slavin adds, so that all students can be successful learners from preschool to high school graduation. All the pieces of the puzzle exist for breakthroughs in student learning, and these pieces are affordable. Instructional design methods have been proven for decades, so there's simply no reason to have failing students in the bottom quartile of good schools and in the lower three quartiles of the inner-city schools. It's time to adopt a new paradigm for both teaching and learning.

The General Education Development certificate, or GED, is rapidly becoming a major educational credential in this country. In 1998, 500,000 Americans obtained a GED, more than doubling the number (231,000) who received the credential in 1971.[41] In fact, one-seventh of the young Americans who report on government surveys that they are high school graduates are actually GED recipients who obtained the credential after dropping out of school. This statistic brings into question the accuracy of the drop-out rates being quoted by schools. GED examinations cover mathematics, reading, social studies, science, and writing. Now, if many of the drop-outs are able to gain a GED certificate, why did they do so poorly in high school and why did they drop out? Once again, many students who are considered slow learners could be successful learners if schools had outstanding learning systems. The GED Testing Service predicts that 1 million students will take the GED certificate test in the year 2002.

## CASE STUDY ON AFFORDABILITY

"The Costs of Sustaining Educational Change Through Comprehensive School Reform," an article by Allan Odden, co-director of the Consortium for Policy

Research in Education (CPRE) and professor of education administration at the University of Wisconsin, appeared in the February 2000 issue of *Phi Delta Kappan* and is useful in testing the concept of affordability.[42] For an elementary school of 500 students (K–5), the estimated costs are listed as follows based on Odden's costs, with some modifications:

| Personnel/Equipment | Cost |
|---|---|
| 1 Principal | $70,000 |
| 1 Curriculum Coordinator (Vice Principal) | 60,000 |
| 1 Technology Coordinator | 50,000 |
| 20 Classroom Teachers | 1,000,000 |
| 4 Teaching Specialists (Art, Music, P.E., Library) | 200,000 |
| 1 Counselor/Family Outreach | 50,000 |
| 1 School Nurse and Supplies | 50,000 |
| 3 Secretaries/Attendance Clerk | 70,000 |
| 5 Classroom Aides (Tutors) | 125,000 |
| 1 Volunteer Coordinator | 25,000 |
| **Subtotal Personnel** | **$1,700,000** |
| Professional Development Institute | 75,000 |
| Technology equipment, network, etc. | 75,000 |
| Courseware and Instructional Materials | |
| ($100 per Student Each Year) | 50,000 |
| **Total** | **$1,900,000** |
| Cost per Student | $3,800 |
| Cost per Student for District Staff | $200 |
| **Total Cost per Student** | **$4,000** |

These estimated costs do not include food services, bus services, custodial services, building maintenance, utilities, insurance, legal, and other miscellaneous expenses. Costs do include a $2,000 laptop computer for each professional educator, computers for the secretaries, and a $1,000 multimedia computer for every four students, which is depreciated over a five-year period. A server, a local area network, a connection to the Internet, and the appropriate software are included in the budget for each school. This estimate assumed that the district is on a wide area network.

The $200 cost per student for the district office is based on a 5,000-student school district with four elementary schools with 500 students, two middle schools with 750 students, and one high school with 1,500 students. The district office would include the following personnel:

| Personnel | Cost |
| --- | ---: |
| 1 District Superintendent | $150,000 |
| 1 Chief Operating/Financial Officer | 100,000 |
| 1 Director of Curriculum | 115,000 |
| 3 Master Teachers for Curriculum and Professional Development | 180,000 |
| 1 Chief Technology Coordinator | 85,000 |
| 2 Accountants | 80,000 |
| 2 Computer Specialists | 80,000 |
| 4 Secretaries | 110,000 |
| Administrative System Expenses | 100,000 |
| **Total** | **$1,000,000** |
| **Cost per Student** | **$200** |

The personnel and benefit costs are close to 95 percent of the total expense. If there were 10,000 students in the school district, district staff costs would drop to below $150 per student, but size does not change the costs at schools because as schools are doubled there is a need for twice the number of people and equipment. Large schools require more master teachers. Class size and salary programs are the two most important factors. Costs would be much higher in New Jersey and Connecticut and much lower in Utah and Mississippi because of salary programs agreed upon for school personnel. Many schools have one or two volunteers per classroom, which is why a volunteer coordinator is included. If properly trained, volunteers are effective tutors.

With learning systems, students are focused on learning, which reduces the attendance and discipline problems. This correlation was proven years ago with the SRA self-study systems and again with interactive tutoring systems. With the proper learning systems, the vice-principal, who is also the curriculum coordinator, should be able to manage the learning performance of 500 students with 20 classroom teachers and the proper assessment systems.

Special education costs, which sometimes require 20 to 30 percent of a school's budget, were not included in this example because the programs vary widely. With learning systems, special education classes should be required only for those students with severe physical and mental handicaps, which is a very small percentage of the total students. In schools that receive immigrant children, additional expenses are incurred for immersion classes for English. Costs for middle school students are often $500 more per student than for elementary school students. Cost for high school students can also be $500 to $1,500 higher per student than for middle schools because of the cost of musical programs, athletic teams, drama productions, extracurricular activities, and more specialization in teaching.[43]

All of this information tells us that the American public school system can well afford personnel, equipment, networks, and course materials required to have an outstanding school system under the current budgets in most school districts.[44]

Some districts are underfunded and some districts have excessive costs, but a lack of funds is not a valid reason for poor student performance in most school districts.[45] Obviously, the management system and teaching methods must be improved to achieve a substantial increase in student learning.

## INCREMENTAL FUNDS IN 1999 AND 2000

In most states, a surplus of revenues over expenses resulted in 1999 and 2000 because of the nationwide prosperity that increased both sales and income taxes. For the first time in decades, governors and state legislatures are faced with the pleasant duty of determining what to do with the extra money. In many states, the governor has recommended major increases in school funding. For example, California's Governor Davis had already provided a $1.8-billion increase in year 2000 over 1999, bringing the total school budget to $30 billion. Then in May 2000, he added another $1.8 billion, which was to be a permanent increase with no strings attached.[46] This additional funding allows school districts to decide how the money will be spent. With $400 million more for computers, California schools are receiving about $4 billion more, or more than 14 percent in additional funding.[47] What a golden opportunity this windfall is to purchase all the new learning systems and technologies required to fix the crisis in student learning, with billions of dollars left over to improve teacher salaries and benefits.

Unfortunately, this money will no doubt have little or no impact on student learning because the school system employees will still be managing and teaching with the current methods. Everyone will be receiving more money, but everyone will claim that California has not provided sufficient funding because the average cost per student in the nation is higher than in California. Only a small fraction of this money will be spent on new learning systems, and most of the new computers will not be used as interactive tutoring systems. The old paradigm is alive and well, but it costs billions of dollars more for the same results. In a small state, $445 million is being added to the education budget with a sales tax increase, but no funds are allocated for new course materials or learning systems.

## INCREASED COMPENSATION FOR TEACHER CREATIVITY

In the 1930s, most teachers were single women and men who devoted their lives to teaching. In fact, if a woman did get married, she often had to resign her teaching position. These devoted teachers spent long hours in the evenings and on weekends creating outstanding lesson plans and presentations. Even the married men who taught in those years had the same time to devote to their classes because their wives were full-time house managers who took the primary responsibility to raise the children.

Few teachers today have these extended hours because 40 percent have an extra job.[48] Another large percentage are house managers, which is like a second job. Most teachers are in the process of raising their own children, which takes a good deal of time. And a high percentage of teachers are enrolled in graduate or continuing education classes. This leaves a small percentage who have the time to create learning systems or to develop outstanding course materials. For those that do create such items that are used throughout their grade, additional compensation should be forthcoming. These creative work products must benefit other teachers in the school or school district to qualify for the bonus and/or recognition.

Teachers who work in the summer to evaluate and/or develop learning systems and courseware should also receive additional compensation. Once again, this work should be for schoolwide systems, not just for tuning up an individual teacher's lesson plans.

## SELECTION OF LEARNING SYSTEMS

The creation and development of learning systems on a centralized basis is the only affordable and practical way to proceed. On the other hand, selection of what learning systems to use in a school district or school should remain a local decision. Teachers and principals must have great confidence in their learning systems, and they should enjoy using the system. In the future, school districts should emphasize the selection of learning systems rather than the trying out of various teaching fads by individual teachers. This approach will eliminate the current problem of inconsistent teaching in the public schools. Learning systems also make new and inexperienced teachers successful performers.

In the music world, few musicians have the talent or training to compose music. In fact, less than 1 percent of all musicians are successful composers. Millions of musicians perform beautifully once the music is selected for them. Teachers will be like musicians in the future. They will deliver outstanding lessons, while a small group of educators develop and compose learning systems.

The director of curriculum in a local school district should organize the experienced and master teachers into committees by grade and subject area to select the learning systems that will most appropriately satisfy the requirements of local schools. The main criteria for selection must be whether more than 90 percent of the students will be successful learners with this system. Considerations such as what system the teachers find easiest to use or what system requires the least amount of change for the staff must be minor factors in the selection process.

Educators who support the concept that all students can be successful learners with the use of a standards-based curriculum and standards-based assessments often do not fully understand how much time, effort, and cost must be invested to achieve this important goal. Too many educators believe that this major change in approach requires just a little more effort on the part of the existing faculties. The motto: "work harder and smarter" is not the solution. To avoid creating an impossible workload for teachers and administrators in schools, the director of curriculum and district staff need to evaluate in detail the capabilities of many schoolwide designs and learning systems.

*The following questions need to be asked:*

1.  Is the design clear and understandable by teachers and administrators?
2.  Has the design been developed into a full-scale learning system or is the work to be done by local teachers and administrators? If so, the school district needs to assemble a full-time development team, which can be costly and time consuming. Does the design utilize instructional systems design methods?
3.  Has an in-depth validation been conducted to provide proof of concept that more than 90 percent of the students will be successful learners with no excuses for race, gender, or economic level? After a learning system is developed by an organization, it should be tested over a period of months with various types of students. There should be an overpowering case that real improvement in student learning will occur.
4.  Are the implementation plan and professional development seminars adequate? If not, the local school must mount an effort to do these tasks.
5.  Does the organization provide adequate customer service and support for the teachers?
6.  Will there be a funded continuous improvement program to enhance the schoolwide design and/or learning system?
7.  Do the students at the installed schools like the new learning systems and do they become motivated learners? Remember, 40 percent of college freshmen said they were bored in high school, which is an increase from 25 percent in 1985.
8.  Do the teachers at the installed schools like the learning system and prefer it to the previous system?

Naturally, the first version of any learning system will not be perfect because schools usually do not have ideal specifications for the developers. Version One may be vastly superior to previous lesson plans, but once a school system implements a learning system for a given grade or subject, teachers will be in a much better position to enhance the specifications for Version Two. Even after

Version Two is implemented, teachers can further define their requirements and create a close-to-ideal Version Three. Of course, all learning systems need to be updated periodically as new knowledge arises. This effort is much like the development process for computer software.

These questions clearly tell a school district that they need to deal with full-service organizations rather than with hobby shops of well-intentioned people. NAS has published a document called *How to Evaluate Comprehensive School Reform Models*.[49] Many of these booklets and papers by other organizations on the selection of schoolwide reform do not focus on learning standards, instructional systems design methods, or student learning assessments.

Another good evaluation method is to look at the talent on the development team and the budget for the design and development. Some companies have invested several hundred million dollars into the development of their schoolwide reforms and/or learning systems. Some school districts are letting every school select their own learning systems rather than make a districtwide decision. This lack of centralization creates inconsistent teaching among schools that feed middle or high schools. In future years, a partnership should be formed between the district staff (director of curriculum) and the schools to make districtwide decisions for learning systems.

Some so-called learning systems, Web sites, and schoolwide reform projects will have little or no impact on student learning. The selection process is as important as the hiring of architects and general contractors for major building projects. Competition among learning system companies and school reform models will be the real "choice" that will improve student learning in future years. Several currently operating organizations will go out of business when their systems do not produce breakthroughs in learning, and a few new organizations will emerge that will learn from the pioneering groups. This is the traditional American way to finally achieve success in most areas of society.

As competition increases, negative stories will surface in which one educator explains why a rival system is not as good as they claim. Robert Slavin wrote a negative article in 1991 about John Henry Martin and his Writing To Read program to prove that his own system was better.[50] In 2000, Stanley Pogrow wrote similar articles in *Phi Delta Kappan*[51] and *Education Week*[52] stating that Slavin's Success for All program is not all that effective either. Dr. Pogrow is the developer of Higher Order Thinking Skills (HOTS) and Supermath, a prealgebra curriculum. Dr. Slavin has also developed a document entitled *Achievement Outcomes of Success for All: A Summary and Reponse to Critics* that answers all of Stanley Pogrow's negative comments in great detail.[53] Dr. Slavin points out that Success for All has been successfully evaluated by several third-party evaluators, and he has plenty of data to support the success. These conflicting articles and opinions encourage educators who do not want to change their current teaching methods. They want total agreement on a perfect system. Debates will continue for decades, and educators must not wait until everyone is in total agreement on how to improve student learning. Debates and critical articles are just part of our country's competitive system.

One activity that will help with this decision is to have reputable independent evaluators conduct comprehensive studies of the academic effectiveness of various learning systems. An example of this analysis method is occurring in Ohio. In 1999, the Ohio legislature funded Governor Robert Taft's OhioReads program aimed at putting 20,000 mentors in Ohio schools to ensure that all children will read at grade level by the end of the fourth grade. More than 200 schools chose to implement the HOSTS learning system using OhioReads funding. Part of the legislation called for independent evaluation of the results of OhioReads programs. Under the leadership of the governor and legislative leaders, the Center for Evaluation Services, a unit of Bowling Green State University, has agreed to gather comprehensive student achievement data from the schools implementing the HOSTS program, as well as from control group schools not having the program, to provide analytical data to the governor and legislature to guide them in future funding of school reform programs.

## LEARNING SYSTEMS FOR MAINSTREAM AND AT-RISK STUDENTS

Learning and tutoring systems fall into two categories: Some are focused on students learning their lessons the first time, whereas others are based on remediation. Title I money has provided more revenues for remediation programs. For example, Sylvan Learning Systems has more than 750 private for-profit tutoring systems in the United States.[54] Middle-class and wealthy parents pay hundreds of millions of dollars each year to Sylvan, Huntington, and other tutoring companies. Sylvan has even been hired with Title I money by more than 100 school districts to provide tutoring within schools. Once again, students learn with a highly structured system and good course materials.

Most of the learning systems that exist today have been developed for the at-risk student who is one or more grade levels behind. *The Directory of Programs for Students At Risk* is 316 pages and lists 45 different programs.[55] There are at least 100 programs for failing students because billions of dollars in Title I money are available for at-risk students. After all, one of the national education goals is to reduce drop-outs. It is interesting that students are able to learn with a second effort that includes structured learning systems that utilize instructional system design methods. Why not learn the first time?

The goal should be to have outstanding learning systems for mainstream classrooms and students. These schools need learning systems if they are to achieve the goal of more than 90 percent of students as successful learners. Companies such as CompassLearning, CCC, Riverdeep, and HOSTS have the creativity to develop outstanding learning systems for the mainstream classroom. Much of what they have learned working with at-risk students gives them a base to achieve breakthroughs in learning for mainstream classroom students. Research and development of programs for the second effort must continue because at the pace that schools are moving to fix the student learning problem, there will be millions of at-risk students for at least another 10 years.

## EMPOWERMENT OF TEACHERS AND ADMINISTRATORS

During the past 18 years, some educators have been more positive than others toward various changes, but most teachers have had a reactive response to various education reform programs. They've implemented various "quick-fix, sound-good" programs when ordered to do so. Unfortunately, almost all of these efforts have resulted in only minor improvements in student learning. It's no wonder that many educators today have little hope for real breakthroughs in student learning.

This attitude and approach must change in the future. With new standards and new accountability systems at the state level, all teachers and administrators must become proactive in developing the means to achieve the state standards for learning. Educators must have a positive attitude toward developing and implementing a new learning-centered paradigm, just as the teachers and principals did at Moss Point, Mississippi. If local educators fail to address the issues of improving student learning, the state departments of education and school district staffs will soon make all of the decisions concerning curriculum, learning systems, and assessment methods. To justify the $200 billion in incremental funding for operating schools and the billions of dollars more for new and better facilities, everyone has promised to fix the schools. Student learning must improve. Failure must not be accepted.

Today's teachers and principals are being asked to do something that has never been accomplished before: Elevate all students to high learning standards. A new paradigm has to be developed and implemented. As Bob Chase, president of the National Education Association, stated in a September 29, 1999 article in *Education Week*, "The challenge is to match our revolutionary goals with equally revolutionary means."[56] Learning systems are that revolutionary means.

---

### NOTES

1. I. Harris and A. Shanker, American Federation of Teachers, "A Million Drowning Children," *New York Times*, 6 June, 1993, E7.
2. L. Armstrong, "Don't Know Much about Multimedia? Your Kids Will," *Business Week*, 21 June, 1993, 150–151.

3. *Fact Sheet* (San Diego, CA: CompassLearning, 2000), 1.

4. *Company Profile* (Sunnyvale, CA: Computer Curriculum Corporation, 1999), 2–4.

5. Riverdeep, www.riverdeep.net, 2000, advertisement in *ASCD Journal*.

6. *Request for Proposals* (Arlington, VA: New American Schools Development Corporation, 1991), 1–59.

7. Letter of the President, "Stellar Schools for a New Century" (Arlington, VA: New American Schools, July 2000).

8. *ERS Blueprints for School Success: A Guide to New American Schools Designs* (Arlington, VA: Educational Research Service, 1998), 1–107.

9. *Working Toward Excellence: Examining the Effectiveness of New American Schools Design* (Arlington, VA: New American Schools, February 1999), 1–50.

10. *ERS Blueprints for School Success: Roots and Wings* (Arlington, VA: Educational Research Service, 1998), 85–94.

11. W. Bulkeley, "Now Johnny Can Read If Teacher Just Keeps Doing What He Is Told," *Wall Street Journal*, 19 July, 1999, A1, A9–12; and R. Herman, *An Educators' Guide to Schoolwide Reform* (Washington, DC: American Institute for Research, 1999), 1–12.

12. R. Herman, *An Educators' Guide to Schoolwide Reform.* (Washington, D.C.: American Institutes for Research, 1999), 106–109, 115–120.

13. Herman, *An Educators' Guide*, 63–65.

14. Herman, *An Educators' Guide*, 76–80

15. J. McChesney and E. Hertling, *The Path to Comprehensive School Reform* (Alexandria, VA: Association of Supervision and Curriculum Development, April 2000), 10–15.

16. D. Feuerstein, *Stellar Schools for a New Century* (Arlington, VA: New American Schools, July 2000), 8.

17. C. Hendril, "New Jersey Schools Put Reform To The Test," *Education Week*, 21 April, 1999, 1, 13–14.

18. *Catalog of School Reform Models* (Washington, DC: Department of Education, July 5, 2000).

19. R. Corrigan et al., *Graduates with Competitive Skills: A Blueprint for Predictable Success* (New Orleans, LA: The Institute of Effective Learning, 1992), 25–35.

20. Corrigan et al., *Graduates with Competitive Skills*, 27.

21. L. Thompson, *Systemwide Education Reform* (Washington, DC: United States General Accounting Office, April 1993), 26–29.

22. Corrigan et al., *Graduates with Competitive Skills*, 15.

23. D. Kearns and J. Harvey, *A Legacy of Learning* (Washington, DC: Brookings Institute Press, 2000), 113–115.

24. *New York Times* News Service, "Bush's Plan Has Gains for Schools on Reservation," *San Diego Union-Tribune*, 20 August, 2000, A6.

25. R. Branson, *An Urgent Plea: Establish a Research and Development Policy* (Tallahassee, FL: Florida State University, June 23, 2000), 16.

26. D. Blom, "Education Vital Signs," *American School Board Journal*, December 1999, A22–A27.

27. D. Blom, "Education Vital Signs."

28. Herman, *An Educators' Guide*, 4–5.

29. *ERS Blueprints for School Success*, 90–91.

30. E. Fatemi, "Building the Digital Curriculum, Milken Exchange on Education Technology," *Education Week*, 23 September, 1999, 5–8, 58–108.

31. Fatemi, "Building the Digital Curriculum," 9.

32. Fatemi, "Building the Digital Curriculum," 13.

33. I. Harris, *Children In Jeopardy* (New Haven, CT: Yale University Press, 1996), 5–209.

34. M. Magee, "Major School Overhaul Proposed," *San Diego Union-Tribune*, 14 December, 1999, A1, A13.

35. P. Crosby, *Quality Is Free* (New York: New American Library, 1979), 1–249.

36. Kearns and Harvey, *A Legacy of Learning*, 14.

37. C. Gewerty, "More Districts Add Summer Coursework," *Education Week*, 7 June, 2000, 1, 12.

38. D. Harrington-Lueker, "Summer Learners," *American School Board Journal*, March 2000, 20–25.

39. Harrington-Lueker, "Summer Learners."

40. R. Slavin, *Success for All* (Arlington, VA: Educational Research Service, 1992), 1.

41. R. Murnane and J. Tyler, "The Increasing Role of the GED in American Education," *Education Week*, 3 May, 2000, 48, 64.

42. A. Odden, "The Costs of Sustaining Change through Comprehensive School Reform," *Phi Delta Kappan*, February 2000, 433–437.

43. Estimates by the author.

44. L. Picus, "Setting Budget Priorities," *American School Board Journal*, May 2000, 30–33.

45. S. Pereus, "Cut Costs without Cutting Quality," *American School Board Journal*, May 2000, 34–42.

46. E. Werner, "Davis Touts Additional Funds for Education," *San Diego Union-Tribune*, 7 May, 2000, 1.

47. E. Mendel, "Davis Gives Schools $1.84 Billion More," *San Diego Union-Tribune*, 10 May, 2000, A1, A18.

48. L. Olson and D. Hoff, "Teaching Tops Agenda at Summit," *Education Week*, 6 October, 1999, 20.

49. S. Ross, *How to Evaluate Comprehensive School Reform Models* (Arlington, VA: New American Schools, 2000), 1–20.

50. R. Slavin, *Reading Effects of IBM's Writing To Read Program: A Review of Evaluations* (Arlington, VA: Educational Research Service, 1991), 1–11.

51. S. Pogrow, "That Unsubstantial "Success" of Success for All," *Phi Delta Kappan*, April 2000, 596–599.

52. S. Pogrow, "Beyond the "Good Start" Mentality," *Education Week*, 19 April, 2000, 44, 46.

53. R. Slavin, *Research on Achievement Outcomes of Success for All: A Summary and Response to Critics* (Baltimore, MD: Johns Hopkins University, June 2000), 1–35.

54. M. Walsh, "Sylvan Learning Shifts Its Focus Online," *Education Week*, 5 April, 2000, 8.

55. T. William, *The Directory of Programs for Students at Risk* (Larchmont, NY: Eye On Education, 1999), 1–316.

56. B. Chase, "Eyes Wide Open," *Education Week*, 29 September, 1999, 34.

# CHAPTER 11

# Need for an Exciting
# New Vision

There's a saying: If you don't know where you are going, any road will get you there. Unfortunately, this adage applies to the education reform movement over the past 18 years. As stated previously, there are two approaches to fixing a major performance problem in any large organization. The initial effort is usually a series of quick-fixes to the existing paradigm with the hope of making the required minor corrections necessary to get back on the road to achieving objectives. When this doesn't work, it is important to develop a vision of where the organization should be to achieve its goals. This vision is often a long way from where the current performance level is. The organization can then develop innovative means for taking a giant leap toward the vision. Clearly, every school district and school that sets a goal to have more than 90 percent of its students achieve as successful learners needs a vision.

Too often, a school reform vision is just a piece of paper filled with unrealistic hopes and dreams. Based on Chapters 7, 8, 9, and 10, it should be clear that school districts can have an exciting vision in which almost all children can be successful learners with a world-class curriculum. The vision can be both practical and affordable.

The new vision for the American school system should be a simple one-page statement embraced by all of the key parties (i.e., board of education, administrators, teachers, students, parents, local business executives, community leaders, taxpayers, and the state department of education). This statement will motivate all of these groups to support the fundamental changes needed to reengineer schools and to achieve new learning standards. The language of a results-oriented vision must be clear to everyone. Too many visions are merely statements of good intentions that have little value or motivation. Ken Blanchard, author of *The One-Minute Manager*, states: "A vision is a picture of the future that produces passion, and it's this passion that people want to follow. An organization without a clear

219

vision is like a river without banks—it stagnates and goes nowhere."[1] The following statement meets all of the criteria for a good vision.

## EXAMPLE OF A NEW VISION

Here is an example of a results-oriented vision:

> The (name of the school district) is organized, staffed, and funded to develop successful learners in a safe and enjoyable environment based on an integrated curriculum of lessons that meets the state and school district learning standards. With the assistance of parents and community leaders, all children, except for those who have a serious physical, mental, or language challenge, will be at grade level during the kindergarten through high school years. Graduates will be prepared to enter the workforce or be able to enroll at institutions of higher learning without the assistance of remediation programs, and they will have the necessary knowledge to become good citizens and lead productive lives. To achieve this vision, (name of the school district) will implement proven learning, assessment, administrative, and management systems that focus primarily on learning and cost containment.

When every American school district can distribute such a vision to parents and political and community leaders, then the education reform movement that started nearly 20 years ago will become a success comparable to landing a man on the moon. All educators want their local school districts to accomplish this important feat.

The graphic in Figure 11–1 clearly shows the difference between continuing with quick-fixes and fine-tuning strategies compared to the systemic change strategy required by an exciting vision. Tinkering around the edges is simply a no-win, very expensive strategy.

## IMPORTANT SUCCESS FACTORS

It's important for those who support a new vision to understand what its success factors will be. In other words, how will anyone know when the vision has been achieved?

*The following 25 success factors will help answer this question:*

1. *All Students Are Successful Learners.* Being realistic, a few students will have serious family, attendance, or attitude problems that temporarily re-

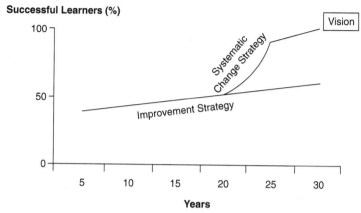

**Figure 11–1** The Road to Success

strict their learning. Thus, a very small number of students must be retained in their current grade because they simply are not prepared to learn the lessons in the next grade. Exceptions would obviously be made for students who have serious physical, mental, or language challenges. These students would be placed in special education classes with an individual learning plan, or in a language immersion class. They would be viewed as successful learners based on their success with their learning plan. More than 90 percent of the students will be promoted as successful learners. With frequent assessments built into learning systems, children will learn the first time or receive immediate help through tutoring systems. Students will not fall behind, get lost, or give up. Students will value education and expect to succeed. The Japanese have only successful students in their classes rather than a successful top half and failure in the bottom half of the class. American schools can achieve this same goal of mass education.

2. ***Traditional Excuses for Poor Performance Are Eliminated.*** School districts will no longer use the excuses of hunger, poverty, minorities, gender, and so forth to justify poor learning performance. A critical mass of schools have proven with more assurance than ever that children can achieve at high standards regardless of race, gender, or economics. Closing the achievement gap must be one of the most important success factors in a new vision. Too often in the past, school reforms that do work seem to work only for college-bound students. The focus of education reform must now be on the bottom half of the class.

3. ***Children Are Ready To Learn in First Grade.*** Preschool (including Head Start) and home schooling programs will be enhanced by a partnership with the school district to prepare children for kindergarten. Children will be

fluent in the English language when they enter first grade. Today, many children enter first grade far below the norm and never catch up, resulting in 12 years of failure and educationally damaged children.

4. ***Successful Neighborhood Schools Are Available.*** When all schools within a district enable all students to meet learning standards, children will once again attend neighborhood schools with their friends. A neighborhood school does not have to be a low-performing school. There is no reason why a neighborhood school cannot be as good as a magnet or charter school. Today, many parents must drive their children to remote schools or the school district must pay for an expensive transportation system to provide choice. The choice between successful schools and failing ones should not pigeonhole students in middle or high schools based on their interests in athletics, drama, science, business, health services, and other specialty programs. Students need a good general education; specialization by profession is more appropriate at the university level.

5. ***World-Class Integrated Curriculum Is Implemented.*** A realistic integrated curriculum that meets the state department of education and school district standards is essential for all students. Enrichment lessons should also be provided to "gifted" students and those who learn quickly.

6. ***Resources for Equal Education Opportunity Exist for All Students.*** The state departments of education should establish standards for the number and quality of administrators, teachers, counselors, aides, and clerical personnel needed to carry out an integrated standards-based curriculum. The budget should be based on adequate personnel, as well as learning, assessment, administrative, and management systems that produce successful learners. With this plan, all schools should be properly funded by state and local governments so they can provide a statewide standard education. Schools and/or school districts should have the freedom to add extra personnel, programs, facilities, and so on if their local taxpayers approve additional funding.

7. ***Teachers and Administrators Will Have High Morale.*** When teachers and administrators work in a school in which more than 90 percent of the students are successful learners, the annual employee opinion survey will reflect good results for morale. Contributions of both teachers and administrators will be celebrated. Professional respect for the teaching profession will be at an all-time high.

8. ***Vision Works In Today's Society.*** The new paradigm must accommodate all family types, including single-parent families, foster children families, families in which both parents work, and the traditional two-parent family. The vision should work in rural communities, inner-cities, urban areas, and suburban schools. The new paradigm must effectively serve a culturally

diverse and mobile population. Last but not least, it must adjust to ever-changing societal conditions.

9. ***Vision Works with Existing Facilities, Staff, and Students.*** Although some buildings will need to be rewired and brought up to code, the proposed vision will not require new facilities, administrators, teachers, administrative personnel, or students. New learning, assessment, administrative, and management systems should be implemented successfully by the current staff with proper training and professional development programs.

10. ***Performance Is Sustainable.*** A culture of learning emerges with high norms for behavior achieved by students. Taxpayers, parents, and faculties are pleased with a cluster of top-performing schools. Therefore, there should be no regression to old teaching methods when a change of administrators or teachers occurs. Change must be institutionalized in order to sustain top performance.

11. ***Improvements Are Continuously Implemented.*** New learning and assessment systems are pilot-tested against the existing system to determine if learning can be increased, costs can be decreased, and/or the curriculum can be enriched. New systems must be based on research and validation studies rather than on "hit-and-miss" attempts to improve the system.

12. ***High Morale Exists Among Students.*** Annual surveys should be implemented to determine if students like how a school is being operated, if they like learning with the current learning systems, and if they like their teachers.

13. ***Attrition Rates Decline.*** If administrators and teachers like the learning, assessment, administrative, and management systems within their schools, they will remain there. Increases in the number of successful learners will lower attrition rates. Successful schools always have low attrition rates. New mentoring systems are also required for new teachers.

14. ***Substitute Teachers Are Effective.*** In too many schools, thousands of substitute teachers arrive in a classroom with little or no training only to find no lesson plan, no seating chart, no guidance from administrators, and disrespectful students. Days, weeks, or even months of so-called teaching is a complete waste of time and another reason why students fall behind, get lost, or give up. Substitute teachers are forced to become child care workers rather than teachers in most schools. Approximately 5 million children have substitute teachers in their classroom on any given day. There are estimated to be almost 1 million substitute teachers, and many of them are not trained to do the job.[2] With learning systems that feature standard assessment systems, substitute teachers can be effective educators, which is an essential requirement for a successful learning institution.

15. ***Discipline Problems Are Reduced.*** Referrals and discipline situations can and should be documented. Successful students rarely cause problems

because they're too busy working at learning. School districts should provide alternative education services, supervision, and counseling for any student who is expelled from a classroom. It is estimated that 1.5 million students miss one or more days because they have been suspended or expelled.[3] In 1994, the Safe and Drug-Free Schools and Communities Act required schools that receive federal funds to expel students who bring weapons or drugs to school. This zero tolerance policy was designed to provide safe, orderly, and drug-free schools for teachers and students. Thanks to this policy and the tremendous effort made by teachers and principals, most schools are safe today. Teachers also need to be protected from discipline-related lawsuits. Children should not have to go to school afraid of being bullied or beaten.

16. *Absenteeism Is Reduced.* Children cannot learn if they do not attend school. Attendance is not a problem at some inner-city schools, but in Detroit, 63,000 of the 180,000 school students missed more than one month's worth of classes during the last school year.[4] This excessive absenteeism occurred in a school system in which barely half the students graduate. It's not a case of chronic illness or not having adequate clothes to wear; in most cases, students are so far behind that they've given up on school. Some cities are threatening fines and jail time for parents, but punishing parents won't be nearly as effective as fixing student learning within the schools. Successful learners attend school regularly, and successful schools have few serious truancy cases.

17. *Drop-out Rate Is Reduced.* The definition of a drop-out is a person of high school age who is not enrolled in school and who is not a high school graduate. Drop-outs have less earning power, fewer job opportunities, reduced job security, and a greater likelihood to enter the welfare and/or prison systems. Clearly, drop-outs hurt the nation grievously in terms of health, wealth, and achievement of our democratic ideals. The national goal needs to be a 90-percent graduation rate, but every school should aim for close to 100 percent. Again, successful learners do not drop out of school. Almost all drop-outs are students who are two or more grades behind and who have experienced serious academic trouble. Rather than sit in a seat feeling lost for two or three more years, they leave school. As stated previously, the General Educational Development (GED) certificate is becoming a major educational credential because of the high rate of drop-outs. It's easy for a school to identify potential drop-outs because at-risk students have low grades, low test scores, high truancy rates, and frequent negative interactions with teachers and principals. These students need remedial tutoring and counseling.

18. *Homework Is Completed On Time.* Ever since the one-room schoolhouse days, students have come up with excuses for not completing homework

assignments. As students fall behind and get lost in a class, they stop doing homework. On the other hand, successful students do their homework because they know it's an essential part of the learning process. Some schools have implemented "homework hotlines" as a solution for students who miss class, "forget" teacher instructions, or leave written assignments in their lockers by mistake. These hotlines enhance parent involvement because they inform parents about what homework assignments have been given. Some teachers assign too much or too little homework, but a well-designed learning system will correct this problem. Learning systems also ensure that homework assignments are more consistent among teachers in the same grade and/or subject.

19. ***Participation in Extracurricular Activities Increases.*** Successful students enjoy school and are more likely to participate in extracurricular activities such as music, art, drama organizations, government clubs, vocational clubs, student newspaper, yearbook, interscholastic groups, and athletic programs. Studies have proven that students who participate in school activities are typically better students who stay in school until graduation. Research also tells us that at-risk, gifted, and average students all have a sense of belonging to a school when they participate in activities. Some schools identify students who do not participate in any extracurricular activity and counsel them to join at least one activity.

20. ***Parent Involvement Is Increased.*** Parents are like anyone else: they want to be part of a successful team. If their children enjoy school and become successful students, parents are more likely to volunteer as tutors, classroom aides, support personnel for extracurricular activities, and field trip supervisors. Satisfied parents also get more involved in assessment systems as well as homework assignments. Even in inner-city schools, parents will make the time to get more involved, despite their long work hours or the various jobs they work in order to support their families.

21. ***Health Problems Decline.*** To make matters worse, school health clinics are often the only affordable health care in poor neighborhoods. Children who fall behind in class or who are lost in a subject have more health problems. They look for excuses to get out of class and school altogether. It was reported on the "Good Morning America" show that 10 million students have frequent headaches.[5] On the other hand, successful students don't want to miss a class because they want to keep up with their classmates. Successful students have fewer unwanted pregnancies and emotional problems.

22. ***The Number of Special Education Students Decreases.*** Special education classes should be reserved for students who have serious physical or mental challenges. It is impossible for these students to keep up with a mainstream class, even if they have special resources. Children with severe disabilities need individual education plans, special learning systems, and teachers who

are trained to work with handicapped students. Unfortunately, some people claim that educators discriminate against children with disabilities if they support special classrooms, learning systems, and teachers for handicapped students. Don Raczka, the president of the Poway, California Federation of Teachers, stated: "Inclusion can work for some children. We see successes every day. But full inclusion as a policy for every child does not seem to meet the test of common sense."[6] Equally important, special education often is not the best remedy for students with simple learning problems. Learning and tutoring systems are a better alternative, in most cases.

**23. *More Graduates Attend Institutions of Higher Education.*** On the national average, more than 60 percent of high school graduates attend a community college or a four-year college/university. This figure is much lower in most inner-city schools. With student aid and scholarship funds, more inner-city students could become college graduates if they succeed in the K–12 grades. In some urban schools today, special programs are available for middle school students who are interested in planning for a college education. Local colleges and universities invite students to spend a few hours on campus so they can learn what it will take to be accepted into an institution of higher learning. They also receive information on financial aid. These special programs motivate students to think about their goals and their future.

**24. *Vision Is Replicable To Other Schools.*** School districts do not need model schools that exist as sideshows. The vision should be implemented in each school within all school districts. If the Edison Schools can currently develop a vision and move it into hundreds of schools across the nation, then a successful vision should be transferrable within a school district and among other school districts.

**25. *Adequate Resources Are Provided.*** The new paradigm must be affordable, which, for most schools, means within 5 percent of the current operating budget. Political leaders and business executives would probably support a 10-percent increase, however, if schools produced more than 90 percent successful learners. With learning systems, school districts can determine precisely the exact costs of operating a school. Money flows to successful schools. The cost of each piece of the puzzle can be determined, and the damage to the learning process can be measured when each puzzle piece is not fully funded.

Let's summarize these 25 important success factors with an action program. School board members, parents, and teachers should meet with their district superintendent to develop a vision for their school district that would enable most students to be successful learners. The vision should then be accompanied by a customized list of important success factors that would tell the school district when the vision has been successfully implemented.

## NO EXCUSE FOR POOR PERFORMANCE

These goals may sound like utopia, but these 25 important success factors can be accomplished by schools that reengineer their teaching and learning systems as outlined in this book. The key is to focus on student learning. Here is more evidence that this vision is possible.

A March 1999 report prepared for the Council of Chief State School Officers by the Education Trust contained these important messages:[7]

> Over the past decade (really several decades), we have watched a kind of creeping malaise infect more and more educators, and, indeed, more and more entire school systems. The clearest manifestation of this malaise is found in the conversations we have had with teachers and principals in high poverty schools who often tell us that, 'these standards you are talking about may be fine for some kids, but certainly not for the kind of kids that we have in our school.' But, the malaise is by no means limited to front-line educators: leaders at all levels—administrators, school boards, legislators—often make policies about things like assignments, graduation requirements, accountability systems and the like, that at their core expect less of poor children (which include minorities) and poor schools. Somewhere along the line somebody decided that poor kids (and minorities) couldn't learn, or, at least, not at a very high level. And everyone fell in line. But the truth is actually quite different. Some poor children have always learned at high levels, and some entire schools get all of their children to levels reached by only a few students in other schools.

In Fall 1998 the Education Trust designed and administered a survey for schools that had been identified by the states as the top-scoring and/or most-improving schools with poverty levels greater than 50 percent.[8] The 366 elementary and secondary schools responding to the survey serve mostly poor student populations in 21 states. They operate in rural isolation and in urban overcrowded schools. They serve every racial and ethnic group in the country, including students who come to school speaking little or no English

***In general, they found that these top-performing, high-poverty schools tend to do the same successful things:***

1. Use state standards extensively to design curriculum and instruction, assess student work, and evaluate teachers.
2. Increase instructional time in reading and mathematics in order to help students meet standards.
3. Devote a larger proportion of funds to support professional development focused on changing instructional practice (many are implementing learning systems).

4. Implement comprehensive systems to monitor individual student progress and provide extra support, including tutoring to students as soon as it's needed.
5. Focus their efforts to involve parents with helping students meet standards.
6. Have state or district accountability systems in place that have real consequences for adults in the schools.

In the May 5, 1999 issue of *Education Week*, Kerry A. White wrote an article entitled "High-Poverty Schools Score Big on Kentucky Assessment Tests."[9] Of the top 20 schools, 13 had 25 to 83 percent of their students receiving free or reduced-price lunches. Susan Perkins Weston, the executive director of the Kentucky Association of School Councils, said Wrigley Elementary's performance (ranked 2nd in the state but with 83 percent poor students) challenges conventional thinking on student achievement and leaves fewer excuses for administrators and teachers at low-achieving schools who view poverty as a virtually insurmountable barrier.[10] These schools show us that it's possible for high-poverty schools to meet tough standards. They also affirm the fundamental philosophy behind Kentucky's wide-ranging 1990 school reform law: All students can learn at high levels.

It's important to remember that high-poverty schools dominate the bottom of the rankings, so the challenge is to transfer the "best practices" from the top-performing schools to the low-performing ones. This responsibility belongs to the state school officer and the state department of education, as well as the superintendents. It also needs to be a formal action program, not just a hope that one school will talk to another.

Many schools across the country are achieving breakthroughs in learning. It's no accident that their achievements are based on more than good intentions. They have a new system for teaching and learning that must be implemented in all schools. These new methods and learning systems should even be implemented in the so-called good schools in which 25 percent of the students are at the bottom of the class, falling behind, and getting lost.

## VISION ACHIEVES BETTER TEACHING

Today, everyone seems to be talking about "better teaching." They quickly admit that they have yet to define what "better teaching" is, which means no action programs have been created to obtain this goal except for additional college courses and professional development seminars. Too many visions have little or no impact on student learning.

*"Better teaching" is achieved by the following:*

- Standards for learning
- Learning objectives to achieve the standards
- Motivational lessons that teach to the learning objectives
- Frequent assessment based on learning objectives
- Professional development workshops that enable successful teaching of the lessons

There is no short-cut or quick-fix to realize "better teaching," except for implementing a world-class curriculum, including learning and tutoring systems.

Compare this plan to the quick-fix idea (Chapter 4) that good teachers in high-performing schools should be transferred to low-performing schools because recent studies tell us that low-performing students need good teachers. Studies show that poor and minority students have a disproportionate share of inexperienced and unqualified teachers.[11] For example, in New York City, the percentage of teachers who have failed national teacher-certification examinations is three times higher than it is elsewhere in the state. Similar patterns are prevalent in other states.[12]

Let's get realistic. Large numbers of top-performing teachers with the most teaching experience in the best schools are not going to volunteer to transfer to inner-city schools, especially when inner-city schools are being ranked as failures and their faculties are being blamed for poor student performance. It will take major bonuses of $10,000 to $25,000 to implement such a program. After the so-called good teachers go to the low-performing schools, the school districts may find that the good teachers are not as successful in the low-performing schools as they were in the top-performing schools.

What happens to the low-performing teachers at inner-city schools? They either must be fired, which is not feasible, or they replace the good teachers in the high-performing schools. How popular will that decision be with parents, students, and taxpayers? Therefore, implementing a new integrated curriculum with new learning and tutoring systems at inner-city schools is the more practical and timely solution.

Recently, there have been recommendations that states should provide an incentive for new teachers to start their careers at low-performing schools. It is not clear how the most inexperienced teachers will be successful in the most difficult teaching environment. Some political leaders want to forgive education loans for new teachers if they will commit to teach at low-performing schools. Another political leader has proposed a $10,000 college scholarship for students in the college of education if they will commit to teach in poor-performing schools.[13]

Fixing the teaching and learning problems in low-performing schools would do more than all of the scholarships and loan forgiveness in the world. New teachers want to work in schools where they feel safe and discipline is not out of control. Most important, they want to work with successful students who are at grade level.

It is important that low-performing schools have very good teachers compared to 40 to 50 percent with less than three years of experience. This situation results from the long and steep learning curve needed to become a successful teacher. There is total agreement that a serious problem exists that must be resolved. Unfortunately, a quick-fix and sound-good solution will not work. The process of learning must be fixed.

There is nothing wrong with paying teachers a bonus to stay in low-performing schools or offering them increased pensions, but the incentives should apply only to very good teachers in this challenging environment. Rewards should not be given to poor-performing teachers who are not qualified to teach at good schools. Providing better working conditions, such as an office or even no restrictions on the use of a copier, makes a positive statement in some schools. Also, giving these teachers their own computers and cell phones could be a positive gesture.

## BENEFITS OF THIS VISION FOR TEACHERS

If the recommendations in Part III (the last five chapters) are implemented, nearly all teachers and administrators could be successful using a new vision in which nearly all students would be successful learners. There is no need or excuse for having a wide bell-curve for teacher performance, which results in the worst attrition rate among all professional jobs. The vision must focus on both the success of teachers and the success of students. Let's look at why teachers will benefit.

First, students will arrive in the classroom at grade level, ready to learn their lessons. Second, new, inexperienced teachers can all be more successful. Third, lesson plans, graphics, case studies, simulations, exercises, and assessments will have been developed by master teachers and other educators, which means teachers will have a reasonable workload. Fourth, an advanced administrative system would exist, which would enable teachers to spend more time teaching. Outstanding professional development workshops would support each learning system. Each teacher would have a cell phone and laptop computer. Students would have multimedia computers for learning and tutoring. Adequate facilities would be available for planning lessons, contacting parents, and meeting with students and other teachers. Taxpayers would support bond issues for outstanding school buildings. Parents would become more involved with schools, and students would enjoy their school years. New professional respect and enhanced job satisfaction would be garnered for teachers.

In the past, wide bell-curves existed for both teachers and students. In the future, teachers will be required to be successful, and more than 90 percent of students will be successful learners. This is the basic message of this exciting new vision. In order to achieve this vision, schools must adopt a new management system and accept more structure, which is the subject of the next chapter. Before proceeding to the next chapter, consider the following story, which is often told at education meetings.

> One day in heaven, the Almighty decided he would visit Earth and take a stroll. When he was walking down the road, he encountered a man who was crying. The Almighty asked, "Why are you crying, my son?" The man said that he was blind and had never seen a sunset. The Almighty touched the man, and he happily could see.
>
> As the Almighty walked further, he met another man crying, and asked him, "Why are you crying, my son?" The man told the Almighty that he had been born crippled and was never able to walk. The Almighty touched him, and the man was able to walk, which made him very happy.
>
> Further down the road, the Almighty met a teacher who was crying, and he asked, "Why are you crying?" The teacher said, "I am trying to find the means to achieve the new standards of learning." The Almighty sat down and cried with the teacher.

This story gets a laugh at these meetings because most teachers and administrators aren't sure they know how to implement "better teaching" to achieve the new learning standards. It is hoped that the first three sections of this book have convinced readers that a method exists by which all children can become successful learners. The four remaining chapters explain how to make this vision a reality.

---

**NOTES**

1. K. Blanchard, "Are You a Leader?" Rancho Bernardo Community Presbyterian Church, San Diego, CA, 20 November, 1999, 2.

2. D. Hill, "Substitutes Unite," *Education Week*, October 6, 1999, 35–39.

3. S. Black, "Locked Out," *American School Board Journal*, January 1999, 34–37.

4. R. Meredith, "School Districts Raise Stakes for Truants, Lay Down Law to Parents," *New York Times* New Service, *San Diego Union-Tribune*, 16 January, 2000, A28–A29.

5. *Good Morning America* TV Show, ABC, New York City, 4 September, 2000.

6. D. Raczka, "Inclusion Is Not The Answer for Everyone," *Rancho Bernardo Journal*, 12 June, 1998, 8.

7. K. Haycock, *Dispelling the Myth: High Poverty Schools Exceeding Expectations* (Washington, DC: Education Trust, March 1999), 1.

8. Haycock, *Dispelling the Myth*, 1–13,

9. K. White, "High Poverty Schools in Kentucky Land in Top 20 on Assessment," *Education Week*, 5 May, 1999, 18, 20.

10. White, "High Poverty Schools," 18.

11. Dialogue Report, "Why Some San Diego Schools Are So Hard To Staff," *San Diego, California Dialogue*, July 2000, 1–4.

12. R. Colvin, "Better Teachers Are Key To Reform," *Los Angeles Times*, 3 December, 1999, A1, A14.

13. L. Joiner, "The Candidates on the Issues," *American School Board Journal*, September 2000, 19.

# PART IV

# How To Institutionalize Change

The transformation from a school system in which more than half of the students are below grade level to one in which more than 90 percent are successful learners will not happen unless the chief state school officers, state departments of education, school board members, district superintendents, and key district staff members provide leadership to school faculties on how to achieve breakthroughs in learning. This leadership requires a new management system at the state, district, and school levels. In addition, a formal change management system must be implemented to institutionalize change. All stakeholders must understand why supporting the new vision is in their interest. As always, great change requires great leadership, which is the message of the final section of this book.

# CHAPTER 12

# Need for a New
# Management System

When the words "management" and "business" are used in connection with schools, they often have a negative connotation for some teachers and administrators. Many educators do not want not-for-profit schools to be managed or measured like a business organization. They want academic freedom and measurements based on good intentions, instead of results.

## SCHOOLS MUST BE MANAGED

Many large and intermediate not-for-profit organizations, including the military services and government agencies, have management systems consisting of the following elements:

- Strategic plans (for multiple years)
- Operating plans (for current year)
- Budgets
- Information technology systems
- Accounting systems
- Human resource programs
- Public relations policies
- Measurement systems.

All the organizations have a service and/or product that is required by large groups of people. These organizations must be managed just like other successful organizations. Schools have the same list of management functions and tasks, and they, too, need to be managed like a business. As stated previously, the output or product of schools is successful learners. Learning must be measured and managed if there is going to be any hope for major improvement in student performance.

***The major differences between schools and successful organizations are as follows:***[1]

1. High rate (25 to 75 percent) of failure is tolerated.
2. Little attention is devoted to the implementation of "best practices."
3. Little focus on productivity through economies of scale, new methods, new technologies, and so forth.
4. Annual increases (3 to 10 percent) in budgets over a 50-year period.

Numerous articles and speakers claim that schools must not be run in the future based on the "factory" model of years past. This is another myth that has evolved over the years. The fact is, schools are not managed like factories at all. Manufacturing organizations constantly focus on higher quality and lower costs, whereas schools tolerate low quality and high costs. Manufacturing executives would never say they are using the "school" model of management.

In most cases, schools have been loosely managed. Without an integrated curriculum and learning standards, most administrators haven't been involved in day-to-day classroom lessons. Instead, they've devoted their time to budgets, physical plant problems, building programs, human resource problems, hiring, public relations, and so on. Classroom teachers have had to develop their own lesson plans and methods. Inconsistency reigns in teaching between grades and even within a particular grade or subject. Little coordination among schools has been orchestrated regarding what lessons need to be taught and when lessons would be presented. Assessment and grading procedures among schools and by teachers of the same subject have differed tremendously. Essentially, most schools have been managed like a collection of one-room schoolhouses. This approach makes it impossible for anyone to manage an education system that focuses primarily on improving student learning. With the current management methods, schools will always have the two (teacher and student) bell-curves and a high failure rate.

This approach will change during the next 10 to 12 years because states are implementing new standards and accountability systems. Schools must be managed like successful organizations that have very low failure rates. A new multilevel partnership must be established between the state departments of education, local school districts, and schools.

## NEW MULTILEVEL ORGANIZATION FOR WORKING PARTNERSHIPS

For decades, split responsibility has resulted in no responsibility. Thousands of people work in state departments of education, school district offices, and school administration offices, but no one takes responsibility for school performance. Teachers should not be the only people held responsible for student learning. It is no longer acceptable for everyone other than classroom teachers to say that they offer professional help, resources, programs, and so on but that only teachers are responsible for student learning. Let's look at each organizational level within the American public school system and review its responsibilities.

### Responsibilities for the Federal Department of Education

Without national standards or accountability systems, the federal government cannot be held responsible for school performance any more than states can be held responsible for national defense. The federal government provides funds for various programs such as breakfasts, lunches, remediation, special education, buildings, and the like, but they do not manage the school system. The federal department of education awards grants for research to various universities and conducts comparative studies among states. In the last election, both presidential candidates claimed that they would provide more funds to local schools, but these funds would require increased accountability. Except for the Native American and Defense Department schools, the federal department of education is only a resource provider to schools and a force for change.

### Responsibilities for the State Department of Education

The states have the constitutional responsibility to manage the public school system. Before World War II, states delegated nearly all of their authority and responsibilities to local school boards. Today, there are about 15,000 local school districts. In the past, schools were almost completely funded by local real estate taxes. This funding system changed during the past 60 years. According to the U.S. Department of Education, the federal government provides 7 percent of the education funds, state governments provide 48 percent, and local governments provide 45 percent.[2] These numbers vary by state. In some places, the entire allocation of funds is now controlled by the state department of education through state legislation.

*Listed as follows are the typical responsibilities of a state department of education:*

- Establish standards of learning in core subjects.
- Establish statewide assessments/rankings.
- Evaluate successful learning systems.
- Communicate, and in some cases fund, "best practices."

- Allocate resources to school districts.
- Reconstitute failing schools and school districts.

The state department of education must have the ability to close school districts and schools that fail to perform. West Virginia is an example where the state department of education took over an entire school district and removed the superintendent.[3] The state also has the power and responsibility to close schools in more than 25 states.[4] The local school district or the state must then reconstitute a failing school. Reconstitution means installing new administrators and new management, learning, assessment, and administrative systems. Teachers and administrative personnel apply to the new management team for positions in the reconstituted school. The objective is to change both education systems and personnel to achieve the state learning standards.

Every year the state provides stronger leadership to local school districts for two reasons: First, the state department of education provides most funds to most school districts; second, and equally important, political leaders have, in many cases, given up on local control and leadership. Governor Davis of California bluntly told a reporter that local control of schools had been an "abject failure." He further stated: "When you have an earthquake or natural disaster, people expect the state to intervene. Well, we have a disaster in our schools."[5]

## Responsibilities for Local School District

*Listed as follows are the typical responsibilities of a successful school district in future years:*

- Determine learning objectives based on state standards.
- Add local learning objectives (history, traditions, etc.).
- Develop integrated curriculum with assessment instruments.
- Select or develop successful learning and tutoring systems.
- Provide administrative, computer, and support systems.
- Provide human resource programs.
- Hire, train, and retain good employees.
- Develop professional development programs for teachers.
- Provide financial control systems.
- Allocate resources to schools.
- Monitor school performance.
- Reconstitute failing schools.

- Develop a long-range facilities plan.
- Supervise building and renovation projects.
- Enhance community relations.

The pressure of states taking over schools and school districts has created a new sense of urgency at the district level to improve low-performing schools. Therefore, the superintendent and the district staff are taking on a greater leadership role. Local control by school districts will only survive if the local school district is able to manage both the finances and student learning.

## Responsibilities for Schools

Schools can be classified as the operating units of this multilevel partnership organization. *Typical future responsibilities for schools will be as follows:*

- Implement successful learning and assessment systems.
- Implement a professional development system for teachers.
- Implement parent involvement programs.
- Maintain the technology system.
- Provide input to administrative systems.
- Handle discipline, truancy, and drop-out problems.
- Maintain students at grade level.
- Operate within a budget.
- Maintain the physical plant.
- Manage the cafeteria, buses, and security.

In some school districts, the principal of a school is responsible for hiring and retaining good employees.

When tasks are documented for the three partnership levels (i.e., state, district and school), it becomes clear that teachers are not the only personnel responsible for student learning. This partnership is an education system. The key word is "system," rather than a one-room-schoolhouse–type method and organization. For example, if an educator at the district level selects the wrong learning system, teachers and students within that district will regress from success to failure. Inadequate technology systems can also prevent teachers and students from succeeding. Every piece of the overall system must be successful in order to achieve the goal that all students can be successful learners. Some people refer to this system as "shared leadership" and "distributed leadership" based on a shared vision. Distributed leadership makes everyone responsible for student learning by assigning specific tasks to each member of the management team and the teachers. If students fail to learn, it must be clear which job is responsible for the failure so corrective action can be taken.

This organization closely resembles the modern successful corporate model in which decisions are made to centralize certain functions because of economies of scale and quality control. Other functions are performed at the local operating unit level. Therefore, discussions of total centralization compared to total decentralization are meaningless exercises; certain functions should be centralized and certain ones should be decentralized. A state school officer once said, "If there is money coming, no one mentions local control. If there is accountability, everyone raises the issue of local control."[6]

In the last century, many schools believed that the district office was a large bureaucracy that failed to serve schools. This situation was often true because the district office was concerned primarily with district office activities. Little was done to help schools. Instead, district administrators "viewed with alarm" any unfavorable occurrence that happened at a school. Schools knew that the state department of education existed, but most classroom teachers viewed it as a total waste of money. This situation must change. In this century, these three organizational levels must work together in a meaningful partnership through distributed leadership before duplicate efforts and costs become unbearable.

When political leaders and educators wave the local control banner, do they really want to maintain the costly one-room-schoolhouse model that has a 25 to 75 percent failure rate? Probably not. The modern organization model provides administrators and classroom teachers with an embraceable responsibility. The one-room-schoolhouse model creates intolerable working conditions for teachers. When all of the functions and tasks that are performed at the state, school district, and school levels are reviewed, it becomes obvious that even if teachers worked 80 hours per week and 12 months every year, they could not accomplish all of the necessary work. For example, teachers do not have time to review each research study, evaluate all courseware, review all learning systems, and read all books written on their grade or subject. A task analysis should be performed to determine what a principal's responsibilities are and what a classroom teacher's responsibilities are. In most cases, it would be obvious that neither has an embraceable responsibility because too many tasks have been delegated to the operating unit level—the school.

Some educators will interpret this chapter as yet another top-down management system. Unfortunately, too many people carry the flag of decentralization as the solution for all school problems. They tell us that if we loosen the grip of bureaucratic rules at the school district and state levels, we will empower the community, teachers, and principals with the ability to run successful schools. Teachers can focus then on helping students learn rather than fulfilling another school mandate. What they do not discuss is how much work must be accomplished by teachers and principals under the local management control model, and they quickly forget the performance statistics of schools that have no oversight.

Don't be fooled by this simplistic approach. New York City has had a 25-year experiment with decentralization. Their 1,000 schools were divided into 32 community school districts. Over the years, some of these schools have become legendary for corruption and indifference to academics. New York City schools were considered some of the worst in the nation, except for the magnet schools that carefully selected the best students and two districts that had outstanding superintendents. Recently, the New York state legislature returned most of the decision-making authority to the School Chancellor.[7]

In most cases, decentralization increases costs and lowers student performance. It was considered a great solution until accountability systems revealed that it was just another quick-fix. Al Shanker, former president of the American Federation of Teachers, once stated:

> The American education system is already the most decentralized in the industrial world, and the result is a system in which some kids get a pretty good education and others get garbage—often in the same school district or school. Decentralization may work when certain things are highly centralized—when there are rigorous, grade-by-grade academic standards set at the state level, assessments based on those standards, and accountability for the way public money is spent, to name a few.[8]

Sixty years ago there were 115,000 school districts in the United States. Today, there are nearly 15,000 districts.[9] There is no indication that states want to create more districts. The organization and management structure outlined in this chapter optimizes the best of all functions by having some functions centralized and others decentralized. Local control is alive and well in this organization structure.

## SYSTEMS APPROACH FOR ACADEMIC PERFORMANCE

The diagram shown in Figure 12–1 outlines the new management system that must be implemented into school districts and schools to both measure and manage learning. For decades, public schools did little to measure learning. Now that learning is being measured, the challenge is to manage learning. For the first time, there is an opportunity to manage learning with a standards-based curriculum and assessments.

This simple but effective management approach starts with learning standards established by the state, local school district, and school faculty. The director of curriculum must work with experienced teachers to convert these standards into

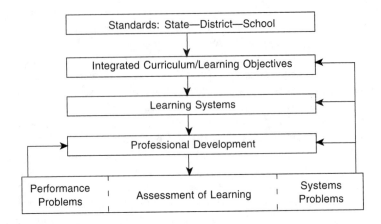

**Figure 12–1** Systems Approach for Academic Performance

learning objectives (lessons) for the K–12 integrated curriculum. Schools must know what lessons need to be taught in each subject and each grade. The director of curriculum and experienced teachers will then select proven learning systems that will achieve these learning objectives and standards. Learning systems can be validated, prepackaged systems from a company or university, or homegrown learning systems like the ones used in Moss Point, Mississippi (Chapter 10). In either case, the system must work for more than 90 percent of the students. This approach supports local control within public schools. Teachers can no longer work in isolation. They must become part of a professional learning community based on a common curriculum and learning system.

The school must then provide adequate professional development programs and resources that enable all teachers to implement the learning systems successfully. This means that the selection of learning systems must include the fundamental question of whether the teachers are able to and will use the system. In other words, teachers must like the learning systems and have confidence in them. Professional development must be schoolwide and consistent throughout a school district rather than hit-and-miss teacher-by-teacher programs.

The final step is to determine by various assessment means whether students have learned their lessons. If the result is less than 90 percent, then the principal and master teachers must report to the director of curriculum that a performance problem and/or a learning system problem is present. If the problem is with performance, then additional professional development training must be implemented for teachers who didn't succeed. The principal will also need to coach these teachers until they're successful. On the other hand, if most teachers failed, then the learning system needs to be modified or replaced. Frequent assessments and reports to the administrators are absolutely essential if learning is to be both measured and managed.

For example, in 1997, the new Dallas Reading Academy unveiled its new reading initiative, but the new methods did not achieve breakthroughs in reading scores by 1999.[10] Therefore, the school district leaders had to decide if their new learning system, which combined the best of phonics and whole-language instruction, was inadequate or if the problem was with their professional development programs. In California, the state school board approved a change from the whole-language approach that was adopted in 1988 to a framework that stressed phonics because the reading scores in second through sixth grades had fallen to a rank of 46th out of 50 states. The goal is now to have successful readers by third grade.[11]

These assessments will ultimately eliminate the bell-curve model for teachers. Teachers will become like pilots in that they will all be required to be successful. Also, teachers will no longer be blamed for poor student performance. The bell-curve model for students will be pushed to the right, and more than 90 percent of them will receive an A or B performance rating. This approach is a radical but much-needed departure from site-based management and the one-room-school-house organizational model.

## "BETTER TEACHING" REQUIRES "BETTER MANAGEMENT"

If professional musicians in an orchestra were playing different musical selections and/or were not on the same place on the sheet music, the orchestra leader would stop the orchestra, ask everyone to use the same sheet music, and play together as a team. This is exactly what the superintendent and principals must do with the help of the director of curriculum in order to achieve the goal of "better teaching."

*Instead, some people have come up with more expensive, quick-fix silver bullets, as follows:*

- Increase teachers' pay.
- Exempt teachers from state income tax.
- Eliminate seniority-based teacher assignments.
- Minimize hiring teachers with emergency permits.
- Provide 11- or 12-month contracts to teachers in low-performing schools.
- Support National Board certification for excellent teachers in low-performing schools.
- Increase funding for professional development workshops.

Once again, the school reform movement is spending millions of dollars on a series of expensive, sound-good programs that may have little or no impact on student learning. The management team must focus on the fundamentals of teaching, tutoring, assessment, and learning in order to fix student performance problems in all schools, but especially in low-performing schools.

*Let's review the actions that are necessary, as follows:*

- Develop and implement an integrated curriculum that is aligned to state and local learning standards.
- Document learning objectives by grade level that enable students to learn their lessons to meet the standards.
- Select, modify, or develop learning systems that enable all teachers to be successful in teaching the lessons required for grade-level performance. The learning system must be interesting and motivational in order for all students to become successful learners.
- Implement assessment and tutoring systems that ensure that students will not fall behind and get lost during the school year. The assessments will test the lessons that achieve the learning objectives.

These actions will not be accomplished unless great leadership is demonstrated from the superintendent, director of curriculum, principals, vice-principals, and master teachers. The director of curriculum and the learning system staff can identify why students are not learning, but the school administrators, with the support of the superintendent, must take corrective action when a serious performance problem in learning becomes apparent. Task forces made up of political leaders and business executives cannot and should not be expected to fix student learning problems.

Principals and vice-principals cannot be leaders of learning and change if these fundamental systems are not implemented in all schools within a district. Education is a system, not just a course or a lesson. School leaders must be systems integrators. Schools are low-performing because the learning, tutoring, and management systems are inadequate. Once again, it is not the fault of teachers, parents, or students when a school is ranked as a failure or low-performing institution. It is wise to remember the following quote from Father Hesburgh, former president of Notre Dame University:

> My basic principle is that you don't make decisions because they are easy; you don't make them because they are cheap; you don't make them because they are popular; you make them because they are right.[12]

Administrators must make the decisions to both measure and manage learning to reach the goal of all students being successful learners.

## NEW STATEWIDE OR DISTRICTWIDE ADMINISTRATIVE SYSTEM

Over the years, massive amounts of time and funds have been invested in thousands of administrative systems. Computers have driven the cost and complexity to an all-time high. Almost all of the administrative systems have the same information: attendance, grades, courses, basic student facts, parent names, addresses, telephone numbers, and a current list of classes. It's costly to develop an administrative system, but a state can well afford to develop a sophisticated one. The country can also well afford to have 50 of these systems, but there is no need to have 15,000 (one per school district) or 90,000 (one per school) systems. The state department of education should design a system that enables it to manage its public school system. The largest state, California lacks such an administrative system to track student and school performance in 1,000 school districts and 8,000 schools, whereas some states such as Texas have implemented such a system.

Too many administrative systems, developed by local computer personnel, require extensive maintenance. Studies have shown that schools spend as much as 30 percent of their budget on clerical personnel and administrative systems. Parochial schools have always maintained tight controls over their administrative costs. The "for-profit" school chains expect to minimize their administrative costs by using one system for all of their schools, with a goal of spending less than 10 percent of their budget. With various mandates from the federal department of education, state department of education, the school districts, and the central offices of the school, classroom teachers are now forced to spend an inordinate amount of time on administrative tasks. The state department of education should reengineer the administrative process to minimize school costs and effort and to achieve economies of scale.

In the past, it was unthinkable for an outside firm to program one of a company's or government agency's key information systems. That belief changed during the past 25 years. Payroll is the best example of this shift. Today, three large companies and a dozen intermediate-size organizations process more than half of the nation's payrolls. Considered one of the most sensitive applications years ago, this basic application is now outsourced by thousands of organizations. A similar approach may soon be taken with the public schools' administrative systems. For example, Philadelphia and other cities use a new identification card that students swipe at school entry doors or in each classroom to automatically record attendance.[13] One school has improved attendance by 6 percent and lowered costs because clerical errors are eliminated and an enhanced system for dealing with students who cut classes or fail to attend school has been implemented.

## THREE BASIC TYPES OF ADMINISTRATORS

For decades, many people believed that principals, vice-principals, superinten-dents, and assistant superintendents were just a necessary evil. After all, a classroom teacher did all the real work and rarely needed help from administra-tors. Recently, this attitude has changed. Today, most leaders within the education reform movement realize that administrators must be leaders of change and learning. In fact, if a school district's senior management team and principals are not enthusiastic supporters of a new vision, it's a waste of time and money to start any education reform programs. Working with only a few teachers creates a "hobby shop" or a model program that lasts only as long as the interested teachers are willing to devote their efforts to the new approach.

Schools, like corporations and government agencies, have three types of executives. The first group is caretakers. They maintain the status quo. Unfortu-nately, with schools, that means a failure rate of 25 to 75 percent. Caretakers avoid education reform; they want someone else to be the pioneer who gets the arrows in the back (criticism from the community). When they foresee only a few risks from proven systems, then they'll consider restructuring their schools. Fortu-nately, there are fewer caretaker administrators in today's schools.

Most administrators have risen to the second category: education reform administrators. They attend meetings, read articles, and discuss books on the subject. They comment positively on education reform. Unfortunately, the deci-sions they make are minor. They let one or two teachers try something new. They let one school in the district experiment with a new program. Site-based manage-ment is one of their favorite reforms. They rarely, if ever, develop schoolwide or districtwide visions. They take a very safe approach in which no one gets blamed for being too aggressive or for huge failures; however, this conservative approach results in only a slight improvement in student learning because they are just tinkering around the edges.

The third group, and its numbers are small, features the true visionary leaders of learning and change. They have existed in Memphis, Seattle, San Diego, and, of course, Moss Point, Mississippi. As mentioned previously, Dr. C. Hines Cronin was such a leader of learning and change who inspired actual breakthroughs in student learning throughout a school district. These leaders have an exciting vision. They're risk takers like their corporate counterparts Jack Welch of General Electric, Andy Grove of Intel, Tom Watson of IBM, Bill Gates of Microsoft, and Steve Jobs of Apple. They have goals, strategies, action programs, learning systems, and measurements to create change. They are committed to long-term improvement in student learning. They accomplish the two aspects of leadership: (1) a visionary role (doing the right thing) and (2) an implementation role (doing things right), which are often quoted by Ken Blanchard, a management consult-ant.[14] Blanchard has also stated: "People look to their leader for vision and direction. While leaders should involve their experienced people in shaping direction, they cannot delegate the responsibility for establishing vision and direction."[15]

Needless to say, there's a vital need to train thousands of these leaders. One factor that will expand this group is a major increase in compensation. Visionary learning and change leaders are worth at least $50,000 more per year than caretakers or education reform administrators because they solve the major problems of a school district. The sum of $50,000 is an arbitrary number, but it is based on the differential pay rates between executives of low-performing organizations and successful organizations.[16]

Many superintendents last, on average, two or three years at their jobs. This statistic shouldn't be surprising because most of these people have no vision, no solution for breakthroughs in student learning, and few action plans to address the 25 success factors listed in the previous chapter. They leap from crisis to crisis as they tinker around the edges of school reform. After a few years, they exhaust their energies and move to another school district.

There are currently nearly 90,000 public school principals in the United States, and it is estimated that 40 percent will retire in this decade.[17] Some will be asked to leave their jobs. The long hours (estimated at 54 hours per week) and the increased job responsibilities are not attracting new candidates.[18] More than 90 percent of teachers have no interest in having a principal's job.[19] The attrition rate for principals is so high now that a critical shortage is developing. Good schools require strong and stable leadership. Principals have enormous influence over the performance of a school. In the past, the pay differential between an experienced teacher and the principal's job was not that great, but this situation is changing. More principals are now earning at least $25,000 to $35,000 more than experienced teachers. Many principals' salaries now exceed $100,000. Outstanding principals, who manage successful schools where student learning is improving, are in great demand and deserve to be well paid.

## OTHER KEY POSITIONS REQUIRED FOR THE NEW VISION

Superintendents and principals must be relieved from the day-to-day business and operating decisions so they can concentrate more on the issue of how to improve student learning. As a result, the assistant superintendent in charge of operations (e.g., budgeting, accounting, information systems, administrative systems, facilities, food services, transportation, purchasing, supplies, custodial services) becomes a key executive on the district staff.

Schools depend on the performance of people, and many superintendents now appoint an assistant superintendent in charge of human resources to handle recruitment, benefits, labor relations, resolution of personnel problems, compensation, and the constant review of new labor laws. If a superintendent does not have a strong person in this job, personnel problems will consume both the superintendent's and principals' schedules, leaving them with little or no time to focus on student learning.

Public relations is another area where superintendents in major urban cities need full-time professional personnel. Many legal problems require a full-functioning legal service office. As stated earlier, the importance of an assistant superintendent for the curriculum position cannot be stressed enough. This person is the Chief Education or Academic Officer of the district.

Schools need an outstanding management team that is well-paid and rewarded when it achieves the school district's goals. The superintendent is a school district's Chief Executive Officer, and assistant superintendents act as its senior vice-presidents. Last but not least, principals are essentially the vice-presidents in a school district.

## ADMINISTRATOR'S INSTITUTE FOR MANAGEMENT

The best-managed organizations in government and the corporate world have a management development program consisting of courses and seminars on key subjects such as organization, work delegation, training the workforce, handling unhappy employees, financial control, public relations, legal issues, performance management systems, recruiting, coaching, attrition, and so on. Although some management development programs are offered by colleges of education, most are a hit-and-miss effort rather than a focused curriculum of lessons.

Each superintendent of a large school district should implement a formal management development program for all levels of school administrators. The program could be a mixture of internal and external programs. Internal courses should clearly communicate the management tasks of each administrator's job within the district. For example, a general course on people management is not as effective as programs that teach how to attract, motivate, retain, and reward outstanding teachers. Superintendents of small districts should carefully evaluate the courses available from colleges of education and business to determine if they achieve the learning objectives required by an outstanding management development program. Very few programs have adequate lessons on management systems, effective organizations, learning systems, assessment systems, instructional design, and change management systems. This instruction is essential if administrators are going to be successful in the new environment of standards-based curriculum and assessment. They must be provided with in-depth lessons on how to improve student learning.

Superior management is not a gift, but rather comes from skills based on a superior management development program, which is lacking in most school districts. Today's attrition rates for administrators are not tolerable, and much of the blame can be placed on ineffective training. In the past, many courses for administrators have been very theoretical, textbook-based, and extremely easy to complete. Courses have been so inadequate that some universities are now trying to establish a partnership with one or more school districts to bring "real-world" training to the program. A maverick principal in Providence, Rhode Island, is trying a new approach by having 10 "distinguished principals" in his program to train new administrators.[20]

"On-the-job" programs sound good, but it is not wise to use "on-the-job" training programs if serious performance problems exist within the organization. Training people on the old paradigm does not lead to breakthroughs in performance. Thousands of well-qualified candidates will step forward to be administrators if they know that adequate management systems and management development programs exist in their school districts and that financial rewards are given for increased responsibilities, but this is not going to happen with the current management methods and inadequate management development programs that exist today.

## REQUIREMENT FOR A NEW POSITION: MASTER TEACHERS

In most schools, teaching is a socialistic career that offers pay increases based on years of education and service. Recently, some recognition awards, such as Teacher of the Year, have been instituted, but for most people, teaching appears to be a dead-end job with low status, uncompetitive salaries, poor working conditions, and an unembraceable task of developing successful learners when many students are not at grade level. Fortunately, the teaching job will greatly improve with the new paradigm of learning and tutoring systems tied to learning standards. With rare exception, teacher salaries are increasing across the nation. New school buildings are being constructed and old buildings are being renovated. Let's look at a new career opportunity.

Similar to other jobs, some superior teachers are well-equipped to take on greater responsibilities. Every school system needs to implement a new teacher category for these people: Master or Lead Teacher.

***Titles will vary, but here are the responsibilities for this new position:[21]***

- Is an acknowledged leader within a grade or subject area.
- Is knowledgeable about research projects and learning systems.
- Is knowledgeable about assessment programs.
- Takes a major role in the development of the integrated curriculum.
- Plays a major role in helping to select learning systems.

- Helps plan professional development programs.
- Teaches in the professional development programs.
- Visits classrooms to observe and mentor other teachers.
- Mentors new and inexperienced teachers.
- Mentors student teachers.
- Serves as a role model for other teachers.
- Transfers "best practices" of teaching.
- Serves as a leader of change.
- Enhances knowledge of subject matter and effective teaching methods by attending conferences and consulting with experts.
- Is responsible for student learning within the grade or grades and subject matter areas.

Teaching is often referred to as a lonely profession. There is a definite need for new and inexperienced teachers to work with a mentor. Too often, this action program is just another "nice to do" program. The Master or Lead Teacher position formalizes the collaboration with measurable results. Master teachers should earn $15,000 more than the top of the teacher salary scale. They should not have a full classroom schedule, but they would have at least a 25- to 50-percent teaching schedule. This enlarged set of responsibilities would be considered a promotion within the teaching ranks. Many master teachers could later be promoted to be a vice-principal or principal. Like deans of colleges, they could return to a full-time teaching position at any time. Restoring the concept of the master teacher would be a major step forward to raising the professional concept of the profession.

This new career opportunity for teachers will enhance their professional growth and ensure that local decision making improves and maintains a high level of student learning. A principal needs a formal working partnership with outstanding teachers in the school. Again, principals need help because they have too many people to supervise. Too often, they have an impossible job. Master teachers would be part of their management team and would have a formal voice in the means for achieving learning standards. Although this position is not a new idea, the responsibilities are more precise and the concept of being a member of the management team is new.

This position and promotion for teachers is more meaningful than the certificate by the National Board for Professional Teaching Standards because the job is enriched to have management responsibilities. The Master or Lead Teacher will make a far greater contribution to the overall performance of other teachers. The National Board certification is a good recognition program, but it does not fix the problem that principals need, which is another layer of management to both measure and manage student learning. The National Board certification is based on videotapes of teachers' classroom performance, a portfolio of their work, and a series of written examinations. In 1999, 6,124 teachers completed the process, and in 2000 a record 9,506 educators are going through the evaluation process. By the fall of 2001, the board plans to offer certification in 33 specialties of teaching.

## REQUIREMENT FOR PARA-EDUCATORS

"Para-educator" is the new name for a teacher's aide in today's schools. Their responsibilities vary from supervising the lunchroom to teaching in the special education classes. Their pay varies from $6 per hour for beginners in low-paying states to $20 per hour in higher-paying states for experienced aides. These people usually do not have a college degree, and most are mothers looking for work during school hours.

In many schools, no job description, little or no training, no evaluation system, and almost no preparation time to do their tasks is given to these people. These para-educators are merely "warm" bodies who do whatever a teacher tells them to do. Many have been hired with Title I funds. In some schools, there are as many or more para-educators than there are certified teachers.

Para-educators should be viewed as members of the instructional team. They need job descriptions, outstanding training programs as well as on-the-job training assignments, and professional evaluations of their work. They will be far more effective in a school that has a standards-based curriculum, learning systems, and standards-based assessment systems.

This lack of guidance for para-educators is another reason for implementing the Master or Lead Teacher position in schools. A master teacher should be responsible for the selection, training, and job performance evaluation of para-educators. Principals and vice-principals rarely have time to work with para-educators, and most teachers are not trained to supervise these people. Para-educators are a major resource in schools, and their performance can be greatly enhanced with the new organizational structure and management system.

## COUNSELING STUDENTS

Another area where split responsibility is often no responsibility asks the question: Who on the faculty is responsible for each child to be a successful student during their middle and high school years? Some schools say it is the homeroom teacher while others say the classroom teachers, and still others say the school counselors. To have students enrolled in the right courses to prevent drop-outs, to have students complete high school on time, reduce discipline problems, and prepare students for college as well as to find help for disturbed students, it should be clear that each student is assigned to a faculty member for their overall success in school.

Too many schools do not have clear responsibility for this important task. How a school accomplishes this task can have an impact on their overall costs. Counselors are expensive, but they provide an important function in schools. The American School Counselor Association recommends a student-counselor ratio of 250 to1. Many schools operate at 500 to 1 or 1,000 to 1. Today, the focus is on fewer students per teacher, but very few educators are discussing the number of students per counselor. The real issue is: How does a school district ensure that their students are assisted through 13 years of schooling to achieve the highest possible number of successful learners?

## JOB TRAINING FOR NONTEACHING STAFF

The workforce within every commercial, government, and not-for-profit organization can be classified into one of the two following categories:

1. *Workforce with Some Training.* The great majority of school districts have a workforce with only some training. This means there are a few courses available and there is a small budget for training that has only a small impact on job performance. Usually, there are no quality measurements other than asking if the participants liked the course.
2. *Well-Trained Professional Workers.* In a very few school districts, there is a focus on job performance within every key job of the organization. These jobs include counselors, medical staff, school secretaries, attendance administrators, accountants, information technology personnel, human resources personnel, food service personnel, custodians, and transportation people as well as teachers and administrators. The goal is simple: Train and develop employees to master their job responsibilities.

*What are the advantages for having a well-trained professional workforce?*

- Increased productivity
- Higher employee morale
- Lower operating expenses
- Lower supervision costs
- Reduced cost for rework
- Lower attrition rates
- Reduced recruitment and employment costs

- Increased job security
- Enhanced cross-training of jobs
- Faster implementation of strategic directions and tactical decisions.

The Human Resources Services department should develop a performance system for every key job within the school district. They should implement a systems approach for workforce performance that starts with the performance requirements of each key job based on the overall strategic and tactical objectives for the school district. A performance system is then developed for each key job including the following:

- Orientation to the district and the school
- Personal development courses and programs
- Performance-based training courses
- On-the-job training experiences
- Basic support system such as job aids.

Then a performance management system is implemented based on job requirements and performance systems. There should be a reward and recognition system that recognizes excellent performers and those who make outstanding contributions to their school and/or school district. Once again, all this sounds like common sense, but it is not common practice in most districts.

## CASE STUDY OF MANAGEMENT

The most notable example of managing a school district that contains inner-city schools was in Community School District 2 in New York City. There were 22,000 students in 24 elementary schools, 7 junior high schools, and 17 alternative schools, with a student body comprising 29 percent white, 14 percent black, 22 percent Hispanic, and 34 percent Asian students. Approximately 50 percent of the students came from families living below the poverty line, with some schools being as high as 95 percent. Nearly 20 percent of these schools' students spoke English as a second language.[22]

Superintendent Anthony Alvarado spent 10 years transforming the district into a learner-centered system that focused 100 percent on improved teaching and student learning. He gave great emphasis to literacy and reading, with the objective that every student must be a good reader. Principals and teachers had to know each student and felt very responsible for their success in learning. Funding for professional development increased from less than 1 percent to about 6 percent. Many outside consultants were used to enhance teaching skills. Distinguished teachers were paid $10,000 more to work with other teachers. All of this effort resulted in the percentage of students meeting New York state's standards rising from 27 percent to 74 percent. District 2 was ranked second in both reading and math within the 32 city school districts.[23]

This transition from failure to success came with major changes in personnel. First, the district staff was downsized, reorganized, and restaffed. Second, Superintendent Alvarado replaced 20 of his 30 principals in the first four years, and about half of the teachers were replaced over a 10-year period. New applicants were carefully reviewed and selected. Alvarado emphasized local control and individual responsibility, with few excuses being accepted for poor performance.[24]

Looking back, no one can say that Alvarado did not improve learning, but the objective was reached through a lot of hard work, stress, and a high turnover of personnel. The question can be asked whether this achievement could be accomplished in future years with less stress and without so much change in personnel with a combination of Alvarado's new management system and learning systems. Dr. Alvarado relies more on "better teaching" than on validated learning systems.

Dr. Alvarado is now the chief academic officer in San Diego, which is six times larger than his New York City district. Dr. Alvarado's reorganizations, management systems, and focus on student learning, as well as "better" teaching, have again improved student learning and test results. Dr. Alvarado has shown that leadership and management make a difference. In San Diego, he works with Alan Bersin, the superintendent of public schools. Both are strong leaders, and they are achieving results. In Oakland, California, the new superintendent has ordered major changes in the low-performing schools. He has moved or demoted one-third of the principals, with 29 schools under new leadership. New curriculum and learning systems are being implemented.[25] There are a few other visionary leaders of change and learning, but the country needs thousands more of these executives during this decade.

Many educators write well-meaning articles and books on how the system cannot be changed, but some people are creating real change within the American public school system. New management and learning systems greatly reduce the politics of education that prevails in so many school districts.

## ACHIEVE TOTAL QUALITY MANAGEMENT IN SCHOOLS

If the implementation of a new management system and organization like the one outlined in this chapter achieves the 25 important success factors documented in the previous chapter, then a school will satisfy the goals of Total Quality Management (TQM)—a common practice used in many large corporations.

In November 1992, the governor of Texas hosted a conference on TQM and National Goals. More than 1,500 educators, parents, business leaders, and government officials from 40 states and five countries attended.[26] Like many other states, Texas had doubled its spending for public schools, but student learning remained low. Lack of results had frustrated students, parents, and teachers who had tried everything they knew to achieve breakthroughs in student learning.

In 1993, David Kearns, a former Deputy Secretary of Education and the former Chief Executive Officer of Xerox, made the following comments in the foreword of a book entitled *Quality & Education: Critical Linkages*:

> The fact is TQM works in any large, complex organization. Indeed, its principles can and should be applied in any organization, large or small. I am convinced, as never before, that we must transform our schools. TQM can be and will be a large part of that transformation. Once upon a time TQM was a novel, even alarming, way to think about running a business. Its insistence on total quality through every step of the process—from design to manufacturing to marketing to customer service—meant a complete transformation of the organization. Easy to say, hard to do. Hard to do because old ways and old habits die hard. They are comfortable, and, in most cases, served the organization well—once upon a time. But no longer. Change becomes necessary when old ways no longer work.[27]

As stated previously, the schools' current organization, management procedures, and teaching methods prevent them from achieving the new quality standard that all students should be successful learners. Schools must have an integrated system for their standards, curriculum, and learning systems and assessments in order to achieve the overall TQM goal: Students learn the first time. This is why a new multilevel partnership with distributed leadership and a new management system—systems approach for academic performance—are essential. New "for-profit" national school chains are already using new management systems and a systems approach to student learning. Soon, not-for-profit public schools will, too.

To achieve the goals of TQM, the education community must accept the implementation of a performance management system that exists in all successful organizations whether they are for-profit or not-for-profit. It is important to remember that the primary goals of a first-class supervision and evaluation system are student learning and teacher professionalism based on standards-based curriculum and assessment systems.

The systems should assess teacher performance on curriculum knowledge, class management skills, instructional methods, and interpersonal skills with students, parents, and faculty. If learning systems are used, it is much easier to evaluate both teachers and administrators because standards of performance are based on "best practices" with the learning systems. In the unstructured world of traditional teaching and learning methods, the challenge to supervise and evaluate is much greater. It may be almost impossible, which is another primary reason for using new management and learning systems.

In most states, there are now laws that require teachers and administrators to be evaluated. Many of the systems are failing because of inadequate implementation and training.[28] Poor evaluations often lead to personnel problems and even to lawsuits or arbitration. The "needs to improve" performer must have a formal improvement program and an opportunity to improve. New and inexperienced teachers should not be allowed to "sink or swim." That is why the Master or Lead Teacher role is so important. Beginning teachers must be partnered with a successful and experienced teacher.[29]

Some people vehemently object to the idea of running school like businesses. If the word "businesses" is replaced with the phrase "successful organizations," perhaps they will feel better. To justify hundreds of billions of dollars in taxpayer funds, schools must operate as successful organizations. To achieve TQM and more than 90 percent successful learners, learning must be managed at all five levels of the education system: state, district, school, teacher, and student. An integrated management and administrative system that serves all five levels must be developed to achieve optimum results in learning and cost containment.

Another visionary leader of learning and change is Dr. Jim Parsley, Superintendent of Vancouver, Washington. He has seven full-time educators on his district staff for quality control and assessment systems in a school district of 22,500 students.[30] This group is similar to an approach by Arthur Andersen & Co., which has a full-time quality control group at its large training center in St. Charles, Illinois. Some institutions of learning do focus on and achieve TQM objectives.

How big is the transition from today's world to tomorrow's world of success? Let's look at the commercial aviation business. In the 1920s, Charles Lindbergh was involved in the design and maintenance of his airplane, the navigation of his flight, the weather evaluations, and the piloting of his aircraft. He "did it all" with little help from other people. Today, pilots are expected only to fly the plane. Engineers design the plane, computer specialists handle communication systems, professional weather experts provide forecasts, electronic systems provide navigation, and an entire team of mechanics maintain the aircraft. Too often, our schools operate on the Charles Lindbergh model. Teachers are expected to "do it all," but it is an impossible task. Therefore, it's time to change, which is the subject of Chapter 13.

## NOTES

1. List developed by the author.
2. R. Johnston and J. Sandham, "States Increasingly Flexing Their Policy Muscle," *Education Week*, 14 April, 1999, 1, 19, 21.
3. B. Keller, "West Virginia Seizes Control of Its Third School District," *Education Week*, 21 June, 2000, 22.
4. Johnston and Sandham, "States Increasingly Flexing," 21.
5. Johnston and Sandham, "States Increasingly Flexing," 21.
6. W. Moloney, Colorado Commission of Education, "States Increasingly Flexing Their Policy Muscle," *Education Week*, 14 April, 1999, 20.
7. A. Shanker, "Where's the Evidence," *New York Times*, 2 February, 1997, E7.
8. Shanker, "Where's the Evidence."
9. M. Wang and H. Walberg, "Decentralize or Disintermediate," *Education Week*, 1 December, 1999, 52.
10. K. Manzo, "Dallas Reading Initiative Produces Limited Results," *Education Week*, 1 March, 2000, 28.
11. J. Kerr, "Phonics Guidelines Approved for Reading," *San Diego Union-Tribune*, 11 December, 1998, A1, A3.
12. Quote by Father Theodore Hesburgh, the former president of Notre Dame University, South Bend, Indiana.
13. M. Jennings, "Attendance Technology Easing Recordkeeping Burden," *Education Week*, 10 May, 2000, 7.
14. K. Blanchard, "Are You a Leader?" Rancho Bernardo Community Presbyterian Church, San Diego, CA, 20 November, 1999, 2.
15. Blanchard, "Are You a Leader?" 2.
16. Estimate by author.
17. L. Olson, "Demand for Principals Growing, But Candidates Are Not Applying," *Education Week*, 3 March, 1999, 1, 20–21.
18. Olson, "Demand for Principals," 20.
19. Olson, "Demand for Principals," 21.
20. B. Keller, "Building on Experience," *Education Week*, 3 May, 2000, 36–40.
21. R. Feiler et al., *Teachers Leading Teachers* (Alexandria, VA: Association for Supervision and Curriculum Development, April 2000), 66–69.
22. R. Wolk, "Strategies for Fixing Failing Schools," *Education Week*, 4 November, 1998; and The Pew Forum on Education Reform, 46.
23. Wolk, "Strategies for Fixing Failing Schools."
24. Wolk, "Strategies for Fixing Failing Schools."
25. R. Harris, "Oakland Shakes Up Worst of Its Schools," *San Diego Union-Tribune*, 24 June, 2000, A3–A4.

26. B. McCormick, *Quality and Education: Critical Linkages* (Princeton Junction, NJ: Eye On Education, 1993), 1–293.

27. McCormick, *Quality and Education*, Foreword, 7.

28. W. Ribas, "Ascending the ELPS to Excellence in Your District's Teacher Evaluation," *Phi Delta Kappan*, April 2000, 585–590.

29. D. Evans, "Assistance for Underqualified Teachers," *Education Week*, 3 February, 1999, 35–36.

30. Author's interview with Dr. J. Parsley, Superintendent of Schools, Vancouver, Washington.

# CHAPTER 13

# Need for a Change Management System

Joel Barker, an expert on changing paradigms, has stated: "A vision without action is merely a dream. Action without a vision just passes time. Vision with action can change the world."[1] It's not necessary to change the world, but there's a critical need to bring systemic change to the American public school system. Fulfilling this need requires both an exciting vision and a realistic plan of action based on change management principles.

## FROM TRADITIONAL MODEL TO A LEARNING-CENTERED MODEL

Years ago in the traditional model, teachers possessed all of the knowledge and experience. At first, teachers passed the knowledge on to students primarily through oral presentations. Eventually, the knowledge base expanded when books and printed materials were introduced. After teachers had delivered a lesson, they asked the students, "Do you understand the lessons?" Those who did raised their hands or responded with an enthusiastic "Yes." Teachers then moved on to the next lesson even though some students were not prepared to learn the lesson (were not at grade level) and others didn't learn the previous lesson at all.

The result of this system has been that some students fall behind and others are totally lost. Some have mentally dropped out of the learning process even though they sit in classrooms until they're 16 years old. In the past, slow learners have been categorized as unmotivated or unintelligent. Recently, students' gender, socioeconomic level, or race has been used as an excuse. In this traditional model, teachers work very hard at teaching, but too often, students do not work hard at learning. This teaching-centered model will never enable 90 percent of all students to become successful, especially at inner-city schools.

The new learning-centered model encourages students to work very hard at learning through a combination of high standards, high-quality course materials, audiotapes, videotapes, interactive tutoring systems, and teacher lectures developed by a team of professional educators. Students learn each lesson or receive immediate tutoring until they do learn. Successful students go on to receive enrichment lessons. Managed by a classroom teacher, this learning system is part of a world-class curriculum that enables students to be successful on state achievement and mastery tests. Students manage more of their own learning and feel responsible for being at grade level. This new learning-centered model is a performance system that will enable both teachers and students to be successful. How does a school move from the traditional model to a learning-centered one? Read on for the answer.

## GUIDELINES FOR CREATING AND MANAGING CHANGE

Almost every major change and successful reengineering project goes through the following five major change phases:

### Phase 1: Develop an Overpowering Case for Change

As Part I of this book indicated, quality and cost problems provide an overpowering case for change in the American school system.

*Each school district and/or school must develop its own case by documenting the following information:*

- What percentage of the students are at grade level?
- How many students are one, two, three, four, five, six, or more years behind in grade level?
- What is the drop-out rate?
- How many students do not attend school on a regular basis?
- How many students are discipline problems?
- What is the mobility rate for students?
- How many years of teaching experience does the staff have?
- Do the teachers have the required education to teach their subjects?
- What is the attrition rate for administrators, teachers, aides, and administrative personnel?
- How good are the professional development programs?

- What is the morale level for administrators, teachers, aides, and administrative personnel?
- What is the quality of course materials?
- How many multimedia computers are used for instruction and tutoring?
- What are the strengths and weaknesses of the current administrative system?
- What are the strengths and weaknesses of the current information technology system?
- What are the scores on key assessment tests?
- What rank does the school have academically?
- Which education reform programs have been implemented in past years and at what level of success?
- How much are parents involved?
- What are the current costs and operating budget?
- What are the measurements for quality performance?
- What are the serious problems facing the school district?

In schools where 50 percent or more students are not at grade level, it's easy to present an overpowering case for change.

## Phase 2: Create an Exciting Vision and Establish Key Goals

An example of an exciting vision was provided in Chapter 11. Remember, the vision should be a commitment to achieve more than 90 percent successful learners. A vision that states schools will improve merely through good intentions is inadequate. Sometimes it's helpful to document four or five goals before the vision is written. Goals should be challenges, not just easy objectives. Bob Galvin, the former Chief Executive Officer of Motorola, tells everyone, "Don't underestimate how much an organization can improve. Most people like to think of improvements on the order of a few percentage points when they should be thinking in terms of 25, 50 or 100 percent. It is important to set high but realistic expectation levels."[2]

*An example of six such goals is as follows:*

*Goal 1:* Utilize a world-class curriculum.

*Goal 2:* Students become successful learners at grade level and achieve superior performance on state and local tests with the utilization of learning and assessment systems.

*Goal 3:* Achieve high teacher and administrator productivity by implementing embraceable responsibilities based on needs and task analysis.

*Goal 4:* Utilize a management system that achieves the goals over a strategic period.

*Goal 5:* Achieve a high level of community relations and parent involvement.

*Goal 6:* Control the cost of education.

The vision and goals must motivate political leaders, business executives, community leaders, educators, parents, and citizens to embrace a shared picture of the future. Vision outcomes with quantifiable goals must be so overwhelmingly positive that the effort to make the necessary changes is seen as worthwhile.

## Phase 3: Document a Blueprint for Change

The detailed plans for reaching goals and achieving the vision should include the following:

- Strategies (that outline how a goal will be achieved over several years)
- Action plans (what will be accomplished each year to implement the strategy)
- Budget for change (by year, what changes need to be made to the standard operating budget)
- Organization chart
- Staff responsibilities (tasks for each team member)
- Project management (when will the work be completed and who is responsible?)

Phases 1 and 2 are accomplished by most education reform projects. Unfortunately, only a few projects do an adequate job in Phase 3 (completing a "blueprint" for realizing the vision and achieving the goals). This phase is where all of the pieces of the puzzle for school reform come together. Everyone works on his or her piece of the puzzle individually, but the overall coherent plan for break-throughs in student learning is never agreed to unanimously. Without a complete and agreed-upon blueprint, there's really no hope for success.

It is important to remember that the blueprint should change only what must be changed. Some education reformers have stated that everything and almost every person must be changed in the schools. This complete overhaul is not necessary and should be avoided.

## Phase 4: Achieving Proof of Concept

Three to six schools should be identified as pilot schools in the district, including at least one elementary, one middle, and one high school. Pilot schools should be used to implement and test new curriculum, learning systems, assessment systems, administrative systems, management systems, human resource practices, information technology systems, and room layouts. Keep in mind that the first systems selected may not be the best ones or may need to be modified based on real-life experience. A series of assessments can determine if the systems need to be changed or if employee performance problems need to be corrected.

As systems and performance problems are resolved, the student body will consist of more than 90 percent successful learners and the school will achieve the important success factors outlined in Chapter 11. Proof of concept will come when all elementary schools that feed into middle schools become successful and when all middle schools that feed into a single high school become successful (in other words, a successful cluster-of-schools model). After all, high schools do not become dysfunctional by themselves. A low-performing high school is usually part of a low-performing cluster of schools.

Every school district should have a set of pilot schools working on a new paradigm to achieve more than 90 percent successful learners. This isn't a high-risk decision professionally or financially for a local board of education or a superintendent; local taxpayers and parents will respect a school board that establishes a schoolwide reform pilot program to achieve learning breakthroughs.

A pilot program also enables teachers and administrators who do not wish to develop a new paradigm to transfer to other schools within the district so they can continue using their traditional teaching methods. All personnel challenges can be solved with a group of pilot schools. In a very small school district, such as Moss Point, Mississippi, a pilot school may not be feasible, but a districtwide system can achieve success in fewer years.

### Phase 5: Institutionalize Change throughout the District

Three key questions must be asked in every school concerning its reform program: (1) Will the reform be sustainable over long periods? (2) Can the reforms be transferred to other schools in the district? and (3) Will other school districts adopt the programs that achieve breakthroughs in student learning?

As soon as proof of concept has been realized, a second cluster (i.e., elementary, middle, and high schools) can be started to implement the new and successful paradigm. In the past, some school districts have made the mistake of selecting the worst schools for this group. The second cluster should include a group of schools where success should be able to be realized because of the good performance of administrators and teachers. Keep in mind that many educators become willing to change once proof of concept has been demonstrated and the risk of failure is perceived to be low.

On the other hand, in every organization, there are always people who must be dragged into the future. A few teachers and administrators will continue to resist, and only a district office mandate will force them to accept the new vision. They always want to be in a position to say, "I never volunteered to implement these new programs." Once several successful clusters have been established, it's easy for schools to practice "tough love" and to say publicly, "We expect you to successfully implement the new learning and assessment systems, and your evaluation will be based on your full cooperation and performance." Although some doubting teachers may continue to whine in private, "late" performers will get the message or they'll leave the system. The management system and accountability programs supervised by the state department of education will help institutionalize change.

It's important that a school district accelerate the pace of systemic change whenever possible. One cannot wait for a perfect world or 100-percent agreement; as soon as a learning system works in the pilot schools, it must be moved into schools that need to show real improvement. The reform must be institutionalized to the level where new teachers and administrators cannot regress to the old traditional method because successful administrators and teachers will receive job offers from other schools and districts.

## WHO IS RESPONSIBLE FOR CREATING CHANGE?

*The following individuals and groups must be identified with clear responsibilities for creating change:*

- Sponsoring executive or executives
- Director of change
- Change team
- Changing personnel
- Change agents.

Let's briefly describe each group. As previously stated, change rolls from the top down. If the Superintendent of Schools refuses to take a public leadership role in the process, then systemic change will not be implemented. Superintendents and assistant superintendents must be *sponsoring executives* of change. Superintendents must embrace the new vision and the new paradigm. They should inspire all members of the district staff, especially the director of curriculum. Pilot school principals should realize that they will receive positive and cooperative support on all school reform issues from the district staff. Superintendents should hold monthly progress meetings with the district staff and pilot school principals to verify that all responsible parties are implementing the action programs outlined in the "blueprint." If the district staff ignores the pilot schools because they're too busy working on other schools' day-to-day operating problems, then pilot schools will be viewed as a sideshow. In this situation, pilot schools will have little impact on other schools. If pilot schools are successful, principals should become candidates for promotion to key positions on the district staff or to schools of greater responsibility. They should also receive a major bonus or significant pay raise for successfully implementing all of the action programs and education reform project strategies.

To ensure success, the superintendent in an intermediate or large school district should promote a principal or assign an assistant superintendent to be the executive director of the education reform project. This individual will serve as the full-time *director of change*, which is essential except in small school districts where the superintendent is the director of change. If successful, this person will be entitled to a promotion, public recognition, and a substantial pay raise.

An education reform *change team* consists of key district staff personnel, principals, and master teachers in the pilot schools. The director of curriculum is also a key member of the team. They make most of the key decisions, reinforcing the concept of local control. Their decisions are then reviewed by the director of change at monthly meetings of the sponsoring executives. The *changing personnel* are, of course, the teachers and students in the pilot schools. The local press, business executives, political leaders, community leaders, and others outside the school district play the role of *change agents*, but they have no responsibility or authority to implement change. They can, however, have a substantially positive impact on the need to create and manage change. The change agents should be included in the public recognition when success is achieved.

One indication that school districts are becoming serious about school reform is the involvement by superintendents, district staffs, and principals in the discussion of how to improve student learning. In the past, change agents did most of the talking and work on this subject.

In large government agencies and corporations, a consulting firm is often hired during a period of great change. Consultants can be helpful when they have a proven track record of creating change within an industry because they're able to avoid costly mistakes made on prior engagements. In other words, a consultant is an insurance policy during a significant period of change. Foundations and government grants could help pay for consultants. Consultants should provide professional advice rather than actually doing the work if superintendents want to create self-sufficient teams at the completion of the pilot project. School districts should not hire consultants who are new to education reform issues. A lot of consultants want to learn how to restructure schools, but school districts should not pay for these professionals' learning curve.

## DIFFERENCE BETWEEN PILOT SCHOOLS AND CHARTER SCHOOLS

Most charter schools do not need to abide by local school district and state department of education regulations. They're islands of experimentation where new ideas and programs can be tested. Many charter schools are not tied to a union contract. In the future, a few—and it will only be a few—charter schools will emerge with successful homegrown curriculum, learning systems, assessment systems, and administrative systems. When it's time to transfer these new systems into all schools in a school district, the unions will probably not agree to the working conditions of the charter schools. The district staff will find fault with their new, innovative approaches. Teachers and principals will view the charter school as a model school that operates in an unrealistic world. Right or wrong, most systems developed by charter schools will never be used in most school districts because district executives will not be able to take any credit for these systems.

A pilot school is different. The superintendent, director of curriculum, director of business affairs, and human resources director will all have ownership in the reform. The new curriculum, learning, assessment, administrative, and management systems will have been developed within the realistic world of state and local regulations as well as within a union contract. The superintendent will get the credit for institutionalizing change throughout his or her school district.

## TRAINING REQUIRED TO CREATE CHANGE

Many professional development sessions on new visions and paradigms are "nice to do" for administrators and teachers. Unfortunately, very few workshops cover the entire subject of how a school district creates an exciting new vision and implements a new paradigm to achieve breakthroughs in student learning. These sessions must not be just lectures; time needs to be allowed for an open and thorough discussion of each issue. The facilitator can use some of these sessions to reach consensus. The reason why so few workshops exist is because so few proven leaders of change are available to teach them.

In the corporate world, the American Society of Training and Development (ASTD) offered a Chief Training Officer Workshop to communicate a new vision and a new management system that enabled companies and government agencies to meet total quality management (TQM) requirements. One or more colleges of education should create such a workshop for a school district's management team. State departments of education or large school districts could also develop workshops. There's no excuse for having 15,000 management teams learning lessons on a "hit-and-miss" basis. Best practices and proven methods should be the workshop's foundation. Again, such a program would not represent a large financial commitment or a high-risk decision. Workshops cannot be simply recycled administration courses. They need to include new course materials on mapping, curriculum design, learning systems development, instructional design methods, learning system selection, administrative system requirements, assessment systems, management systems, change management systems, interpersonal skills, people management skills, financial control systems, tradeoff planning methods, and public relations.

## LESSONS OF CHANGE FROM NEW AMERICAN SCHOOLS

The New American Schools (NAS) is a 10-year-old organization that has created change in schools and school districts. Its 1999 booklet *Working Toward Excellence* identified the following situations as potential hindrances to an education reform project:[3]

- Leadership is not stable or is likely to turn over soon.
- The reform efforts are not central to the district's goals.
- The district is in the midst of a budget or redistricting crisis.
- The district has a history of broken promises to schools concerning support for reform.
- The district forces the decisions on school reform issues without input from the schools.
- The principalship is experiencing turnover.

The booklet goes on to say, "If implementation is to succeed, district offices, principals, teachers, and design (change) teams must work together towards common goals and a shared vision. As in an orchestra, performers in the string, brass, and percussion sections must follow the same score and stay in tune."[4]

Teachers who are accustomed to being "solo" performers must adjust to working within a team. Remember, the entire education organization (i.e., the state education department, school district staff, and school principals) must develop a working partnership that focuses on the new learning-centered paradigm in order to eliminate the two bell-curves for teachers and students.

## WHAT ROLE DOES TECHNOLOGY PLAY IN THE CHANGE PROCESS?

It's been said that if you took a surgeon who practiced medicine 100 years ago and put him in a modern operating room, about all he would recognize would be the human body. Everything else has changed. If you took a teacher from 100 years ago and put her in a modern classroom, she would recognize just about everything. She would be surprised to see white boards rather than blackboards and the absence of ink wells on desks. Student dress would probably be a surprise, but overall, not much in our schools has changed until recently.[5] Schools will change dramatically over the next decade, however.

What role has technology played in other industries? Computers are used throughout the airline industry to raise safety standards, increase the quality of customer service, and lower costs. Food stores could not operate without automated checkout stations using scanners rather than having a clerk add up items on a brown paper bag. Manufacturing companies use computers from the front door to the back door to achieve TQM objectives and to lower costs. Financial service firms use technology, such as ATMs, to provide more customer services. It has been said that every American would have to be a switchboard operator if technology had not entered the communication industry.

Almost every industry goes through an initial phase where computers are "nice to have" for some experimental applications, but they keep their old manual systems in the mainstream processes. In the next phase, they resystematize their basic processes to improve performance, reduce workload, and to contain costs. Technology has become so essential to government agencies and business organizations that there is now one personal computer for every 1.3 employees. It is estimated that 60 percent of American households will have one or more personal computers by 2003. Internet access is forecasted to grow to 320 million users in 2002, up from 14 million in 1995.[6] A recent study by the Grunwald Associates research firm reported in an April 5, 2000 *Education Week* article that the reason most parents and children buy computers and use the Internet from home is to pursue education opportunities.[7] Use of e-mail was a distant second reason. After playing around with personal computers for 20 years, it is now time for the public school system to enter the next phase.

***The need for technology in schools is driven by at least the following 12 factors:***

1. Quality must improve to achieve more than 90 percent successful learners.
2. Teaching must be more consistent.
3. All teachers must be successful.
4. Tutoring is essential.
5. Enrichment lessons are required.
6. Lessons must be more motivational.
7. Costs must be contained.
8. New cost-effective administrative systems are required.
9. Improved partnership with parents is essential.
10. A working partnership among states, districts, and schools is essential.

11. Improved assessment systems are required to measure learning.
12. Instruction and learning must be managed.

These 12 objectives will never be realized until the latest and finest technology systems are implemented in the schools. The key to achieving a true payback in the investment of computers is to ensure that they're used properly. Computers can be used for drill and practice or as a reward for doing favorable work in a subject, but there are far more productive ways to use a classroom computer. Computers should feature courseware that's part of a learning system for simulations, case studies, and lessons based on learning objectives. Computers also bring more information into the classroom through the Internet and through encyclopedia courseware for term paper research. Two-way interaction with students is promoted by computers—a benefit that promotes learning. Students can also use computers to design World Wide Web pages. Students learn faster and retain more knowledge when they complete interactive computer exercises in a learning system. Computers improve problem-solving skills, individualized instruction, and time on task. As a result, technology enhances the role of teachers.

Technology standards must be established at the district and/or state level. Microsoft is currently working with 18 other software companies to establish a set of technical standards.[8] Another challenge is to integrate technology into all schools and the district staff. How do you know when technology has been integrated? The August 1998 issue of *Technology and Learning Journal* identified the following 10 indications of an integrated system:[9]

1. An outside observer views the use of technology as a seamless lesson component.
2. Students work toward a relevant goal in the lesson.
3. The technology activity is a logical extension of the lesson.
4. A real problem is being solved by the use of technology.
5. You can describe how a particular student is benefiting from the technology.
6. You'd have trouble accomplishing your learning goals if the technology were removed.
7. You can explain what the technology is supposed to do in a few minutes.
8. All students are able to participate and learn.
9. Students are genuinely interested and enthusiastic about learning.
10. More cool stuff is happening than you expected.

Many students have personal computers at home, but inner-city children rarely have a home computer. Their computer experiences are limited to class and afterschool programs. For that reason, inner-city schools need more technology than suburban schools. Congress is providing more than $1 billion in grants to city schools to further technology use.[10] A few school districts in New York City and

South Carolina are offering home computers on a $10 or $35 per month lease.[11] The hope is that children and their families will treat their computers just as carefully as they do their band instruments.

Some educators do not want to spend one dime on technology. They want more teachers, aides, and volunteers in each classroom. They want all funds to be invested in salaries and benefits. This nontechnology plan will only be feasible if the failure rate of 25 to 75 percent remains acceptable in the future, and that will not happen. The "no-technology" strategy also requires at least 5- to 10-percent annual increases in school budgets, which will eventually prompt a taxpayer backlash. Educators who oppose computers are standing in the way of a low-cost interactive tutoring system that's essential for creating student learning breakthroughs and for developing cost-effective administrative systems.

These educators need to take a look at the agricultural industry. In Russia, production quotas are rarely met and food is of the lowest quality. For decades, the Soviet government tried to repair its agricultural system with quick-fix and sound-good programs. Even if the Russian government doubled farmers' salaries, built them new houses and barns, and gave out awards such as "Farmer of the Year," there still would be a massive cost increase in farming with almost no change in farm output. Why? When you compare farming in the United States to the Russian system, it's obvious that new farming methods, improved seeds and fertilizers, and new technologies have provided the United States with a vastly superior system. The key word is "system." Farmers work physically harder in Russia and have the best of intentions, but their good intentions alone cannot feed the country. In the United States, only 1 to 2 percent of the population feeds more than 98 percent of our people as well as millions overseas. American farmers' working conditions and standard of living are far superior to those in Russia, thanks to their modern farming methods and systems. Computers are used successfully throughout farming and every industry, but not in most K–12 public schools.

A few educators always maintain that an outstanding teacher can do anything that a computer could do in a classroom. In today's world, that's like saying a farmer with a shovel and a wheelbarrow can do anything that farm machinery does. This statement is true, but it takes dozens of farmers at several times the cost over many more hours to do what one farmer with the help of farm machinery can do. When the cost, quality, and time of a task is measured, technology with a skilled person is usually the most efficient and cost-effective method. Too many educators do not consider the cost, time, or quality issues when they evaluate the use of technology in the classroom.

The cost of advancing technologies continues to decline annually, and the capabilities of various technology systems improve each year. For example, thousands of teachers are beginning to use the Internet to develop a daily partnership with parents. Parents and teachers can now communicate by e-mail at any time instead of waiting for formal conferences. Students (and parents) no longer have excuses for not knowing when assignments are due or what homework has been assigned. In some schools, parents can access an electronic gradebook with a password. Some teachers also post comments on a student's behavior, attentiveness, and attendance in these gradebooks.

Recently, some dramatic developments have been made in the area of thin computers—low-cost, stripped-down personal computers that run applications and courseware off a school's central server or via an application service provider (ASP) on the Internet. As a result, maintenance, upgrading, and file management can be accomplished by the server, which makes the computers easier to use. New education service providers (ESPs) are being created to serve school districts.[12] Once again, technology is moving faster than schools. In the world of high-bandwidth, multimedia courseware will be available from the server and the Internet. America Online (AOL) is offering a free service to schools that will make it easier for students to use the Internet. AOLSchool will have separate portals for elementary, middle, and high school students that will help students reach the best educational Web sites. No advertisements will be posted on this free service to avoid exposing students to some of the less seemly elements of the Internet.[13]

Information systems provide a steel framework for consistent performance. Principals, master teachers, and the director of curriculum can monitor how well learning systems are being applied by various reports. Constant teacher supervision is unnecessary. Effort and cost of supervision decline with good management and learning systems. Supervision will be made on an exception basis in future years as it becomes a collaborative partnership.

Computers bring together curriculum design, learning system applications, assessments, administrative systems, and management systems. Every school district will need a director of information technology and a staff to implement communications and computer systems. Each school will need at least a part-time technology coordinator. Technology budgets must become as important as funds for utilities. Begging for used computers must stop; schools need first-class, modern computers. Every teacher should have a cell phone and a notebook/laptop computer that can be used throughout the school building and at home. Remarkably, this technology would raise the cost of a teacher by only 1 percent.

To improve the use of technology, a new on-line National Library of Education is being proposed by the federal Department of Education. Its vision is a future in which all teachers and students have equal access to the information necessary for their personal and professional growth. To accomplish this goal, the National Library of Education will become the major national network providing access to education information through collections and other education-related material.[14] This program and the Internet clearly point the way to a future in which knowledge will be stored in electronic media. Electronic textbooks are expensive today, but they could become affordable and widely used by the end of this decade. Textbook publishers generate revenues in excess of $2 billion annually from the

K–12 schools. With desktop publishing, electronic books, courseware, distance learning, and learning systems coming into the classroom, the traditional textbook may not last unless it's part of a successful learning system that produces more than 90 percent successful learners. In the future, publishers will need to take on more responsibility for student learning.

The education community will undoubtedly study the effectiveness of technology for the next 50 years; however, there's already ample evidence that when technology is combined with instructional design methods, students learn at a faster rate and retain lessons longer. Computers have been available to schools for 20 years; it's time for their benefits to be fully utilized. Technology won't replace a classroom teacher, but it will enable teachers to be successful in achieving the new learning standards established by the state department of education and the local school district. Computers will also reduce administrative tasks for a teacher, thus providing more teaching time. The message is simple: Schools need good teachers and good technology with the proper resources.

Advancing technology will have a great impact on future learning systems. For example, it took six fibers in a fiberoptic line in 1985 to carry a single program broadcast. Today, one fiber can handle 700 such broadcasts.[15] This advance in technology means that eventually full-fledged television and audiotapes will be viewable from the Internet. Bandwidth has been a barrier in the past, but it will be an advantage in the future. Schools are now installing networks that will handle high-quality telephone, digital video, and data signals on the same network.[16] Electronic books are expensive today, but the concept has the advantage of each learning system customizing the various pieces of text from several books and journals for students to study. Backpacks in the future may weigh less but contain several times the information because of electronic books.[17] The prediction is that by the year 2005, the bookpad will cost approximately $20 and weigh no more than 6 ounces. It could contain up to 500 books and articles.

Several futurists, such as Ian Jukes, Geoffrey Meridith, Rick Smolan, David Snyder, and Ted McCain, offered their opinions to the *Technology and Learning Journal* at the beginning of our new century on what education would be like in the future. Listed below are 10 predictions:[18]

1. Education will not be confined to a single place.
2. Education will not be confined to a specific time.
3. Education will not be confined to a single person like a classroom teacher.
4. Education will not be confined to human teachers.
5. Education will not be confined to memorization.
6. Education will not be confined to paper-based information.
7. Education will not be confined to linear learning.
8. Education will not be confined to the intellectual elite.

9. Education will not be confined to childhood.
10. Education will not be confined to controlling learners.

These predictions suggest that state departments of education and school districts need to focus on learning systems or they are going to lose their influence on educating children. Technology creates great freedoms to perform a task or a process in a different way. It is hoped that the public schools will utilize technology to improve student learning rather than as another excuse for why millions of children are not achieving at grade level.

One motivation for increased use of technology in the classroom will be outstanding courseware on a teacher's computer for professional development. Training could be delivered anywhere at any time and customized for each teacher. Video segments on how to and how not to teach a lesson can be more effective than a pedantic classroom lecture. Most important, the state department of education can communicate with every administrator and teacher in all school districts. Most educators agree that professional development workshops need major improvements. This may be an opportunity to provide "choice" to local faculties.

The use of computers in the classroom has passed the point of no return. Society has embraced technology, and schools eventually mirror society.[19] One company, Net Schools, has made it feasible and affordable to give a laptop computer to each student and teacher in the K–12 grades.[20] This was made possible by using wireless infrared technology to circumvent some of the most expensive and problematic elements of the traditional school-based computing infrastructure, including wiring, special furniture, and space requirements. Students can now use their laptops any time to complete individual assignments, communicate with students and others online, work on projects collaboratively, simulate real-life situations, and develop critical-thinking and problem-solving skills. Schools in El Paso, Texas, and Connecticut are already using these new computers and learning systems. They are achieving more than 90 percent successful learners by teaching academics with the aid of technology.[21]

Another signal that technology is finally moving into the K-12 learning process is the "virtual high schools" that are being developed in Florida, Hawaii, Kentucky, Louisiana, New Mexico, and Utah. The plan is to offer complete online courses to students in school or at home. Teachers work with 20 to 30 remote students who can be anywhere in the state. Most of the courseware has been provided by course development companies. An article in *Education Week* (October 25, 2000) stated that California, Michigan, Illinois, and West Virginia were also moving in this direction.

Advancing technology will someday include speech recognition, electronic books, video simulations, experts providing part of the lesson, and tutoring.

Learning systems will be embedded into the technology. What seems too expensive today will be affordable during this decade. When technology is combined with instructional design methods, learning systems, assessment systems, and good teaching, most of the current learning problems will disappear. Computers will be able to generate numerous assessments, which will make classroom cheating disappear as well.

In the May/June 1993 issue of *Education Today*, Dr. Terrell Bell, the former Secretary of Education when the *A Nation At Risk* report was published, made the following comment on the 10th anniversary of that famous report:

> We don't have the vision we should have for the schools of tomorrow. I don't think Americans see the incongruity between today's schools, which operate as if they were back in the 1950s, compared to today's workplace, which is influenced on all levels by technology. We've got to join the technological revolution that is sweeping all corners of our country—except education.[22]

If Dr. Bell were alive today, he would be pleased that some progress has been made, but he would no doubt be disappointed at the slow pace of change.

## CASE STUDY FOR AN INSTRUCTIONAL TECHNOLOGY PROGRAM

The West Virginia state department of education conducted a study in conjunction with the Milken Family Foundation a few years ago on the state's Basic Skills/Computer Education Program.[23] The overall conclusion was that across-the-board increases in statewide assessment scores for all basic skills areas as well as improvements in their National Assessment of Educational Progress (NAEP) scores had been made. The report also stated that the researchers had seen the faces of children light with excitement and learning, and teachers exhibited renewed enthusiasm when technology was integrated into the curriculum.

In West Virginia, articulated learning objectives in reading, mathematics, and composition was the first step in achieving learning breakthroughs. Learning systems from CompassLearning and IBM that were aligned with the West Virginia Instructional Goals and Objectives was the next important step. Implementation, which began in the earliest grades, moved up every year over an eight-year period as the students moved up one grade. Teachers attended outstanding professional development sessions, which was the next step, and the final step provided frequent assessments to ensure that students did not fall behind or get lost in the learning process. The entire program was based on best practices identified by solid education research. Structure and measurements replaced teacher-centered learning in the classrooms.[24] The study was based on 950 fifth graders who have used learning systems in all five grades and 290 teachers.[25] The data indicated that this program helped the neediest children the most, which would be expected, and boys did as well as girls.[26] Seventy-eight percent of West Virginia's fifth-grade students thought that the learning systems and technology had helped make them become more successful students.[27] Ninety-two percent of the teachers concluded that instructional technology was not just another fad.[28] The cohort's fourth-grade reading scores in 1997 were reported to be the second highest among southern states, with only North Carolina ahead by one point.[29]

The program cost $7 million annually to add technology and to provide teacher training to one grade level across the state. For comparison purposes, the cost of reducing class size in West Virginia from the current level of 21 students per class to 15 would be $191,670,140 annually in operating expenses. This is based on 301,314 students in K–12 and 14,348 teachers (assuming one teacher per class). Not only 5,739 additional teachers but also at least 100 new schools would be needed at a cost of more than $1 billion in capital expense.[30] The vision outlined in Part III of this book is far more practical, affordable, and effective than many of the quick-fix and sound-good programs that are being implemented to fix the crisis in student learning.

## SIZE WILL EVOLVE TO BE AN ADVANTAGE

Before the age of new computer and communication systems, size was not always an advantage because most tasks had to be performed in every operating unit of an organization. This is not true today. A single payroll or a single administrative system can be used nationwide throughout an organization. Measurement systems are used throughout an organization to control quality and costs. Quality control systems ensure a high level of performance by all of the major jobs within an organization. Senior executives are able to communicate directly with "front-line" employees at the operating units without relying on layers of middle management, who often failed to communicate or delivered the wrong messages. Large organizations can afford more research and development. After key decisions are made, they achieve lower costs for essential services and supplies for large-volume purchases. Best practices and standards of performance are institutionalized through performance systems.

Large school districts and chains of schools that are managed by not-for-profit or for-profit companies will have major cost advantages over local charter schools and small school districts. With new learning and management systems, they will also have a major advantage in quality and student learning.

## CASE STUDY OF CHANGE

For-profit schools are emerging as a successful case study on how to create and manage change. They realize that their curriculum must be world-class. Their number of successful learners must be far superior to the public schools, and the cost of their administrative systems must be far below the public schools, so they can earn a profit. They also reduce their instruction costs by using fewer aides and administrators. For-profit schools often operate on a five-year contract, which is renewed only when administrators, teachers, parents, and students approve the school's courses and operations. In other words, for-profit schools must be successful to survive.

Their goal is simple: Be different and better than public schools. Just being different or just being better is not sufficient, however. Some schools offer longer school days or more school days. Others offer more interactive tutoring systems. All of them use new high-quality course materials. Their goal is to manage large chains of schools with a proprietary curriculum. An article in *Business Week* predicted that, by 2009, the for-profit schools could capture as much as 10 percent of the $360 billion education market. The Edison Company's founder, H. Christopher Whittle, recently said, "In 20 years, 20% to 30% of the U.S. public schools will be run by successful chains of for-profit schools."[31] That means a market share of more than $100 billion. No one knows for sure whether these organizations will achieve their growth targets, but their success could bring far more competition to public education than the current voucher systems have.

Evidence also suggests that for-profit companies are learning how to develop and manage successful school systems. They're using new integrated curriculum, learning systems, assessment systems, administrative systems, and management systems in addition to effective change management systems. For-profit schools are being managed like any other successful organization. Charter school rules allow them to be funded by school districts and to use existing school buildings. Making a profit may not be as big of a challenge as some educators think because costs in many school districts are out of control. For-profit schools are going to contain costs like church schools do, and they hope to be as successful as church schools in terms of satisfying learning objectives. Competition in the future may well be between not-for-profit public schools and for-profit schools. Some educators have a difficult time understanding how a for-profit company can achieve lower costs and higher quality than a not-for-profit organization. They need to look no further than Federal Express, which has consistently outperformed the U.S. Postal Service. A competitive model can often outperform a government monopoly.

Today, there are six major for-profit school management companies:[32]

- Advantage Schools (16 schools and 9,000 students)

- Beacon Education Management (26 schools and 4,700 students)
- Edison Schools (110 schools and 58,000 students)
- Leona Schools (35 schools and 10,000 students)
- National Heritage Academies (22 schools and 8,000 students)
- Tesseract Group (36 schools and 7,000 students)

These numbers may seem small, but most of the numbers have been accumulated during a five-year start-up period. The pace is accelerating. More and more states as well as school districts are turning to these for-profit companies to take over their low-performing schools. New York City is even considering the option of having 50 chronically low-performing schools operated as privately managed charter schools beginning in the fall of 2001.[33] This is a long way from 10 years ago when Miami offered one school as a pilot program.

Edison Schools has signed a five-year contract with IBM to provide personal computers for classrooms, teachers' desks, and student homes. IBM will also manage Edison's computer networks and will work with Edison to develop a new type of computing device for use by students.[34] The contract is believed to be worth approximately $350 million. Edison spends roughly $500 per child per school year on technology, which is far more than most public schools spend.[35] The sole reason for this investment is to achieve breakthroughs in student learning.

For-profit school chains will discover that it's in their best interest to develop proprietary learning and assessment systems because they will cost less and provide a strategic marketing advantage. How will their learning systems cost less? Let's assume that the for-profit school system invests $1 million into a learning system. If the chain has 100,000 students, then the cost is $10 per student. The Edison Schools are already halfway to that number. The price will decrease further to $1 per student when the chain has 1 million students—a goal it could reach in this decade. A for-profit company also has no marketing expenses for its own learning systems, which is a major line item for courseware and learning system companies. Eventually, quality within their learning systems will establish their professional reputation as a school system in which all students become successful learners. If that happens, for-profit companies could achieve explosive growth.

There's no reason that not-for-profit public schools cannot change as fast or faster than for-profit school chains, but the pace for systemic change must be accelerated. Today it's occurring at a snail's pace. Maryland's state department of education has taken over Baltimore's three failing schools. Their 1,500 students will attend reconstituted schools managed by a for-profit school system where previous teachers can apply for a job, but will be hired only if they are considered to be qualified teachers. Maryland may reconstitute 96 more schools in the near future.[36] In the Baltimore situation, the state had given the local school board a couple of years to fix the problems, but when they failed to improve, the state took responsibility for fixing the schools. Baltimore tried a for-profit company once before and dismissed it on the basis that the city could operate its not-for-profit schools without the for-profit company. Now 83 Baltimore schools are on the state failure list. A state school officer said, "No child should have to attend a failing school by accident of where he or she lives." Edison Schools has been hired to manage three Baltimore schools.[37]

The pressure is on. School boards may decide that it is easier to buy a successful school system than to resystematize their existing school districts when the price is the same. State school officers and boards of education are going to try to partner with any organization that can fix schools. Remember, the key word is "fix," not "improve" schools. The Inkster, Michigan, school board recently gave Edison Schools a five-year contract to run all schools in its district.[38] This suburb near Detroit has had serious problems for years and was often used as an example of how vouchers would close a school district. As predicted, they are going to be fixed rather than closed.

## WHAT HAPPENS IF CHANGE MANAGEMENT PRINCIPLES ARE NOT USED?

In recent years, considerable research has been accomplished by people such as Daryl Conner, president of ODR, Inc. in Atlanta on how to create and manage change. Unfortunately, the lessons from the research have not been taught at most education, business, law, and liberal arts colleges. In addition, the messages have not been well communicated to political, business, and education leaders. Therefore, the education reform movement has become a classic case of how not to create and manage change. For example, if you want people in an organization to make fundamental change, increased compensation and awards are given only after people have committed themselves to a new paradigm. In schools, massive amounts of money have been given to schools, administrators, and teachers who are committed only to the current methods of teaching and managing schools.

In recent years, large sums of money have been given to low-performing schools in several states on the belief that the administrators and teachers in those schools know what to do to fix the learning problems of their students, which is not a good assumption. If they knew what to do, they would have implemented new teaching and learning methods that would have already fixed the problem.

Some years ago, the Business Roundtable adopted the state of Connecticut in an attempt to improve its schools. The Connecticut Business for Education Coalition invested months of effort and created an outstanding report entitled *From Vision To Reality*.[39] The state legislature also created a task force of business leaders, political leaders, union leaders, media personnel, and educators (including the state school officer). Union Carbide's Chief Executive Officer also appointed his own personal task force and commissioned a report. Overall, nearly four years of effort were invested, and the best consultants were involved. Reports were right on target for what must be done. Unfortunately, this effort ended in total failure when the Connecticut state legislature refused to vote on the proposed education reform bill.

One reason given for the failure of this proposal was that the process moved too fast. It's hard to believe that four years is a short period to study a problem and recommend solutions. A more concrete reason was that school administrators became concerned about the recommendations for new accountability systems when there were no means by which to reach the proposed learning standards. Administrators just sat on the sidelines during the whole debate. Teachers turned negative because they didn't want to be measured on student performance, and they didn't like the site-based management recommendation. Another recommendation implied that all students should learn their lessons, which some parents interpreted as a "dumbing down" strategy. The task force wasn't prepared for this opposition, and it was never able to explain to the education community or to parents how a world-class education system would be implemented in all Connecticut schools.

What lessons were learned from this failure? First, a series of recommendations about improving learning must be embraced by administrators and teachers. These recommendations must avoid the subject of tenure, teacher certification, school councils, merit pay, evaluation systems, and anything else that erodes the support of the only people who can create change within a school system. Second, numerous pilot programs to achieve world-class performance standards must be funded so that educators can learn how to reach world-class objectives. Third, the most successful schools or the worst schools cannot be changed first. One must start instead with schools that have a high potential for success.

Today, Connecticut ranks second in the nation for education expenditures. Fortunately, the large compensation increases there were packaged with mastery tests for students. Connecticut has achieved real improvements with these mastery tests. The lesson is simple: Deliver the funds at the time that new reforms are agreed upon. Wage increases should not be given with just a hope for cooperation.

## CHANGE IS NOT EASY, BUT IT DOES HAPPEN

One reason that the United States is a world leader today is Americans' ability to embrace major changes. In World War II, Americans built the greatest military production system in the world and completely changed it into peacetime production after the war. Our buildup of superior weapon systems and military services has enabled the United States to be the world's most powerful nation for 60 years. Our interstate highway system is accepted today as the status quo, but it was a major accomplishment when the nation had only two-lane roads winding through every small town. Our nation moved from segregation to equal rights through various proactive programs. Recently, the national deficits have been replaced by balanced budgets and surpluses. Our corporations have created many of the world's greatest products, and today the United States leads in computer and communications technology. Change and success take several years, and everyone should be prepared for the long haul.

As the famous Serenity Prayer states, "Grant me the serenity to accept the things I cannot change, the courage to change the things I can, and the wisdom to know the difference." Unfortunately, many educators believe that they cannot improve the procedures and methods now being used in the public schools. It is hoped that readers of this book will realize that great changes can take place and must be implemented in order for the United States to have a world-class public school system. It does take courage to leave the current paradigm and embrace systemic change.

Each group affected by change must understand why a reengineered school system is in its personal best interest. This concept is so important that the next chapter is devoted to the benefits of change for each major stakeholder group.

---

## NOTES

1. J. Barker, *Discovering the Future: The Business of Paradigms* (St. Paul, MN: ILI Press, 1989).

2. D. Kearns and J. Harvey, *A Legacy of Learning* (Washington, DC: Brookings Institute Press, 2000), 70.

3. *Working toward Excellence: Examining the Effectiveness of New American Schools Designs* (Arlington, VA: New American Schools, February 1999), 1–11.

4. *Working toward Excellence*, 5.

5. S. Forbes, *Training Minds and Hearts: Principle-Centered Education Reform* (Hillsdale, MI: Imprimis, October 1999), 4.

6. "Seven Megatrends That Will Affect the Profession," *ASTD Training and Development Journal*, November 1999, 38.

7. A. Trotter, "Home Computers Used Primarily for Learning, Families Say in Survey," *Education Week*, 5 April, 2000, 6.

8. A. Trotter, "Software Companies Working on Technical Standards for Schools," *Education Week*, 3 March, 1999, 1, 24–25.

9. M. Milone, "Master Class," *Technology and Learning Journal*, August 1998, 7.

10. A. Trotter, "Congress Expected To Put High Priority on Technology," *Education Week*, February 1999, 34.

11. A. Amato, "Equity and Access," Presentation given at Discover '99 Conference, April 8, 1999.

12. E. O'Donovan, "The Skinny on Thin Clients," *Technology and Learning Journal*, May 2000, 52–58.

13. P. Tolme, "America Online To Offer Free Service to Schools," *San Diego Union-Tribune*, 17 May, 2000, C3.

14. B. Dessy, *Access for All: A New National Library for Tomorrow's Learners* (Washington, DC: U.S. Department of Education, February 1997), 1–40.

15. K. Maney, "The Next Big Bang," *USA Today*, 8 October, 1998, B1–B2.

16. S. Bosak, "Future-Proof Network," *American School Board Journal*, June 1999, A26–A27.

17. C. Vinzant, "Electronic Books Are Coming at Last," *Fortune*, 6 July, 1998, 119–124.

18. J. Jukes and T. McCain, *Technology and Learning Journal*, December 1999, 72–79.

19. T. Greaves, "Looking Ahead with Technology," *School Planning and Management*, January 1998, 1–5.

20. Greaves, "Looking Ahead."

21. Interview with C. Zamora, Principal of Rio Brava Middle School, El Paso, TX, 2000.

22. T. Bell, "Ten Years Later, Are We Still 'a Nation at Risk?'" *Education Today*, May/June 1993, 4.

23. D. Mann et al., *West Virginia Story* (Huntington, NY: Interactive, Inc., 1998), 5.

24. Mann et al., *West Virginia Story*, 5.

25. Mann et al., *West Virginia Story*, 11.

26. Mann et al., *West Virginia Story*, 13.

27. Mann et al., *West Virginia Story*, 17.

28. Mann et al., *West Virginia Story*, 19.

29. Mann et al., *West Virginia Story*, 20.

30. Mann et al., *West Virginia Story*, 37.

31. W. Symonds et al., "For-Profit Schools," *Business Week*, 7 February, 2000, 64–79.

32. Symonds et al., "For-Profit Schools," 67.

33. D. Bowman, "Companies, Nonprofits Jump at Chance To Manage New York City Schools," *Education Week*, 6 September, 2000, 3.

34. M. Walsh, "Edison Schools Joins with IBM in Technology Alliance," *Education Week*, 21 June, 2000, 9.

35. Walsh, "Edison Schools Joins," 9.

36. D. Bowman, "Private Firms Tapped To Fix Maryland Schools," *Education Week*, 9 February, 2000, 1, 22.

37. D. Bowman, "Maryland Picks Edison To Run Three Baltimore Schools," *Education Week*, 29 March, 2000, 3.

38. D. Bowman, "Michigan District Hires Edison To Manage Its School," *Education Week*, 23 February, 2000, 3.

39. *From Vision To Reality* (Danbury, CT: Connecticut Business for Education Coalition, 1992), 1–29.

# CHAPTER 14

# Why Stakeholders Will Endorse the New Paradigm

Based on the failed education reform efforts and programs of the past 18 years, many people inside the public schools and the education reform movement are convinced that schools will never change. With this book, there is now a new vision, new paradigm, and new management system for achieving breakthroughs in learning. This book provides a "win-win" situation for all stakeholders because its action programs and strategies will improve student learning and will benefit each group connected with the American public school system. Let's examine each group's "win-win" situation and understand why urban school districts will change in this decade.

## POLITICAL LEADERS

The President of the United States, all Congressional members, governors, members of state assemblies, mayors, and city council members want to fix the school systems, especially in their urban communities. They realize that urban ghettos cannot be eliminated unless schools are fixed. When most urban high school graduates obtain a real high school education, crime and social services costs will be dramatically reduced. Twenty years ago, mayors tried to distance themselves from the poor performance of schools when they thought that the billions and trillions of dollars from "War on Poverty" programs would solve all city problems. Now Chicago's Richard Daley, New York City's Rudy Giuliani, Oakland's Jerry Brown, Los Angeles' Richard Riordan, Boston's Thomas Menino, Detroit's Dennis Archer, Cleveland's Mike White, and Anthony Williams in Washington, D.C. are all asking for more control of their school systems.[1]

To stem further middle-class flight to the suburbs and to repopulate their cities, mayors know that city schools must be as good as suburban ones. In many situations, the budget per student is nearly the same, except for a few very wealthy suburbs. Retaining businesses and employment opportunities also requires good schools. A city with failed schools will not attract new business opportunities. Unlike most political leaders, mayors understand that vouchers will not fix their schools. Therefore, they encourage embattled and weak superintendents to leave. In too many cases, though, they have not hired a new management team that knows how to create and manage change that produces student learning breakthroughs.

Governors have also involved themselves in school reform. In fact, they are becoming visionary leaders of learning and change. They know they will weaken their chances of being reelected if they cannot show that student learning has improved as a result of enormous increases in school budgets and taxes. Governor Davis of California has said that he does not expect to be reelected if schools do not improve. Like other governors, he is doing far more than speaking from a "bully pulpit." He knows that the school system has fundamental problems that must be fixed, and he is involved in the details of how to fix them. Most members of the state legislatures and Congress follow the leadership of their governor or President because no one wants to be viewed as negative on school reform.

Governors are also aware that when the next recession hits, large tax increases will be needed to sustain the high spending level that has been approved during this period of state budget surpluses. Property taxes are only 30 percent of the total state and local income. Seventy percent of the tax revenues depend on the prosperity of the economy.[2] Therefore, governors must continue to emphasize standards and accountability. Political leaders are the most effective change agents because they greatly influence the budget and regulations for operating schools. In the past, they have thrown millions and billions of dollars into school systems with just a hope for improvement. Now, they have the overall plan outlined in this book to fix schools and to show taxpayers that a positive return is being made on all the money being invested in schools.

Another encouraging sign is the bipartisan efforts by a series of leaders within a state. Texas is a good example. Education reform was started by H. Ross Perot. Governor Richards (Democrat) and Governor Bush (Republican) have both supported years of reforms to improve learning in Texas schools.

## BUSINESS LEADERS

Business executives are dissatisfied with quick-fix and sound-good solutions that do not work. They want a new vision as well as a new management system that will ensure breakthroughs in student learning. Executives now realize that schools have a very complex performance problem that must be fixed. It is important to convince business leaders who have turned away from public school reform in recent years to reenter the process of fixing the American public school system. Vouchers are not the answer; schools need a new paradigm that brings measurable results. Executives will support the concept that learning must be both measured and managed. Business leaders need to support the development and implementation of learning systems. Executives are extremely effective as change agents because most tax increases and bond issues require their endorsements. They also employ graduates, so they are entitled to a strong voice on public school issues.

## MEDIA

All aspects of the media have been involved in school reform during the past 18 years. As stated previously, *Fortune* magazine sponsored annual summits on education, and all of the major magazines have written dozens of articles about education reform over the years. Newspapers feature almost a daily article or articles on various programs that are aimed at improving student learning. The major television networks have aired many specials devoted to education issues. The media truly wants to be an effective change agent for this issue.

Like so many others, the media is frustrated with the slow pace of education reform and the minor improvements in student learning. The media needs to obtain in-depth knowledge on this subject so they can ask penetrating questions whenever a quick-fix and sound-good solution is proposed. They also need to promote the longer-term programs that will achieve breakthroughs in student learning. This new paradigm, in which learning is not only measured but also managed at all levels (i.e., school, district, and state), should be communicated to the general public to build awareness that the American public school system can be fixed.

## ADVOCACY GROUPS

The primary barrier for minorities to achieve equal opportunity in this country is the performance of inner-city schools. The Urban League, the National Association for Advancement of Colored People (NAACP), the Mexican American Legal Defense Fund (MALDF), and the National Council of La Raza organizations can significantly influence school reform if they endorse a new paradigm. They must demand the finest learning systems for inner-city schools. With the cost of retention being in the millions of dollars in city schools, enough money is available to fund effective learning systems that encourage minority children to learn the first time. Minority children can be successful students in a resystematized school system, but not in schools as they are operated and managed today. Meaningful school reform is the main program that will bring great change to the people who support their organizations. Racism cannot be eliminated until most minorities are successful learners in the American public school system.

## COLLEGES OF EDUCATION

This is the moment of opportunity for the more than 1,000 colleges and universities and their departments of education. For years, they have been held in low regard by the other colleges on campus. Many articles have been written about how out-of-touch their professors are.

The old cry that a summa cum laude Ivy League history graduate cannot teach history in a public high school is right on target because the typical Liberal Arts graduate has not learned instructional design methods, teaching methods, education technology programs, learning systems, curriculum design, class management, administrative systems, learning theory, and course development. Most of these graduates have no practice-teaching experience either. They are not trained to be professional teachers who can ensure that more than 90 percent of their students will learn the lessons. They do have in-depth subject matter knowledge and they are qualified to communicate this information, but that is only part of the teaching job. Too many people believe that the ability to communicate large amounts of information is the only requirement to become an effective teacher. Such is the case at the university level because the bottom half of the public school students do not attend college. Even the top half, though, for several reasons, have a 50 percent drop-out rate at universities. One key reason is poor teaching.

Outstanding high school graduates should be encouraged to enroll in colleges of education to become professional public school teachers. They should receive a blended subject content curriculum, including all of the education subjects previously listed, so they can become successful teachers. Many studies have been conducted on whether teachers should have a degree in the subject they are teaching, but the major problem for beginning teachers is a lack of class management and teaching skills. Very few people can remember having teachers who did not know their subjects, but graduates remember too many K–16 teachers who were failures at teaching.

Unfortunately, the colleges of education have done a poor job lately in communicating why teachers needed education courses. In 1999, the American Council on Education and a task force on teacher education made some key recommendations in their report entitled *Transforming the Way Teachers Are Taught: An Action Agenda for College and University Presidents*.[3] Most of the task force members were university presidents or chancellors. The report said, "Colleges and universities have educated virtually every teacher in every classroom in every school in the country. Only about two-thirds of the newly prepared teachers graduating from the nation's colleges and universities enter the profession immediately after graduation." With another 15 to 20 percent drop-out rate in the first two years, there is a 50 percent attrition rate, which is unheard of in other professions. That statistic alone tells us that something must be done to enhance teacher education.

The report went on to say, "Strong teacher education programs tend to share several characteristics: a common vision of what good teaching actually is; well-defined standards of practice and performance; a vigorous core curriculum; extensive use of problem-based methods such as case studies and portfolio evaluation; and strong relationships between the teacher education program and reform-minded schools."

*The task force recommended that colleges and university presidents take these 10 action steps:[4]*

1. College and university presidents must take the lead in moving the education of teachers to the center of the instructional agenda. (Colleges of Education should have the same status as business, engineering, law, and medicine.)
2. Presidents need to clarify and articulate the strategic connection of teacher education to the mission of the institutions.
3. Presidents should mandate a campus-wide review of the quality in their institutions' teacher education programs.
4. Presidents and governing boards should commission rigorous periodic, independent appraisals of the quality of their institutions' teacher education programs. (Secure some reliable form of third-party assessment.)
5. Presidents must require that education faculty and courses are coordinated with arts and sciences faculty and courses.
6. Presidents should ensure that their teacher education programs have the equipment, facilities, and personnel necessary to educate future teachers in the use of technology. (Think beyond connecting schools to the Internet.)
7. Presidents of graduate and research universities have a special responsibility to be advocates for graduate education, scholarship, and research in the education of teachers.
8. College and university leaders should strengthen inter-institutional transfer and recruitment processes. (Many future teachers start in community colleges.)
9. Presidents should ensure that graduates of their teacher education programs are supported, monitored, and mentored. (A partnership with school districts is essential for both recent graduates and professional development programs.)
10. Presidents should speak out on issues associated with teachers and teaching and should join with other opinion leaders to shape public policy. (Join with

governors, business and opinion leaders, public policy makers, and teachers themselves to reform the system.)

Dr. Charles Reed, chancellor of the 23-campus California State University (CSU) system, has stated that one of CSU's top priorities today should be to help improve the public schools. After all, CSU trains 60 percent of the teachers in the state, and 85 percent of their students are from the California public school systems.[5] This number is similar to other state universities. Dr. Reed's objectives are easy to understand: The more high-quality teachers that they train, the better prepared their college students will be, which means fewer remedial courses. He advocates the following five action programs:[6]

1.  Train better teachers.
2.  Train more teachers.
3.  Enter into more partnerships with schools.
4.  Offer greater support for teachers.
5.  Offer early diagnostic testing.

Once again, it will take more than a little improvement for most colleges of education to emerge as education reform movement leaders. Every college of education should have a working partnership with a cluster of pilot schools in which the latest and finest teaching methods and learning systems can be practiced, similar to a teaching hospital that enables medical students and residents to work with patients. They must make fundamental changes in their curriculum and courses. New teaching methods, such as using short case studies on videotape to teach class management skills, will also be needed. It is hoped that at least a few leading colleges and universities will develop outstanding programs for both new and existing administrators. Once this happens, colleges of education will become major change agents for the new paradigm.

Dr. Arthur Levine, president of Teachers College at Columbia University in New York City, stated, "I think education schools have too often become ivory towers. They have modeled themselves after graduate schools of arts and science rather than professional schools like business and medical."[7]

The National Council for Accreditation of Teacher Education by 2001 will approve education programs at colleges only if professors prove they are graduating candidates capable of helping children learn. The proof will include how many graduates pass state teachers' license examinations, what principals and superintendents have to say about the candidates' internships and job performances, and graduates' rating of how well university programs prepared them for the classroom. Colleges will also have to prove that the graduates have been trained to work with many types of children, including minorities, and that candidates can use technology to teach.[8]

Every college of education should have a course on the issues of school reform. *Lessons would include the following topics:*

- Overall history of reforms
- What programs have been successful
- What programs failed and why
- Potential breakthroughs, strategies, and programs to improve student learning
- Role of teachers to create change
- Long-term impact on the profession.

Today, most colleges of education have specialists in nearly every subject area as well as school administration. Unfortunately, they are weak on systems design and system integration methods to develop a vision of how public schools can and should be restructured. Therefore, the colleges have been ineffective during the past 18 years to create change and to solve the crisis in student learning, which has reduced their overall professional reputation. Even teacher unions are calling for major changes in the curriculum within colleges of education.[9]

Another motivation for colleges of education to enhance their curriculum is competition from the for-profit schools. Sylvan Learning Systems has entered the field in selected school districts to provide programs leading to state licenses for teachers who are already working in the classroom. The Sylvan Teachers Institute hopes to expand its program across the nation. The University of Phoenix is expanding the number of states in which it is permitted to prepare teachers for licensure.[10] Edison Schools is a recent entry into this field because they need a steady supply of new teachers for their national chain of schools and school districts.[11] Sylvan and others will be using the innovative methods that are afforded by distance learning. Distance learning could have a major impact on the market share of universities because a few colleges of education and a few for-profit institutions could emerge in this decade with superior programs for preparing college graduates to become outstanding teachers.

It is interesting to note that some of the most famous private universities in the United States have no college of education. The University of Chicago, which at one time had 40 full-time education professors, is closing its college of education this year.[12] Yale closed its college of education, but Harvard reopened its school with more teacher training in 1983.[13] In the past, too many colleges of education focused on public policy rather than on new teaching and learning methods. Today, leading colleges of education are usually found at state universities. Most of the field's research money is being given to these schools. As teacher and administrator salaries increase to six figures, alumni will be in a position to support colleges of education just as they do colleges of law, business, engineering, and medicine. In the future, successful colleges of education will contribute to their universities' overall positive reputations.

## SECRETARY OF EDUCATION AND FEDERAL DEPARTMENT OF EDUCATION

The Secretary of Education position was created at the end of President Carter's administration. Dr. Terrell Bell, Secretary of Education under President Reagan, rang the alarm bell for education reform in 1983. Lamar Alexander, who served under President Bush, and Richard Riley, who served under President Clinton, have received high marks over the past 12 years for helping create standards and accountability systems at the state level. It is hoped that the next Secretary of Education will direct the existing research funds of more than $200 million toward applied research projects, including better learning systems and assessment programs. The federal government is a great change agent, but in the past, their programs have rewarded failure. As previously stated, when poverty and poor reading skills are rewarded with federal funds, millions of students suddenly qualify. Instead, future federal dollars should reward successful programs, schools, teachers, and students.

The Secretary of Education has one of the great management challenges of all times. He or she is expected to influence the equivalent of 50 large organizations that spend more than $300 billion annually, but the chief executive officers of these 50 state departments of education do not report directly to the Secretary of Education. They report to their respective governors, with only a dotted-line relationship to the federal Department of Education. Fortunately, the 50 organizations are doing similar work and have similar goals.

*To wield any real influence, however, the Secretary of Education should consider instituting a formal review system for states that would answer the following questions:*

1. Are the standards of learning realistic?
2. Is an effective accountability system in place?
3. What is the blueprint for achieving the learning objectives and what chance is there for real breakthroughs in student learning?
4. Is the state capable of reconstituting schools and school districts that are failures?
5. Are federal funds for education being used properly?
6. What additional federal programs and funds are necessary, if any, to fix the American public school system?

The governors could use this annual review as a second professional opinion for their statewide programs. This approach would be much more effective than just serving as a cheerleader for better education who uses the "bully pulpit" to criticize states and school districts. The Secretary of Education needs to support new programs and strategies to achieve breakthroughs in learning, or the President will be in deep trouble on this issue at the next election.


## STATE SCHOOL OFFICER AND STATE DEPARTMENT OF EDUCATION

In most state capitals, the largest building belongs to the state department of education. The 50 state school officers, whose responsibilities were outlined in Chapter 12, must evolve into visionary leaders of learning and change. Their focus must be on achieving learning breakthroughs as well as obtaining budget allocations from the governor and legislature. They have been helpful in establishing learning and accountability system standards, but now they must focus on the means to achieve these standards.

*When a school has serious performance problems over several years, the state has the following five alternatives:*

1. Demand that the local school district reconstitute the school (but remember, the school district has had several years to fix the problem, so this action may not be successful).
2. Hire a for-profit or not-for-profit organization that has a proven track record of reconstituting failed schools into successful learning organizations.
3. Use the state department of education's resources and talent to reconstitute the failed school as a charter school.
4. Inject external educators (consultants) into the management team of the school for a limited period to correct the crisis in student learning.
5. Do nothing and continue to list the failed schools in the state. (Closing a school is not a realistic alternative during a period in which there is a shortage of classroom seats within a school district.)


Simply put, state school officers and education departments need to step up and become sponsoring executives for change. They could hire one or more colleges of education that are on the leading edge of school reform to help them reconstitute their schools. The future reputation of state school officers and their departments of education will depend on whether they help create the means for local school districts to achieve state learning standards. Today, the state school officer is as important to a governor as the Secretaries of State and Defense are to the President. They need a new paradigm to succeed in their job and to make the governor successful on the issue of education.

## ACCREDITATION AGENCIES

For decades, accreditation agencies have reviewed schools based on brick-and-mortar credentials because there were no agreed-upon standards and objectives. "How big is the library?" was a typical evaluation question. Now they must focus on curriculum issues, learning systems, accountability programs, and teaching methods. Their review must include a new vision for student learning. Accreditation agencies can have an enlarged role as change agents and, in turn, enhance their mission. The Commission on Public Secondary Schools, a branch of the New England Association of Schools and Colleges, has taken a major step in the right direction by developing a plan of action to emphasize instructional factors at future reviews.[14]

## SCHOOL BOARDS

A seat on the local school board used to be a prestigious position for a community leader. Unfortunately, most members knew little about learning theory, instructional design methods, integrated curriculum, teaching methods, learning systems, tutoring systems, assessment programs, education technology, administrative systems, information systems, and management systems. As a result, most school boards have not been a force for change. Instead, they have approved "caretaker" leadership by a superintendent and, in many cases, quick-fix and sound-good education reform programs. Their big crisis was closing schools in one decade and building schools in the next decade because no one had developed a flexible plan of action for declining or increasing enrollment years. This attitude is changing now because the school budget is often much larger than the city budget for police, fire, emergency medical, sewers, parks, streets, and the like. Taxpayers have finally realized that school boards can spend twice as much money to run a school system but still produce the same student learning results.

The 80,000 school board members need training on all subjects that impact their district. No corporation would appoint people to its board of directors whose only knowledge of the company was that they had been customers using its products and services. As this book has shown, managing a school district is as great a challenge as managing any other large, complex organization. It is not a place for do-gooders and amateurs because learning on the job can create costly mistakes.

School boards should be sponsoring executives for change and learning breakthroughs. Who they hire determines whether the schools will succeed or fail. School boards can be a great force for education reform programs. No district will achieve systemic reform without visionary leaders of change on its school board. The board must not let the district's daily problems divert their attention from the primary mission: academic excellence. Board members must insist on the development of a vision and a plan of action to fix student learning. They need to implement the paradigm outlined in this book. School boards must be held accountable for student learning.

## SUPERINTENDENT AND DISTRICT STAFF

A superintendent is the chief executive officer of a school district and is, therefore, the sponsoring executive for change. A superintendent and all assistant superintendents need to embrace the vision that includes an integrated curriculum, learning systems, tutoring systems, assessment systems, administrative systems, and management systems in order to succeed over the next decade. Being a "caretaker" superintendent is not a long-term successful strategy, and leaping from crisis to crisis is a sure road to losing your job. Tinkering around the edges may have been acceptable in the past, but it will not be viewed as leadership in this decade. Even higher superintendent attrition rates will accrue during the next 10 years as visionary leaders of change and learning replace the caretakers.

Many superintendents will say they have an impossible job, but their jobs will actually become more embraceable as new systems are implemented. Pressure will be greater than ever on school districts to improve student learning, and successful superintendents will be in great demand. Except for stock options, their compensation packages can match the salaries of senior executives in other successful organizations if they implement systemic change. The superintendent of Houston public schools now earns $275,000 in base salary and up to $25,000 in incentives based on improved test scores for a total of $300,000. He has been the superintendent in that city since 1994.[15] On average, corporate chief executive officers last nine years.[16] Because of the demands of their positions, school districts need superintendents who can be effective for at least 6 to10 years.

## PRINCIPALS AND VICE-PRINCIPALS

Being a principal is not an impossible job either. Principals must become leaders of learning and change, and they must have in-depth knowledge of learning and assessment systems. Like other operating unit managers, their job is to oversee the entire learning process. Working with their master teachers, a principal or vice-principal must be the lead coach for new and inexperienced teachers. They cannot do the entire coaching job, which is why the master teacher position is so important. To be successful, principals must demand an integrated curriculum as well as outstanding learning and assessment systems. Like their superintendent counterparts, principals who are leaders of learning will be paid well in the future. On the other hand, "caretaker" principals will slowly disappear as the focus on student learning becomes more intense.

Once again, the attrition rate must be lowered for this important job, and the success rate of new principals must be raised. That goal will not be achieved if principals continue to work within the old paradigm. At the end of school year 2000, the state of Washington had 300 openings for new principals, which was one-sixth of the state's total, and New York City was trying to hire 163 principals.[17] Many schools opened in the fall of 2000 with only an acting principal because of a shortage of candidates. Principals need to adopt the new paradigm in order to survive in this new world of accountability.

## TEACHERS

Teachers will be blamed for poor student performance as long as they continue to use traditional teaching methods and accept the current management system in which they alone take full responsibility for student learning. Many people do not realize that teachers need help in order to succeed. Trying to do it all, like the one-room-schoolhouse teachers of days past, is a guarantee for failure. Like principals, teachers must demand an integrated curriculum that is tied to state and school district learning standards. Teachers need new learning and assessment systems that enable students to achieve the standards. They should also demand tutoring systems. Their world will completely change when students become successful learners at grade level, and they will be proud to be part of a respected profession.

It is important to realize how large a step this change will be for teachers because even new teachers have been sold on the concept that actions outside the classroom are the answer to their problems and working conditions.

*For example, a recent survey provided the following responses to ways for improving teaching quality:*[18]

86%  Reduce the class size.
59%  Require teachers to major in the subject they teach.
57%  Increase professional development opportunities.
52%  Increase teacher salaries.
51%  Provide more mentoring from experienced teachers.
20%  Require a graduate degree in education.

Teachers are not focused on how to improve student learning as a way to improve the quality of their jobs. Teachers did report that their jobs are made even more difficult because they lack the skills to maintain disciplined classrooms. Most new teachers blamed their teacher preparation programs for their inadequacies.[19]

In the past, a teacher's job was known for low pay, minimum respect, poor job satisfaction, poor working conditions, high attrition, low morale, and few career opportunities. This view is going to change during the next decade. In many school districts where there are good schools, good facilities, and supportive parents, beginning teacher salaries will be more than $30,000, which is the same as entry-level positions in business and engineering. With 15 to 20 years of experience, salaries for successful teachers in successful schools will approach $60,000 to $75,000, as long as the teacher obtains a master's degree and continues to take professional development courses.[20] With benefits, teachers will earn close to $100,000 in some states by the end of the decade. There are few "merit pay" systems in the corporate world and in government with such potential growth for nonmanagement positions. In addition, teachers have approximately 12 weeks of school holidays and vacations, allowing for time with the family or for personal development.

Beginning teachers now have a contract and some well-defined employment rights. Within a few years, they can earn tenure, which provides a high degree of job security that is not easily, if ever, obtained in the corporate world. Teachers will have an embraceable job if they work for schools that have outstanding learning and assessment systems. They will enjoy their job as a teacher, and they will be respected by the community, parents, students, and other professions when more than 90 percent of their students are successful learners. Future compensation will be greatly influenced by student success. Taxpayers and parents will vote to improve salary schedules if schools are successful. Future success will happen when schools evolve from the one-room-schoolhouse model to the learning-centered model using the latest methodologies and technologies.

If teachers wish to take on greater responsibilities, they can progress to positions within the administration ranks, including master teacher, department head, dean, assistant principal, principal, assistant superintendent, and district superintendent. Management position salaries will range from $75,000 to $200,000. A few large city superintendents will earn more than $300,000 when housing and automobile allowances are included, which is $100,000 more than in 1994.[21] Top performers will earn close to $400,000 by the end of this decade. In other words, teaching will no longer be a dead-end job. Teaching can be an outstanding career.

In the future, other career opportunities in the education field will include instructional designers, education technologists, assessment specialists, learning system specialists, and course developers. These high-paying positions will feature excellent job satisfaction because of the demand for new and enhanced learning systems, including multimedia tutoring systems. It is time for the education profession to quit complaining about its past problems and to publicize these future opportunities.

This new attitude can happen while teachers experience the thrill of watching children learn lessons and develop skills. Or they can resist change and cling to traditional teaching and learning methods. This practice will enable them to continue saying, "No one gives us our proper respect." Teachers must realize that in the United States, people rarely get respect when their organization does not achieve operating goals and objectives. High failure rates are not a winning strategy.

## TEACHER UNIONS

It is amazing how many citizens are convinced that teacher unions are the fundamental cause for most problems within the public schools. Articles have communicated this message, and numerous people who have failed to improve student learning with quick-fix and sound-good programs blame the unions as well. The Save Our Schools Research and Education Foundation has published a book entitled *Who's Ruining Our Schools: The Case Against the NEA Teacher Union*.[22] This organization was founded in 1980 by Dan Alexander to educate parents and taxpayers on how he believed the National Education Association (NEA) was ruining schools and teachers. Sadly, this book has been endorsed by several congressmen. And who can forget when, at a national political convention, a former senator running for President blamed teacher unions for poor school performance.[23] Many business executives, who now support choice and vouchers, are also convinced that the unions have blocked progress in school reform.

Do teacher unions deserve this blame? Let's try to put it into perspective. First, teachers are not responsible for the low performance of inner-city schools when they are doing what management (i.e., superintendents, principals, and school board members) asks them to do under the traditional one-room-schoolhouse model. It is rare to find an integrated curriculum in a school district or any agreed-upon learning systems. Instead, most schools use old books, inadequate course materials, and some out-of-date computers. Clearly, the message to teachers is, "Do the best you can with our limited resources and do not expect too much from minority students who are below the poverty line." A teacher rarely can be successful at inner-city schools with the current management practices. Therefore, unions should not take the blame for poor performance. By the way, it is interesting to compare nonunion school districts to union school districts in this country on the issue of student learning. Both groups have the same problems and the same poor performance by students.

Union leadership falls into the same two categories as management. Many union leaders are "caretakers" who resist change. In good faith, they believe they are protecting teachers from administrators, political leaders, community leaders, and business executives who want to change the current teaching and learning methods. By resisting change in these situations, unions are forcing their members to continue functioning in an environment that has intolerable working conditions, low pay, few career opportunities, and a reputation for failure. The fact that 50 percent of new teachers either do not accept a teaching position or leave the field within two years tells us that maintaining the status quo is a "lose-lose" strategy. Unfortunately, some local union leaders have adopted this strategy to protect their members from any fundamental change.

Many union leaders, however, recognize that the current student learning problems in schools present a great opportunity to increase the professionalism and earnings of teachers who are willing to participate actively in the school reform movement. The late Al Shanker, president of the American Federation of Teachers (AFT), was this type of leader in the education reform movement who motivated many teachers to get involved and look for breakthrough solutions. In recent years, the NEA leadership has also become an advocate for change within public schools. Both unions recognize that continuous failure is the wrong road to travel. At the same time, they are not going to support every quick-fix and sound-good program because changes are too often approved without any evidence that the new program will work. Part II of this book illustrates why teachers must be careful about adopting new, untried programs. Rightfully, they are insisting on proven reform methods that will increase the professionalism of teaching.

For example, they support standards and accountability movements at the state level, as well as a behavior code. Unless there is order and civility in the classroom, very little learning will take place. Focusing on safe and orderly schools with high academic standards makes sense.

***Listed below are the AFT Bill of Rights and Responsibilities for Learning:***[24]

1. All students and school staff have a right to schools that are safe, orderly, and drug free.
2. All students and school staff have a right to learn and work in school districts and schools that have clear discipline codes with fair and consistently enforced consequences for misbehavior.
3. All students and school staff have a right to learn and work in school districts that have alternative educational placements for violent or chronically disruptive students.
4. All students and school staff have a right to be treated with courtesy and respect.
5. All students and school staff have a right to learn and work in school districts, schools, and classrooms that have clearly stated and rigorous academic standards.
6. All students and school staff have a right to learn and work in well-equipped schools that have the instructional materials needed to carry out a rigorous academic program.
7. All students and school staff have a right to learn and work in schools where teachers know their subject matter and how to teach it.

8. All students and school staff have a right to learn and work in school districts, schools, and classrooms where high grades stand for high achievement and promotion is earned.
9. All students and school staff have a right to learn and work in school districts and schools where getting a high school diploma means having the knowledge and skills essential for college or a good job.
10. All students and school staff have a right to be supported by parents, the community, public officials, and business in their efforts to uphold high standards of conduct and achievement.

The NEA leadership has no basic disagreement with this list, but the challenge is how to achieve the 10 objectives. Just the motto of "improved teaching" and/or good intentions is insufficient. This bill of rights will never be attained unless an integrated curriculum is created and tied to state and school district learning standards. New learning, tutoring, assessment, and administrative systems are essential to give teachers more time to work with students. A new management system will also be needed, and union leadership should not insist on approving every decision made by administrators. A strong working partnership needs to develop between union leaders and administrators. If a collaborative partnership is not established, then serious systemic change will be impossible as the two sides constantly run to the media to claim they are the only party interested in teachers and students. Both management and union leaders must have a shared vision, an approved blueprint to restructure schools, and an agreed-upon set of quality measurements.

Critics believe that the senior executives of the two unions are enlightened, but local union chapter presidents continue to live in the past and resist change. Such is the case in some communities, but many local union leaders have demonstrated progressive leadership. For example, the Teacher Union Reform Network (TURN) of the NEA and AFT local chapters was organized four years ago to restructure teacher unions in order to promote changes that improve student achievement. TURN comprises 24 local unions from both the AFT and NEA. TURN represents unions in Albuquerque, Bellevue (Washington), Boston, Cincinnati, Columbus (Ohio), Denver, Hammond (Indiana), Memphis, Minneapolis, Montgomery County (Maryland), Pinellas County (Florida), Pittsburgh, Poway (California), Rochester (New York), San Diego, San Juan (California), Seattle, Syracuse, Toledo, San Francisco, New York City, Los Angeles, and Westerly (Rhode Island).[25] Adam Urbanski, a co-director of TURN and president of the AFT in Rochester, New York, is pressing the union leaders to draft local action plans for school reform. Local action programs vary, but the common goal to improve student performance is the same. Unfortunately, like other education reform movement areas, no plan of action has been agreed upon as yet.

The local union leader must recognize a visionary leader of learning and change when a school district is blessed with such a person. Being realistic, the new leader may have some ideas and plans that are different from what exists in the system. But, it is in the union's interest to develop a working partnership with the new superintendent to help create and manage change to improve the working conditions and future compensation for its members. The new superintendent also needs to be a good "people manager" and do all that is possible to achieve a working partnership with the leaders of local unions. The art of persuasion is far more effective than a series of direct orders from the central office.

Enlightened union leaders now realize that they need good relationships with the state departments of education, district administrators, school boards, community leaders, and colleges of education. They retain their jobs far longer than district superintendents, giving them a powerful voice. Although they need to continue to enforce teachers' contracts and negotiate for better compensation and working conditions, it is time for the unions to encourage teachers to accept changes that achieve learning breakthroughs. Union leaders need to convince community members, business executives, and political leaders that better learning systems, tutoring systems, assessment systems, and administrative systems are desperately needed. Some union members will always want every budget dollar to be allocated to additional employees and benefits, but that strategy will never achieve student learning breakthroughs.

Unions are also helping to modify the tenure system. The president of the NEA said, "We as an association cannot continue to sidestep accountability for the quality of our members' work. We cannot tolerate—and we certainly shouldn't protect—that small minority of school employees who fail to measure up professionally."[26] Good teachers are beginning to raise their voices on this issue because they now realize that if their schools shelter incompetent teachers, the students that they receive will not be at grade level. Therefore, the students will receive low scores on state assessment tests.

In April 2000, the AFT proposed a national test and rigorous new standards for those who want to become teachers. Sandra Feldman, the president of the AFT, believes that the test and enhanced standards can bring teachers to a professional level similar to that of accountants, lawyers, and doctors. Now 39 states are considering some form of improved teacher standards. The AFT proposal would require that prospective teachers pass two tests, one after their sophomore year in college and a second before becoming classroom teachers. This report also calls for creating a national core curriculum explaining what teachers need to know. This new testing process would enable teachers to move from one state to another without being recertified.[27]

In addition, the AFT president urged her local union leaders to negotiate contracts that would give professionals in schools the flexibility on decisions affecting instruction in a standards-based system. She wants them to adopt programs, strategies, and schedules that increase student learning.[28]

The NEA is promoting a new agenda with three priorities: (1) teacher quality, (2) student achievement, and (3) school systems capacity, which is the infrastructure necessary for a quality education. The NEA appears to have a new willingness to experiment with new concepts based on emerging research in the education field. They want to adopt new methods and programs that improve student learning. Bob Chase, the NEA president, has called for local affiliates to negotiate contracts that empower and enable teachers to do their jobs better in cooperation with superintendents and school boards that are willing to think differently.[29]

In both unions, many teachers are against standards and accountability. The leadership of the unions has supported standards-based curriculum and assessments, but they are now rightfully demanding new curriculum and course materials to reach the standards. If school administrators and school boards do not provide the means to reach the standards, the union leadership will eventually be forced to reduce its support. Then the unions will be blamed for the failure of the standards. It is a real lose-lose situation, but the real losers will be the students in the bottom quartile of the schools. Sandra Feldman of the AFT made the following statements at her 2000 convention: "They promised we'd get new curriculum aligned with new standards. Where is it? They said tests would be better and used more responsibly. In how many places is that true?"[30]

Bashing teacher unions may never end, but it certainly doesn't help bring fundamental change to the public schools. Union leaders must become positive partners on issues of school reform. Successful for-profit school management companies should also be supported. After all, millions of union workers are employed in for-profit companies. It is in the unions' self-interest and that of their members to move urban schools from the low-performing to high-performing category with any organization that achieves breakthroughs in student learning.

## PARENTS

Wealthy parents of students who rank in the top half of their classes have little or no interest in education reform issues unless they improve the curriculum. After all, their children will leave high school with a good grade point average and will be accepted at a fine college or university. Four years later, these students will receive a good job offer. This is also the case for parents at inner-city schools whose children are at grade level, meaning the top quartile of the class.

The parents of children who are not at grade level need to speak out and demand to understand why a school does not have an integrated curriculum or learning systems to achieve the learning standards. They should demand tutoring systems to keep their children at grade level and better assessment systems to warn teachers when a student has not learned the lessons. Parents are not asking too much when they want their children to be at grade level and enjoy school.

**Parents should ask the following penetrating questions at "Parents' Night" or when they enroll their child in a school:**

1. Could I have a copy of the curriculum that describes the lessons that my child will learn this year, which will enable him or her to be successful on local and state assessment tests?
2. Are the lessons tied to the learning standards of the state and local school district?
3. What percentage of the students in this school are at grade level?
4. Will I be told when my child is not at grade level? And what tutoring programs do you have for students who are not at grade level?
5. How much experience does the teacher have and what percent of his or her students stay at grade level?
6. Does this school utilize validated learning systems or homegrown lesson plans?
7. What are the dress code and behavior guidelines?
8. What does the school expect me to do as a parent?

Every parent of every student in every school has a right to ask these questions. Teachers and administrators should have no problems answering these questions. In fact, they should prepare this information long before parents start asking the questions. When parents ask these questions, the school will have achieved a working partnership with parents. It will be a win-win situation. Almost every school can improve the quantity and quality of information provided to parents to enhance their support and involvement.

Fixing schools first is important to ensure parental involvement. Unfortunately, many inner-city parents are scared of teachers. A trip to school is a traumatic experience because they endured 13 years of failure and humiliation when they were students. These parents are the school drop-outs and failures from the last generation. It's no wonder that they are not as supportive as suburban parents, who were successful students and enjoyed school.

Most parents are not aware that poor-performing schools have a direct impact on the price of a college education. Only so much money is allocated for education in state and local budgets, and welfare and crime costs have diverted money in recent years from state universities and colleges. The $200 billion that has been added on an annual basis since 1983 to the K–12 school budgets represents more money directed from state universities.[31] The social service costs for prison, judicial, and welfare systems that handle millions of "hard-core" unemployables have also transferred more money away from state universities.[32] As a result, expenses at state universities are now between $10,000 and $15,000 per year.

Obviously, it is in the interest of state universities and parents to fix schools as soon as possible.

## TAXPAYERS

Most taxpayers know that public school costs rise annually from a few percentage points to 10 percent. Yet, very few people keep track of how much the incremental dollars amount to over a 10- or 20-year span. That is why many taxpayers are shocked to hear that public schools now cost an additional $200 billion annually since the 1983 *A Nation At Risk* report was published. They shake their heads when they hear how even more spending is planned during the next few years. Most taxpayers want our nation's children to have a good education, but they are rightfully upset that few people take any interest in cost containment. The for-profit schools understand these financial issues and will educate the public on how costs are out of control in many school districts when they present their proposals to local school boards. Taxpayers will always vote for good schools that enable children to be successful learners and that maintain financial control over taxpayer funds.

A taxpayer backlash will result during the next recession when major state and local tax increases will be required to maintain costly programs, such as small class sizes, which were approved during prosperous years. Annual rankings of school performance will encourage taxpayers to ask why students are not learning more when school budgets have doubled and/or tripled since 1983. Taxpayers will bring intense pressure on political leaders to install an integrated curriculum as well as new learning and assessment systems. They will have no problem approving charter schools, for-profit schools, magnet schools, or any other type of school that enables children to be successful learners at reasonable costs.

## STUDENTS

Students need the K–12 years to be an integrated education system instead of a series of one-room schoolhouses with an excellent teacher one year, an average teacher the next, and an unsatisfactory teacher in the third year. Once again, the bell-curve for teacher performance helps to create the bell-curve for student performance. Students need to be at grade level throughout their 13 school years. Every student cannot be a superior performer in every subject in each grade because students learn at different paces and with different learning styles. Therefore, they need interactive tutoring systems when they fall behind and enrichment lessons when they soar ahead of their classmates. Children want to enjoy school, succeed at their studies, and bring home good report cards. These goals will be possible when the paradigm outlined in this book is implemented during the next decade.

In the prosperity of the past decade, thousands of outstanding jobs are going to skilled foreign workers with temporary work visas. Thousands of other jobs have been exported overseas. In the future, American graduates need to be educated to a level where they can qualify for the best job opportunities.

## THE CHALLENGE

Before his death in 1997, Al Shanker delivered the following message in his final column:

> Public schools played a big role in holding our nation together. They brought together children of different races, languages, religions, and cultures and gave them a common language and sense of common purpose. We have not outgrown our need for this; far from it. Today, Americans come from more different countries and speak more different languages then ever before. Whenever the problems connected with school reform seem especially tough, I think about this. I think about what public education gave me—a kid who couldn't even speak English when I entered first grade. I think about what it has given me and can give to countless numbers of other kids like me. And I know that keeping public education together is worth whatever effort it takes.[33]

With all of the diverse interests discussed in this chapter, it is a great challenge to pull everyone together for a shared vision and an agreed-upon blueprint to enable most children to become successful students. How all of these groups can be brought together is the subject of the next and final chapter of the book.

---

## NOTES

1. M. Kirst and K. Bulkley, "New, Improved Mayors Take Over City Schools," *Phi Delta Kappan*, March 2000, 538–545.

2. "State and Local Tax Revenues," *Business Week*, 27 March, 2000, 234.

3. M. Baer, *To Touch the Future: Transforming the Way Teachers Are Taught* (Washington, DC: American Council on Education, 1999), 1–38, Executive Summary.

4. Baer, *To Touch the Future*, 3–5, Executive Summary.

5. C. Reed, "Taking Action on K-12, University Cooperation," *Education Week*, 24 March, 1999, 53, 72.

6. Reed, "Taking Action on K-12," 53, 72.

7. A. Levine, "Are Teachers of Teachers Out of Touch?" *New York Times*, 22 October, 1997, B8.

8. S. Gembrowski, "Art of Teaching, As Well As Subject To Be Required," *San Diego Union-Tribune*, 16 May, 2000, 8.

9. S. Feldman, "Building a Profession," *Education Week*, 7 June, 2000, 32.

10. A. Bradley, "For-Profits Tapping into Teacher Training," *Education Week*, 29 March, 2000, 1, 14.

11. M. Walsh, "Edison To Explore Expansion into Teacher Preparation," *Education Week*, 3 May, 2000, 11.

12. E. Bronner, "End of Chicago's Education School Stirs Debate," *New York Times*, 17 September, 1997, 12.

13. Bronner, "End of Chicago's Education."

14. K. Manzo, "Secondary Accreditation To Target Academics," *Education Week*, 23 February, 2000, 14.

15. A. Richard, "Houston's Paige Becomes Top-Paid Superintendent," *Education Week*, 17 May, 2000, 8.

16. "The 21st Century Corporation," *Business Week*, 12 August, 2000, 106.

17. C. Moran, "A Matter of Principals: Schools Looking for Leaders," *San Diego Union-Tribune*, 12 September, 2000, A1, A15.

18. J. Blair, "Teachers' Idealism Tempered by Frustration," *Education Week*, 31 May, 2000, 6.

19. Blair, "Teachers' Idealism."

20. E. Mendel, "Davis Turns His Focus To Teachers' Paychecks," *San Diego Union-Tribune*, 20 May, 2000, A1, A20.

21. J. Bowsher, "An Outstanding Career," *Westport News*, 6 December, 1994, A27.

22. D. Alexander, *Who's Ruining Our Schools: The Case Against The NEA Teacher Union* (Washington, DC: Save Our Schools Research and Education Foundation, 1986), 1–147.

23. A. Shanker, American Federation of Teachers, "Blaming Unions," *New York Times*, 8 September, 1996, E7.

24. A. Shanker, American Federation of Teachers, "It Works," *New York Times*, 10 September, 1995, E7.

25. A. Bradley, "Unions Turn Critical Eye on Themselves," *Education Week*, 16 February, 2000, 1, 14–15.

26. R. Cedeno, "NEA's New Unionism in Pursuit of Quality," *ASTD Training and Development Journal*, February 2000, 66.

27. J. Blair, "AFT Urges New Tests, Expanded Training for Teachers," *Education Week*, 19 April, 2000, 11.

28. M. McCain, "AFT and the Baldrige," *ASTD Training and Development Journal*, February 2000, 64.

29. Cedeno, "NEA's New Unionism," 66.

30. A. Bradley, "Union Heads Issue Standards Warnings," *Education Week*, 12 July, 2000, 1, 20.

31. E. Mendel, "Cut UC, CSU To Fund K-12, Analyst Urges," *San Diego Union-Tribune*, February 18, 2000, A1, A4.

32. F. Butterfield, *New Prisons Cast Shadow Over Higher Education*, 12 April, 1995, *New York Times*, A21.

33. A. Shanker, American Federation of Teachers, "Keeping Public Education Together," *New York Times*, 2 March, 1997, E7.

# CHAPTER 15

# Call for Dynamic Leadership and Action

Civil rights leaders often asked, "Oh, Lord, how long must we wait?" To answer that question for school reform, we must examine why the reform movement has made such minimal progress despite great talent working on this issue and so much incremental funding being invested in our public schools.

## REASONS FOR SLOW PROGRESS

*Listed as follows are the key reasons why today's public schools have not changed much since 1983:*

1. The initial education reform focus was not on improving student learning; the goal to improve schools was hazy at best.
2. It took an inordinate amount of time to establish goals, standards, and accountability.
3. Too many quick-fix programs were tried to aid an organization that has serious and complex performance problems.
4. Large sums of incremental funds were invested to fix the deficiencies with the hope that billions of dollars alone would improve student learning.
5. The goal has always been to *improve* student learning rather than to *fix* student learning.
6. Most efforts have been made to improve teaching rather than to improve student learning. There is a major difference between these two objectives.
7. Most reformers believed that the responsibility for fixing the schools belonged to the more than 2 million teachers without involving the management team of state school officers, superintendents, district staff, and principals.

8. The reformers' modus operandi has been tinkering around the edges rather than designing learning and management systems for schools.

Once again, Americans have been masters at spending money and approving quick-fix programs to solve a problem. This activity and spending has been confused with making real progress on finding a solution to the crisis of student learning. In this decade, the focus must be on systemic change that measures and manages breakthroughs in student learning.

## WHY TEACHERS CANNOT LEAD THE REQUIRED CHANGES

If someone studies major performance problems in other organizations, they will quickly learn that the "front-line" employees are not in a position to fix an organization's problems. For example, no one expects the engineers at General Motors to solve all of the problems that have reduced their market share by nearly 50 percent. When IBM encountered rough times after 70 years of no layoffs and had to move more than 150,000 employees out of the company, there was no thought that the sales personnel alone could fix the problems. When Sears, Roebuck and Co. had to abandon the catalog order side of the business, no one suggested that better order picking by their employees would have saved what was once a great business. Even doctors have not been able to fix the fundamental quality and cost problems of the American health care system. In fact, in all of these situations, a new management team with a new vision and a new paradigm was or is required.

Although their teaching is very important, teachers alone are not in a position to fix student learning. Unfortunately, some education reformers believe that new teachers from colleges of education with a revised curriculum can fix the schools' learning crisis. This solution is unrealistic because new employees are never able to create much change in any large organization. New employees are quickly influenced by experienced employees who use the old paradigm. This pattern is seen year after year in schools. If the top 5 percent of the finest university graduates were processed through the colleges of education and into urban school districts over the next 10 years, there would probably be little or no improvement in student performance.

Quality in teacher preparation, recruitment, mentoring, and professional development will not be successful unless the integrated curriculum, learning systems, tutoring systems, assessment systems, and new management systems are implemented throughout a school district. We should not expect a miracle from more than 4 million teachers who work hard each day trying to survive in an almost impossible situation where students are not at grade level.

In most school districts, more than 95 percent of the teachers are currently rated as "outstanding" or "exceeds expectations"; usually 2 or 3 percent are rated as "meets expectations"; less than 1 percent are rated as "below expectations"; and none are rated "unsatisfactory." In the nontenured ranks, percentages change by 1 or 2 percent, with almost no nontenured teachers rated as unsatisfactory.[1] Therefore, most teachers have a difficult time understanding the phrase: we need "better" teaching. They believe that they are doing exactly what their school districts and school administrators have asked them to do, and the performance management system backs up their beliefs. In addition, the teachers receive an annual increase each year for their hard work and good intentions. Of course, the product they create (successful learners) has more than a 50-percent defect rate. The problem is in the education system, not in the teaching ranks. Administrators need to lead the change in the student learning system.

To go back to the aviation analogy, consider six airlines: American, Delta, and United are the leaders in the United States airline industry today. Three other airlines went out of business: Pan American, Eastern, and People Express. Based on accident records, pilots in all six airlines performed satisfactorily. The reasons for the three airlines' success were that they had better strategic plans, cost controls, information systems, communication systems, marketing programs, reservation systems, and customer relations. Pilots cannot succeed by themselves; they need outstanding systems and an excellent management team to support their efforts.

## REQUIREMENTS FOR AN OUTSTANDING MANAGEMENT TEAM

During the Cold War, the Secretaries of State and Defense were by far the most important appointments made by various U.S. Presidents. In the 1990s, the Secretary of Treasury was elevated to the status of State and Defense as our country regained its world economic leadership role. In this decade, the Secretary of Education should be ranked at the same level as State, Defense, and Treasury because the primary domestic crisis is student learning. Although it is the constitutional responsibility of 50 state school officers to fix our public school system, the President with an outstanding leader in the Secretary of Education cabinet position can greatly influence school performance with the "bully pulpit," accountability system, ranking reports, and allocation of funds. The focus must be on low-performing schools, and the federal government appears to have a bipartisan agreement to demand improvement in student learning for all the billions of dollars being invested in schools. No President has yet insisted on a detailed plan of action from a Secretary of Education to fix rather than just improve student learning in the public schools. This President may do just that.

The new Secretary of Education should consider establishing a closer working partnership with the 50 state school officers. An annual national meeting of these 50 key senior education executives should be held, in which states would review their plans for how the public school system would eventually have more than 90 percent successful learners. Awards could be given by the U.S. President for each state that reaches its goal. The meeting could also include presentations by various superintendents on how they reached their goal of 90 percent successful learners. This approach would send a message that the school reform pace needs to go into high gear. There must be a sense of urgency during this decade to fix schools.

*Chapter 12 offered the following descriptions of three types of superintendents:*

- Caretaker (maintains the status quo)
- Education reform administrators (tinkers around the edges with quick-fixes)
- Visionary leaders of learning and change (committed to fixing the student learning problem)

Great change requires great leadership. Our decentralized public school system must have visionary leaders of learning and change in the 50 state school officer positions and the 15,000 district superintendent jobs. These senior executives are in charge of our public schools and are the only individuals who have the authority and responsibility to create systemic change. There is high turnover in these jobs.

*As each position becomes available, the state board of education (and governor) or the local school board (and mayor) should ask the following key questions to be certain that they are not hiring another caretaker or just an education reform administrator:*

1. What percentage of students in your current district or school are at grade level?
2. What percentage of your high school students drop out?
3. What programs did you implement to help students in the bottom half of the class?
4. Did you have an integrated curriculum and do you believe in having such a curriculum?
5. Did you tie the integrated curriculum to the state and district standards?
6. What percentage of students do you think can stay at grade level and receive a real K–12 education?
7. How would you use learning systems to ensure that all teachers are successful?
8. How will you know when students are not learning their lessons? What assessment systems do you plan to use to keep students at grade level?
9. Do you insist on instructional design methods for your recommended learning systems?

10. What tutoring systems do you use?
11. How do you build a working partnership with your management team and teachers?
12. How do you build a working partnership with your unions?
13. What is your overall vision for a successful school system?
14. What type of change management system do you use to reach the vision?
15. How effective are you at making tradeoff decisions to fund strategic changes in the system?
16. How effective are you and what programs do you use to develop a working partnership with parents?
17. What programs do you use to develop a partnership with public officials, business executives, and the media?
18. What methods do you use to focus on cost containment?
19. What administrative systems do you feel are necessary in future years?
20. What is your overall management system for operating a successful school system?

Many administrators will think that these questions are too detailed, but if a school board is going to hire leaders of learning and change for its senior management team, then it needs to ask a series of penetrating questions to determine if the candidate is a caretaker or a visionary leader. A similar set of questions should be asked of candidates who are applying for their first superintendent job.

## WHAT ARE THE SOURCES FOR OUTSTANDING CANDIDATES?

In the 1960s and 1970s, corporations and government agencies decided they needed a change leader to implement outstanding information and communication systems. They created a new executive position called Chief Information Officer (CIO). The question became, "Do we promote someone from inside the information technology department or do we hire a proven executive of change from outside the computer organization?" Some companies and government agencies promoted technical computer managers and tried to develop these individuals into executives of change. Some were successful, but many of these managers failed. It was too big a jump into the executive ranks, and they never gained the respect of other executives. They leaped from crisis to crisis until they resigned in exhaustion. Other organizations decided to promote proven executives of change with the understanding that they would be tutored on the position's technical issues. In these situations, the person who was second in command was often a strong manager of technology. The success rate was higher with this approach. Failures in both situations could be attributed to the lack of a vision and management system. To make matters worse, the graduate schools of business were slow in developing courses and workshops for new Chief Information Officers.

In the past decade, many corporations and government agencies decided to create a new executive position for education and training called Chief Training Officer (CTO) or Chief Learning Officer (CLO). Once again, the issue became, "Do we promote someone from the training department or do we promote a proven executive of change?" The third alternative was to hire someone from the outside who was a proven performer as a Chief Training Officer. Unfortunately, in this situation, very few proven performers were available, so the decision was whether to use a proven executive of change (and tutor that individual on education issues) or to promote an educator. There were both successes and failures, and again, the failures lacked a vision and management system. Graduate schools of business again have not developed courses or workshops for this important position.

In a few school systems (e.g., Chicago, San Diego, Los Angeles, Seattle, New York City), the school boards have hired a noneducator who was a proven executive. These people have come from the business world, the military, and the legal profession. Last year, former Governor Roy Romer of Colorado was hired by the 710,000 student Los Angeles Unified School District to be the superintendent in one of the most challenging school districts in the country.[2] All of these executives have created change and improved their school systems, but they have yet to fix a school system to the point where more than 90 percent of the students are successful learners.

Unfortunately for this group, no consulting firm or college of education is available that could advise them on how to transform their school systems into a major success. It is hoped that this book will help future superintendents who are hired from outside of the education field because there is no reason why they cannot be successful. In the future, it would also be beneficial if more consulting firms and colleges of education are able to help new superintendents. Even though most new superintendents come from the ranks of assistant superintendents and successful principals, they, too, need the help of consultants and colleges of education. There is a critical requirement for training new and existing superintendents on a new paradigm in which all students can be successful learners.

Because of the high failure rate and turnover in the school districts of major cities, a trend may develop to have a proven leader of change as the superintendent and a proven educator that knows how to increase student learning as the Chief Education Officer or Chief Academic Officer. In Philadelphia, a well-known education reform–oriented superintendent resigned after six years of effort. This city appears to be looking for four key people. The Chief Executive Officer will be responsible for managing the district in a way that focuses and leverages all district resources toward the core mission of educating children. The Chief

Academic Officer will be responsible for improving student learning, which includes the curriculum, learning systems, tutoring systems, and assessment systems, as well as professional development programs. There will also be a Chief Operating Officer and a Chief Financial Officer.[3] This type of governance system also appears to be working well in Chicago and San Diego.

In the meantime, school boards should ask their existing superintendents to give them a vision and management system that will enable their schools to have more than 90 percent of their students as successful learners. They should ask their superintendents the aforementioned 20 questions, and governors should ask the same questions of every state school officer. It's time to motivate the caretaker superintendents to become leaders of learning and change.

## PERFORMANCE AUDIT OF A SCHOOL DISTRICT

When new superintendents are hired, it's important that they take inventory of the major processes within a school district. Fortunately, at least one group is well qualified to conduct a performance audit: the National Curriculum Audit Center sponsored by the well-known Phi Delta Kappa professional education organization. The name of the center is misleading, however, because the audit includes all of the major areas of a district, such as the following:

- Organization
- Formulae for allocating resources
- Personnel programs and policies
- Performance and evaluation system
- Financial control
- Budget process
- Turnover of key management positions
- Long-range strategic plan
- Allocation and assignment of personnel
- Curriculum and subjects taught
- Alignment of curriculum to standards
- Professional and staff development
- Use of effective teaching practices
- Links between the written, taught, and tested curriculum
- Inventory control of assets and supplies
- Student test scores and assessment methods
- Improvement programs based on assessments

- Long-range master plan for facilities and sites
- Long-range technology plan
- Current use of technology
- Administrative and clerical systems
- Attendance systems
- Communication systems
- Basic statistics on student population
- Basic statistics on the community.

The first curriculum audit was described in 1970 in Dr. Leon Tessinger's best-selling book, *Every Kid a Winner*. The audit was first implemented by Dr. Fenwick English in 1979 in the Columbus, Ohio, public school district. The audit is based on generally accepted concepts pertaining to effective instruction and curriculum design and delivery, some of which have been popularly referred to as "effective schools research." Each major section of the audit starts with what the auditors expected to find, which are the generally accepted standards. The entire process is similar to a General Accounting Office (GAO) program audit of a major government agency. It is important to note that the audit focuses on the systems within a school district, not on individual schools.

The audit does not examine any aspect of school system operations unless it pertains to the design and delivery of curriculum. For example, auditors do not examine the cafeteria function unless students are hungry and, therefore, not learning. It is not concerned with custodial matters unless schools appear unclean or unsafe. In the future, the audit should include a review of learning and assessment systems.

The auditors are administrators, former administrators, and professors (who have been administrators) who are trained through an intensive national program. They have conducted hundreds of audits across the nation in small, intermediate, and large school districts. They are often hired by a state school officer to review a low-performing school district. Their professional fees are affordable by any school district that requires their services. Fees vary from $20,000 to $100,000 based on the size of the district and the number of schools to be visited.

Every new superintendent should start with this objective information rather than saying, "What can I help you do?" Too often, the new superintendent becomes a servant of the old paradigm with no hope of accomplishing a break-through in student learning.

Texas has had more audits of school districts than any other state. The Texas Curriculum Management Audit Center is affiliated with the Texas Association of School Administrators (TASA), which is one reason why Texas has witnessed major improvements in student performance. In addition, Texas' current state comptroller has expanded her school management review program.[4] She has budgeted $1 million to conduct audits, and she does not wait to be invited into a school district. Her department has reviewed 32 school districts, and the goal is 20 per year. Auditors return to the school district 18 months later to determine if their recommendations have been implemented. Texas is managing its schools like a business, and they expect every school to be successful on student learning. Texas also has had bipartisan support from its political leaders. A state-by-state analysis by the RAND Corp. ranked Texas as the second state for improvement in student learning on the NAEP math examinations.[5] Pennsylvania has ordered its auditor general to initiate audits. California also has a California Curriculum Management Audit Center that is affiliated with the Association of California School Administrators. The key to the audit is to have a focus on improving student learning rather than just counting the petty cash fund.

## THE NEED FOR OUTSTANDING PRINCIPALS

Fortunately, most people in the education reform movement understand that schoolwide reform is impossible without the creative leadership of very good principals. Teacher quality is important, but the overall collective performance of all teachers and administrators within a school transforms a low-performing school into a higher rating. Gerry Tirozzi's article "The Principalship" in *Education Week* stated it well: "Reform strategists who concentrate only on improving teachers are captives of celebrating small 'victory gardens' when the need is for an 'amber waves of grain' approach to whole-school reform. Schools cannot be transformed, restructured, or reconstituted without leadership."[6]

The principal is the key executive for implementing the vision, but the district superintendent, district staff, and pilot schools must create the new vision and paradigm. Of course, the principals in the pilot schools are deeply involved in the development of the vision and paradigm. It is a big transition from being the school building operating manager to also being the leader of student learning. Many principals need to be trained for their new responsibilities because instructional leadership is a complex challenge that is not easily achieved by most principals.[7]

Today, 73 percent of all teachers are women, but only 35 percent of the principals are women. This number of female principals may seem small, but remember that in 1987–1988, only 2 percent of the principals were women or from minority groups. School districts need to focus on these groups to determine if more successful teachers can evolve to be qualified principals. As more women and minorities become successful principals, there will be a change in both gender and race in the district superintendent's job, which today is 96 percent white male.

Forty percent of the nation's principals are nearing retirement.[8] A principal's job is a giant step forward in an education career. As stated previously, top-performing principals should be well-paid because they work a full year and have major responsibilities. Many school districts should reevaluate their compensation programs for principals and make the necessary adjustments.

The enormous demands placed on today's principals attract very few qualified candidates to take on the burdens and responsibilities of the job. But with the implementation of new management and learning systems, this executive position will have enough candidates. It is time to stop leaping from crisis to crisis and to use modern management methods and a revised organization structure to govern a successful organization.

## NEW ROLE OF THE SCHOOL BOARD

In the March 2000 *American School Board Journal*, John Carver wrote a thought-provoking article entitled "Remaking Governance." He stated: "The familiar—even cherished—practices of school boards are strangling public education. Most of what school boards currently do is a travesty of their important role."[9] He believes that the board should govern the system, rather than try to manage pieces of the organization. The board should demand educational (student learning) results rather than probe into the educational and administrative processes. The Board of Education should have at least two meetings per year devoted solely to the question of what the administrators and teachers are doing to raise student learning assessments.

The board should work with the superintendent and the general public. The superintendent works for the board of education, which represents the taxpayers who fund the school district. Parents do not own and should not control the schools. They are an important voice to the board of education, and they represent their children, who are the customers of the system, but the superintendent is the chief executive officer. Only the superintendent gives direction to employees of the school district, and only the board evaluates the superintendent. The board should demand great performance and then get out of the way. This enables the superintendent to manage an education system rather than a series of one-room schoolhouses. If these lessons are implemented, board of education members will also have embraceable jobs rather than attending frequent meetings that extend into the early hours of the morning. John Carver also said that "Visionary leadership is not forged in a flurry of trivia, micromanagement and administrative detail."[10] It is time for public school superintendents to take control of their organizations and achieve breakthrough results.

## ORGANIZATION LEADERSHIP IS REQUIRED

Organization leadership is going to be a key factor in the transformation of a traditional public school district to a new paradigm in which more than 90 percent of the students are successful learners. A great leader does not stop with a mission and vision. The leader knows that the fundamental processes must achieve the vision's goals. That is why a world-class integrated curriculum, learning systems, tutoring systems, assessment systems, and administrative systems must be implemented in all schools.

If the right systems are in place, then leaders do not have to make every decision and attend every meeting. In fact, leaders do not have to be the smartest people in the organization or even do most of the work. With an outstanding management system, superintendents can delegate most of the decisions to their staff, the principals, and the master teachers. Leadership filters down through all school district levels. This type of management will enable superintendents to be in their jobs six to ten years, which permits them to achieve significant changes in student learning.[11]

When all systems are in place, there is less chance that schools will regress to the old paradigm of good intentions and excuses for poor performance. It is important that all of us realize there is great pressure to return to the "good old days."

Administrators continue to identify instructional supervision as their most difficult responsibility.[12] With the old paradigm, it is an almost impossible responsibility. With a new integrated curriculum, learning systems, and assessment systems, the job of supervision is reasonable and embraceable. The management system and all of the other basic processes enable the management team (administrators) to lead without giving direct orders or acting as if they know it all. Everyone in the organization takes responsibility to make the necessary important decisions during the various selection and implementation phases. Both teachers and administrators must be trained to lead during the great transition to a new paradigm. Everyone needs to step up to more challenging goals.

## ROLE OF FOUNDATIONS TO SOLVE LEADERSHIP CHALLENGE

Once again, foundations and government agencies are ready to invest large sums of incremental dollars into various programs. The policy and research director for the Broad Foundation is planning to invest $100 million into the training of urban superintendents, principals, school board members, district-level executives, and union leadership.[13] This grant is a giant step in the right direction if the courses contain the necessary lessons. Several other foundations, including Readers' Digest grants, are working with various universities and educational organizations to establish new training programs for school administrators. The previous Secretary of Education discussed the idea of having a national school leadership academy similar to West Point for school administrators. Unfortunately, many of these new management development programs will result in failure and become a waste of time because they will be developed based on the old paradigm of operating schools with the hope of "better teaching."

As stated in Chapter 2, foundations have already invested hundreds of millions of dollars in various programs to improve schools, and much of it has been a total waste. Foundations are beginning to be educated on education issues. It is hoped that their future grants will yield a higher return on their investment. The Price Foundation in San Diego has contributed $18 million to a partnership that includes San Diego State University (SDSU), the San Diego Unified School District, and the local National Education Association (NEA) union.[14] SDSU has the leadership responsibility, and the superintendent has given SDSU three pilot schools (one each of elementary, middle, and high schools) to try new methods and systems. Key players are already in place, including a positive university president and a new dean of the college of education who has a proven record in school reform programs. Time will tell if this partnership achieves breakthroughs in student learning, but it represents one of the first foundation grants aimed at fixing schools rather than just improving student learning by a few percentage points.

In 1998, the San Diego Unified School District's board of education hired Alan Bersin, a former U.S. Attorney, to become district superintendent after community leaders decided that they wanted to achieve major improvements in student learning. Mr. Bersin then hired Dr. Anthony J. Alvarado, a former New York City district superintendent who had a proven record for increasing student learning. With strong leadership, these two men are bringing fundamental change to the San Diego school system in which inner-city students are often behind several grade levels. The sole purpose of their vision is student learning. Dr. Alvarado has set a goal to have 75 percent of the students at grade level, which is what the best schools seem to accomplish using traditional teaching methods. His primary strategy is to enhance teacher performance through an emphasis on new and better professional development programs. The superintendent is working with several foundations to help create these programs, which include San Diego Reads and a new management development program for school administrators.

In future years, the superintendents and chief academic officers should document how they achieved breakthroughs in student learning in books and case studies in order to enable the advanced management programs in education to be as effective as they have been in the field of business administration. The current programs lack successful case studies and textbooks based on successful new paradigms. Educators who are qualified to teach the new paradigm are also in short supply.

## SUCCESSFUL CASE STUDIES OF LEADERSHIP

Hartford, Connecticut has consistently ranked among the worst school districts in the country. Hartford has had nine superintendents in the past 10 years, according to Jeff Archer's article in *Education Week.*[15] The city has tried everything, including a "for-profit" management company that almost destroyed the "for-profit" firm. In 1997, Hartford's school board disbanded, and a state-appointed board took over. In addition, the city has had a long-running desegregation lawsuit, resulting in the state supreme court ordering a better plan to integrate area schools. Finally, in 1999, the new school board hired a former New York City district superintendent to manage its 24,000-student district.

Dr. Anthony S. Amato took over the lowest-performing school district in New York City in 1987 and elevated it to become one of the better-performing districts by 1999. In 1999, Dr. Amato subsequently took over the lowest-performing school district in Connecticut, in which 50 percent of the ninth graders dropped out of school, and by the end of high school, only 30 percent of the entering freshman class would graduate. Some of the Hartford schools had only 3, 8, or 11 percent of the students passing the state mastery tests.

Dr. Amato sees himself as half chief executive officer and half instructional leader. He truly is a visionary leader of learning and change. He has set measurable goals and is implementing learning systems from CompassLearning. With an 80-percent approval rating by teachers, Hartford also installed Success for All as well as other learning systems. These systems provide students with high-quality course materials and interactive tutoring systems. Student mobility problems are being solved by a districtwide integrated curriculum and learning systems. Students throughout the district have at least 40 minutes per day to work on computer-guided tutorials on literacy and numeracy skills. Beyond regular school days, students who are not at grade level have the option of attending an extended-day program called "Power Hour," and summer sessions if necessary. Dr. Amato is a visionary leader who believes in structure, standards, measurements, assessments, and new management systems. With learning systems, he is helping his teachers and principals to become successful without the high turnover rates and stress that have occurred in some other school districts.

Although a few teachers still believe that the superintendent is trying to "teacher proof" the curriculum, Dr. Amato develops standards, structure, and measurements to ensure that all students have the opportunity to be successful learners. Dr. Amato has also won the support of the American Federation of

Teachers (AFT) union, which has backed the new curriculum, learning systems, education programs, and assessments. Teachers see hope for their students and are proud that their school now ranks above four other school districts in the state. This success was accomplished in one year, proving that progress can be achieved in a short period. Hartford still has many challenges to face, but it now has a vision and blueprint for significantly improving student performance. Leadership has made the difference. Connecticut's mastery tests are widely recognized as among the country's most vigorous accountability methods, and Dr. Amato has committed his school district to achieving major improvements in test results.[16] The American Federation of Teachers has published a report, *Doing What Works* to show that several large urban school districts deserve recognition for raising test scores.

In another turnaround story, Nathaniel Anderson, who is in his second year as the superintendent in East St. Louis, has posed some of the most dramatic gains on last year's standardized tests in the state of Illinois.[17] This district was featured in Jonathan Kozol's 1991 book *Savage Inequalities* as a community that was so deep into poverty that a good school system was impossible. It does take money to turn around a school system, but even more important is the leadership of the school board and school administrators. Mr. Anderson has set new course materials and teacher training as priorities. Once again, fundamental change must take place within the classroom.

## IS PUBLIC SHAMING REALLY NEEDED FOR ACCOUNTABILITY?

This all-important question was raised by Suzanne Tingley, a school superintendent, in her *Education Week* article entitled "Weighing the Cattle."[18] The answer would have been "no" in 1989 if educators had determined what the problems were in student learning and fixed the education system to achieve at least 90 percent successful learners. Today, 18 years after educators rang the alarm bell and requested billions of dollars of incremental funds, the answer is "yes." Political leaders, taxpayers, and business executives who supported the massive increases in funding are no longer going to allow educators to get by with little or no improvement in student learning.

There is a saying that real pain must occur in order to create real change. Unfortunately, the pain will continue to increase each year until the student learning crisis is resolved. Therefore, it is in the interest of every school district to raise the subject of student learning to the highest priority. Pain and shaming will quickly disappear when the lessons of Part III in this book are implemented. Americans are not going to settle for child care centers where a little learning takes place; they want true institutions of learning.

The 10 major education problems outlined in Chapter 3 and repeated in Chapter 9 existed in 1983 when the *A Nation At Risk* report was published. If those problems had been identified in 1984, which would have occurred if a thorough review of the learning process had been conducted, then work could have started in 1985 on the following issues:

- Learning standards
- Integrated curriculum
- Learning systems
- Tutoring systems
- Assessment systems
- Administrative systems
- Management systems.

The development work and proof of concept in pilot schools could have been completed by 1990. This means that the current generation of K–12 students (50 million children) could have had the benefit of a first-class education system in which more than 90 percent of students are successful. Unfortunately, these 50 million students have had to drag through the old paradigm for 13 years, and 50 percent (approximately 25 million students) of them have not received a real K–12 education because they are not at grade level.

Without the standards-based curriculum and assessments that have been established in 49 states, another 50 million students could go through a third-class education system during the next 13 years. To save this travesty from occurring, pain and shaming must be invoked to motivate educators to fix the American public school system. Our country should not damage millions of children in this next generation because some people want to take another dozen years to debate the issues of education reform. It is time to achieve the eight national education goals by the year 2010 with no excuses for poor performance.

On the other hand, if the education reform movement cannot convince administrators and teachers to resystematize schools to achieve breakthroughs in learning, then there is always the alternative to reduce school budgets and expectations. If this occurs, teachers and administrators are in for many years of shame, but the real losers will be the next generation of children. In addition, the teaching profession must be ready to accept years of poor working conditions and, at best, only cost-of-living raises. Financial support for schools will be at an all-time low.


## NEW LAWSUITS WILL MOTIVATE CHANGE

Chapter 2 stated that more than 20 state school systems have been declared unconstitutional because of the inequities of funding the operating expenses of school districts. Last year, the American Civil Liberties Union (ACLU) filed a class-action lawsuit on behalf of students in 18 low-performing schools in California.[19] The ACLU claims that students cannot learn and teachers cannot teach in these schools. They are "the shame" of California. The lawsuit was filed on the 46th anniversary of the landmark Brown v. Board of Education Supreme Court decision.

Once again, the courts are being told that the state has reneged on its constitutional obligation to provide at least the bare essentials for students to be successful learners. The lawsuit is not about money. It is about having a meaningful learning system that enables all California students to achieve a real K–12 education. Of course, some people immediately say that the solution is vouchers,[20] but there are not enough seats in the "good" schools to handle thousands of students from the 18 failing schools. Therefore, schools must be fixed. When lawyers learn that standards, best practices, learning systems, tutoring systems, and assessment systems are available for good schools to emerge out of failed schools, the number of lawsuits across the nation will sharply increase. A similar suit has been filed by the National Association for the Advancement of Colored People (NAACP) and the League of United Latin American Citizens in Florida. Other cases exist in Alabama, North Carolina, and Ohio.[21] It is hoped that leaders of the K–12 public school system will not wait for additional lawsuits before they start an aggressive program to fix their low-performing schools.

## NEED FOR DYNAMIC ACTION PLANS

In the commercial world, a company goes out of business when it can no longer pay its employees and/or its creditors. The term for this condition is bankruptcy. In a few situations, the government steps in to reconstitute the organization for national defense or for other national interests. The Chrysler Automobile Company and the government of New York City were two beneficiaries of government intervention. New management, new systems, and new funding helped return the organizations to financial and operating health. Nearly 10 years ago, the federal government closed about one-third of the 1,200 savings and loan institutions when they could not pay their depositors. Federal deposit insurance enabled most depositors to receive their money at a cost of $250 billion in taxpayer funds. Because this bailout was not a scheduled item on the budget, the government had to pay another $250 billion in interest payments, thus requiring a total investment of approximately $500 billion.[22]

After 18 years of local school boards trying to improve student learning, it is time for state school officers and governors to give these local boards one last chance to fix schools with the systemic changes outlined in this book and other documents. If school boards and superintendents are still not successful, then the state should take over the "bankrupt" schools that cannot produce successful learners. The state department of education should then reconstitute the failed schools with new management, learning, tutoring, assessment, and administrative systems. The state departments of education need to develop these new systems as part of their plan of action. It will probably cost the larger states somewhere between $25 and $50 million to evaluate existing learning systems, modify them, and, in a few cases, develop new ones. All of the larger states can afford this plan of action. The federal Department of Education should enact a similar plan to help smaller states. The cost is petty cash compared to the savings and loan crisis. In this situation, however, the leadership effort by state governments will need to be greater because the challenge is to reopen successful schools rather than just close a savings and loan association.

Hugh Price, president of the National Urban League, is calling for an even bolder plan. In the *Education Week* article entitled "Urban Education: A Radical Plan," he called for the elimination of local school boards.[23] He wants the state school officers to hire district superintendents because he believes that local school boards have failed to fix student learning problems after years of effort and billions of dollars in incremental funding. This idea may seem radical, but by 2008 (the 25th anniversary of the *A Nation At Risk* report), it may be a proper course of action if Americans want to spare another generation from enduring a third-class education system.

If state governments cannot live up to their constitutional responsibilities to provide a school system in which more than 90 percent of students are successful learners, then the federal government may have to handle the responsibility just as it did with the failed banks during the Depression in the 1930s. This situation can be avoided by the states providing adequate funds and leadership for building a successful public school system. Our country simply cannot have a third-rate school system, behind those of Europe and Asia, after spending close to $400 billion annually. Some level of government must fix the student learning crisis in our schools.

## STOP THE BACKLASH ON STANDARDS

There are polls and studies that state that a large majority of parents support the establishment of learning standards and tests that determine if the students have learned their lessons. There is less support for the standardized tests that are given in many states. Parents are more for tests that determine if lessons have been mastered. There is a minority group of educators who want to avoid testing and accountability because the inconsistency of teaching is revealed. No one is for low standards and the current failure rates of learning, but that is exactly what happens when there are no standards and assessments.

Many educators wish that all talk about education reform would fade. In fact, a few educators make a full-time living bashing the standards movement. For the sake of millions of students in the bottom quartiles of their classes, it is important to stop this backlash. How will that happen? It can happen only by implementing the vision and management systems outlined in Parts III and IV of this book or by another vision that achieves the same success factors outlined in Chapter 11.

On the other hand, it is understandable that some educators are having a difficult time giving up the belief that most learning problems are caused by poverty, broken homes, minorities, immigrants, and poor-performing parents. After all, studies conducted over the past 40 years have supported this way of thinking. The media has also been a major contributor toward this way of thinking with scores of articles that communicate the message that high-income areas will always produce superior students. In many communities, newspapers often publish articles before the statewide test scores are released reminding the area that no one should expect good scores from certain schools because of the low economic status of the families who live there. These facts are only true when schools are managed using the old paradigm with traditional teaching methods.

This lose-lose situation must be changed, but change will occur only if teachers and administrators demand resources and elements of the new paradigm. If they continue to sit on the sidelines waiting for the "gift of success and respect" from their political leaders, business executives, or community leaders, then the moment of opportunity will pass and they will have decades of insufficient resources, low respect, and many wild and ineffective ideas about how to apply a quick-fix to the schools. Once again, educators will lose, and students will lose, too, if the backlash against standards is successful.

## BRIEF REVIEW OF OTHER COUNTRIES

In most other countries, the national governments establish learning standards. *Most countries also have a national curriculum for the following reasons:*

1. As students reach adulthood, they move around the country, which means that they need an education that enables them to live and work anywhere in the country.
2. When students apply for higher education, colleges and universities know what students have learned in their K–12 years. No remedial courses are offered at the university level.
3. When employers interview students for employment, they know what students learned in their K–12 years. Again, no remedial courses in reading, writing, and basic arithmetic are provided for those who didn't learn the first time.

4. When students move from one school to another, they are able to do so without falling behind in their studies because consistent lessons are taught at each grade level.
5. Teachers and administrators are able to work in any school system throughout the country.

The exception to this system is Canada, where the provinces control the curriculum, much like our state school officers and state departments of education do. In fact, Canada does not have an equivalent of our federal Department of Education.

Contrary to rumor, education systems in other countries do not have a high drop-out rate, and they do have a low truancy rate. Class sizes are often larger than in the United States, with Japan having nearly 40 students per class. Teacher compensation is quite similar to the United States, but teachers in other countries rarely work second jobs. Teaching is considered a full-time position in most other countries. Canada has the highest teacher salaries. In most countries, high school and gymnasium (high school) teachers earn more than elementary school teachers. Teachers in other nations are afforded great respect because a high percentage of their students are successful learners.[24]

Children in other countries attend neighborhood schools that they walk to or take a short ride on public transportation. There are few discipline problems. There are usually more school days, but days are shorter and include more field trips, which means that the hours spent on learning are quite similar. Japan, for instance, has 240 school days. Only 20 to 30 percent of students in other countries graduate from college, about the same as in the United States; however, more than 60 percent of American high school graduates enroll in institutions of higher learning. Thus, our country has a much higher drop-out rate at the university level. Teachers and administrators enjoy more collegial relationships in other nations than do their American counterparts.[25]

In Japan, large classrooms are supported by tutoring: first by the mother and then by "cram" schools. Based on lessons learned, Japan and Korea have two outstanding education systems. Germany is famous for its vocational and apprentice system that prepares young people to become productive workers in key jobs. England is finally getting its education system up to the level of other European countries. The British schools have had high levels of local control and inconsistent teaching, resulting in bell-curve performance problems. In recent years, the government has implemented a national curriculum and student assessment program. England has parental choice, but that means that the schools can reject students as well. The English system also has implemented structure and measurements that are improving student learning.[26] Canada's western provinces have also implemented more structure and measurement in an effort to upgrade school performance. Ireland is also having economic successes because of a world-class school system in which unemployment has fallen from 16 to 4 percent in the last decade.[27]

New Zealand implemented a new decentralized education system in 1989 with vouchers for all parents. With no learning standards and no accountability system based on standards, they now have a mixture of schools. Some are very good and only the most motivated students are accepted, whereas others are terrible and are attended by poor and minority children. They have proven with their "Tomorrow's Schools" that competition does not fix quality problems. It is an interesting experiment to study, but not one that should be copied.[28]

For many years, critics have dismissed results of international studies, suggesting that the results are meaningless because the United States educates the masses and other countries school only their elite learners. This statement is not true. Late in 1998, the Paris-based Organization for Economic Cooperation and Development (OECD) issued a report comparing high school graduate rates in leading industrialized nations. The United States, once thought to be a world leader in high school completions, is now lagging behind 22 other leading industrial countries.[29] In the Third International Mathematics and Science Study (TIMSS), the United States had a poor performance compared to other nations when our best students represented our country.[30]

Asian countries are making major investments and implementing systemic change in their education systems. Remember, Korea invested $17 million over eight years in the 1970s and achieved breakthroughs in student learning.[31] In Singapore, a small country where English is the republic's primary language, their school system is investing $2 billion for a master technology plan with learning systems. Their goal is to have all schools fully networked by 2002, with one multimedia computer for every two teachers and every two students. They plan to have their students using interactive tutoring systems 30 percent of their curriculum time. A new paradigm for teaching and learning will be implemented.[32]

The United States has a third-class education system within our cities compared to Europe and Asia. If our country continues with the current paradigm, our students will have the same opportunities as children in India. Wealthy and middle-class students will attend good schools, and students in working-class and poor neighborhoods will go to child care centers called "schools" where they will learn just enough to be minimum wage earners.[33] On the other hand, the United States could be the world's leading education system. Our educators know more about learning theory, instructional design, integrated curricula, learning systems, assessment systems, multimedia courseware, distance learning, and management systems than do educators in other countries. This knowledge just needs to be implemented in our schools. Simply put, there is no excuse for our country to have a third-class public education system in any community.

We can learn a great deal by studying the education systems in other countries. For example, a number of mathematics teachers are studying the textbooks and teaching methods used in Singapore which was the top performer in international tests. We can discover not only how they achieve higher student performance but also how their schools have created and managed change to achieve world-class standards. It is important to stress that American children are not inferior learners compared to European and Asian children; however, American students need a better education system that enables them to become successful learners.

## CONCLUSION

Many teachers and administrators want to believe that all children can become successful learners. Few, however, actually believe that statement because they have never experienced such a success rate. Why didn't a state school officer or a district superintendent or a dean from a college of education write this type of book soon after the famous *A Nation At Risk* report was published in 1983? In fairness to these important educators, they've been buried in the existing paradigm's daily operating challenges. They have had little time to stand back and determine how the public schools should be resystematized to achieve learning break-throughs. These education leaders have also been part of the current paradigm for 20 to 40 years. It is difficult to develop a new paradigm when one has so many years and so much authorship invested in the old one. Some years ago, Bill Bennett, a former Secretary of Education, said: "Those who led us into this crisis may not lead us out. We should listen to some new people who have new ideas."[34]

I have had more than 30 years of experience as an instructor, course developer, manager (principal) of an education center, and chief training officer (the equivalent of a state school officer) of a large global corporation. In addition, I have received valuable feedback from hundreds of educators, business executives, and public officials on the goal of all students becoming successful learners.

There are days when I wish I could have written a smaller, simpler book such as Spencer Johnson's bestseller *Who Moved My Cheese?*, which is an allegory about change and has been read by more than 1 million people.[35] School reform issues are complex, however, and readers must understand why a new systems approach to learning must be developed and implemented. The education "cheese" will be moved many times over the next decade, and educators need to understand why change is necessary and how to create and manage it.

During the past 18 years, many educators, political leaders, business executives, and community leaders have said: "We know how to fix schools, just give us the resources and let us get on with the tasks to be done." This is another myth! Very few people—and it is very few—know how to resystematize the inner-city public schools to a level where more than 90 percent of students are at grade level. I make this statement based on the performance of those schools during the past 18 years and having read more than 100 books and more than 1,000 articles, as well as attending scores of meetings, on school reform. That is why so few detailed plans have been formulated to achieve breakthroughs in student learning. After all, if educators knew how to fix the crisis of student learning, they would have done the job during the past 18 years because no educator enjoys watching students fail or get behind in their studies.

*It is hoped that educators who have read this book have answered the following three questions that were raised at the end of the Introduction:*

1. What messages and facts in the book do you agree with?
2. What messages do you disagree with and why?
3. What changes are necessary to modify the blueprint at your school to achieve the learning standards that have been established by the local school district and the state department of education?

The country needs a vision and a detailed plan of action within each school district to achieve learning standards established by the state department of education and the local school district. In this decade, it appears multibillion dollar increases of incremental funds over the base of $330 billion in year 2000 will be invested by political leaders and taxpayers. By the end of the decade, the annual operating budget for the American public schools could be close to $500 billion at the rate of spending being projected at the federal, state, and local levels. For that amount of investment, the American public schools have the funds to create fundamental change with a new paradigm to achieve breakthroughs in student learning. Hopefully, this book will help political leaders and educators spend the incremental funds on programs that really work rather than merely sound good.

Mr. Raymond F. Bacchetti, a program officer at the Hewlett Foundation in Menlo Park, California, made an important observation in an article concerning staying power. He said: "If we are to reform public education, we have to accept its complexity and have the patience and determination—indeed, the collective courage—to analyze, understand, and respond to that complexity. With Albert Einstein, we should seek to make things as simple as possible but not simpler."[36] That is, of course, the intention of this book. Bacchetti also said that "Improving schools is difficult but not mysterious work." Perhaps THE READERS can now agree with that statement.

Almost a decade ago, Peter Drucker, a well-known professor of management said: "The lesson for school leaders in this social climate is clear. You must start looking at taxpayers and parents as customers, and the schools must sell results."[37] He also said that

> The big challenge will be to find leaders for our public school system. There may be "born leaders," but there surely are too few to depend on them. Leadership must be learned and can be learned. All the effective leaders I have encountered—both those I worked with and those I merely watched—knew four simple things:[38]

1. The only definition of a leader is someone who has followers. Some people are thinkers. Some are prophets. Both roles are important and badly needed. But without followers, there can be no leaders.
2. An effective leader is not someone who is loved or admired. Popularity is not leadership. Results are.
3. Leaders are highly visible. They, therefore, set examples.
4. Leadership is not rank, privileges, title, or money. It is responsibility.

Drucker also said that "Effective leaders are not preachers; they are doers." Over the next 10 years, the United States will need thousands of these doers in the public school system's top management positions. They'll also need to remember the following three alternatives for future education reform programs that were listed in Chapter 3:

1. Give up and accept schools as they are.
2. Continue looking for "silver bullets."
3. Adopt a new paradigm with systemic change.

Everyone agrees that looking for more "silver bullets" is a waste of time. *Therefore, the leaders of our public schools system have the following simple choice:*

1. *Go back to having one of the most expensive child care systems for half of the students where a little learning takes place and society continues to have*
   - millions of functional illiterates
   - millions of hard-core unemployables
   - millions of welfare cases
   - millions of people in various prisons
   - millions of ex-convicts
2. *Go forward to having the finest public school system in the world that helps to provide Americans with an above-average standard of living and world leadership.*

After reading this book, it should be clear that school reform is not "rocket science" or an impossible task. Again, a new paradigm with systemic change is both feasible and affordable. It is time to move at an accelerated pace toward the new paradigm in which all students, with few exceptions, become successful learners. "Fix schools first" should be a rallying cry for this decade. As stated in the Introduction, much has been learned during the past 18 years on how to fix the crisis of student learning.

Now, almost every school district must take two giant steps forward. First, they must recognize that inconsistent teaching will only be eliminated by implementing learning systems in the classrooms. Second, a new management system must be implemented in both schools and the school district to measure and manage learning. The good news is that all of the knowledge, experience, methodologies, and technologies necessary to take these two giant steps exists today. Continuous improvement will need to be made over the years, but there are no valid reasons to wait for any more inventions or research studies. Every school needs a thermometer similar to the one that the United Way uses for fundraising to show how it is progressing toward its goal of 100 percent. The education thermometer would, of course, show the percentage of successful learners.

The United States has had great leadership over the years, which is why our country enjoys such high standards of living. Our country has also been generous to developing nations. When we have developed a superior education system with new learning, tutoring, and assessment systems, we could export it to developing countries as we did with Korea in the 1970s. The gift of a successful education system could mean even more than the foreign aid we are already giving to underdeveloped countries because billions of children need to be educated.[39]

In 1993, the Conference Board wrote an excellent publication entitled *Ten Years After a Nation at Risk*. Many leaders in the education reform movement are quoted in this document, including the author of this book.[40] Terrel Bell, the former U.S. Secretary of Education who commissioned the well-known report, contributed the following words in this follow-up book:

> The 10 years since the publication of *A Nation At Risk* have been a splendid misery for American education. We have learned much. We have suffered many disappointments. But we have not given up the quest to shape education into the super-efficient enterprise that it must become if America is to keep its proud place of leadership in the marvelous information age of this decade and beyond. Perhaps we should have made much more progress than we have. But at least we have stayed with the task.[41]

Unfortunately, the report *Twenty Years After a Nation at Risk* could open with the same words as its predecessor because all of the money and efforts of the past 20 years have not produced documented widescale improvements in student learning. Lee Iacocca also commented in 1993 that, "In spite of the big bucks contributed to education by the private sector, I don't see much improvement. We need to put more energy and human resources into schools and stop throwing money at the problem." Precisely. It's time to end the pain and suffering in the bottom half of our urban school district classes. It's time to turn the jobs of teacher and administrator into embraceable responsibilities and enjoyable experiences.

Too often in the past, everyone waited for some other person or group (e.g., political leaders, corporations, community leaders, colleges of education, teachers, or parents) to fix the schools. It is important to remember that only the school board members, administrators, and teachers can bring systemic change into the classrooms to fix learning problems in the public schools. Let the work begin. Our country must achieve the eight national education goals by 2010.

As this book is being printed, a new President, Secretary of Education, and many new governors as well as school board members are taking up the heavy responsibilities of government. All are committed to fixing the American public school system. It is hoped that they will focus on the real problem of student learning and meaningful solutions to this problem. Just throwing money into schools will not solve the student learning crisis.

This book is intended to recharge the education reform movement so that the American public school system and especially the inner-city schools can be fixed in this decade. Americans want their schools to be successful.[42] Restructuring our public school system will be a unifying experience for this country just as the space program, the national highway system, and wartime victories have been. It seems appropriate to end this book with the following quotation by Mark Twain:

> The secret to getting ahead is getting started. The secret to getting started is breaking your complex overwhelming tasks into small manageable tasks, and then starting on the first one.[43]

Let us constantly remind ourselves during this decade that every child deserves a good school with an effective teacher who has a validated learning system which teaches every lesson of the integrated curriculum to the level where each student in the classroom learns all the lessons required to successfully complete each grade level of school. When our schools are at this level of performance, the rallying cry "Fix Schools First," can be ended.

---

## NOTES

1. B. McCormick, *Quality and Education: Critical Linkages* (Princeton Junction, NJ: Eye On Education, 1993), 32.

2. A. Richard, "Los Angeles Board Taps Romer for Top Job," *Education Week*, 14 June, 2000, 1–2.

3. K. Reid, "Corporate-Style Team Sought To Take Charge of Philadelphia District," *Education Week*, 2 September, 2000, 11.

4. B. Keller, "Tough Grandma Steps Up Audits in Texas," *Education Week*, 8 March, 2000, 24–28.

5. D. Viadero, "RAND Report Tracks State NAEP Gains," *Education Week*, 2 August, 2000, 8.

6. G. Tirozzi, "The Principalship," *Education Week*, 29 March, 2000, 44, 68.

7. L. Olson, "New Thinking on What Makes a Leader," *Education Week*, 19 January, 2000, 1, 14–15.

8. L. Fenwick and M. Blackman, "Looking for Leaders in a Time of Change," *Education Week*, 28 March, 2000, 46, 68.

9. J. Carver, "Remaking Governance," *American School Board Journal*, March 2000, 26–30.

10. Carver, "Remaking Governance," 30.

11. L. Cuban, "The Superintendent Contradiction," *Education Week*, 14 October, 1998, 43, 56.

12. D. Arredondo et al., *Pushing the Envelope in Supervision* (Alexandria, VA: Association of Supervision and Curriculum Development, November 1995), 74–78.

13. L. Olson, "Policy Focus Converges on Leadership," *Education Week*, 12 January, 2000, 1, 16.

14. Interview with Sol and Robert Price.

15. J. Archer, "Under Amato, Hartford Schools Show Progress," *Education Week*, 1 March, 2000, 1, 18–19.

16. Archer, "Under Amato," 18.

17. R. Johnston, "Test Scores in East St. Louis Raise Hopes of a Turnaround," *Education Week*, 14 June, 2000, 7.

18. S. Tingley, "Weighing the Cattle: Is a Public Shaming Really Needed for Accountability?" *Education Week*, 4 August, 1999, 44.

19. J. Soundham, "California Schools Lack Basics, Suit Alleges," *Education Week*, 24 May, 2000, 1, 29.

20. J. Perkins, "The Best Way To Fix Failing Public Schools," *San Diego Union-Tribune*, 2 June, 2000 (Editorial).

21. J. Sandham, "Florida Sued over Educational Adequacy," *Education Week*, 20 January, 1999, 14.

22. Interview with the former Comptroller General of the United States.

23. H. Price, "Urban Education: A Radical Plan," *Education Week*, 8 December, 1999, 29, 44.

24. R. McAdams, *Lessons from Abroad* (Lancaster, England: Technomic Publishing, 1993), 1–327.

25. McAdams, *Lessons from Abroad*.

26. C. Tell, *Whose Curriculum? A Conversation with Nicholas Tate* (Alexandria, VA: Association for Supervision and Curriculum Development, October 1998), 64–69.

27. R. Kuttner, "Ireland's Miracle: The Market Didn't Do It Alone," *Business Week*, 10 July, 2000, 33.

28. E. Fiske, and H. Ladd, "A Distant Laboratory: Learning Cautionary Lessons from New Zealand's Schools," *Education Week*, 17 May, 2000, 38, 56.

29. D. Hoff, "U. S. Graduation Rates Starting To Fall Behind," *Education Week*, 25 November, 1998, 1, 11.

30. C. Callahan et al., "TIMSS and High Ability Students," *Phi Delta Kappan*, June 2000, 787–790.

31. R. Morgan, *The Korean Educational Development Institute* (New York: United Nations Educational Scientific and Cultural Organization, January 1979).

32. F. McGinn, "An Education Exchange in Singapore," *Technology and Learning Journal*, August 2000, 20.

33. S. Dallas, "Why India's Poor Pay for Private School," *Business Week*, 24 April, 2000, 22E14.

34. Presentation by Bill Bennett, Secretary of Education, at 1988 Education Summit by *Fortune* magazine.

35. S. Johnson, *Who Moved My Cheese?* (New York: G. Putnam's Son, 1999), 1–94.

36. R. Bacchetti, "Stay Power: The Most Important Reform Objective," *Education Week*, 10 November, 1999, 4.

37. P. Drucker, "Performance Accountability and Results," *American School Board Journal*, March 1992, A4–A11.

38. P. Drucker, Foreword to *The Leaders of the Future* (San Francisco, CA: Jossey-Bass, October 1995), 11–15 in Foreword.

39. Associated Press, "World Total Is Now Put at 6 Billion," *San Diego Union-Tribune*, 12 April, 2000, 4.

40. L. Lund and C. Wild, *Ten Years After a Nation at Risk* (New York: The Conference Board, July 1993), 20, 26–28.

41. Lund and Wild, *Ten Years After.*

42. A. Coles, "Gallup Poll Finds Americans Committed to Public Schools," *Education Week*, 8 September, 1999, 12.

43. *Bartlett's Book of Quotations.*

# Suggested Readings

Alexander, D.C. Jr. 1988. *Who's ruining our schools? The case against the NEA Teacher Union*. Washington, DC: Save Our Children Foundation.

Ashby, D., and Krug, S. 1998. *Thinking through the principalship*. Princeton, NJ: Eye On Education.

Bennett, W.J. *James Madison High School: A curriculum for American studies*. Washington, DC: Department of Education.

Bennett, W.J. et al. 1999. *The educated child: A parent's guide from preschool through eighth grade*. New York: The Free Press.

Bernardt, V.L. 1998. *Data analysis for comprehensive schoolwide reform*. Princeton, NJ: Eye On Education.

Bloom, A. 1987. *The closing of the American mind: How higher education has failed democracy and impoverished today's students*. New York: Simon and Schuster.

Bracey, G.W. 1997. *Setting the record straight: Responses to misconceptions about public education in the United States*. Alexandria, VA: Association for Supervision and Curriculum Development.

Burden, P.R. 2000. *Powerful classroom management strategies: Motivating students to learn*. Thousand Oaks, CA: Corwin Press.

Caine, R.N. 1991. *Making connections: Teaching and the human brain*. Alexandria, VA: Association for Supervision and Curriculum Development.

Cetron, M. 1985. *Schools of the future: How American business and education can cooperate to save our schools*. New York: McGraw-Hill.

Chubb, J.E., and T.M. Moe. 1990. *Politics, markets, and America's schools*. Washington, DC: The Brookings Institute Press.

Colfax, D., and M. Colfax. 1988. *Homeschooling for excellence: How to take charge of your child's education and why you absolutely must*. New York: Warner Books.

335

Crane, T., and A.G. Spoon. 1999. *The CEO forum: School technology and readiness*. Washington, DC: CEO Forum on Education and Technology.

Deming, W.E. 1986. *Crisis*. Cambridge, MA: MIT Center for Advanced Engineering Study.

Dick, W., and L. Carey. 1990. *The systematic design of instruction*. Glenview, IL: Scott Foresman.

Dryfoos, J.G. 1998. *Full-service schools: A revolution in health and social services for children, youth, and families*. San Francisco: Jossey-Bass.

Education Week. 1999. *Quality counts '99: Rewarding results, punishing failure*. Bethesda, MD: Education, Inc.

Education Week. 1999. *Technology counts '99: Building the digital curriculum*. Bethesda, MD: Education, Inc.

Education Week. 2000. *Lessons of a century: A nation's schools come of age*. Bethesda, MD: Editorial Projects in Education.

Education Week. 2000. *Who should teach?* Bethesda, MD: Education, Inc.

Ellis, A.K., and J.T. Fouts. 1994. *Research on school restructuring*. Princeton, NJ: Eye On Education.

English, F.W. 2000. *Deciding what to teach and test: Developing, aligning, and auditing the curriculum*. Thousand Oaks, CA: Corwin Press.

Feistritzer, C.E. 1999. *The making of a teacher: A report on teacher preparation in the U.S.* Washington, DC: Center for Education Information.

Finn, C.E. Jr. 1991. *We must take charge: Our schools and our future*. New York: Free Press.

Finn, C.E. Jr., and T. Rebarber. 1992. *Education reform in the '90s*. New York: Macmillan.

Fiske, E.B. 1992. *Smart schools, smart kids: Why do some schools work?* New York: Simon & Schuster.

Fosler, R.S. 1990. *The business role in state education reform*. Washington, DC: The Business Roundtable.

Frankel, D.B. 1996. *True needs: True partners*. Washington, DC: Institute of Museum and Library Services.

Frazier, G.G., and H.Sickles 1993. *The directory of innovations in high schools*. Princeton, NJ: Eye On Education.

Friedman, M. 1962. *Capitalism and freedom*. Chicago: University of Chicago Press.

Gadsden, V.L., and D.A. Wagner. 1995. *Literacy among African-American youth*. Cresskill, NJ: Hampton Press.

George, P.S. et al. 1992. *The middle school and beyond*. Alexandria, VA: Association for Supervision and Curriculum Development.

Gerstner, L.V. Jr. 1994. *Reinventing education: Entrepreneurship in America's public schools*. New York: Dutton.

Glatthorn, A.A. 1997. *The principal as curriculum leader.* Thousand Oaks, CA: Corwin Press.

Glennan, T.K. Jr. 1998. *New American schools after six years.* Santa Monica, CA: Rand Education.

Goodlad, J.I. 1984. *A place called school: Prospects for the future.* New York: McGraw-Hill.

Goodlad, J.I. 1990. *Teachers for our nation's schools.* San Francisco: Jossey-Bass.

Goodlad, J.I., and R.H. Anderson. 1987. *The nongraded elementary school.* New York: Teacher's College Press.

Goodman, R.H. et al. 1997. *Getting there from here: Creating a school governance team capable of raising student achievement.* Arlington, VA: Educational Research Service.

Gordon, S.P., and S. Maxey. 2000. *How to help beginning teachers succeed.* Alexandria, VA: Association for Supervision and Curriculum Development.

Gross, B., and R. Gross. 1985. *The great school debate.* New York: Simon and Schuster.

Guskey, T.R. 1985. *Implementing mastery learning.* Belmont, CA: Wadsworth.

Hamburg, S.K. 1987. *Children in need: Investment strategies for the educationally disadvantaged.* New York: Committee For Economic Development.

Hammer, M., and J. Champy. 1993. *Reengineering the corporation: A manifesto for business revolution.* New York: Harper Business.

Harless, J. 1998. *The Eden conspiracy: Educating for accomplished citizenship.* Wheaton, IL: Guild Publications.

Harry, M., and R. Schroeder. 1999. *Six sigma.* New York: Doubleday.

Heerman, B. 1988. *Teaching and learning with computers.* San Francisco: Jossey-Bass.

Hess, F.M. 2000. *Spinning wheels: The politics of urban school reform.* Washington, DC: The Brookings Institute Press.

Hesselbein, F. et al. 1996. *The leader of the future.* San Francisco: Jossey-Bass.

Hesselbein, F. et al. 1997. *The organization of the future.* San Francisco: Jossey-Bass.

Hesselbein, F. et al. 1999. *Leading beyond the walls.* San Francisco: Jossey-Bass.

Hill, P. et al. 1997. *Reinventing public education: How contracting can transform America's schools.* Chicago: University of Chicago Press.

Hirsch, E.D. Jr. 1987. *Cultural literacy: What every American needs to know.* New York: Houghton Mifflin.

Hirsch, E.D. Jr. 1999. *The schools we need: And why we don't have them.* New York: Anchor Books.

Hoerr, T. 2000. *Becoming a multiple intelligences school.* Alexandria, VA: ASCD Books.

Hunt, B. Jr. 1983. *Action for excellence: Task force on education for economic growth.* Denver, CO: Education Commission of the States.

Ikenberry, S.O. 1999. *To touch the future: Transforming the way teachers are taught.* Washington, DC: American Council on Education.

Jacobs, H.H. 1989. *Interdisciplinary curriculum: Design and implementation.* Alexandria, VA: Association for Supervision and Curriculum Development.

Jacobs, H.H. 1997. *Mapping the big picture: Integrating curriculum and assessment K-12.* Alexandria, VA: Association for Supervision and Curriculum Development.

Johns Hopkins University. 2000. *Ten promising programs for educating all children: Evidence of impact.* Arlington, VA: Educational Research Service.

Johnson, D., and R. Johnson. 1994. *Leading the cooperative school.* Edina, MN: Interaction Book Company.

Kaufman, R. *Mapping educational success: Strategic thinking and planning for school administrators.* Thousand Oaks, CA: Corwin Press.

Kearns, D.T., and D.P. Doyle. 1988. *Winning the brain race: A bold plan to make our schools competitive.* San Francisco: Institute for Contemporary Studies.

Kearns, D.T., and J. Harvey. 2000. *A legacy of learning,* Washington, DC: Brookings Institute Press.

Kohn, A. 2000. *The case against standardized testing.* Westport, CT: Heinemann.

Kozol, J. 1991. *Savage inequalities.* New York: Crown.

Lenn, P.D. 1993. *Active learning.* New York: Penguin Putnam.

Levine, M., and R. Trachtman. 1988. *American business and the public school: Case studies of corporate involvement in public education.* New York: Teachers College Press, Columbia University.

Lowman, J. 1995. *Mastering the techniques of teaching.* San Francisco: Jossey-Bass.

Manning, R.C. 1994. *Schools for all learners: Beyond the bell curve.* Princeton, NJ: Eye On Education.

Marsh, D.D. 1999. *Preparing our schools for the 21st century.* Alexandria, VA: Association for Supervision and Curriculum Development.

May, W.F. 1985. *Investing in our children: Business and the public schools.* New York: Committee for Economic Development.

McAdams, R.P. 1993. *Lessons from abroad: How other countries educate their children.* Lancaster, PA: Technomic Publishing.

McAdams, D.R. 2000. *Fighting to save our urban schools . . . and winning!: Lessons from Houston.* New York: Teachers College Press.

McCormick, B.L. 1993. *Quality and education: Critical linkages.* Princeton, NJ: Eye On Education.

Mitchell, W. 1986. *The power of positive students.* New York: Bantam Books.

Nathan, J. 1998. *Charter schools.* San Francisco: Jossey-Bass.

National Alliance of Business. 1990. *A primer for business on education.* Washington, DC: The Business Roundtable.

National Commission on Excellence in Education. 1983. *A nation at risk.* Washington, DC: U.S. Government Printing Office.

National Research Council. 1999. *How people learn: Brain, mind, experience, and school.* Washington, DC: National Academy Press.

Oblinger, D.G., and S.C. Rush. 1998. *The future compatible campus: Planning, designing, and implementing information technology in the academy.* Bolton, MA: Anker Publishing.

Pankratz, R.S., and J.M. Petrosko. 2000. *All children can learn,* San Francisco: Jossey-Bass.

Papert, S. 1993. *Children's machines.* New York: Basic Books.

Perelman, L.J. 1992. *School's out: Hyperlearning, the new technology and the end of education.* New York: William Morrow & Company.

Pinnell, G.S. et al. 2000. *Reading recovery: Early intervention for at-risk first graders.* Arlington, VA: Educational Research Service.

Podsen, I.J., and V.M. Denmark. 2000. *Coaching and mentoring first-year and student teachers.* Larchmont, NY: Eye On Education.

Provenzo, E.F. Jr. 1998. *The educator's brief guide to the Internet and the World Wide Web.* Princeton, NJ: Eye On Education.

Ravitch, D. 1985. *The schools we deserve: Reflections on the education crisis of our time.* New York: Harper Collins.

Ravitch, D. 2000. *Left back: A century of failed school reforms.* New York: Simon and Schuster.

Ravitch, D., and J.P. Viteritti. 1997. *New schools for a new century: The redesign of urban education.* New Haven, CT: Yale Press.

Reigeluth, C.M., and R.J. Garfinkle. 1994. *Systemic change in education.* Englewood Cliffs, NJ: Educational Technology Publications.

Rich, D. 1988. *Mega skills: How families can help children succeed in school and beyond.* Boston: Houghton Mifflin.

Rioux, J.W., and N. Berla. 1993. *Innovations in parent and family involvement.* Princeton, NJ: Eye On Education.

Rosenblum-Lowden, R. 2000. *You have to go to school: You're the teacher.* Thousand Oaks, CA: Corwin Press.

Rothchild, E. 1993. *Risktaker, caretaker, surgeon, undertaker: The four faces of strategic leadership.* New York: John Wiley & Sons.

Rubin, S.E. 1994. *Public schools should learn to ski: A systems approach to education.* Milwaukee, WI: ASQC Quality Press.

Sarason, S.B. 1998. *Charter schools: Another flawed education reform.* New York: Teachers College Press.

Schlechty, P.C. 1990. *Schools for the 21st century: Leadership imperative for education reform.* San Francisco: Jossey-Bass.

Schlechty, P.C. 1997. *Inventory better schools: An action plan for education reform.* San Francisco: Jossey-Bass.

Schlechty, P.C. 2000. *Shaking up the school house*, San Francisco: Jossey-Bass.

Schmoker, M. 1996. *Results: The key to continuous school improvement*. Alexandria, VA: Association for Supervision and Curriculum Development.

Schumaker, D.R., and W.A. Sommers. 2000. *Being a successful principal*. Thousand Oaks, CA: Corwin Press.

Sizer, T.R. 1992. *Horace's school: Redesigning the American high school*. Boston: Houghton-Mifflin.

Slavin, R. 1986. *Educational psychology: Theory into practice*. Englewood Cliffs, NJ: Prentice Hall.

Sniegoski, S.J. 1988. *The department of education: Know your government*. Washington, DC: Chelsea House Publishers.

Stanley, S.J., and W.J. Popham. 1988. *Teacher evaluation: Six prescriptions for success*. Alexandria, VA: Association for Supervision and Curriculum Development.

Thompson, D.C., and R.C. Wood. 1998. *Money and schools*. Princeton, NJ: Eye On Education.

Timpane, M.P., and L.S. White. 1998. *Higher education and school reform*. San Francisco: Jossey-Bass.

Toch, T. 1991. *In the name of excellence: The struggle to reform the nation's schools and why it's failing and what should be done*. New York: Oxford University Press.

Tucker, M.S., and J.B. Codding. 1998. *Standards for our schools: How to set them, measure them, and reach them*. San Francisco: Jossey-Bass.

Venezky, R.L. et al. 1990. *Toward defining literacy*. Newark, DE: International Reading Association.

Walberg, H.J. 1985. *Examining the theory, practice, and outcomes of mastery learning*. San Francisco: Jossey-Bass.

Wells, A.S., and R.L. Crain. 1997. *Stepping over the color line*. New Haven, CT: Yale Press.

Wenglinsky, H. 2000. *How teaching matters: Bringing the classroom back into discussions of teacher quality*. Princeton, NJ: Education Testing Service.

Whitaker, T. et al. 2000. *Motivating and inspiring teachers: The education leader's guide for building staff morale*. Larchmont, NY: Eye On Education.

Williams, T.L. 1999. *The directory of programs for students at risk*. Larchmont, NY: Eye On Education.

Woods, G. 1986. *Drug use and drug abuse*. New York: Franklin Watts.

Yankelovich, D. 1999. *The magic of dialogue: Transforming conflict into cooperation*. New York: Simon & Schuster.

---

# Definitions of Various Systems Used throughout an Education System

The word *system* is defined as a group of interacting elements with a common purpose. Throughout this book, the words "system" and "systems" are often used.

*Administrative System:* An administrative system is a collection of clerical tasks and computer programs that tie together all of the information required to manage a school system from the school to the state department of education, including the district staff. The system has a complete record on each student (i.e., name, student number, telephone number, address, parent(s) or guardian(s), work location and telephone number, attendance record, courses completed, grades, courses for current semester, grades to date) and each member of the staff (i.e., name, social security number, telephone number, address, payroll information, education). All of the financial records and budgets, as well as planning data, are kept in the system.

*Assessment System:* The intent of the assessment system is to measure what students know and can do. The system may include exercises and tests administered at the end of each lesson. In some courses, a portfolio of work by the student is a major part of the assessment. In some grades and courses, a final examination is given at the end of the semester or school year. Several school districts and some states are now implementing a final (exit) examination at the end of elementary school (grades K–4), middle school (grades 5–8), and high school (grades 9–12). Many states use norm-referenced standardized achievement tests, but these tools are being replaced in several states by mastery tests that test students on the lessons that are aligned to the state and district learning standards. There are national tests for Advanced Placement courses. The assessment system is the quality control system for public schools.

*Budget and Financial Control System:* All of the transactions of a school and school district must be recorded in an accounting system that enables all units of

341

a school district to plan, budget, and control their resources. Many operating and statistical reports are generated by the system for management control purposes.

*Communication System:* With advancing technology, many new devices are being installed at nearly every school with new or enhanced software. E-mail, Internet connections, cell phones, and other forms of technology are part of every organization, including schools. The communication system ties together parents, students, teachers, administrators, schools, district staff, and the state department of education for improved communications.

*Facilities Management System:* School districts utilize buildings and facilities that are valued in the millions of dollars. Building and maintaining the facilities are major responsibilities for school administrators.

*Human Resource System:* Human resources programs include job descriptions, compensation plans, evaluation programs, benefit programs, and databases that maintain adequate records for each employee.

*Information Technology System:* Schools have or will have computers in most rooms in the building. Computers may be stand-alone units or they may be tied together through networks using servers. Most of the computers are connected to the Internet. Constant change is the result of new software, software releases, courseware, hardware, and networks, which require a professional staff to maintain the overall information technology system.

*Inventory Control System:* Schools are major purchasers of books, supplies, food, capital items (e.g., buses), furniture, and utilities. This requires a full inventory control system to maintain control of these assets.

*Learning System:* A learning system integrates systems design principles and instructional design methods to produce a set of group learning sessions, individual learning models, interactive tutoring sessions, and high-quality motivational course materials. All of these elements are essential to enable all students to become successful learners by achieving learning objectives derived from educational standards.

*Management System:* A management system is defined as a process for managing resources (i.e., people, capital funds, facilities, operating funds, learning, assessment) to achieve the operating objective of an organization. A management system is required within each school, district, and state department of education.

***Staff Development System:*** Public schools employ nearly 5 million people as custodians, bus drivers, food service employees, secretaries, nurses, counselors, technology specialists, teacher aides, teachers, vice-principals, and principals. All of these critical jobs require performance-based training programs, on-the-job training assignments, and employee development programs. The teaching staff require formal professional development programs in each subject they teach. Administrators need to have management development programs. Records must be maintained on past training, and each employee deserves to have an individual development program.

***Tutoring System:*** Educators at all levels are implementing various mentoring systems, which may be one tutor with one student or one tutor with a few students. New, interactive computer systems also provide tutoring sessions. Each student is assessed to determine the required instructional level and learning objectives. Then an individual plan is developed for each student.

\* \* \* \*

### *Summary of Overall Integration of Systems*

If a school is a high-performing institution of learning, there are always 12 successful systems within the organization because the basic systems of a school are all essential for achieving high standards. In low-performing schools, one or more systems are ineffective, or some systems may not even exist. Students struggle to learn in schools that have missing, incomplete, or ineffective systems. Administrators must integrate and manage the 12 basic systems to achieve the objective that all students can be successful learners.

# Index

# ABOUT THE AUTHOR

*Jack Bowsher* is the former chief training officer of IBM Corporation. For more than 30 years he has worked as a teacher, course developer, education center manager, consultant, and executive in the fields of workplace training and education. As a former director of management development at IBM, he has been associated with many of the leading professionals in the field of management methods and organization structures. He has been an active member in the school reform movement since 1987. Based on his extensive research, he has been asked to be a general session speaker and panel member at numerous meetings on how to improve student learning within the American public school system.

Mr. Bowsher is one of the few educators who has experience in successfully designing education systems in which more than 99 percent of the students are successful learners. He has worked with course developers on utilizing self-study materials, computer-based training programs, multimedia programs, satellite classrooms, traditional classrooms, and advanced technology classrooms. He has experience with every teaching method from the traditional classroom to the most sophisticated electronic techniques. With his background in finance, information technology, human resource development, marketing, and training, he has the experience to create and manage fundamental change within education institutions. In fact, he has more than 40 years of experience in creating change within large organizations. Jack Bowsher is the master teacher on ways to restructure corporate and government training programs to achieve breakthroughs in workforce performance. He was the developer of the American Society For Training and Development (ASTD's) Chief Training Officer Workshop and the author of *Revolutionizing Workforce Performance.*

Now, Mr. Bowsher emerges as a leader in the school reform movement on how to restructure the public school system with a new vision, an integrated curriculum, learning systems, tutoring systems, assessment systems, and a new management system for school administrators. He is also the author of *Educating America: Lessons Learned in the Nation's Corporations*. His undergraduate degree is from the University of Illinois, and he earned an MBA at the University of Chicago. For several years, his column "Education Breakthroughs" appeared in a Connecticut newspaper.

The author has been described as a long-term educator but not someone who is tied to the history and methods of the public school system. Some people refer to him as a sympathetic outsider who really understands the process of learning and management methods currently used in public schools. With this knowledge and experience, he has developed new teaching and management methods that will achieve breakthroughs in student learning. He now resides in San Diego, California, where he continues as a guest lecturer and consultant.